STONE SOUP

FOR THE WORLD

MARIANNE LARNED

Three Rivers Press

New York

STONE SOUP

FOR THE WORLD

LIFE-CHANGING STORIES OF

EVERYDAY HEROES

A complete list of credits appears on page 397.

Published by Three Rivers Press, New York, New York.
Member of the Crown Publishing Group, a division of Random House, Inc.
www.randomhouse.com
Originally published in different form by Conari Press, Berkeley, in 1998.
THREE RIVERS PRESS and the Tugboat design are registered trademarks of Random House, Inc.

Printed in the United States of America
Design by Jo Anne Metsch

Library of Congress Cataloging-in-Publication Data

Larned, Marianne.
Stone soup for the world : life-changing stories of everyday heroes /
Marianne Larned ; foreword by Jack Canfield. — [Updated].
Includes bibliographical references.
(trade paperback)
1. Spiritual life.   2. Social action.   I. Title.
BL624 .L363   2002
                        2002004332
                        177'.7 — dc21

ISBN 0-609-80969-5

10 9 8 7 6 5 4 3 2 1

First Edition

DEDICATION

To my brother Chris, the tenth and last child in our family. From the moment he was born, he was larger than life, weighing eleven pounds, with curly blond hair and a twinkle in his eye. With his take-charge attitude and great sense of humor, he lived life to the fullest. What I remember most are his hugs. Real ones, as though he meant it.

Chris would do anything for his friends. He always stood up for what he believed in, and he challenged people to live up to his high standards. As captain of his high school football team, he got his teammates to quit drinking and taking drugs when he did. Once he sent a letter to a wayward teacher, challenging him to set a better example for his students.

Chris had a fierce loyalty to his family and brought us together in times of trouble. Just before he died, he organized a family reunion. It turned out to be his own going-away party.

Chris wasn't always this way. When he was just five years old, our dad died, leaving him with a hole in his heart and a chip on his shoulder. Without a father to guide and stand up for him, he struggled to find his way in the world. Growing up, he protected himself with his temper, so no one would get too close.

Until one summer, when he went to camp. Chris always loved being with his friends—playing basketball, sailing, water-skiing, and climbing mountains. But that summer he had a revelation that helped him put things in perspective and began to fill the hole in his heart: The words "God so loved us, that he gave . . ." really clicked with him. From that summer on, Chris came to see that life was about giving. When he gave to others, his life became more meaningful, purposeful, and fulfilling.

Just before Chris died, he wrote a letter to his friend Toby:

Sitting here, talking to my roommate, listening to Pink Floyd, eating round Doritos. Midterms are coming up this week. I'm hoping for the best. I'm also working for the best, too. Tonight I asked God to show me the right ways to go about preparing for each test, to help me avoid distractions and to give me the strength to do my best. I think He listened. I really ask a lot of Him . . . and often feel that I have too little to offer in thanks. I think that by helping other people in this world to utilize the unique assets He gave them, I could help Him as He has helped me. It is easy to say.

Through the ups and downs of his brief life, Chris became a young hero in our community. He believed that if we each pitched in, we could all do just about anything. With his infectious smile, he invited you to join him. When he was killed at nineteen in a car crash, his high school created the Chris Larned award, presented each year to the student who gave the most of him- or herself.

Losing my brother at such a young age left a huge hole in my heart, but his spirit now lives on in the hearts of those lives he touched, through every generous act. His tragic death reminded me of the preciousness of life and inspired me to live mine more fully. It also challenged me to do whatever I could to help build a better world for our children. Chris was and is my hero; he gave me the courage to write this book and guided me in my quest to help other young people open, as he did, the gift of giving.

ACKNOWLEDGMENTS

Writing this book has been an amazing Stone Soup experience. Many people generously gave of themselves, their time, their ideas, their support. A special thanks to those featured in this book for your trust in me, your faith in the process, and your commitment to building a better world.

To Claire Nuer, who touched my heart and strengthened my commitment to help build a more humane world. To Nathan Gray for opening my eyes to the fragile beauty of the global village. To my mentors Willis Harmon, John Gardner, and John McKnight for learning to build healthy communities. To my parents for inspiring my lifelong commitment to service, especially to my mother for her profound faith and courage.

Thanks to Three Rivers Press, especially my editor, Stephanie Higgs, for championing this book. To my literary agency, Lit West, Linda Mead, Nancy Ellis, Andrea Brown, and Robert Preskill for helping to make the dream come true.

With sincere appreciation to the Stone Soup Leadership Institute Board of Directors: Nane Alejandrez, Hulas King, and Terry Mollner, and advisers Ray Gatchalian, Will Morales, and Marty Rogol. Many thanks to Janet Hulstrand for her editorial assistance and those who helped run the Stone Soup Leadership Institute, especially Randi Vega, Elizabeth Knox, and Shirley Bickel for her support over the miles and the years.

Special thanks to the early supporters and friends of the Stone Soup Leadership Institute, especially Gale Smith, Don and Ann Brown, Richard Goodwin, Lucy and Sheldon Hackney, and Ralph and Lou Davidson, with special thanks to Frank Logan and George del Fierro.

A heartfelt thanks to special friends for their extra caring and enduring support during this incredible journey, and to Karen Stone McCowen and Kristen Pauly for their generous support and for always believing in me and this book.

Thanks to the hundreds of friends and colleagues who generously gave their ideas, suggestions, and support. To the community of Martha's Vineyard, especially Nancy Aronie, Susan Fieldsmith, Pam Benjamin, and Doris Gaffney. To Jack Canfield and the Chicken Soup staff for encouraging me to write this book. To story nominators, story reviewers, and everyone whose lives have been touched by these stories. For all those who provided this project a home: Charles and Marion Guggenheim, Doris Hutchings, Nancy Michelson, Gail Evanari, Laurie Anne and Kevin Waddell, with special thanks to Carol Saysette and Bob Reynolds.

The following organizations nominated a story for this book: Co-op America, the Robert Wood Johnson Foundation's Community Leadership Project, The American News Service, The Business Enterprise Trust, The Giraffe Project, The Fellowship of Reconciliation, The Independent Sector, The Points of Light Foundation, and the World Business Academy.

To my family for their love over the years, with much appreciation for all the children in my life, especially my nieces and nephews. You are my greatest teachers—showing me how to laugh at life, sing for joy, and give from my heart. May God bless each and every one of you.

CONTENTS

INTRODUCTION
Walter Cronkite

As we begin a new millennium, and face a critical time in our nation's history, it's a good time to take stock and ask ourselves some important questions: "Where have we been? Where are we going? What do we want to accomplish in the next hundred years—for ourselves and for our families? And who will chart our course?"

Creating an educated constituency of Americans is the most critical issue of our time. Our country needs people prepared to address the urgent challenges facing our world.

We wonder how the events of September 11, 2001, could have happened. We wonder why "they" hate us so much. It's hard for most Americans to imagine how people on the other side of the world live—in desperate poverty, without hope, without opportunities. We are separated from them geographically, and by the growing distance between the haves and the have-nots. As we strive to build a more peaceful world, we must learn more how to work with all other people on this planet.

Throughout history, we've thought that fighting wars would bring peace. We've passed this legacy of war on to our children. After September 11, we wonder if, in the long term, this approach will really work. Polls tell us that our children believe that the world will be less safe and prosperous when they grow up. What can we do now to change things so that they can have a more hopeful vision of their future?

We've all been touched by the power of the examples set by legendary heroes like Gandhi, Martin Luther King Jr., Cesar Chavez, Nelson Mandela, Eleanor

Roosevelt, John and Robert F. Kennedy, and Mother Teresa. These men and women of kindness, courage, and action set the course for the twentieth century, yet they are famous not because they possessed superhuman brains, wealth, or privilege, but because they embraced humanity and dedicated their lives to empowering every human being. They did this with hope, self-sacrifice, and hard work. They envisioned a better world, and left a legacy of service for us to follow.

Stone Soup for the World is a blueprint for building a better world. Its heroes are ordinary folks in America and twenty-nine other countries who, by conviction, imagination, innovation, persistence, frequently hard work and not infrequently moral or physical courage, have lifted neighbors and their communities. They challenge each of us to respond in kind. By their actions, neighborhood by neighborhood, village by village, they break from the destructive patterns of our past and transform the world. The secret to their greatness is the magic ingredients in *Stone Soup for the World*—the simple truth that by working together we can accomplish much more than any of us could have on our own.

In today's world, young people are hungry for role models and modern-day heroes they can look up to and follow. Marianne Larned works with the Stone Soup Leadership Institute, training young people to become heroes. Future and emerging leaders work side by side with heroes from the book who share their time, their life stories, and their insights into the toughest issues facing their communities and our world. I've enjoyed working with Marianne and her team. Grounded in local values, her work is spreading across the country.

As the only superpower, we must be the best country and the best global citizens we can be. That means offering a hand up to the good guys—and forging new directions for the global economy. In the last century we've shown the world how we can attack and solve perplexing problems with technology. Imagine if we were to apply that same intellectual power to solving the world's greatest problems—poverty, overpopulation, pollution, and medical insufficiency, as well as our dependence on nonrenewable energy sources. With the resurgence of patriotism in America, this is an ideal time to launch such a bold national initiative. It could become this generation's version of putting a man on the moon.

Around the world, revolutionary forces are already at work, and they have humankind's dreams on their side. It is up to us to assume leadership of that revolution, to channel it in a direction that will ensure freedom's future. We can help assure success by celebrating the heroes in our midst who by their example can lift up the spirit of our people. Their leadership will realize the true values of humankind and put to shame the false values that simultaneously exalt and trivialize our society. Their spirit is the spirit of America, and of the human experience. For humans will be nothing if they are not their brothers' and sisters' keepers.

We all can take the hero's journey. It begins with a single step, the moment we decide to stand up for something we believe in. *Stone Soup for the World* asks each of us to take that first step. It's time to roll up our sleeves. It's a time to share our stories and teach our children that they too can be heroes. It's time to build a better, safer place for all people. It's time to take action—and chart the course for our future.

And that's the way it is.

FOREWORD

Edward James Olmos,
Actor and Activist

Growing up in East L.A.'s barrio of Boyle Heights, I was blessed by people who showed me that helping others is a way of life. My mother, Eleanor, worked for twenty years in the Los Angeles County General Hospital AIDS ward and my father, Pedro, helped coordinate Little League baseball. For our family, these were labors of love.

Over the years, I've met many everyday Latino heroes who, by the power of their example, taught this important life lesson. Like math teacher Jaime Escalante, the real star I played in the movie *Stand and Deliver*, who gave Hispanic youth the opportunity to get real jobs, with a real future. Carlos Santana, Rita Moreno, and I work with the Hispanic Education and Media Group to honor our heroes and educate our communities, to promote Hispanic culture and ways of life.

And like my friend Cesar Chavez, one of the greatest Latino heroes of our time. Cesar dedicated his life to helping our people. A humble leader, he told us, "Only by giving our lives do we find life." Even in the toughest times, Cesar would remind us, *"Sí se puede!* Yes, we can!" *Stone Soup for the World: Life-Changing Stories of Everyday Heroes* honors Cesar Chavez and the can-do spirit of many other Latino heroes.

Nane Alejandrez carries on Cesar's legacy at Barrios Unidos. He gets kids off the street, gives them jobs, and helps them make something of themselves. When Nane saw what Cesar did, he said to himself, "I can do this," and he's found that, given the chance, young people agree they can, too.

Alejandro Obando is a hero to some of the six thousand Nicaraguan children left orphaned and homeless by their country's long civil war, since he and his New York City students and their families built them a school.

At La Clinica del Pueblo in Washington, D.C., Dr. Juan Romagoza helps people from Central America heal themselves by helping one another. "We are a people of weavers," he says, quoting Guatamelan Rigoberta Menchu, "weaving a better future from our suffering and pain." People return to the clinic with a passion for giving back. "*Se tiran la casa por la ventana.*"

Don Francisco unites 100 million Spanish-speaking television viewers around the world every Saturday night on *Sabado Gigante*. At a time when too many TV shows prosper by exploiting human frailties, Don Francisco's shows, such as *An American Family* on PBS, teach people the value of giving and helping others, and the strength of community roots.

The stories in *Stone Soup for the World* testify to the Latino tradition of giving back. I am honored that mine is one of them. One of the most important gifts we can give our children is to read stories about those who went before them. Our children need to know about the sacrifices Cesar Chavez and others made for them, and their responsibility to give back to future generations. Who will they learn this from, if not from us?

The Cesar Chavez Day of Service and Learning in California is the first state holiday dedicated to a Latino. Teachers share stories about Cesar's life from the *Stone Soup for the World* educational curriculum and, on March 31, they initiate cultural, artistic, environmental, and human service projects to help their communities. If other states follow California's example, we can pass Cesar's legacy on to all of our nation's youth and inspire them to be heroes, too.

Young people need hope, and hope comes with a vision of the future. With 31 million Hispanic people in America, we can create a great future. My hope is that after reading these stories, each one of you will be inspired to move beyond what you already think is possible by helping one another take ownership of your lives and your futures. I hope that with me, with *Stone Soup for the World*, you will hear Cesar's words: "*Sí se puede!* Yes, we can!"

"*Nos estamos moviendo para adelante.*" As we say, we are all moving forward.

FOREWORD

Jack Canfield,

coauthor of *Chicken Soup for the Soul*

The world is hungry for positive, uplifting, and inspirational stories. I know this because, over the last decade, the *Chicken Soup for the Soul* books have struck a powerful chord with millions of people all across the country and around the world.

Everywhere Mark and I go, people now ask us, "What's next? I feel so much better about myself and my life; I want to give something back—but I'm not sure how." Once we feel better about ourselves, we naturally want to reach out to help others.

Stone Soup for the World: Life-Changing Stories of Everyday Heroes is a handbook for humanitarians, showing us how we can contribute to our communities, giving us hundreds of ideas for what's next and where to start making the world a better place.

In these hundred stories, you will meet ordinary people doing extraordinary things, and extraordinary people doing ordinary things. They remind us that we can each make a difference, and that when we work together, we *can* change the world.

These encourage us all to stretch ourselves and our own little worlds and reach out to our fellow human beings. They show us that with a little imagination, teamwork, and cooperation, we can do things we never thought possible.

Over the twenty-five years that I've known Marianne Larned, we've become great friends, connected by our shared search for practical ways to inspire people to help make the world a better place. Marianne is one of those people who truly believes that we can solve the world's problems. Whenever we get together,

Marianne shares inspiring stories about people she's worked with across America and in faraway countries, who are doing great things. Until now, many of those stories have not been widely known. Thanks to *Stone Soup for the World*, millions of people will tune in to these stories and be inspired to take action, to join in and help build a world that works for everyone.

From the millions of teens who have read our books, we know that young people love these kinds of stories. They yearn to know that their lives matter and that the world will be a better place because of them and their efforts. I encourage all of you who read this book to share these stories with kids. Read them these stories, give them this book, and challenge them to find their own ways to contribute.

After you read these stories, you'll have lots of new ideas. So pick up the phone or a pen and get involved today. But wait—I'm getting ahead of myself. First you need to read the book you are holding in your hands. You are in for a wonderful treat, a wonderful meal of *Stone Soup for the World*.

Enjoy!

THE STONE SOUP FOLKTALE

There was once a man who had been traveling for a long time. Having run out of food, he was weary and hungry from his journey. When he came upon a small village, he thought, "Maybe someone could share some food."

When the man knocked at the first house, he asked the woman who answered the door, "Could you spare a bit of food? I've traveled a long way and am very hungry." The woman replied, "I'm sorry, but I have nothing to give you."

So the traveler went to the next door and asked again. The answer was the same. He went from door to door and each time he was turned away. Each of the villagers had good reasons.

But then one villager said, "I have some water." "Oh, good," said the traveler. "We can make stone soup."

He then went to the center of the village and started building a small fire. From his backpack he pulled out a small pot and his magic stone and placed them in the pot. As the water started boiling, a passing villager stopped and asked him what he was doing. "I'm making stone soup," the traveler replied.

"What does it taste like?" the man asked curiously. "Well, it would be better with a few onions," the traveler admitted. "Oh, I have some onions," he replied, heading off to his home.

People from the village heard about this strange man who was making soup from a stone. They started gathering around the fire. One of the villagers offered, "I have a few carrots from last year's harvest." Someone else said, "I'll get some potatoes from my garden."

One by one, each villager brought something special to add to the pot. Pretty soon, right before their eyes there was a delicious soup—enough to feed the whole village. They all sat down together to enjoy their soup—and the miracle they'd help to create.

ANONYMOUS,
adapted from a sixteenth-century folktale

INTRODUCTION

Marianne Larned

Can we really change the world? From the youngest child to the oldest senior, each of us wants to make a difference in the world. We want to feed the hungry, care for the elderly, and teach the children. We sometimes wonder how to start. With too little time and money to solve all the world's problems, one person can feel alone. We may even feel like giving up.

Since September 11, 2001, though, more people have been asking, "What can I do?" We looked for ways to help. We gave our blood, our money, and our time. And each time we did, we felt just a little better.

With each holiday after September 11, we found new meaning in our giving. At Halloween, American children raised $4 million for Afghani kids by trick-or-treating for UNICEF. On Veterans Day we all felt a profound sense of gratitude to those who'd helped protect our country and preserve our precious freedom over the years. When local food banks were struggling at Thanksgiving, people responded with a last-minute flood of donations. And in New York City, a Secret Santa from Kansas City gave out hundred-dollar bills to thousands of people on the streets. A New York City woman thanked him with all her heart: "You are doing God's work in the most personal ways, seeking out hurting eyes and faces and replacing them with bright smiles and thankful hearts."

The children's story "Stone Soup" reminds us that when we each give something, we can feed both the hungry of the world and the hunger in our souls. In this simple story, a hungry traveler makes soup from just a stone and invites each poor villager to give something to the pot. Together they cook up a feast, more than enough to feed the entire village. It's a story that is shared in many lands.

Stone Soup for the World is a collection of one hundred stories of ordinary people doing extraordinary things. Their stories show us that greatness grows out of simple acts of giving. They remind us that with a little imagination, cooperation, and goodwill, we really can make the world a better place for everyone. Magic happens.

When 11,500 ordinary local heroes carried the Olympic torch across America, it was one of the first truly joyous national events since September 11. I was privileged to see it twice—with my family in Montpelier, Vermont, and again, with the Mill Valley, California, community. We smiled brightly into the sun as history passed before us. The Olympic flame has always been a symbol of our global unity, our common humanity, and our collective possibility for a more hopeful future. This year we held the torch especially high.

Now, more than ever, we need this kind of hope in the world. Since September 11, we are examining our lives and changing our priorities. We are realizing that having money isn't enough; we want more meaning and purpose. We want to spend more time with our loved ones, living each day as if it could be our last. We are grateful just to be alive.

How the world changes depends on each one of us. The decisions we make *today* will determine our future, for our children and for our children's children. We do have a choice: to be paralyzed by fear, to protect ourselves from "them," or to remember that we're all in this together and we all want to live in a safer, healthier world. Did September 11 change us forever? Let's hope so. Let's face the challenge and make the choices for all humanity.

There is a deep reservoir of energy and goodwill in our country and in the world. With more funds being spent on disaster relief, increased security, antiterrorism efforts, and rebooting the economy, there are fewer resources available for local communities. Now, more than ever, we need to work together with our neighbors, to help each other, and to invest in our communities, especially in our children. The greatest gift we can give them is to teach them, by example, to give back, to show them how to make democracy work for everyone.

This book is a collection of stories about what is working in the world. Use it as a toolbox and a guide, for in it you will find all the hope and ideas and direction you'll need to change the world. Like the hungry traveler in the folktale, we each have a magic stone: the power to give, the joy of getting together and getting involved. The time is now; the place is here and everywhere you go; and the everyday heroes in this book will light the way.

I hope these stories will fuel the flame of hope burning in your hearts. Carry the torch of possibility, hold it high, and pass it to the next generation.

Somewhere on this planet,
someone has a solution to each of the world's problems.
It just might be you!
What can you do today, tomorrow, next week, next year to build a better world?
Remember the Stone Soup folktale:
When we each give a little, we can feed the whole world.

I

ONE PERSON'S VOICE

The heroes of all time have gone before us.

We have only to follow the thread of the hero path.

Where we had thought to travel outward,

we will come to the center of our own existence.

And where we had thought to be alone, we will be with all the world.

JOSEPH CAMPBELL

Have you ever wondered if just one person can really make a difference? Sometimes the problems around us can seem overwhelming. But think about it: one person first walked on the moon and one person discovered electricity.

There are thousands of ways each of us can make a difference. A helping hand extended to a neighbor or a stranger creates a more caring world. Reading to children enriches their present and opens up their future. A gift to a church or a charity helps those helping others. One kind word or a thoughtful deed can change someone's day—or make history. It's amazing what one person can do!

There's a lot that needs changing in this world. We've been looking for heroes. On September 11, we found them: the "ordinary" people who risked their lives to help others, especially the firefighters, police, and EMT workers. As people were running for their lives away from the fireball, the firefighters ran toward it, never thinking that the World Trade Center buildings would collapse. Their code for the day was "Before we save ourselves, we save others." Selflessly risking their lives, they kept their promise to "preserve life and property"—and saved over 25,000 people. Actually, they'd been doing this all along. Everyday heroes are less often celebrated, but they're still heroes. Maybe more so.

Oakland fire captain Ray Gatachalian, who went to New York City to help in the aftermath of the attack, was moved to tears when he heard Bette Midler sing "Did you ever know that you're my hero?" at the Yankee Stadium memorial service for the victims' families. "They showed us what it means to be a hero," Ray says. "They exemplify the best in all of us."

The stories in this chapter show how ordinary people can become heroes with acts of human kindness and courageous acts of service. "A hero is someone who responds to a 'call to service' and gives his life to something bigger than himself," said Joseph Campbell, after helping George Lucas with *Star Wars*. In the movie, young Luke Skywalker responds to a call, goes on a quest, battles demons, both inside himself and out, and returns to his people victorious, with a gift. So he becomes a hero. In training one day, Obi-Wan Kenobi coaches Luke, "Turn off your computer, turn off your machine, and do it yourself; follow your heart, trust your feelings." When Luke does this, he succeeds, and the audience breaks out in applause.

Like Luke Skywalker, when the heroes in this chapter responded to a "call," their lives changed as they changed the world. People from all walks of life—firefighters and ministers; nurses and doctors; artists and musicians; mothers, fathers, students, and seniors; presidents of countries and companies—all set out on journeys along paths of self-discovery. They overcame obstacles and discovered the resources to fulfill their destinies. Good Samaritans and great humanitarians, dedicated volunteers and corporate champions followed their hearts and trusted their instincts to help others. Along the way, they found the kind of joy and fulfillment others only dream of—and an exciting, lifelong adventure.

"The ultimate aim of the quest must be the wisdom and the power to serve others," says Campbell. He describes "legendary heroes" as those who dedicate their entire lives to a new way of life, a new age, a new religion, a new world order. The legendary heroes in this chapter and throughout the book—Mother Teresa, Nelson Mandela, Jimmy Carter, Eleanor Roosevelt and others—have left exemplary footsteps for others to follow.

Every one of us can be a hero. We, too, can embrace the courage of our convictions. We can step up, make our mark, help make history, and, with it, a better world.

As you read these stories, let your imagination take *you* on a hero's journey. What has been calling to *you*? Remember, it's your choice. There's always something one person can do. As Dr. Martin Luther King Jr. said, "Everyone can be great because everyone can serve."

If you had one day or even one hour

to make a difference in someone's life

what would you do?

When you take time to listen for your "call," you may be surprised.

You may begin an adventure more exciting than any you could imagine!

May the force be with you.

STARFISH

A young girl was walking along a beach after a terrible storm. She was upset to find thousands of starfish washed up on the shore.

When she came to each starfish, she picked it up, and threw it back into the ocean.

After she'd been doing this for some time, a man approached her. "Little girl, why are you doing this?" he asked. "Look at this beach! You can't save all these starfish. You'll never make a difference!"

At first the girl was crushed, suddenly discouraged. After a few moments she bent down, picked up another starfish, and hurled it as far as she could into the ocean.

She then looked up at the man and replied, "Well, I made a difference to that one."

GOD DIDN'T MEAN FOR THEM TO BE HUNGRY

Told by David Murcott

Sometimes big things come in little packages. Take Isis Johnson, for example. At the tender age of four, she took her first step toward making a gigantic impact in her community. "Grandma," she asked, "can we send the chicken we have left to the children in Ethiopia? God didn't mean for them to be hungry." Isis had just seen pictures of starving children in the news on TV, as she was finishing her supper, and she wanted to do something to help them.

"Isis," her grandmother said tenderly, "Ethiopia is too far away. The chicken would spoil before it got there." Not ready to give up so easily, Isis asked, "Well, are there any hungry girls and boys in New Orleans?" Her grandmother told her the sad truth. "Yes, I'm sure there are." That was all Isis needed to know. "Then let's send our chicken to them," she said.

That's how it all started. Isis went door to door, asking her neighbors if they would donate food for hungry children. Then she and her grandmother drove around town, gathering even more. Isis put a sign in the window of their home asking people to feed the hungry. Soon people started bringing food to them. Their home became a small warehouse of donated food and supplies.

Isis and her grandmother decided to give the food away on a Saturday, just before Christmas. They told the Salvation Army what they were doing. In turn, the Salvation Army told needy families. That year, Isis gave out over one thousand items of food to hundreds of people, attracting the attention of the media. *NBC Nightly News* and Black Entertainment Television, to name just two, covered the story. People were surprised to hear how much one little girl could do.

Isis received calls of support from all over New Orleans. Everyone wanted to help. Some people gave money to buy goods, and others continued to bring food to her house. The following year, Isis helped collect 1,300 items. The Salvation Army, which had agreed to distribute them, had to send seven men to load it all into a truck. The next year her donations totaled four thousand; and each year they multiply.

A few years ago, when Hurricane Andrew hit Louisiana, Isis was upset by the amount of suffering she saw. She promptly collected over 1,600 pieces of clothing for the Red Cross to distribute to needy families. Whenever Isis hears stories that make her sad, she tries to find a way to help.

One day, for example, she heard about a New Orleans child who was killed in the crossfire of a drive-by shooting. When Isis learned that the parents couldn't afford the child's burial expenses, she collected money for the funeral and gave it to the family. Now Isis, the parents, and the child can be more at peace.

So many people have made contributions to Isis's projects that her grandmother and a lawyer helped create the Isis Johnson Foundation. Now her donors receive tax credit for giving money, food, or clothes. Sometimes it's still hard for Isis to believe she has a foundation named after her. She has received numerous awards of recognition such as induction into the Mickey Mouse Hall of Fame.

Some children envy her fame and popularity. Isis simply tells them, "If I can do it, so can you. You can get involved in projects like mine, or start a special one of your own. But, no matter how you do it, when you help people, you feel good about yourself." She's only human, but for her that's enough to give.

Isis is now a seventeen-year-old peer mediator, working with teens to solve their problems. She's often asked to speak at local schools, inspiring students to help people in their communities. There are many ways to help people, she explains: "No matter who you are or where you come from, you can make a difference. You don't have to be old to make things better, you only have to care." For those who still don't know where to begin, Isis suggests they listen to a child. For, as she has proven, the youngest will show us the way.

Good habits formed at youth make all the difference.

ARISTOTLE

Organize a food or clothing drive for those in need in your community. If you want to help Isis in her war on hunger, write or call her grandmother, Claudette Jones, at the **Isis T. Johnson Foundation,** 3340 Fawn Drive, Apt. 7, Memphis, TN 38127; 901-354-8582.

WORKING IN THE SCHOOLS
Told by Jonathan Alter

Sometimes hope is born of fear. In this case, it was the fear that volunteer tutors would be robbed as they walked to their cars.

In 1991 the Byrd Academy was an inner-city public school, overcrowded and understaffed like many others. The school was located in the Cabrini-Green neighborhood of Chicago, one of the most infamous housing projects in the United States. Only a mile away from Chicago's glittering lakefront, it was rotting with poverty and violence. Children couldn't walk across playgrounds without fear of crime, injury, or worse. Not long ago, a young boy was actually dropped to his death from a window by some older children.

The apartment buildings in Cabrini-Green were mostly occupied by young mothers and their children, most on public assistance, some with drug problems, others so young themselves that they had little idea how to raise children. Fathers, for the most part, were nowhere to be seen. They'd abandoned the area, and left it for gangs to rule.

Joanne Alter was well aware of the problems in Chicago's public schools; as a county officeholder she sometimes visited them. The first woman elected to county-wide office, she was ending an eighteen-year career in elective politics. In her mid-sixties, it was time for her to retire.

One day she talked with a third-grade teacher at the Byrd Academy. The teacher was concerned that her students were struggling to learn, oppressed by fear, and starving for love and positive role models. On an impulse, Joanne volunteered to help the kids learn to read and—just as important—to let them know that someone besides their teacher believed in them, too.

On Joanne's first day of class, as she was leaving home, she met her neighbor, Marion Stone, in the elevator of her apartment building. Joanne explained the school's need and invited Marion to join her, and the two decided to go together. They had a terrific time in the classroom. The young children, delighted to have their attention, begged them to come back. That was the modest beginning of a program called Working in the Schools (WITS).

"We help the teachers with some of their most challenging students," Joanne says. "We come up with two hundred ways to say to the child, 'You look wonderful today!' 'Your math is so much better!' 'Aren't you terrific?' and so on. The point is to let kids know 'We're here for you—and we're coming back.'

"To our surprise, we found that the kids weren't the only ones who benefited. We discovered the tremendous payback to the volunteers."

But as WITS began to grow, a problem emerged. Volunteers feared driving to the school, especially walking to the parking lot after school. Unfortunately, the very things that put Cabrini-Green so desperately in need of help were turning the helpers away.

It occurred to Joanne that if children could take a bus to school, so could the tutors. So now, in the mornings and afternoons, WITS buses transport volunteer from their middle-class neighborhoods to inner-city schools and back. Volunteers feel safe and secure. In WITS's ten-year history, there have been no incidents.

The program rented a minibus for the first eleven volunteers. By 1996, two hundred volunteers were taking buses to all five elementary schools in Cabrini-Green. Today there are more than eight hundred WITS volunteers, and they use the biggest buses they can find. En route, the buses fill with chatter about this class or that kid, and a remarkable camaraderie develops, not to mention the occasional romance. One widow met a widower on the bus and married him.

What started as a tutoring program staffed by older, often semiretired volunteers now includes mid-career professionals. Companies in the community, like Salomon Smith Barney and UBS Warburg, grant their employees "release time," which lets them tutor twice a month on company time.

"Whether they go one morning a week or more, once the volunteers get hooked, they almost never leave," Joanne says. "The kids really give you unconditional love. The volunteers are nourished by it, and they keep coming back." One little boy in particular still stands out in her mind. "Moncell was a good student," she recalls. "He tried hard, but he was in the third grade and had never learned to read." Joanne worked with him often, but he still wasn't making much progress.

"One day I asked him if he was reading his books at home after class. He sheepishly said no. I reminded him that practice makes perfect, and he smiled and said he would try harder." The next week, the class recited poems they had memorized for their visiting parents. Moncell's poem was short and not too difficult, and he delivered it brilliantly. His mother had come to hear him and was deeply touched.

After the program, Joanne asked Moncell's mother if she read to him at night. "There was a group of people near us, so she mumbled something about not having enough time and quickly walked away." Later that morning Joanne felt a tug on her sleeve and turned around to face Moncell's mother. "I'm sorry," she said, with tears in her eyes. "I don't know how to read." Now it was Joanne who was touched. "I told her that was okay, and suggested that she have Moncell read to her at night." Moncell's mother promised she would.

The next week Moncell came to class all excited. "Guess what, guess what," he said. "My mom read with me last night. Now I'm gonna read like a pro!" Moncell started to improve that very day.

Give a few hours of your time to help a child learn to read and feel the rewards. **Working in the Schools** is a tutoring and mentoring program involving community members, area businesses, and local high school students, providing volunteers to support the education and development of children in the Chicago Public Schools. To volunteer or to become a corporate partner, visit <u>www. witsontheweb.org</u>, or write WITS, 150 East Huron, Suite 900, Chicago, IL 60611.

SIDEWALK SAM

In Los Angeles, celebrities immortalize their names by placing their hands in wet cement at Grauman's Chinese Theater. In communities across New England, children immortalize their names, along with their visions for the world of tomorrow. "In times like these, when America is being challenged, we have to declare our faith in America and in each other," says Bob Guillemin, a popular New England artist known as Sidewalk Sam. "Who better to do this than our children? For they are our future."

Sidewalk Sam is a sort of Pied Piper who brings people of all ages together to create art that symbolizes the hopes and dreams of the entire community. For the Children's Community Monuments, he gives children a one-foot square of colored wet cement—and a mission. "Draw anything that expresses yourself," he tells them, "a message for the future, something your parents have taught you, something people can believe in." They write innocent, uplifting messages in the wet cement, and draw puppy dogs, flowers, and images that represent the ethnic, religious, and cultural diversity in their communities.

Then Sam and his group assemble the brightly colored red, white, and blue squares like patchwork in front of town halls, and in schoolyards, community parks, and city walkways, knowing these beautiful works may last for a hundred years.

Children's Community Monuments take three to six months to plan and a day or two to build. The entire community rallies around the children, and all kinds of people get involved. Children, teachers, parents, school janitors, and masons work to install the monuments. Others chip in a dollar or two to cover the cost of the concrete squares.

Through this project, children become spokespeople for the spirit of their communities. "The children become community leaders, drawing the adults together," says Sam. "Children of all faiths and backgrounds create these art monuments in their communities, where there are monuments to past wars but none for the future."

People can see children's artwork sites at the Mary Lyon School in Brighton, Massachusetts, or at Prairie College Elementary School in Canton, Ohio, where teacher Joyce Appleman said, "The students develop an understanding of other cultures and learn that we can get along with everyone around the world."

Sidewalk Sam's other community art projects are more ephemeral. Some wash away in a day or so, but they're not forgotten. Chalk One Up for the Arts is an annual event that started in 1996 when Boston's mayor, Thomas Menino, asked Sam to create a "celebration of goodness" for the city. Each year, hundreds of corporations send their employees outside during their lunch hour. They each get a block of sidewalk and a box of colored chalk. On a beautiful summer day in the third week of August, lawyers, bankers, accountants, and salespeople turned artists-for-an-hour, and drew the work of their imaginations in vibrant colors on the sidewalk. Pinstriped men and power-suited women crouching on the sidewalk are a sight to behold, and even more so are their sidewalk chalk designs, thousands of which, all over town, transform Boston's pedestrian paths into banners proclaiming the city's goodness and sense of fun.

It is a major city celebration. As one of the featured summer festivals, Chalk One Up infuses Boston with art for a whole week from City Hall, Copley Plaza, and Faneuil Hall to the waterfront and the business district. Some companies hold friendly sidewalk art competitions, offering their employees small prizes. The city expects ten thousand people to participate in 2002, with 200,000 pedestrians watching. "Everyone is an artist," says Sam. "I love to create new ways for people to express the beauty locked up inside them."

Sidewalk Sam also invites seventy arts and cultural organizations to join in the celebration, as a way of thanking their audiences. Each year the prestigious

Boston Museum of Fine Arts, the Boston Symphony Orchestra, and the Institute for Contemporary Art attend. "For years audiences have applauded the arts," Sidewalk Sam said. "We thought it would be good to have the arts applaud their audiences, and thank them for their years of support."

Sidewalk Sam is happiest when he's in his work jeans and blue denim shirt, working on projects that bring the best of people out into their communities. "Art isn't just for the wealthy and the privileged," he says. "Art is for everyone." He has been doing his unique brand of community-centered art for thirty-eight years, though he started out traditionally. He studied in Paris, Chicago, and Boston, and his work appeared in galleries and museums across the country. That was fun for a while, but he wanted to bring art out of the museums and into the streets, where it could enrich people's daily lives.

"Sidewalks are a natural medium," he thought. "I want to reach out to everyone, rich or poor." So Sidewalk Sam, as he became known, spent the next few years bent over city streets, a milk crate full of chalks beside him. He's done a Sidewalk Mona Lisa and a Sidewalk Whistler's Mother. "I love to go out early on a summer day, crouch down on the sidewalk for ten or twelve hours, and re-create a Van Gogh or a Rembrandt," he says. "By the end of the day my back is sore, my knees hurt, and I feel as tired as a ditch digger, but I'm rewarded. People stop and enjoy the art. They get involved. They have wonderful things to say."

Over the years, Sidewalk Sam has become a living legend. In the beginning, the city of Boston didn't know quite what to do about him. He was accused of defacing public property with graffiti, and threatened with arrest. But once officials saw the entire community behind him, and then with him, they started inviting him to draw everywhere. For Earth Day in 1990, Boston authorities shut down Storrow Drive, and Sam, along with some sixty thousand helpers, painted the city's busiest highway bright green. Participants took up their colored chalk to draw in honor of Mother Earth, so birds, flowers, and bumblebees appeared, and chalk children played in the fields.

For the last several years, Sidewalk Sam has been working on his biggest project ever, decorating a new highway. The Big Dig, as it is called, is a ten-year, $16-billion construction project and the largest and most complicated highway project in the world. While the Dig rearranges the face of Boston, Sidewalk Sam is beautifying the construction zone and entertaining inconvenienced pedestrians with vivid murals covering the walls, benches of bright flowers, and overhead beams transformed into a blue sky with puffy clouds complete with flying cherubs.

"We have been changing meadows into highways for decades," says Sidewalk Sam. "I thought it would be nice if we could change a highway back into a meadow."

We think too much. We feel too little.
More than machines, we need humanity.

CHARLIE CHAPLIN

Discover how art can help bring your community to life in exciting, colorful new ways. To learn how, contact **Art Street, Inc.** Visit www.sidewalksam.com.

HIDDEN TREASURE

Told by John McKnight

Most of the really valuable things in the world are hard to find. Gold, oil, diamonds, and other precious materials reveal themselves to the dedicated, inventive, and reaching. The same is true of people. More often than not, the most valuable thing a person has to offer isn't in plain view. Unfortunately, many of us do not take the time or have the patience to search for the human gems the eyes can't see. John McKnight tells the story of a remarkable woman who does just that:

In her work for a service agency in southern Georgia, she was responsible for assisting developmentally disabled people. Over time, she and her colleagues became concerned over their field's focus on people's disabilities instead of their possibilities. She realized that they rarely thought about the gifts, talents, and capabilities of those entrusted to their care.

This woman decided to spend more time with her clients, to see if she could uncover the treasures each of them had to offer. She went first to the home of a man named Joe. At forty-two, he was the product of a system that, despite its best intentions, had labeled and limited him most of his life. Despite years of special education, there was still no place in society for someone like Joe, and he returned home to his family's pig farm. Every day he did two things. He fed the pigs each morning and night, and he sat in the living room, listening to the radio. After four days at Joe's house and apparently no sign of Joe's gift, my friend was thoroughly dejected. Then, on the fifth day, she saw that it was right in front of her. "Joe listens to the radio," she mused.

It might not sound like much, but to her it was a treasure whose value had not been estimated. "I found out there were three people in town who listened to the radio and got paid for it," she said. "One was in the sheriff's office, one was in the police department, and the third was in the local civil defense and volunteer ambulance office." She went to each of those places to see if she could match one of them with Joe.

The civil defense and ambulance office occupied a donated house that doubled as the neighborhood community center. It was a busy place, full of activity. Somebody was always there. People came in to talk and drink coffee in the dining room. Sometimes they showed movies. My friend thought that Joe would feel right at, well, home. She noticed a young woman monitoring the radio for emergency calls, dispatching ambulances as needed. She told the dispatcher, "I know somebody who likes to listen to the radio as much as you do. I'd like to introduce him to you."

They put a chair out for Joe. Now, every day, he listens to the radio and helps the dispatcher. That first year, when Christmas came, the volunteers at the ambulance station gave him his own CB scanner to listen to at home in the evening. Joe has found his place, and he is a valued member of the community.

"Hey, Joe, what's happening?" the owner of the local diner casually asked Joe one day when he came in. Joe replied, "A house over in Boonesville burned down this morning. And out on Route 90, at that turnoff where you can have picnics, there was a drug bust. And Mr. Schiller over in Athens had a heart attack." The diner fell silent, as all eyes turned to Joe, and all at once everyone in the diner recognized that if they wanted to know what was happening, Joe was the man to see. To the best of my knowledge, this is the only town in the United States that now has the benefit of a bona fide, old-fashioned town crier.

When John last spoke to his friend, she told him she had taken Joe to meet the editor of the local newspaper. Every day by noon, Joe knows the story, so now he is a stringer for the paper.

Thanks to his friend's efforts, Joe, a man society had practically written off, has become an inspiration—and a valuable resource to his community. It would never have happened if one person hadn't dug a little deeper, searched a little longer, and tried a little harder to find Joe's possibilities. There must be many more Joes out there. If you look hard enough, there's treasure to be found in each of us.

Those among you who will be truly happy
are the ones who have sought and found how to serve.

ALBERT SCHWEITZER

Learn how you can uncover the hidden resources in your community by seeing people as assets instead of problems. To find useful guides, publications, and information about their training faculty and current training events, visit www.northwestern.edu/ipr/abcd.html, the Web site of the **Asset-Based Community Development Institute** at Northwestern University.

THE FORGIVENESS PARTY

Told by Jo Claire Hartsig

Adapted from "The Forgiveness Party" in *Fellowship,*
the Magazine of the Fellowship for Reconciliation

Bess Lyn Sannino felt like any nine-year-old whose house has been burglarized. She was hurt and confused. The thieves had not just stolen her favorite things, they had also vandalized her home in Virginia Beach, Virginia, pelting it with raw eggs. From the graffiti sprayed on the garage door, young Bess had a good idea it was some older children from the neighborhood who had broken into her home.

Bess's shock gave way to anger. Her first impulse was for revenge: "I felt like going over to their houses and killing them." They had been in her room and gone through her personal things. It was wrong. In fierce detail, she could list every item that was taken, including seventeen dollars in allowance money, her Valentine's Day candy, and her tape player.

Her mother, Grace, wrestled with the decision of whether to call the police, since the vandals were kids from the neighborhood. She called the father of one of the teens she suspected, who identified the others involved. He encouraged her to work with the police to make this a lesson for the youngsters, and she did.

When Grace called the police, a compassionate and understanding officer responded. He spent a whole week locating the parents of all four burglars. One of the mothers worked two jobs and was rarely home before eleven o'clock at night. Another family was lost in the midst of its own trauma, since the father had been hospitalized after a fight.

Yet eventually the police, the parents, the teens, and Bess's family all agreed to try to avoid forcing criminal records on the kids. Instead they set curfews and other restrictions, and the teens would work to pay back their neighbors. They returned the things they'd stolen. They painted over graffiti, scrubbed the eggs off the door, and helped out with yard work and chores around the house. One of the perpetrators even wrote an essay on integrity and read it to Bess.

Bess wasn't angry anymore, but something was still missing, and she felt unsettled. In her child's heart, she struggled with the grown-up truth that restitution is not the same as reconciliation. Though she and her neighbors had gotten to know each other better, she regretted the awkwardness and distance between them. She kept thinking about this, until an idea formed out of her confusion: she decided to throw a party—not just any party, but a "forgiveness party," as she called it. Her mother agreed to help her host the people who only weeks ago had pried open a window to her house and helped themselves to her special things.

Bess made a piñata and decorated the house and yard with lights and balloons. The party was a huge success. The teens from the break-in brought their families, and people got to know one another in new ways. As they danced to music from the formerly stolen tape player, they moved from anger and shame to compassion and joy. That day, enemies became friends.

How lovely to think that no one need wait a moment: we can start now, start slowly changing the world! How lovely that everyone, great and small, can make a contribution toward introducing justice straightaway!

ANNE FRANK

Teach your children conflict-resolution skills. Learn how to create nonviolent solutions to conflict with the Children's Creative Response to Conflict at the **Fellowship of Reconciliation,** P.O. Box 271, Nyack, NY 10960, or visit their Web site, www.forusa.org.

TEACHING JAZZ,
CREATING COMMUNITY
Told by Leslie R. Crutchfield

Adapted from "Democracy-Participation with Style" in *Who Cares Magazine*

Most people know Wynton Marsalis as a musician. But for students in Washington, D.C., he's a special kind of teacher. When he's not touring the country, he spends much of his time teaching jazz to kids, but he doesn't just show them how to play a few notes. Instead, he uses jazz to teach them about life.

Roberto Perez has always admired Marsalis as a great trumpet player. Roberto's been studying the instrument himself for the past eight years, and he thinks Wynton is the best. One day, Roberto's music teacher at Washington's Duke Ellington School of Arts surprised him by taking him to the local NPR station to meet his hero. The next day, Wynton gave him a free trumpet lesson. Wynton's honest critiques, not to mention two hours of concentrated attention and shared love of music, gave Roberto the encouragement he needed to do his best.

Five months later, they had another lesson over the phone. "We talked for three hours," Roberto says. This time they expanded their range: they talked about life, and about the importance of persistence, dedication, concentration, and consistent practice. Through this conversation, Roberto discovered that his favorite trumpet player was also a real person. "He's very giving, always making time for you," he says.

Over the past decade, Wynton has visited more than one thousand schools and mentored several students like Roberto. "What a kid learns from jazz is how to express his individuality without stepping on somebody else's," he says. Wynton teaches them two main ideas. "The first thing I tell them is 'Play anything you want, as long as it sounds like you. It's important to develop yourself and your own vision.' It's about finding purpose in life," he says. "Kids need to learn to walk their own path."

The second lesson is that individualism has a flip side: "While pursuing your individuality, recognize that other people are also pursuing theirs." So he teaches them how to control their self-expression. "Don't just blurt something out. Adapt it to what the other guy is doing. Take your freedom and put it into the service of somebody else's," he tells the kids. "Being a good neighbor, that's what jazz is all about."

As a young child, Wynton learned some pretty tough lessons about being a good neighbor. He was born in New Orleans in 1961, the second of six sons. He remembers people calling him "nigger," and being forced to integrate into hostile white schools. He was shocked to discover that the better a black student did, the more he was attacked.

Nonetheless, he bravely worked for straight-As and won every musical competition he entered. At seventeen, he was admitted to New York's elite Juilliard School—one of the youngest musicians ever to enter. But the school didn't fit his style, and Wynton left after his first year. He later joined Art Blakey's Jazz Messengers, eventually becoming the first artist to win Grammy awards in both the classical and jazz categories. The rest is musical history.

Although Wynton's father, the great jazz pianist Ellis Marsalis, had the greatest influence on his music, it was his mother who taught him the most about life. He remembers her saying, "You better develop your mind, show some humility, and act like you had some home-training." Wynton says that, next to his parents, the writer Albert Murray had the most influence on him. "Murray said, 'To hell with whining,' " Wynton explains. "Humanity doesn't move forward by complaining about the fact that life is hard. You can't discard the whole apple because one section is rotten." Optimistic to the core, he adds, "You gotta cut that rotten section away and eat the rest."

Wynton says his greatest gift is the ability to listen to the soul of a musician. That's how he can teach students after hearing them play only once. "When they play and I hear their sound, I can tell what kind of grades they make in school and what kind of habits they have. I can just hear it in their sound. I know what they're saying. Sometimes, they're saying 'Help'." Wynton reaches out to them with more than a helping hand. Through jazz, he shows them a richer, fuller life.

Roberto is now a junior at Howard University and still playing his trumpet. Whenever Wynton comes to town, Roberto goes to see him perform. It's been two years since they first met—and Wynton still gives him direction and advice—about the jazz world and the world in general. "Wynton is the best teacher I've ever had," says Roberto. "He's taught me, 'If you love what you do you'll always succeed.'" By example, he's also shown Roberto how to work for that success. Roberto says, "If he wants something, he'll do whatever it takes to accomplish his goal."

To help bring music into the lives of children:

- Support music events in your community.
- Attend concerts given as fund-raisers for school music programs or scholarships.
- Invite people in your community to donate old musical instruments to schools.
- Call Rotary Clubs to learn how to donate instruments to developing countries.

To learn more about Wynton Marsalis and his Jazz for Young People program, visit www.jazzatlincolncenter.org/jazz/arti/lcjo/marsalis.html.

FATHER JOE

Told by Dennis Morgigno

At San Diego's newest and most exclusive shopping center, home to Cartier, Ferragamo, Gucci, and Dunhill, on the third floor, around the balcony that circles the atrium, the clinking of fine crystal mixed with the easy laughter of the revelers at yet another grand opening. Among the guests that night was a large man dressed in black, though not quite like the others in their tuxedos and evening gowns.

The caterer was about to call the guests to his steaming pans of hors d'oeuvres and entrees when he noticed the man in black. He replaced the lid on one of the large warming pans and walked over to him. "Father Joe?" the caterer asked. "I once stood in your food line. Now I want you to be the first to stand in mine."

It's the kind of story Father Joe Carroll never tires of telling. In the fifteen years since opening his revolutionary St. Vincent de Paul Village in San Diego, he's seen thousands of people leave the streets, regain their dignity, and return to productive lives. There's no better example than the caterer Jim Miller, a former construction worker whose alcohol and cocaine abuse led to his sleeping under cardboard by San Diego Bay. One day Miller stumbled onto the food line outside St. Vincent's. He took nourishment for his body while he sorted out his soul. "You have to be ready to kick," he says. "And when you are, you're really thankful for the programs and the support they offer here."

For Father Joe Carroll, a warm and friendly visionary of a man, his role at St. Vincent's is nothing short of divine irony. "From the time I was five until I was twelve, every Christmas present was from the St. Vincent de Paul thrift store in the Bronx. We were a poor family; and when we ran out of food, my mother would go to St. Vincent's. It's funny how God works. I was the one chosen to give back what my family had received all those years."

Not that young Father Joe didn't need a little push. "I never really wanted to do it," Carroll says. "But Leo [the late Bishop Leo Maher] called me in one day and said, 'Tomorrow, you're the new head of St. Vincent's. You're the biggest New York hustler we have. We need you there.'"

Father Joe soon realized the old man had seen the real Joe Carroll, a young priest others would follow, someone who would not be afraid to use his peculiar powers of persuasion to build St. Vincent's into a force in the community. He eventually became known far and wide as "the hustler priest," picking the pockets of average citizens and major philanthropists alike to turn his down-to-earth vision into reality.

The first test came at a local parish, where the pastor issued a challenge. He would support Father Joe's plan for St. Vincent's if Carroll could raise five thousand dollars from the second collection at a mass, always the hardest. Father Joe rose to the challenge. "Homelessness is a social disease," he preached. "It destroys communities like a cancer." The kid from the Bronx had their attention. "The cancer spreads. It gets neighbors fighting neighbors and pretty soon no one's working together."

Joe Carroll raised twenty thousand dollars that day—at one church. Other churches followed, joined by members of the community. Helen Copley, owner of San Diego's largest daily newspaper, was St. Vincent's first major benefactor. Her $250,000 donation gave the project credibility. McDonald's matriarch and former San Diego Padres owner Joan Kroc sealed the deal, giving Carroll $3 million to finish the first phase of the Village.

Father Joe did more than build a shelter; he changed the way a whole city dealt with homelessness. He insisted that communities "break the cycle of homelessness," not just offer indigent people an occasional meal and a place to park their bedrolls at night. When he began his crusade in late 1982, San Diego was doing nothing more than that for the legions of homeless attracted to its warm weather.

The few shelters that existed protected people overnight from the storm drains and underpasses; the meal programs offered peanut-butter breakfasts and dismal soup lines—better than nothing, but not good enough. Carroll ignored those who said his Village was "too nice" for homeless people. He believed that feeding and clothing the homeless was only half the battle. By restoring people's dignity, you can help them reclaim their lives.

St. Vincent de Paul Village is a community where dignity and hope are reborn every day. He built apartments where homeless families would have privacy, and large, clean dormitories for single men and women. The Village now has a medical clinic, job training programs, a school for children, and financial counseling for their parents. A huge central kitchen churns out three meals a day for everyone who calls the Village home.

In September, nine years after the first residence opened its doors, St. Vincent's served its ten-millionth meal. The records show that after a year in Father Joe's program, more than 80 percent of families live in homes of their own and have a positive cash flow.

Father Joe has become a San Diego celebrity and an international symbol as a champion for the homeless. In January 1988, the United Nations gave him the International World Habitat Award. He has opened villages in Las Vegas, Nevada, and Indio, Cailfornia, and has plans for a ranch for 240 boys and girls who have lost their families. "Father Joe's Villages" have truly become a beacon of hope.

But he never forgets his roots. "We have a policy here that, no matter what the size of the donation, if I'm here, you can give it to me personally. We used to have a little old lady who got five-pound blocks of cheese from the federal food program. She would cut them in half every month and give half to us. My staff would call me out of a meeting and she'd hand it to me. Those people are just as important to what we do as the big donors," says Father Joe, and you can tell he really means it.

"Father Joe's Villages have become a catalyst for people who care," Joe says with more than a touch of awe and gratitude in his voice. "We're giving them an opportunity to give back, and people like Jim Miller an opportunity to live again."

The only solution is to love.

DOROTHY DAY

Help end the cycle of poverty for the homeless. Visit **Father Joe's Village** and see how its "continuum of care" supports over four thousand residents and nonresidents with housing, meals, counseling, drug and alcohol programs, medical and dental care, children's services, job training—all at one site. Call 619-687-1066 for inspiration or for a tour, or visit their Web page, www.father joesvillages.org.

OAKLAND'S FIREFIGHTING PEACEMAKER

On Sunday, September 23, 2001, New York City honored the six thousand* victims of the September 11 terrorist attacks on the World Trade Center, the Pentagon, and United Airlines Flight 93, in a mass memorial service at Yankee Stadium. When Bette Midler sang "Did I ever tell you you're my hero?" she gave words to people who were speechless with grief. She expressed the pride and gratitude people felt, especially for the 344 firefighters who'd lost their lives that day, "just doing their jobs," that is, selflessly risking their lives, to keep their promise to "preserve life and property," and saving over 25,000 people.

*At the time, this was the estimated number of missing and dead. The number has since been revised downward to under three thousand.

Oakland's fire captain, Ray Gatchalian, joined his "brothers," some of the twelve thousand New York City firefighters and their families, that day. "They showed us what it means to be a hero," says Ray. "They exemplify the best in all of us."

Ray had been at "Ground Zero" that week, along with thousands of other fire-fighters from across the country and around the world, who came to help New York City firefighters search night and day for their colleagues. "It's about show-ing up when things get tough," says Ray. "The courage and the kindness that I experienced there was incredible." Local firefighters appreciated the help; one New York City fireman said simply, "Thanks for being here." Ray couldn't have imagined being anywhere else. Through all his years as a firefighter, his ears had become very sensitive to the call of duty. Ten years earlier, on October 20, 1991, he'd shown up for what became known as the largest wildland urban fire in U.S. history.

Exhausted from fighting a five-alarm grass fire the day before, Ray was at home resting when he was rudely interrupted. His electricity went out. Fierce winds outside his window shrieked at him in a voice all too familiar. From his deck Ray could see the smoke and flames. There was the sound of a helicopter overhead, and a voice from a loudspeaker: "Evacuate the area! Evacuate the area, now!"

Ray thought of his wife, their daughter, their home and elderly neighbors, and for a few moments, he was torn: "Do I stay here with them, or do I go and fight the fire?" After securing their safety, Ray closed the door to his house, thinking it might be for the last time. He climbed into Oscar, his faithful '65 Chevy pickup truck, and headed to Fire Station 15, where he and another off-duty firefighter, John Arnerich, loaded up the few remaining hoses and nozzles and made Oscar their honorary fire engine.

They sped to the edge of the fire, where it was threatening to jump into the next canyon. In the intense heat of the first hour, the fire was consuming homes at the rate of one every five seconds. By the end of that day, twenty-five people would lose their lives, 3,276 homes would be destroyed, 1,520 acres would be scarred, and in its ashes the fire would leave an estimated $1.52 billion in damages, the largest wildland urban fire in U.S. history.

In all his years, Ray had never seen a fire burn with such ferocity. He recalls, "I had fought in Vietnam. I'd witnessed the destruction of civil war in El Salvador, and pulled bodies from earthquakes in San Francisco and Oakland. But I wasn't prepared to see the devastation of my own community. I was stunned, in total shock."

Ray called the fire department dispatcher and pleaded for help, but there was nothing left to send. All twenty-three fire engines and seven fire trucks were already on the fire lines. When the dispatcher replied, he realized they were on their own: "Ray, I will do the best I can to get someone up there, but I can't promise. God bless."

By now the fire threatened to engulf the entire neighborhood if they didn't somehow slow it down. Several onlookers offered to help, and Ray quickly organized them into a makeshift fire brigade. He looked warily at his volunteers—a dozen young, untrained, unprepared people—but what they lacked in experience, they made up for with spirit.

With nothing but the spare equipment they'd loaded onto Oscar, Ray led his makeshift crew in a courageous three-hour stand against the fire. The angry red monster roared, ready to turn on the firefighters without a moment's notice, but they roared back, saving many homes in the vicinity and preventing its advance to the adjacent canyon, where it would have gained even more strength. But their work was far from over.

When the fire engines finally arrived to relieve them, one of Ray's volunteers, Rich Stover, heard that his own mother's home was on fire. His new brothers, as firefighters come to know one another, were not about to let the fire destroy one of their own. So, exhausted but determined, they took their limited resources and regrouped to save Rich's mother's home and six of her neighbors'. In the heat of those critical hours, Rich, a twenty-eight-year-old general contractor, decided to become a firefighter. He explained, "Fighting the fire with Ray changed my life. It rekindled my desire to help others."

TV cameras from around the world captured dramatic footage showing the magnitude of the devastation, but they missed the selfless heroism of these volunteers and hundreds of others like them, without whom the loss of life and property would have been catastrophic. "Some say they were stupid, while some would say it was valor," Ray says now. "But once you face such a monstrous thing, your life is transformed."

Ray has other battles to fight and people to rally. A Vietnam Green Beret veteran now dedicated to peace, he once got doctors to donate their services to refugees, and then influenced Congress with his award-winning documentary film to stop military aid to El Salvador. He's organized a month-long, round-the-clock, torch-bearing vigil in his Oakland community to build solidarity against violence and create peace. He now works with incarcerated young people in Alameda County and provides scholarships to street children in Mongolia. Upon his return from New York City, Ray invited the Oakland community to create "Celebrate Courage" and raised $75,000 for the 15,000 children who lost a parent in the tragedy.

Ray would be the first to tell you he's just a regular guy. You decide. He credits his father with instilling in him the desire to help others. "We're here to inspire one another, to bring out the best in each other," his father told him. On September 11, the New York City firefighters did just that, and their example will inspire thousands of young people to become firefighters.

Help Ray provide hope and opportunities to orphaned and abandoned children in developing countries. Your donations will help fund the college education of those most in need. For more information, contact Ray via e-mail at rgatch@dnai.com.

Firefighter's Prayer

When I am called to duty,
Wherever flames may rage,
Give me the strength to save a life
Whatever be its age.

Help me embrace a little child
Before it is too late,
Or save an older person from
The horror of that fate.

Enable me to be alert
And hear the weakest shout,
And quickly and efficiently
To put the fire out.

I want to fill my calling and
To give the best in me,
To guard my every neighbor and
Protect his property.

And if according to God's will
I must answer death's call,
Bless with your protecting hand,
My family one and all.

THE POWER OF AN IDEA

Told by Jeb Bush and Brian Yablonski

One Sunday morning in the spring of 1993, eleven-year-old David Levitt read "The Power of an Idea" in *Parade* magazine. The story was about a Kentucky man named Stan Curtis, who founded USA Harvest, a network of volunteers to transport donations of food to hungry people. David was so intrigued, particularly by their motto, "Feeding the Hungry Without Money," that he paid a visit to his local Harvest in Tampa, Florida, to find out more.

He learned about USA Harvest's more than eighty chapters across the nation and gathered plenty of information about Stan Curtis's food donor program, called "Operation Food for Thought," in Louisville, Kentucky, where school cafeterias donate and Operation Food delivers leftover food to the hungry. David wondered if a similar program could be created in his school, so that leftover food could feed the homeless in local soup kitchens.

The sixth-grader first approached his school principal with the idea, but the principal told David that government regulations had previously prevented programs like this from ever getting off the ground. But David was not discouraged.

Over the next few weeks David collected facts and figures from Tampa Bay Harvest and Operation Food for Thought. He researched Florida's laws regarding food donations, then he wrote a proposal, made eight copies of it, and personally delivered it to the superintendent and all seven members of the Pinellas County School Board.

While he was at the school board office, David asked to see their meeting room. Photographs of each of the board members hung on the wall, and as he looked at them, he wondered how an eleven-year-old would be able to sway these powerful people when others had failed. Still, David was not discouraged. What if he called each of them personally to share his idea? No one had ever taken the time to do this before. The school board members were impressed indeed by David's determination.

David's twelfth birthday was a big one. He found himself standing before the Pinellas County School Board in the same awesome room he had been in only weeks before. His persistence and hard work had paid off. The school board unanimously approved his plan! David smiled in victory. "It just took a kid to help them see that this matters," he mused.

Five months went by, however, without any action. David was getting impatient, knowing food was being wasted and people were going hungry, so he called the president of Tampa Bay Harvest to see what could be done. It turned out that they needed airtight containers to ship the food, but neither the school system's budget nor Tampa Bay Harvest could afford them. Again, David would not be discouraged. He set out on a quest for containers. From his local supermarket, he got the addresses of companies that made containers, and sent letters to every one of them. Publix responded with a one-hundred-dollar gift certificate to buy containers. He was making progress, but it wasn't nearly enough, until he received a letter from an executive at First Brands Company, maker of Glad plastic bags. They were so impressed with his project that they sent him eight cases of airtight storage bags, and later committed to providing an ongoing supply. David was delighted.

The program was finally ready to begin. It had taken just about a year from the time David met with the school board for the first school-lunch food to find its way to the hungry. At first, ten schools donated their leftover lunches to soup kitchens and local shelters. Today, 110 schools in Pinellas County participate. By the time David graduated from high school in 2000, they'd donated over a million pounds of food.

Now a junior, majoring in business at the University of Florida, David challenges, "Can you imagine how much food there would be for the homeless if all the food servers throughout the U.S. participated in food donation programs?"

For his part, he keeps finding ways to make this happen. In 1998 he helped pass legislation to extend Florida's Good Samaritan Law to protect transporters as well as donors and recipients of donated food. The State Department of Agriculture created a brochure informing restaurants and hotels of the law, encouraging them to participate in the food donation program. Florida state universities now require students getting a food management degree to take a course on the food donation program.

When David tells others about his experience, he says, "Kids *can* make a difference, and adults *will* take the time to listen to kids." And he's always looking for creative ways to get more food to the people who need it. At his bar mitzvah, he asked guests to bring canned foods for Tampa Bay Harvest, and his friends and family responded with over five hundred pounds of food. Mindy, his former babysitter, couldn't afford to buy him a present. She was struggling to pay for her own college education. But her gift to David—time donated in his honor to a shelter for the homeless near her campus—couldn't have come closer to his heart.

"The most important thing I've learned is how good it makes you feel when you do something to help others," David said in his bar mitzvah speech. "Working with the Harvest program has made me a better person." He adds, "I want to champion causes like this as long as I live."

> *Fortunately for us and our world, youth is not easily discouraged. Youth, with their clear vista and boundless faith and optimism, are uninhibited by the thousands of considerations that always bedevil man in his progress. The hopes of the world rest on the flexibility, vigor, capacity for new thought, and fresh outlook of the young.*
>
> DWIGHT D. EISENHOWER

Empower yourself to help feed the hungry! Call **USA Harvest** at 800-USA-4FOOD, or **Tampa Bay Harvest** at 813-538-7777; or visit www.tampabay harvest.org.

A LITTLE EXTRA

Sometimes tragedy brings out the best in people, spurring the more fortunate to give to others what they've received themselves. After the bombing of the Alfred P. Murrah Federal Building in Oklahoma City, one young man wanted to help the children who had lost their parents. His generosity has made it a little easier for 207 children to get on with their lives.

Ronnie Fields and his parents had always been close. They did everything together: they worked on their fifteen-acre farm, danced the two-step on Saturdays, and went to church on Sundays. On Friday nights they ate Ronnie's mother's delicious homemade pizza.

Carroll Fields was only eighteen years old when she married Ron Fields and started working at the Oklahoma Drug Enforcement Administration—over thirty years ago. Ronnie dearly loved his mother. When he started college, they talked nearly every day. She told him often how much she loved him. What he remembers most about his mother is her laughter. Just two weeks earlier, she'd come to the Mother's Day festivities at his fraternity at Oklahoma University. The pictures they took together that day turned out to be their last.

One morning Ronnie came down for breakfast at his fraternity house, and someone asked him if he'd heard the news. When he turned on the TV, he knew right away it was his mom's office building that had been bombed. The roof to the top floor, where her office had been, was now flapping in the wind.

Ronnie called his dad and then drove home, the longest fifty miles of his life. As he passed by the building on his way home, he couldn't even look at it. It took over a week to find out if his mother was dead or alive, while rescuers worked around the clock to clear rubble and recover victims. The news, when it came, confirmed their worst fear: Carroll Fields was one of the 168 people who died that horrible day, April 19, 1995.

People all over the country were shocked and moved, and deeply needed to do something to help someone, somehow. They prayed and sent donations, washed cars, wrote letters, and gave blood. In Lubbock, Texas, a young child put a dollar in an envelope and addressed it to "Big Help" in Oklahoma City.

In Santa Clara, California, Chris Gross couldn't stop thinking about the children. "I kept seeing the building and the images of the children who died in the day-care center," he said. He kept thinking about them and the others, the ones who had lost their parents. "Imagine being one of them," Chris thought. "Put yourself in their shoes. They're going to be missing their parents for the rest of their lives."

Like Ronnie Fields, Chris had been close with his own parents. He had grown up knowing he was lucky and feeling grateful for his life. At an early age his parents had instilled in him the Jewish tradition of *tsdaka*, giving to others. Chris remembers how his mother would always buy too many cookies from the Girl Scouts. "When young people are trying, give them an opportunity to succeed," she would say. "Never turn them away."

Chris's parents also fostered an appreciation for learning, and worked hard to put Chris and his brother through college. "I always thought that if most parents had a dying wish for their children, they would say, 'Go to college, make something of yourselves,'" says Chris. He thought the Oklahoma parents would have wanted this for their children, too. He wondered how he could help make this wish come true.

He started by talking with his friends. "Wouldn't it be great if we created a scholarship fund and raised a million dollars to give these kids some hope for their future?" Chris asked them. "Right now, everyone is making them dinners and offering them clothes. But in five or ten years, will anyone really be there to help? If we start now, we could make a big difference in these kids' lives."

Chris searched for ways to jump-start a scholarship fund. Having graduated only a few years earlier, he knew how expensive it was to go to college. As a financial analyst at Applied Materials, a semiconductor equipment company, his yearly salary was $54,000. It was a good salary for a young man, but not enough to finance the education of so many children. Even if he gave it all, he would only have enough for one scholarship. But what if he could get others to match his salary? Chris decided to share his idea with Tom Hayes, vice-president of corporate affairs, and ask for his help. "What if we could get eighteen other Silicon Valley companies to match my salary?" Chris proposed. "We could raise a million dollars!"

"A couple of years earlier, I wouldn't have had the money. In a couple more years, I'd be married with lots of responsibilities," Chris reflects. "I was at an optimal point in my life." He calculated his finances: he had $12,000 in the bank, with no car payments or debt. He figured if he cut way back on his spending and planned things carefully, he could live on his savings for one year. So Chris learned to live with less: he slowed down his fast-paced life, gave up his cell phone, and wore the same clothes instead of buying new ones. He kept up his social life by going out with friends for dessert, instead of an entire meal.

When Chris's employer decided to match his salary, he was on his way toward meeting his goal. For the next several weeks he spent many long days faxing and telephoning people in other Silicon Valley companies, inviting them to participate in the scholarship fund. When he felt tired, he gained strength knowing he would someday be able to help children in Oklahoma City.

His persistence paid off. Chris succeeded beyond his wildest dreams. After about a year, he'd raised $400,000 from twelve of the eighteen corporations he had contacted. When the press ran a story, hundreds of people across the country wrote letters and sent checks, adding another $300,000 to the fund. Oklahoma's governor, Frank Keating, was so impressed with Chris's scholarship fund that he added another $3 million to it from the general donation fund. "Giving people the chance to succeed stuck with me," Chris says. "I just wondered what one person could do."

The Oklahoma City Scholarship Fund is hope for 224 children who know they will receive all the support they need when it's time to go to college. Ronnie Fields was one of the first to receive a scholarship. After the bombing, he didn't know if he could continue his college education. Before his mom was killed, she had paid his college tuition. Ronnie worked after school, but he couldn't take on any more debts. At times he thought of dropping out of school. When the Oklahoma City Community Foundation called him with the good news about the scholarship fund, he knew his prayers had been answered. He had prayed for something good to come out of the tragedy.

In turn, Ronnie thought long and hard about his future and how he could share his gifts with others. He had enjoyed working with young people as a peer counselor. An easygoing, fun-loving, and patient guy, he connected easily with them. He could also relate. "When I was a teen, sometimes I was a real jerk, thinking I was too cool to be with my parents," he remembers with regret, "and I have a video to prove it!"

Ronnie decided he could help young people build a strong foundation for their lives if he went to graduate school and became a youth minister. He graduated from Brite Divinity School at Texas Christian University in Fort Worth, and now serves a congregation in Texas. He works with youth councils to plan local and statewide youth events. "Live life to the fullest, don't get stressed out about the little things, and don't wait to enjoy your life," he counsels young people. "Do as much good as you can—and have some fun."

After September 11, Ronnie spoke to youth groups in Texas about finding hope in tragic situations. "I still believe more good can come out of bad situations," he told them. "We only have to look for the opportunities."

Ronnie thinks about his mother every day, and often feels her loving spirit with him. "You never know when any of us are going to go," he tells young people. "So appreciate the time you have with your parents."

One day Ronnie hopes to meet Chris and thank him for helping to make all this possible. "I wouldn't be here if it weren't for him," Ronnie says gratefully. "It's done wonders for me. It's changed my whole life."

If God is watching us, the least we can do is be entertaining.

RONNIE FIELDS

If you know of some children who especially need more encouragement and support, you could start a scholarship fund. To get started, just call your local community foundation or bank trust department.

SHE KEPT HER PROMISES
Told by Trude Lash

In her time, Eleanor Roosevelt became the most trusted woman in the world, and not because she was the president's wife, or because she was born into one of the country's leading families. Eleanor Roosevelt earned people's trust by always keeping her promises.

When she was a very young child, Eleanor's father promised her that when she was a little older, the two of them would live together again. She lived for that day. After her mother died, she was very lonely, living with her grandmother, who was very old, strict, and old-fashioned. When her father broke his promise, it broke her heart. At ten years old, she realized that she had to become strong in herself if she wanted to go on living, and she vowed that she would never break a promise. For the rest of her life, she could always be counted on to keep her word.

The soldiers in the hospitals in the Pacific islands that she visited during World War II believed her when she said she would telephone their families the moment she got home. Something in her manner made people know they could trust her.

The moment I met her, my life changed. I was married with three children, living a very comfortable life. I didn't think there was anything I could really contribute. "Well, that's very silly," she remarked. Since I had a good education, she expected me not only to be a good wife and mother, but to go out and work. She convinced me that I had work to do, so I concentrated on doing what I could do. I started by using my knowledge and my training, and then taking a leadership role and working hard. She always helped people to become stronger. She expected her friends to grow up and grow better, because they owed that to themselves.

In the early days of the United Nations, I was acting secretary to her Human Rights Commission. Later I became executive director of the Citizens' Committee for Children. I was twenty-four years younger than she was, and worked with her whenever possible. In the beginning I stood in awe of her, but eventually we worked together easily, though my admiration for her never changed.

She visited handicapped war veterans, who expected her to work miracles, to straighten out their cases with the Veterans Administration, to provide a wheelchair or help them find a special job. And she often did. I know of one man, crippled in the war, whom she encouraged when he had given up. She stayed in touch with him, and he became a leader in the veterans' organizations. Because she believed in him and helped him, both practically and financially, he was able to believe in himself.

"Mrs. Roosevelt, I have lost my job and can't find another," some would say. "If you help me think through what kind of job you would like," she would respond, "we could try and find one." The strange thing is that of all the impossible things she was asked for, she quite often did the most impossible ones. She was a woman of much influence, and was quite willing to use that influence to help others. She never hesitated to write to the secretary of state or members of Congress if she thought they could do something and she felt that what she was asking for was important. She never tried to force people, or to throw her weight around. She just used her influence to get people what she really believed they deserved.

There was no stronger foe of racial discrimination. She would say, "As long as we leave out some large number of people, we are not yet one nation." When the Daughters of the American Revolution denied the great African-American contralto Marian Anderson the use of their property, Washington's Constitution Hall, for a concert, Mrs. Roosevelt got Secretary of the Interior Harold Ickes to arrange for Anderson to sing at the Lincoln Memorial. And then she resigned from the DAR. During World War II, she fought for equal rights in the armed forces. Once, when she arrived to speak at a meeting in the South, she found that the white audience members sat on one side of the aisle, and blacks on the other. She put her chair in the middle of the aisle and spoke from there. When a leading African-American educator, Mary McLeod Bethune, needed help for her fledgling Bethune College for women, she invited her to the White House. She received an avalanche of hostile reactions for arranging for Bethune to meet people who could help her, yet she carried on.

She also felt that women's rights had been neglected—that women had fewer rights than men—and she worked for them tirelessly. When she first came to Washington, the president was having press conferences—just for men. She held press conferences just for women. And at her press conferences she gave the women real news. Loath to miss the scoop, the men would come and ask, "What did she say? What did she say?"

She was often called a "do-gooder," but she found companionship with other do-gooders like Gandhi, who also expected much of himself—and who moved through difficult situations so he could free people. Sometimes officials would say, "Mrs. Roosevelt is a bother." Sometimes I'm sure she was, the way people who believe in doing things are bothers to others who don't really feel like it. It's necessary to be bothersome sometimes. She used to say that if you have power, you can contribute somehow. She felt it was always worth trying, and she would do that very quietly without claiming recognition.

When her husband became president, the expectations for a first lady were very limited. Through her significant contributions to her husband's administra-

tion, she changed all that and became a role model for the rest of this country—
and for future presidents' wives.

She did an invaluable service for the president when he wasn't able to travel.
She would scout things out for him and help people and give them comfort and
bring back the important information to him about what was happening in the
country. She had started to serve as the president's "legs" when he was governor
of New York, where she inspected state institutions. The president trained her
well. "I don't want any indirect reports," he would say to her. "You go and see for
yourself." In the beginning he would ask her questions she couldn't answer after
her visits. That didn't last. She learned quickly to observe carefully, to look
behind the door to see where the dirty dishtowels were hidden, and to look for
the special staff menu. She was often the one who had to bring the president the
bad news when others wanted to please him.

Her heart went out to families who were refugees from Nazi terror. She visited
refugee camps in Europe, Israel, and Africa, and raised funds for services to their
children. She led the fight for legislation that would have admitted thousands of
children from beleaguered Great Britain to the U.S. The desperate political
refugees often said that Mrs. Roosevelt was the one person who gave them the
feeling that life was worth living. She believed in them—and she believed that
the fight against Hitler was the absolute fight at that time. She arranged for an
endless number of affidavits for people to come to this country.

She considered the United Nations her husband's greatest achievement. After
his death, she became his surrogate, the most powerful advocate for the UN. As
chairman of the Human Rights Commission, she labored ceaselessly to develop
the Human Rights Declaration and to bring the underdeveloped and Western
nations together. When she first became a member of the U.S. delegation, the
men shrugged her off and gave her the unimportant assignments. But they came
to respect her as the most thoughtful, hard-working, admired member of the delegation, the one most concerned about the inclusion of all—not only the powerful nations—in planning for the future.

Over time, she became a leader in her own right. She remained her own un-assuming self, and her majesty combined with her modesty were irresistible to all who met her. She was a realist and knew how much struggle, how many battles between nations and factions, lay in the path of progress, what hard efforts would be needed for even the smallest step ahead. Yet she remained a believer. Her love for people was undiminished, her beliefs were passionate, her work was strong to the end of her days. Even grim disappointments did not discourage her. She simply tried harder next time—her commitment and conviction that you had to fight for your beliefs were for life.

She never gave up. One thing she couldn't stand was someone saying, "But what can I do? I can't do anything." She would say, "We have gotten ourselves in a nice big hole and we have lost a lot of power, but that's because we weren't working hard enough for our country."

She often spoke of individual responsibility and thought we shouldn't blame everything on Washington, or look for someone else to blame. "Let's look at our-selves," she would say. Maybe we did not live up to what we were supposed to do. Discuss it, talk about it, but do something about it.

She's been gone now for thirty-five years, yet she is still with us. Last year a statue of Eleanor was unveiled in a beautiful spot in New York's Riverside Park. It is amazing that there hadn't been one before commemorating her—or any other American woman. Thousands streamed into the surrounding streets and stood quietly through the dedication ceremonies. Even though they couldn't hear or see very much, they wanted to be there. They came to pay respect to a great woman who was important to them. And it's quite amazing to see the people who come and spend a while sitting on one of the benches, looking at the statue, honoring her work and her legacy.

To many of us, it was her being there as an example of what one person could do that changed and enhanced our expectations of ourselves; to others it was the love and care she gave to those she saw as the most needy and lonely. To all, it was her courage and untiring effort, her total dedication to service to others, that were so inspiring. When she died, a columnist friend wrote, "While she was with us, no man had to feel entirely alone."

You must do the thing you think you cannot do.

ELEANOR ROOSEVELT

The next time you're in New York, take some time to visit the Eleanor Roosevelt statue at 72nd Street and Riverside Drive. The **Eleanor Roosevelt Center** at Van Kill, New York, continues her work, especially improving race relations and developing community spirit. For more information, call 914-229-5302.

ASKING FOR HELP

Minutes after they first met in New York City, Mother Teresa asked John F. Kennedy Jr. to drive her to the airport to receive a shipment of donated clothing from New Delhi. "You see," she said, "I ask everyone for help all the time. I ask and I ask and just when they think they've done enough and are fed up with me, I ask for more."

"It was thrilling to help her," John said. "How many times have you jumped at the chance to drive someone to the airport through some of the worst traffic in the northern hemisphere?"

Princess Diana asked Mother Teresa how she could overcome the depression that haunted her. Mother Teresa asked Diana, in turn, to reach outside her troubled self to help others, especially the poorest of the poor. After that, Diana took up humanitarian work with gusto, and indeed found new joy and meaning in meeting, helping, and *loving* people all over the world.

In Ethiopia in 1981, hundreds of thousands of people were starving to death during a drought. The few hundred kilos of medicine and food Mother Teresa had brought from Calcutta were a tiny drop in that vast ocean of need, compounded by the confusion and lack of coordination among many international relief agencies. And the roads were so bad, she couldn't reach villages in the interior where the supplies were desperately needed.

Together with her sisters in Calcutta, she prayed and fasted, asking God to help the Ethiopian people, their animals and their land.

She also wrote a letter to the president of the United States. About a week later she received a telephone call from the White House, and President Reagan came on the line. He thanked her for her letter and assured her that on behalf of the American people he would do everything possible to see that help arrived quickly. "After that, thank God," she said, "the supplies started to flow, and helicopters got food to the villages."

When I met Mother Teresa in the Philippines in 1988, her eyes radiated the love that kept her going, and I saw how this one little woman was able to help so many, when with a glance she touched my life.

Hers was a shining example of the power of unconditional love, enduring faith, and inexhaustible joy. Fearlessly, she embraced the hungry, the homeless, the sick and the dying, the children of every faith and country. Her simple acts of love were contagious. Presidents and CEOs couldn't say no to her humble requests. People went to India and all around the world just to be with her and learn how to love.

Someone once told her that she was the most powerful woman in the world. She replied with a smile, "I wish I was. Then I would bring peace to the whole world."

Join Mother Teresa's revolution of the heart by caring for the poor in your community. To support Mother Teresa's work around the world directly, please write to the **Missionaries of Charity,** 54-A, AJC Bose Road, Calcutta 7000016, India.

EVERYBODY IN AMERICA IS HELPING

Told by Ram Dass

Adapted from the book *How Can I Help?* by Ram Dass and Paul Gorman

I am talking to a woman who is working for the Gallup poll. She's actually doing a poll on how much time people spend helping. She's trying to explain the criteria. I finally start to crack up, seeing something of the absurdity of it all.

"You all are crazy! 'How much time are people helping?' What kind of question is that? Tell Gallup he's nuts!"

She started to laugh as well. "I know. That's what I said, too. What can I tell you? It's a job." She was sort of whispering, which made me laugh more. We got into this conspiratorial, infectious laughter at it all. When we stopped laughing, I asked, "Was that helping?" She said, "I guess so, sort of. Why was it?"

I said, "That's *your* job. You tell *me* why." And then I threw in, "We were trying to make the best of a nutty situation. In fact, that's what I'm trying to do all the time. That's it—I want you to put me down in the Gallup poll as someone who helps all the time."

More laughter. She said, "We don't have a category for 'all the time.' "

"Oh ye of little faith."

"But we do have a line here that says 'all of the above.' " (At this point I didn't know if she was kidding, but I went for it.) "Perfect. Put me down under 'all of the above.' I am very all-of-the-above. In fact, you have to put everybody down under 'all of the above.' Everybody's trying to make the best of a nutty situation. Gallup can release a poll saying, 'Everybody in America is helping.'"

"God," she said, "I wish I had the nerve. Maybe I'll do it with an alternate answer. 'One out of every two people in America is helping.' The other half is being helped."

By this point we were just in love with the idea of throwing the topic back into blessed confusion, which is where it really is anyhow. Finally we said good-bye.

"It's been great," I said.

"Very helpful," she agreed.

Months later, there's a story in the newspaper: "Gallup Poll Reveals Half of All Americans Help Out as Volunteers." Right there in the paper. She did it! She pulled it off!

I rush into the kitchen, reading the headline to my wife. "That's me!" I exclaim. "Which half?" says my very formidable and wonderful wife.

"All of the above!" I answer triumphantly. "Just wash the dishes," she replies.

To learn more about Ram Dass's work and projects, visit his Web site, www.ram dasstapes.org.

ONE PERSON'S VOICE
Adapted from *The Weight of Nothing*

"Tell me the weight of a snowflake," a blackbird asked a wild dove.

"Nothing more than nothing," was the answer.

"In that case I must tell you a marvelous story," the blackbird said.

"I sat on the branch of a fir, close to its trunk, when it began to snow. . . . Since I didn't have anything better to do, I counted the snowflakes setting on the twigs and needles of my branch. Their number was exactly 3,741,952.

"When the next snowflake dropped onto the branch—nothing more than nothing, as you say—the branch broke off."

The dove, since Noah's time an authority on the matter, thought about the story for a while and finally said to herself, "Perhaps there is only one person's voice lacking for peace to come about in the world."

II

—

CULTURAL HEALING

Just think what could happen if the nightly news featured

as many stories about people who are committing acts of goodness

as those who are committing acts of violence.

What a powerful and transforming message we could give to our children!

T

he history of America is one of the most remarkable Stone Soup stories of all. In just three hundred years, people from all parts of the world have come to live together, forming the most culturally diverse country on the planet. We're here with our struggles and challenges, our talents and idiosyncrasies, as well as our hopes and dreams, the color, pattern, subject, and structure of our precious mosaic of nationalities, races, religions, and cultures. As a multicultural nation, while we have our own problems, we have an advantage in the world.

The victims of September 11 came from a cross-section of America, and of the world. They were black, white, Hispanic, Christian, Muslim, Jewish, rich, poor, and middle class—and that same diverse cross-section of people has helped with the relief efforts.

We're all in this together. It doesn't matter how much money you have, or what your religion is, or the color of your skin. Arab Americans in Ohio, Laotian Americans in Wisconsin, and Hispanic Americans in Iowa all feel a sense of pride when they say "I am an American." And in the days immediately after September 11, Cuban and Haitian refugees in Miami willingly worked overtime to keep up with the sudden demand for American flags.

After September 11, America's most famous Muslim, Muhammad Ali, pleaded for tolerance. And while hate crimes against Arab-looking people increased in some communities, so did acts of tolerance and solidarity. Proud of being the melting pot of the world, New Yorkers hung signs in their shop windows proclaiming "United We Stand," and "We Shall Overcome." In Toledo,

Ohio, the non-Muslim community joined hands with Muslims to form a protective circle around the Islamic Center's mosque.

The cultural heroes in this chapter show us that when we teach tolerance, learn forgiveness, and practice compassion, we can heal our collective wounds and move forward. When we bring people from different heritages together, we find ourselves on common ground, facing common problems. We can accept and even appreciate our differences, and we can rise above the distinctions that divide us. As individuals and as a people, we suffer injuries, but we can heal.

The Dalai Lama teaches tolerance, using the power of "truth, courage, and determination" to fight evil and, perhaps more important, to transform it. "If we wage war against our natural instinct for revenge, we will have done something very special," he says. "Then the world will recognize our stand against the endless cycle of violence—and there will be justice."

"We are one human race," Gandhi said. "Religion must unify us, not divide us." After a Hindi man he knew had lost his family in a horrific act of religious hatred, Gandhi asked him to set aside his anger and vengeance and learn how to forgive. "Go and find an orphan Muslim baby and nurture the baby as your own," he advised him. "You must allow the baby to grow up in its own faith."

The stories in this chapter honor people from every culture. Amazing as their protagonists are, they are human—real-life heroes for you to identify with, setting real-life standards we can work to uphold. These are compelling stories of African Americans, Native Americans, Hispanic Americans, Asian Americans, and European Americans who overcame obstacles, endured personal sacrifices, and courageously persevered to better the lives of their people. They have dispelled negative stereotypes, worked for justice, and restored cultural pride. These are powerful lessons about how we can heal our culture, of our country and the world.

The Civil Rights Movement in America offers hundreds of stories of courage and cooperation. These heroes remind us of what it takes to stand up for what we believe in, in the face of injustice. They show us the power of committing ourselves to a noble goal: once we decide to work for justice, somehow we find the strength to make tough choices and hard sacrifices. They show us how to become heroes: by transforming obstacles—despair and hatred, oppression and resentment—into opportunities to do better. They teach us never to give up hope.

Cultural healing sometimes requires humility and honesty. Healing can be painful. Some of the stories in this chapter remind us that terrible mistakes have been made, often by well-intentioned people. Everyone likes to be right, and no one wants to admit he was wrong. Alabama governor George Wallace's ability to admit his mistakes, to apologize for his hateful words and deeds against the Civil Rights Movement and to try to make amends, took great courage. It also took courage for others to forgive him, to allow him to join the thirtieth anniversary commemoration of the march from Selma to Montgomery.

Other stories show how one person can turn the tide against racism. In Montana, one Christian mother began the healing process in her community by rallying her neighbors to stand together and stop the hate crimes against their Jewish neighbors. An African-American minister teaches tolerance—to be willing and able to accept others and their differences so "that all different colors of hands reach down to help each other."

Some cultural healers broke free from the vicious cycle of poverty and then reached back to help others. Through their stories, we come to understand their struggles and celebrate their victories. It often takes tremendous courage, especially to realize that struggle and victory must start with ourselves. In the story about Edward James Olmos's work with young gangs in Los Angeles, George Sarabia says, "If I'm not able to forgive, when will it ever stop?"

Every culture has a long history and a rich tradition of helping others. In the Native American culture, children are taught to think about how their actions will affect the next seven generations. The African proverb "It takes a whole village to raise a child" reminds us that we are *all* responsible for raising *all* of our nation's children. The Jewish tradition of *tikkun olam* encourages people to carry out their responsibility of mending the world. In Puerto Rico, people say, *"Nos estamos moviendo nos para adelante."* ("By working together we can move forward.")

While not everyone can be a Martin Luther King Jr., a Gandhi or a Cesar Chavez, we can all learn from them and can help carry on their legacy. When we help one another, we bring out the best in ourselves and each other. Together, we can keep our promise to be "one nation, indivisible, with liberty and justice for all."

Let America be the dream the dreamers dreamed—
Let it be that great strong land of love . . .
Oh, let America be America again—
The land that never has been yet—
And yet must be. . . .

LANGSTON HUGHES,
from *Let America Be America Again*

When you hear of stories about people from different cultures who are committing acts of goodness, spread the good news. Share these stories with your friends, your newspaper editor, your TV reporter. Challenge your friends and family to practice greater tolerance. Take small steps toward healing our country and the world.

YOUNG ACTS OF COURAGE
Told by Melba Pattillo Beals
Adapted from the book *Warriors Don't Cry*

My grandmother India always said God had pointed a finger at our family, asking of us just a bit more discipline, more praying, and more hard work because He had blessed us with good health and good brains. My mother was one of the first few blacks to integrate the University of Arkansas, graduating in 1954. Three years later, I was one of nine black teenagers who integrated Central High School in Little Rock, Arkansas.

It was not yet eight o'clock in the morning when Mama and I parked at the curb just outside Mrs. Bates's home. Everybody spoke in whispers. I was ushered through the crowd and into the living room, where radio and news reports about the integration held everyone's attention.

As we filed silently out of the house, I waved good-bye to my mother. I wanted to hug her, but I didn't want everyone to think I was a baby. Other parents milled about, looking as if we were being carted off to be hanged. As we started to walk to the cars, they clutched at us as though they weren't completely certain we'd be coming back.

When we arrived at the school, the driver urged us to get out quickly. The white hand of a uniformed officer reached out toward the car, opened the door, and pulled me toward him as his urgent voice ordered me to hurry. The roar coming from the front of the building made me glance to my right. Only half a block away, I saw hundreds of white people, their bodies in motion, their mouths wide open as they shouted their anger. "The niggers! Keep the niggers out!" The shouts came closer. The roar swelled, as though their frenzy had been fired up by something. It took a moment to digest the fact that it was the sight of us that had upset them.

"The principal's office is this way," whispered a petite woman with dark hair and glasses. "Hurry, now, hurry." We were shoved into an office where a row of white people, mostly women, stood staring at us as though we were the world's eighth wonder. "Here are your class schedules and home-room assignments. Wait for your guides," said Mrs. Huckaby, the vice-principal. Each of us was assigned to a different home room. "Why can't any of us be in the same home room or take classes together?" I asked. From behind the long desk, a man spoke in an unkind, booming voice. "You wanted integration . . . you got integration."

I turned to see the hallway swallow up my friends. None of us had an opportunity to say a real good-bye or make plans to meet. I was alone, in a daze, following a white woman up the stairs. Frightened does not describe my state of mind at the time; I had moved on to being terrified. I had fantasized about how wonderful it would be to get inside the huge, beautiful castle I knew as Central High School. But the reality was so much bigger, darker, and more treacherous than I had imagined.

Suddenly I felt the sting of a hand slapping the side of my cheek, and then warm, slimy saliva on my face, dropping to the collar of my blouse. It was the first time I had ever been spat upon. I felt hurt, embarrassed. I wondered if I'd catch her germs. Before I could wipe it off, my guide's harsh command summoned me to move. "Get going. Now. Do you hear me? Move! Now!" I brushed the saliva off my nose with my hand, and stumbled after her.

As I entered a classroom, a hush fell over the students. The guide pointed me to an empty seat, and I walked toward it. Students sitting nearby quickly moved away. I sat down surrounded by empty seats, feeling unbearably self-conscious. One of the boys kept shouting ugly words at me throughout the class. I waited for the teacher to speak up, but she said nothing. My heart was weeping, but I squeezed back the tears. I squared my shoulders and tried to remember what Grandma had said: "God loves you, child. No matter what, He sees you as His precious idea."

Walking the gauntlet to my next class was even more harrowing. "You'd better watch yourself," the guide warned as we moved at high speed through the hostile students. The next class was gym. Out on the playing field, groups of girls were tossing a volleyball. It took me a moment to realize it was whizzing awfully close to my head. I ducked, but they hit me real hard, shouting and cheering as they found their target. And even as I was struggling to escape their cruelty, I was at the same time more terrified by the sound of the angry crowd approaching in the distance. Suddenly things got out of control. "Get inside, Melba. Now!" The face of the gym teacher showed both compassion and alarm as she quietly pointed to a group of women jumping over the rear fence as they shouted obscenities at me.

I was in tears, ready to give up, paralyzed by my fear. Suddenly Grandma's voice came into my head: "God never loses one of His flock." *Shepherd, show me how to go,* I said. I stood still and repeated those words over and over again until I gained some composure.

"I've been looking for you." My stocky guide's voice was angry, but I was so glad to see her that I almost forgot myself and reached to hug her. "Let's go to the shorthand class." She didn't know it, but she was the answer to my prayer. I looked over my shoulder to see the group of mothers standing still, obviously unwilling to come after me with a school official at my side. I choked back tears and speeded my steps.

As I headed for the last row of empty seats by the window, my shorthand teacher called out to me, "Melba, stay away from the window." Her voice was sympathetic, as though she really cared what happened to me. The ocean of people outside stretched farther than I could see—waves of people ebbing and flowing, shoving the sawhorses and the policemen who were trying to keep them in place. From my seat I could hear the crowd shouting, "Get the niggers," and "Two, four, six, eight, we ain't gonna integrate."

I looked up from my notes to see my guide entering the classroom. "Come with me now. To the principal's office," she called out nervously. I heard her frantic tone of voice, heard someone say the mob was out of control, that they would have to call for help. "There must be a thousand people out there, armed and coming this way." "Some of these patrolmen are throwing down their badges," another breathless voice said. "We gotta get these children out of here."

I heard footsteps coming closer. A tall, dark-haired man came toward us. "I'm Gene Smith, from the Little Rock Police Department. It's time for you to leave for today. Come with me now." Right away, I had a good feeling about him. He urged us to move faster, and acted as though it mattered to him whether or not we got out. I decided to remember this man forever in my prayers.

Outside, two cars were sitting with engines running, lights on, hoods pointing toward the door. "Hurry, now. Get in," Smith said as he held open one of the doors. Their expressions told me we were in a kind of trouble I hadn't even imagined before. "Hold on and keep your heads down," the driver shouted. The deafening noise of the mob engulfed us. That's when the car really began moving fast, faster than I'd ever ridden before. Finally there were fewer hands and faces on the car windows, and the noises subsided. I took a deep breath. I wanted to say, "Thanks for risking your life to save mine." It was an awkward moment with a stranger, a decent white man. He took me home, dropping me off right at my door. "Get in the house now—go," he said, pausing for an instant, then gunning his engine and pulling away. He was the second white man I would pray for God to protect.

That night in my diary I wrote, "There seems to be no space for me at Central High. I don't want integration to be like the merry-go-round. Please, God, make space for me."

Speaking from the White House that night on national television, President Eisenhower said he'd sent troops because "mob rule in Little Rock menaces the very safety of the United States and the free world." That night a man handed my mother an envelope from the president and said to her, "Let your daughter go back to school, and she will be protected." The next morning I saw them, about fifty uniformed soldiers from the 101st Infantry with well-shined boots and rifles at their sides. There were tears in my mother's eyes as she whispered good-bye. "Make this day the best you can," she said.

For the next several months I got up every morning, polished my saddle shoes, and went off to war. I entered Central High School, a building I remember only as a hellish torture chamber—a place that was meant to nourish us and prepare us for adulthood. Instead, it was like being a soldier on a battlefield.

I had always imagined that my last day of the term at Central High School would be marked by a grand ceremony, with a massive choir singing "Hallelu-jah," or perhaps some wonderful award from my community—a parade maybe. But it was the same as any other day. "It's over," my brother Conrad said. "You don't have to integrate anymore."

The next September we waited in vain to return to Central High. But Gover-nor Faubus closed all of Little Rock's high schools. Segregationists were squeez-ing the life out of the NAACP, the Bateses' newspaper, and the state press. Our people continued to lose their jobs, their businesses, and their homes to force us into withdrawing voluntarily from Central High. In despair, NAACP officials sent an announcement to chapters across the country, asking for families that would volunteer to give us safe harbor and support us in finishing our education. I was fortunate enough to go to the Santa Rosa, California, home of Dr. George McCabe and his wife, Ruth, and their four children. They were a family of polit-ically conscious Quakers committed to racial equality. More than their guid-ance, it was their unconditional love that taught me the true meaning of equality. Their love helped to heal my wounds and inspired me to launch a new life for myself.

Inspired by those journalists I had met during the integration, I followed my dream and became a news reporter. I always remembered it was the truth told by those reporters who came to Little Rock that kept me alive. Later, as an NBC television reporter, I would take special care to look into those unexposed cor-ners where otherwise invisible people are forced to hide as their truth is ignored.

Forty years later, Little Rock's Central High School is peacefully integrated. I look back on my Little Rock integration experience as a positive force that ultimately shaped the course of my life. Because we dared to challenge the Southern tradition of segregration, this school became, instead, a furnace that consumed our youth and forged us into reluctant warriors for civil rights. As Grandma India had promised, it taught me to have courage and patience.

I for one am grateful for the courage of youth.

ELEANOR ROOSEVELT

To learn more about Melba Beals, visit www.melbabeals.com.

To learn more about the Little Rock Nine, visit www.centralhigh57.org.

Smile at a neighbor. Help a stranger. Be grateful for your blessings, share them with others. Every child deserves a loving home. Join with Melba and those who work with **Aid to Adoption of Special Kids,** who have placed eleven thousand special children in caring homes over the last twenty years. Call 510-451-1748 or visit www.adoptaspecialkid.org.

A MIRACLE IN MONTGOMERY

Told by Reverend Joseph Lowery

Adapted from "God Makes the Crooked Places Straight" in *Fellowship, the Magazine of the Fellowship of Reconciliation*

In March 1996, many of us from the Civil Rights Movement, who had walked the historic path to freedom so long ago, retraced our steps from Selma to Montgomery, Alabama. This sacred trail, forever stained with the blood of martyrs, is hallowed by the hopes and dreams of those for whom we walked. We marched again to remind ourselves of the bitter price we paid thirty years ago for the right of all Americans, black and white, to vote, and the painful cost we pay today for failing to exercise that right.

With this march, we hoped to encourage a heightened level of voter activism and a revived sense of energy. We sought to gain support from politicians and dignitaries, from businesspeople and journalists. We accomplished all of those things, and much more. For on this day we were witnesses to a miracle.

In 1965, Martin Luther King Jr. appointed me to chair a committee of marchers assigned to present our demands to Alabama's governor, George Wallace. This was the man whose troops had brutalized us. He was the man who had called out snarling dogs on black marchers. He was the man who had stood in front of the schoolhouse door, to stop blacks from attending the University of Alabama.

As a Methodist preacher, speaking to a Methodist layman, I told him that God would hold him accountable for his hateful words, which others had transformed into hateful deeds. Those deeds took a heavy toll on people like Viola Liuzzo, Jimmie Lee Jackson, and many others who lost their lives in the struggle. At the time his response was, at best, indifferent. Yet thirty years later, in 1996, this man welcomed us back to Montgomery!

While some were opposed to granting Governor Wallace's request to participate in the march, I did not dare stand in the door against an act of repentance. Since he had nothing to gain politically, I appreciated his offer of reconciliation. That he wanted to join us and affirm our purpose was like the flash of lightning that shines across a way filled with shadows of malice.

By car, it's less than three hours from the University of Tuscaloosa to St. Jude High School, the beginning to the end of the march. But, by way of the heart, it has taken more than thirty years. That's the tortured distance traveled by Governor Wallace that day. At the end of that journey, here he was, paying honor to those he had stood against.

In 1972, Governor Wallace was shot and paralyzed by an enraged citizen. Later he said, "In a way that was impossible before the shooting, I think I can understand something of the pain that black people have come to endure. I know I contributed to that pain, and I can only ask forgiveness." In his last term as governor, in the late 1980s, he appointed more than 160 blacks to state governing boards, and doubled the number of black voter registrars in Alabama's counties.

Remembering the angry days of the 1960s, the hate, violence, intolerance, and stubbornness of this man, I am amazed at the governor's transformation. None of us could ever have dreamed that Wallace would come to embrace our cause, hold our hands, and sing our songs.

Well, almost none. Martin Luther King Jr., that dreamer whose life was cut short, had a vision.

> *I have a dream that one day, down in Alabama, with its vicious racists, with its governor having his lips dripping with interposition and nullification, that one day, right there in Alabama, little black boys and little black girls will be able to join hands with little white boys and girls as brothers and sisters. I have a dream today!*
>
> Dr. Martin Luther King Jr.

Encourage racial harmony in your school, your community, and your world. Learn how from the **Racial Dialogue and Reconciliation Program** at the Fellowship of Reconciliation, P.O. Box 271, Nyack, NY 10960; or visit their Web site at www.forusa.org.

LETTER FROM A BIRMINGHAM JAIL

Told by Andrew Young

Adapted from his book *An Easy Burden*

After some initial setbacks in the struggle for civil rights, some said we were beaten, but in fact we were more ready than ever to wage our nonviolent campaign. So we set our sights on the toughest town in the South—Birmingham, Alabama.

The Birmingham campaign was a turning point for the national Civil Rights Movement. It was also a turning point for our leader. Until then, Martin Luther King Jr. had always been cautious, even reluctant, about being a leader. It had been thrust upon him, and occasionally he would try to retreat from it all. But in Birmingham, I believe he finally came to accept that he could never walk away from the awesome responsibility that had fallen upon his shoulders.

Shortly after our campaign began, the city of Birmingham got a state court injunction against demonstrations. We knew that marches would result in certain imprisonment.

One morning about a dozen of us were squeezed into the living room of Martin's hotel room. We were facing a difficult decision and our unity of purpose began to fray as each person argued from his or her own viewpoint. "Martin, you've done all you can do here," one said. "Forget Birmingham for a while." Another one explained, "You can't put more people in jail now. We can't bail out the ones already in there. Sending more people to jail is just out of the question."

In this atmosphere of utter depression, Martin said very little. He just listened, as was his habit in high-pressure situations. Suddenly, he rose and retired into the rear bedroom. When he was gone for a while, the discussion finally slowed to a halt. Almost on cue, Martin and Ralph Abernathy came out dressed in denim jackets and jeans, our "work" uniform in Birmingham, which we wore to dramatize our solidarity with working people. "The only thing for me to do is go to jail, and join those people already there," Martin said. "And stay there until people see what we're dealing with. Those who're going with me, get ready."

Martin's decision to go to jail on Good Friday, 1963, made it possible for us to sustain both the Birmingham campaign and the movement throughout the South. But of course, we didn't know that yet. The march on that Good Friday did not last long. Martin, Ralph, and some fifty others strode past Kelly Ingram Park. A huge crowd of black citizens gathered around the march. We were stunned by the aggressiveness of the police, who began to push and shove the marchers, including Martin, onto the paddy wagon. "Don't rough up Dr. King like that," the bystanders screamed at the police.

Martin led the marchers along the sidewalk and stopped for red lights; still the marchers were arrested for parading without a permit and their bonds were set as if their offense were first-degree murder. One of the intimidating tactics used by the city of Birmingham was to set the bond at one thousand dollars or more for each marcher. This was incredibly high for what was essentially jaywalking. Martin was placed in an isolation cell, and no one was allowed to see him for a day or so. He couldn't even make a call to his wife, Coretta, who had just given birth to their fourth child.

Martin did not like being in jail: it was a cross he had agreed to bear, but it made him very moody. So he put tremendous pressure on us to maximize the impact and significance of his time in jail. "You must resume demonstrations immediately," he said. "Don't let the local support committee stop you. We have got to keep the pressure on Birmingham."

Despite Martin's impatience, the situation was already changing for the better. The news and the images of the Good Friday arrests were sinking in. Photographs of Martin and Ralph Abernathy being hustled off to jail were shown on television and published all over the world. The reaction was tremendous. For the first time, the Birmingham campaign was being taken seriously. It was not long before we began receiving pledges of support from all over.

That same weekend, singer Harry Belafonte, a committed supporter of our cause and a close friend, was hard at work in New York securing new funds to replenish the critically short bail money. By Monday, Harry reported he had raised fifty thousand dollars and that more would be forthcoming. To us this sounded like a miracle.

From his cell, the week after Easter, Martin began what would become his famous "Letter from a Birmingham Jail." He wrote in the margins of newspapers, and on the back of legal papers, and slipped us the text bit by bit. In this letter, he provided us with comprehensive, far-ranging answers to all the objections to our campaign. He also articulated the religious basis for the nonviolent protest movement in Christian theology. Martin's letter answered the charges of "ill-timing" by reminding our critics that blacks had waited more than three hundred years for justice in America; we could afford to wait no longer. It has always moved me to think about what Martin was able to create out of what most people would consider a painful period of deprivation.

Within a few weeks, thousands of copies of Martin's letter were distributed around the country, published in national and European journals, and quoted from as the rationale behind the Civil Rights Movement. This letter helped establish a strong moral and intellectual basis not only for our struggle in Birmingham, but for all subsequent movement campaigns in the South. It has since become a classic in American literature.

The intense media attention, combined with the effective economic boycott, began to put a lot of pressure on the power structure in Birmingham. For nearly two months, black citizens purchased very little but food and medicine. The lack of retail sales during the Easter season was visibly hurting our targeted stores, just as we had hoped. In Birmingham, blacks spent a lot of money downtown, but businessmen didn't seem to appreciate just how much until their black patronage was withdrawn.

Part of what made Martin's leadership so powerful was his ability to put our movement, and our trials in Birmingham, into its proper context as a world movement. He was able to make us feel as if we were more than our daily selves, more than we had been—a part of a beautiful and glorious vision that was enabling us to transcend ourselves—to lift the people to another place so that they could almost feel themselves moving. Each night of the campaign, after Martin concluded his speeches to tumultuous applause, we would all rise, join hands, and sing "We Shall Overcome."

> We shall overcome
> We shall overcome
> We shall overcome some day

Oh, deep in my heart I do believe
We shall overcome some day.

As usual, Martin was right. And the work we did in Birmingham did help launch a worldwide movement. The model we developed for nonviolent social change in this small Southern town has since been used to help campaigns for human rights and freedom in Poland, South Africa, and other countries. Trusting in Martin's wisdom helped us persist in the struggle. Now, looking back, it's very rewarding to know that the suffering we lived through was not in vain. It was all an integral part of God's plan for a better tomorrow.

In the spirit of Dr. King's commitment to service, the King Holiday in January is now a national day of service, interracial cooperation, and youth anti-violence initiatives. People and organizations are keeping the "Dream" alive by opening their hearts and offering their hands to bring diverse peoples together. Call the Office of Public Liaison at the Corporation for National Service at 202-606-5000. You can learn more about Dr. King's life and his works by visiting www.thekingcenter.org.

FULFILLING MARTIN'S DREAM
Told by Rosalind Barnes

On the morning of August 18, 1963, Frank Carr got up at 2:00 A.M. to join a bus bound for his nation's capital. This white businessman from Chicago wasn't quite sure why he was going. He'd read about Reverend Martin Luther King Jr. and the March on Washington. He'd heard about the call to action for equal rights for all Americans. He just knew he had to go. Later, standing among a quarter of a million other people, he listened to Dr. King's awe-inspiring speech "I Have a Dream!" For the first time in his life, he knew why he was here.

> . . . Now is the time to open the doors of opportunity to all God's children. Now is the time to lift our nation from the quicksands of racial injustice to the solid rock of brotherhood. . . . When we let freedom ring, when we let it ring from every village and every hamlet, from every state and every city, we will be able to speed up that day when all of God's children, black men and white men, Jews and Gentiles, Protestants and Catholics, will be able to join hands and sing in the words of the old Negro spiritual, "Free at last! Free at last! Thank God Almighty, we are free at last!"

After hearing these words, Frank knew in his heart that he had to do something to help make Martin's dream come true. When he arrived back home, he talked with his friends, people in business, people with influence. He spoke with a new confidence. "There are students in the ghettos and barrios with real talent," he said. "They can play important roles in our corporations and our communities, if we give them a chance." Frank urged them to see what they could do.

His friends and colleagues knew he was right. They'd all seen young people with a wealth of potential, who were denied opportunities simply because of the color of their skin. They knew about racism in corporate America, and they decided to see what they could do about it.

The key to their own success had been mentors, people who had taken time to listen to their hopes and dreams, show them the ropes, and introduce them to the "old boys' network." So they each made a commitment to mentor one student, and get their companies to place them in summer internships. In 1970 they opened the first INROADS office in Chicago, with seventeen corporate sponsors and twenty-five eager students. "We had no track record, just a dream, and enough people willing to take some risks," says Carr.

Juan was one of the first twenty-five students. Originally from a small village in Mexico, he had grown up like thousands of boys before him, with very few opportunities. Everyone who knew him would tell you there was something special about Juan.

When he was in the sixth grade, he joined his father, who was working hard in Chicago to improve his family's life. At first, Juan was thrilled, thinking that in this new world he could accomplish just about anything. On the unfriendly streets of Chicago, however, Juan discovered that life was pretty tough.

Here, he wasn't special, just another poor Hispanic kid, speaking in broken English. In his Mexican village he had been revered as a leader. In Chicago he was an outsider. But despite the difficulties he faced, Juan persevered, something he had learned from his father.

Within three years he graduated with honors from his high school. He was proud to be the first in his family to enter college. But, once again, Juan discovered that reality was less hospitable than he'd imagined. College students were expected to be self-sufficient, and those who struggled with the language or anything else got no special help. Juan did his best, but his first year was rough. Some days he even thought of quitting.

Then, one day, Juan's life took an unexpected step forward. "During my freshman year, I met a remarkable man," he says. "To my surprise, this white man picked me out of the many students passing through a hallway, and said, 'Would you like to intern with a major corporation this summer?'" Juan couldn't believe his ears. "I thought, *Summer job? Major corporation?* 'Sure. What do I have to do?'"

The man in the hall was Frank Carr. He took Juan under his wing and introduced him to INROADS. That summer, Juan got a great job and, for the first time in his life, opportunities to work with business leaders. "These people became my mentors, showed me the ropes, guided me throughout the summer," he recalls. "They really wanted me to make it in the business world."

That summer's work experience with the Wrigley Corporation convinced Juan that he really could, too. "For the first time since I was a boy in Mexico," he says, "I knew I could be somebody!"

When Juan met Frank, he bore the weight of his family's future on his young shoulders. "At the lowest point of my life, Frank gave me the support, encouragement, and financial assistance I needed to finish school."

Today, Juan is a manager at Wrigley, and has joined the INROADS/Chicago board of directors. Knowing what a difference a mentor made in his life, he's working with sixth- and seventh-graders of Mexican descent.

Juan will never forget Frank Carr. "His idea is as right today as it was all those years ago," Juan says. "There is so much talent in our youth. We all need to take the time to harvest it and help them realize their dreams."

For more than thirty years, INROADS has connected the nation's brightest young minds with the world's best companies through salaried internships. Each summer it places nearly seven thousand college students of color in paid positions with Fortune 500 companies in thirty-eight states and Mexico City, Mexico; Toronto, Canada; and Johannesburg, South Africa. And it all started when one man woke up to another man's dream.

If you are interested in becoming an INROADS student, or if your company would like to learn about sponsoring INROADS students, call **INROADS** at 800-642-9865 or visit their Web site, www.INROADS.org.

SHINE ON IN MONTANA

Told by Jo Claire Hartsig

Adapted from "Shine On in Montana" in *Fellowship, the Magazine
of the Fellowship of Reconciliation*

Early in December, Tammie Schnitzer helped her little son, Isaac, stencil a menorah on his bedroom window in Billings, Montana. Like any five-year-old, he was proud of his holiday decorations. The family was celebrating Hanukkah, the Jewish festival of lights. Many non-Jews don't know the meaning of the holiday, or of the menorah, the candleholder with nine (or seven) candles. If you asked Tammie and Isaac, they'd be proud to tell you about it.

The story began over two thousand years ago, when Judea was invaded by the Syrian Greeks. A small yet determined band of Jewish freedom fighters waged an incredible, and victorious, guerrilla war against the Syrian army. During the bitter conflict, the Greeks tried to destroy the Jewish culture and religion. They ransacked the holy temple and extinguished the altar's eternal flame.

The Jewish people worked day and night to clean and restore their place of worship. Then they consecrated the temple once again. All that remained was to light the eternal flame. But they had only enough sacred oil to keep the lamp alight for one day.

Nevertheless, the Jews were committed. If they could burn the lamp for only one day, so be it. But, miraculously, the light didn't die on that day, or the next. For eight days the lamp burned, as brightly as it had on the very first day, shining on the altar. In commemoration of the miracle, Jewish families celebrate Hanukkah with the menorah. They remember the miracle of the wondrous little lamp that kept the altar lit for eight amazing nights.

Shortly after Tammie and Isaac had finished stenciling their menorah, a brick flew through the decorated window and shattered it. The image of his menorah lay in bits and pieces, dangerously sharp, on the bed. The next day the *Billings Gazette* described the incident. Tammie was reported to be troubled by the advice of the investigating officer. "You'd better remove the symbol from your house," he had told her. But could a mother explain this to her son? Tammie thought Isaac was too young to be introduced to hatred like that.

As Margaret MacDonald, another Billings mother, read the paper that day, she was deeply touched by Tammie's question. She imagined having to explain to her own children that they couldn't have a Christmas tree in the window, because it wasn't safe. That was no way for a little boy to remember the holidays. She wanted Isaac to know this as a season of love, not hate and fear.

She remembered a story about the king of Denmark during the Nazi occupation of World War II. When Hitler ordered King Christian to force all Danish Jews to wear the Star of David on their chests, the king refused. In an act of courageous defiance, he placed the yellow star over his own heart, declaring that he and all his people were one. If Hitler wanted to persecute the Jews, he would have to take the king as well. The king was not to stand alone. His example inspired his countrymen, and Danes of all religions wore stars in solidarity with the Jews. The Nazis couldn't pick out their "enemies." In Denmark there were no Jews, no Gentiles, only Danes.

It happened that Margaret had been reading *When Hate Groups Come to Town*, a book about how other communities had overcome similar challenges. She wanted to make a powerful statement against hate for Tammie and Isaac, and for all the children of Billings. She phoned her pastor, asking him to tell the Danish story during his Sunday sermon and pass out paper menorahs so that families could hang them in their windows. The pastor agreed, and spread the word to other churches. That Sunday, members of the congregation all over town began hanging menorahs in their windows. By the following weekend, other churches, businesses, and human rights and community groups had followed suit. Soon, menorahs shone from the windows of hundreds of non-Jewish homes. When Tammie and Isaac drove past them on the way to school, they felt a special connection with their community.

Concerned citizens called the police department, asking if they wouldn't be inviting danger with this action. They were told, in no uncertain terms, by Chief Wayne Inman, "There's greater risk in not doing it." Hate crimes in Billings had been on the rise. A small contingent of skinheads, Klan members, and other white supremacists had targeted Jews, nonwhites, gays, and lesbians for harassment, vandalism, and personal injury. If there was a time to stand together, it was now.

The townspeople of Billings rallied around Tammie and Isaac and all Jewish people, and not just in their living rooms. A sporting-goods store proclaimed NOT IN OUR TOWN! NO HATE. NO VIOLENCE. PEACE ON EARTH, on its large billboard. A local high school posted a sign reading HAPPY HANUKKAH TO OUR

JEWISH FRIENDS. People gathered for a vigil outside the synagogue during Sabbath services to protect those who worshiped inside.

But the battle of light against darkness was not easily won. Someone shot at the store's large billboard, and bullets riddled the high school's windows. Two United Methodist churches, adorned with menorahs, had their windows broken. Six non-Jewish families had car windows smashed; a note was left behind saying "Jew lover." The violence continued, but so did the love.

One day the *Gazette* published a full-page drawing of a menorah with an invitation to its readers to cut out the picture and place it in their windows. In this town with fewer than a hundred Jewish families, the menorah was proudly displayed in thousands of homes. Now the hate groups couldn't find their enemies. In Billings there were no Jews, no Gentiles, only friends.

As the holidays wore on, there were fewer incidents of violence. New friendships formed, and greater understanding developed. Ironically, the violence intended to rip that community apart only served to make it stronger. Now the people of Billings have new reasons to celebrate. If you ask them about their menorahs and what Hanukkah means to them, they'll be proud to tell you. It's about standing together in the face of hatred, overcoming violence with love, and the miracle of the light shining through the darkness.

> *Darkness cannot drive out darkness; only light can do that.*
> *Hate cannot drive out hate; only love can do that.*

> DR. MARTIN LUTHER KING JR.

Want to help your church foster better relations in your community and undermine the appeal of hate groups? The Interfaith Department at the **Fellowship of Reconciliation** will show you how. Write to them at P.O. Box 271, Nyack, NY 10960; or visit their Web site, www.forusa.org.

WE WALK OUR TALK

Told by Reverend Cecil Williams

Adapted from his book *No Hiding Place*, written with Rebecca Laird

In the heart of San Francisco is the Glide Memorial Church. Glide is much more than a church, it's a community, a place of unconditional love and support. For thousands—rich and poor, young and old—Glide is a place of healing, of starting over. My African ancestors, who endured slavery, carried with them across the Atlantic a tradition that remains solidly rooted in African-American culture today. At Glide, we speak our truth by storytelling, engaging one another through dialogue and immersing ourselves in the Spirit.

We estimate that 80 percent of the people who come to us are in recovery. One of the first things we learned about fighting the war on addiction was that traditional drug-treatment programs didn't work for most African Americans. Twelve Step programs focus on individual recovery, as if independently getting clean and sober were the ultimate goal. But African Americans are a communal people—we fight for our freedom together.

I grew up in San Angelo, Texas, a segregated town prior to the Civil Rights Movement. The buses, the drinking fountains, the railroad tracks, the rest rooms, everything in San Angelo, constantly reminded me that I was colored, black, a nigger. When I grew up and became a minister, I wanted to change that—to make life better for my people. Over 65 percent of blacks in San Francisco live in crime-ridden, boarded-up, graffiti-plastered housing projects. Many folks are on drugs. And even if they manage to stay drug-free during the day, they eventually have to go home to projects that have become havens for every imaginable habit. The temptations are great. Since our people were living in the projects, Glide had to go there, too.

One of the things I preach at Glide is to "walk the talk that you talk." So we walked our talk and decided to march on the most troubled housing projects in San Francisco, Valencia Gardens. We decided to march and call out the good news of recovery to our brothers and sisters. We spent dozens of hours gathering together people from the community; the public-housing tenants' association, the mayor's office, and about six hundred people from Glide. We also decided not to be stupid with our faith. We took the police with us, too.

We created a human force to influence the people in the projects. Our goal was not to run the pushers, pimps, and drug users out of public housing. We were coming to embrace them with unconditional love and declare that there was another way to live. So we boarded buses, drove up Market Street, and turned on to Valencia Street, singing songs of freedom. When we arrived, we got off the buses and marched around the projects. Those in the front carried a street-wide banner that declared our nonviolent battle cry, IT'S RECOVERY TIME. Others carried placards reading THE USER NEEDS RECOVERY and WELCOME HOME TO RECOVERY.

We marched as a posse of lovers, heralding freedom from drugs, addiction, and despair. As Jesus has said to each of us, "I'm with you." Glide marched to say to our hurting extended family, "We are with you." Each heart bore a commitment to accepting those we met. No one marched empty-handed, either. Some carried paintbrushes and gallons of paint. Others bore heaping plates of fried chicken and potato salad. It does no good to go in shouting and screaming for change with your empty hand shaking in the air. You've got to have something to offer.

When the hundreds of marchers had converged in the center of the housing complex, I took a bullhorn and began to shout to those peeking out of the top-floor apartments: "C'mon down. Join us. It's recovery time! We know who you are. You're our sons and daughters. It's time for you to take control of your lives!"

Slowly people started coming down, some from apartments currently serving as crack houses. We put them right up on stage and gave them the microphone. They talked about their lives. Then, late in the day, one of my staff members came up to me and said a group of pushers wanted to play a tape over our public-address system. I said okay, seeing it as an opening to talk with the young men. I walked up to the door where these young pushers were holed up. Someone from the crowd yelled to me, "You ought not do that, Cecil." But I did it anyway, and that's how I met Alex.

Earlier in the week, Alex had begun to reflect on his life. He later told us, "I had been taught by my father that if I was going to live, then I should be the best at whatever I was doin'. I took the bad road, being crooked, a criminal, and I was good at it. I had no mercy or concern for another's physical well-being. I did some time in jail. I was growing tired of life.

"I was thinking, 'I can get a job and if I don't make it, I can always turn back to what I was doin'—selling drugs.' But the one who is always by my side, my baby's mother, said, 'You can make an honest living.' So I started thinking about it. That Saturday was the day Cecil and all the people came in marching.

"I listened to Cecil. What he was talking about was what I wanted to be about. After the walls at Valencia Gardens got painted, I realized that the march wasn't about covering up the dirty walls; it was about the people. There was a total change in the people who lived in the projects. People in the projects who never talked to each other were now talking. There had been so much bad around V.G., I wanted to help make some good."

Soon after, Alex started coming to Glide. Many months later he spoke about the march on Valencia Gardens to some visitors who were interested in our recovery program. Alex said, "I remember my father telling me so many times that by being born in 1968 I missed out on everything: Malcolm X, the Reverend Martin Luther King Jr., Vietnam, the hippie movement, and the Black Panthers. After I came to Glide, I began to see that I hadn't missed everything. I've lived to see Glide and to know the Reverend Cecil Williams, who is not a killer but a saver. Glide saved me and my family from the madness. One of the coolest things about finding myself is that I never had to go find Glide. Glide came to my home and found me."

Alex now has a job, and he's good at it. He's a new man. "Coming to Glide was like facing a mountain where there weren't any stairs or a clearcut path. Instead there were hands, all different colors of hands, reaching down to help me. All I had to do was hang on and keep climbing until I got to the top. When I reached the top, then I looked back and saw how far I'd come. It was, and is, a beautiful view—this is recovery."

Lift up your eyes upon this day breaking for you. Give birth to the dream.

MAYA ANGELOU

Join the Sunday celebrations at **Glide Church** with Reverend Cecil Williams and inspirational gospel music from the Glide Ensemble. To support Glide's thirty-seven comprehensive programs that serve thousands of homeless, drug-addicted, downtrodden, hopeless, or outcast people, including its Daily Free Meals Program, which serves three free meals a day, 365 days a year, over a million meals annually, visit the church's Web site, www.glide.org.

A MAN WITH A PAST GIVES BACK
Told by Diane Saunders

It's ironic, Will agrees, that a man with his past now works with the police, some of whom have become his best friends. And it's sad, he tells young people, that it took his brother's death for him to find life. He often looks back to the turning point. Though he wishes it had come sooner and more peacefully, he's grateful it came at all.

William Morales was in solitary confinement—"the Hole"—where all he could do was think. There wasn't much else to do. Screaming, bragging, blaming, tripping on the past, plotting revenge, he'd done all that. It had gotten him nowhere, and had gotten his young brother, Hector, dead, shot during a gun battle with the police.

Will could never change that fact. As he sat alone in the Hole, thinking over his life, and Hector's death, he finally realized things would never change for him unless he changed himself. With a determination he had never felt before, he decided to let go of his past and start working on his future, and he knew that it was the best decision he had ever made.

Up to that point, his life was made of one bad choice after another. When he was only sixteen, he founded a gang, the X-Men, on the lucrative profits of cocaine trafficking in Boston. Known for their targeted attacks on police officers, other gangs knew better than to mess with the X-Men. Will went from infamy to incarceration within a year. By the age of seventeen, he was quite literally a prisoner of his own bad choices.

On his long road to self-rehabilitation, he met his first mentor, Perez, a lifer who'd gotten his master's in education inside the walls, who agreed to teach him to read. Starting with Little Bo Peep coloring books, Will devoured words, then sentences, then paragraphs and chapters, and after a while he wanted to share his fulfillment with others. He joined a speaking program so he could talk to troubled teens, in real street terms, about his brother's death and how it had changed him. The kids listened. Will began to understand that intervention at the right time, and from the right person, could keep a teenager out of trouble.

Four years after Hector's death, and six years after Will was locked up, he was released. He got a job at a pizza company. One day he met up with his friend Luis, who had also been paroled. Together they formed a group called X-Hoods and made plans to give presentations to high-school kids.

Will and Luis knew they would always be associated with their former violent gang, the infamous X-Men, so they decided to twist that association to teach kids. They told Boston students that the "X" was a symbol for crossing out drugs, gangs, violence, and all the other bad elements in their community. "Hoods," they said, stands for Helping Out Our Dysfunctional Society. They added the caution that if not used wisely, the "X" could be the mark of poison, ruining a young life. But the same "X" could also mark the spot where you'll find the buried treasure within yourself.

When Will met the Reverend Wesley Williams, a Methodist minister who directed an urban youth service program, the reverend was working on bringing the kids, the police, and the church together with "tough love," strong values, and open communication. Out of their collaboration, the Boston Youth and Police Partnership was born, a breakthrough in community relations and the first outreach program in Boston's history created by teenagers. They organize and run a crime watch in the city and lead workshops to teach adults how to start crime watch groups.

Still on that good road, Will got the Massachusetts School of Law in Andover to create a special curriculum for his kids. The school teaches them to think and act like lawyers. "Now when the kids see a problem they can analyze it in their minds, then verbally say, 'This is why that's wrong.' They can state their arguments clearly and defend themselves with words, not fists, knives, and guns." Will tells them, "Hey, I still carry a gun, but, it's not a physical gun, it's a mental gun. And what I'm shooting for is the sky—the hope, peace, and freedom in the sky."

On some nights, Will visits gang members to talk about jobs and other opportunities. Occasionally he meets with the police to mediate and resolve problems. Officer Juan Torres, who coordinates the Youth and Police Partnership program, says, "There is definitely a new trust between us and the kids. They get to know us, in and out of uniform, as real people. We're constantly reminded these are good kids who want to make a difference. They just need to know someone cares." Torres continues, "When they see a guy like Will let old wounds heal and move ahead, then they can also trust us and work with us to make the community a safe place where they'll have opportunities for personal growth."

As a law student, homeowner, husband, and father of a three-year-old son, Will is an inspiring role model for young people who are looking for a better future. He is now the executive director of the YMCA of Greater Boston, Egleston Square Youth Center, directly across the street from where his brother was killed. "Some days it's kind of tough," he admits. "I see ghosts—the ghost of my brother and of my former life." Then he adds proudly, "I want to live this life for both of us."

> *There are two ways of exerting one's strength: one is pushing down, the other is pulling up.*
>
> BOOKER T. WASHINGTON

Learn how you can bring the youth and police in your community together to build healthy relationships and teach children how to prevent violence through problem-solving forums and recreational activities. E-mail Will Morales at wmorales@ymcaboston.

A JOURNEY TO HEALING

The next time you go to Washington, D.C., visit 1470 Irving Street, NW. While this cultural center isn't on any city tour maps, it is a home away from home for 200,000 refugees from war-torn countries in Central and South America.

To some, it looks like any old school building. To others it's a symbol of hope and healing. On the outside, a colorful mural combines vivid images from the rich life of rural Latino communities with religious icons and pictures of the indigenous peoples' struggle. A sign over the door, BIENVENIDOS, welcomes everyone. Climb up a few flights of stairs and you'll find the heart of this center, La Clinica del Pueblo, bustling with energy.

Dr. Juan Romagoza, the clinic's director, has an ambitious goal: to help his people manage their own health care, and be in charge of their lives. A picture of the martyred peace activist Archbishop Oscar Romero hangs near Dr. Juan's desk. Like his patron saint, Dr. Juan's calling is to be "a blessing on the land." At the clinic he is their Cesar Chavez, leading them toward a healthy and hopeful future.

As a surgeon in his homeland of El Salvador, Dr. Juan felt it was his sacred duty to heal the sick. He worked in the countryside, helping the *campesinos*, peasants who desperately needed his services. For this, he was accused of being a communist. In 1983, soldiers machine-gunned Dr. Juan's clinic in San Antonio Los Ranchos in Chalatengo, and imprisoned him.

To make sure that he would never perform surgery again, they slit Dr. Juan's wrists, severing vital tendons in his hands. Then they shot him and left him to die. "You'll never return to help these people," they said. "They're right about one thing," Dr. Juan says calmly. "Since I can't practice surgery anymore, I've discovered other ways to help my people."

Dr. Juan and thousands of others escaped from El Salvador's regime of terror. Many came to the Mount Pleasant neighborhood, a sanctuary community in Washington, D.C. Many were victims of torture themselves; others were forced to watch as loved ones were murdered. The collective trauma in this community is almost beyond imagination.

Dr. Juan has devoted his life to helping his people heal from the pains of war. Instead of dwelling bitterly on his own experiences, he offers his gift of healing. He knows only too well that the horrors of war include not only physical ailments but also alcoholism, depression, post-traumatic stress disorder, and domestic violence. He began by training the displaced, educating them on how to provide basic services to one another.

Dr. Juan's small office doubles as a health-education center, where he dispenses a unique mix of Western medicine, indigenous wisdom, and respect for the role of the family. Now, instead of using his skills as a surgeon, he practices a more holistic approach to health care, tending to bodies, minds, and souls. Remembering his own once-poor dietary habits, he asks a young, single Latino who isn't feeling well, "How many eggs do you eat each week?" When the young man replies, "Three dozen," Dr. Juan takes the opportunity to talk about how some foods increase our cholesterol count. "Juan understands our needs and finds ways to meet them," people say.

When Dr. Juan arrived, the clinic was open only on Tuesday nights. Today it serves seven thousand residents a year on a full-time basis, providing free medical care, health education, and counseling services for 60 to 70 percent of the District's Latino community.

Those whom he helps in turn become grateful givers. Some give their time, such as the Salvadoran artist who painted the clinic's beautiful mural; the woman who, every day, brings rice and beans, chicken and tortillas, and *atol*, a warm, comforting custard drink; and the young Latina TV reporter who buys toys for the Christmas celebration known as the Posada.

"People are on fire, wanting to give back," says Dr. Juan. The Clinic nurtures a passion for doing good, and their generosity knows no limits. "They exemplify the Latino compliment '*Se tiran la casa por la ventana*'—they throw the house out the window, they give their all," says Dr. Juan.

This spirit of generosity is the magic that keeps La Clinica working. More than one hundred community volunteers—including doctors, nurses, and staff volunteers from major hospitals—donate their time. Often you will see Ivan Menjivar, an emergency medical technician from Georgetown University Medical Center. On Tuesday nights you may find him at the clinic, taking vital signs, translating, and counseling people. "La Clinica is the heart of our community," he says.

Trained laypersons called "health promoters" offer education and counseling. A teacher at Lincoln Junior High School, Jamie Fischman, volunteers once a week. "It's important to know where people are coming from," she says, "so I can better help their children."

Volunteers organize monthly health fairs that offer free screening and education about diabetes, hypertension, and HIV. More than one thousand people attended a recent diabetes health fair, at which a panel of Latinos talked about their experiences with diabetes.

These days, Dr. Juan asks everyone to help with the AIDS crisis. "It's a time bomb in our community," he says. La Clinica has the largest Latino HIV/AIDS program in the area. "Traditionally, we've taken care of our own problems," Dr. Juan explains. "When we are sick, we first turn to our families, to our grandmother, our mother. AIDS is a new problem—as a people, we are just learning how to deal with it. We must educate, break down the barriers, and integrate everyone," he says. Clinic counselors go from door to door and to neighborhood soccer matches to distribute flyers about the virus.

La Clinica is much more than a medical facility. It is also a social center, one of the few places where these people can go and feel at home. The Posada, La Clinica's annual Christmas fiesta for patients and their children, dramatizes Mary and Joseph's journey to Bethlehem. People walk in a candlelit procession from place to place, asking in song, "Have you room for us to spend the night?" Finally, someone welcomes them into their home; often it is the poorest family. The story of Mary and Joseph traveling to a strange land and staying with the shepherds echoes the lives of these Latino people who are far away from their homes, seeking shelter and healing in a new land.

La Clinica's brand of community medicine also includes advocacy. "Come, participate and talk about your health concerns," urges a flyer for a clinic-sponsored public meeting. "If La Clinica didn't exist, more people [would be] in the expensive ER at hospitals," Dr. Juan reminds the policymakers, government officials, and a variety of funders that help support La Clinica's programs. When the Robert Wood Johnson Foundation's Community Health Leadership Program honored Dr. Juan with one of their prestigious $100,000 awards, he received national recognition. More important, it helped to keep the clinic's mental-health program going at a time of government cuts.

Dr. Juan is well-loved in his neighborhood, and he can't walk down the street without getting stopped by people who want to talk with him. One day a drunken man staggered to his side. A strange feeling came over Juan. After a moment he realized that this was Arturo, a man from the torture squad who had slit his wrists, the man who had shot him and left him to die.

Juan stood in stunned silence for a moment. But all he saw in the broken man before him was another member of his devastated community, in need of healing. "I'm still doing the same work I did before the torture cell," he said calmly to Arturo. "As a physician, I offer to help you, too."

Arturo healed deeply that day. Juan's ability to forgive him gave Arturo a whole new outlook on life. It was a tremendous moment for Juan, too. "In spite of having suffered, we can pardon our torturers, so they can heal themselves." He adds, "People like Arturo need a special love, they need more compassion—and they need a democratic system so they can relearn how to be human again." Now, when Arturo sees Juan in the streets, he always asks, with deep respect, "How are you, Doctor?"

Those who had survived the unthinkable found a source of healing and renewal they would never have dreamed possible.

We are a people of weavers, weaving a better future from our suffering and pain.

RIGOBERTA MENCHU

Volunteer at your local free clinic and give the gift of health. Medical professionals and bilingual translators who want to help Dr. Juan provide free medical care, health education, mental health, and social services to immigrant Latinos at **La Clinica del Pueblo,** contact the clinic at 1470 Irving St., NW, Washington, DC 20010; 202-462-4788.

VIVA! BARRIOS UNIDOS

Told by Peggy R. Townsend

His grandmother called him Nane, meaning "Walks in Peace." It's an
unusual name for one who spends his days in the toughest neighborhoods of the
country. Then again, Nane is a rather unusual man. His real name is Daniel Alejandrez. In barrios throughout the nation, he fights the violence and addictions
that are killing America's youth.

The barrio where he started his work lies in the shadow of the Giant Dipper
rollercoaster in Santa Cruz, California. It's a tiny neighborhood filled with rundown homes and broken dreams. Drug dealers stand on every corner, gang graffiti litters the walls, and most of the tourists who pass by on their way to the
nearby amusement park don't even notice it exists.

It is here that Nane began Barrios Unidos. He combines messages of hope and
understanding with practical programs like job training and computer courses,
as well as art classes. "Kids aren't born gang members or racists," he says. "They
become that way." But Nane can tell you from personal experience that they
don't have to.

His voice is so soft that a listener has to lean in very close to hear the story of
his life, but it is definitely worth the effort. He was born in Merigold, Mississippi,
the child of migrant workers who followed the crops through America's heart-
land. By the age of five, he was picking cotton, asparagus, and beets alongside his
family. Living in noisy labor camps, dusty tents, and once even under a tree, was
the norm. "I just accepted it," says Nane. What else could he do? He'd never
known anything different.

The day his grandfather died, a life that was simply hard turned bad. The
patriarch, Don Pancho, returned home from a long day of chopping beets with

a short-handled hoe. Soon after, he collapsed. Twelve-year-old Nane held his seventy-two-year-old grandfather in his arms, begging him not to die, but it was too late.

After Don Pancho's death, Nane's family fell apart. His father began to drink, and jobs became more scarce. Nane felt his father's pain as he bowed his head before the bosses and searched for work. He wanted nothing more than to escape, but there was nowhere to go. He decided if he couldn't run from his pain, he'd numb it. At twelve years of age, he started sniffing glue. By thirteen he'd smoked his first joint. When he was seventeen he tried LSD. He returned from Vietnam a heroin addict.

During a short jail sentence for drug use, he took a hard look at himself. He knew if he didn't change his path, he'd wind up like the gangsters and drug deal-ers around him: in prison for a very long time, or dead.

When he got out of jail, Nane used the GI Bill to attend Fresno City College and transfer to the University of California, Santa Cruz. As he studied, he gained perspective on his life. He understood that the same despair that had nearly destroyed him was running rampant in the barrios. Without help, and with few choices, many young boys were destined to repeat the mistakes he had lived, and kill each other or self-destruct.

Nane chose to help. He went out into the streets and started talking to kids. It was that simple. He hung out with them, counseled them, and talked to them about better ways of living, alternatives to prison or death. To reach the kids bet-ter, he decided to walk his talk: he conquered his own drug addictions.

But the way out of addiction and despair was "one step forward and two steps back." One day Nane reached the low point in his life. He had lost twelve rela-tives and friends in twelve years, including his two brothers; his childhood hero, Uncle Pancho; and his grandmother. Finally, all he could feel was the pain. "I didn't know how to let go of the tragedies in my life," he said. Desperate to escape, Nane overdosed and was near death.

As he was rushed to the hospital's emergency room, Nane had a vision in which he could actually see his brother Leo at the end of a tunnel of flashing light. "Go back, go back," Leo said. "It's not your time." Then he saw his other brother, Tavo, who said the same thing.

"When I finally woke up, I realized the Creator had given me the opportunity to see my brothers and to know they were okay," Nane remembers. "After that I could let go of the pain."

The next day he went to the cemetery and prayed quietly with his brothers. "I realized that I needed to deal with my own life—to move forward," he said. From then on, Nane found strength from being spiritually connected through traditional Native American ceremonies. He sought guidance from tribal elders, and also spoke more with people of different faiths. "I began to focus on my own mission in life," Nane says, "to better our communities and to stop the violence among our young people."

Nane founded Barrios Unidos working from the trunk of his car. The group was to provide new role models for the youth of America. It was 1977, and he was twenty-seven years old. While his wife sold tacos to make ends meet, he and his small band of volunteers pursued their dream: providing youth with a world free of violence, drugs, and alcohol abuse. They went to schools, walked the barrios, and worked late into the night. After a while, Barrios Unidos moved into a small office, then used grant money to buy a computer so they could write applications for other grants. Soon their message spread, as did their impact.

Today, Barrios Unidos has a room full of computers and a staff of twenty-six people in several chapters across the country. They offer extensive programs and free food and counseling to those in need. Three summer Kids' Klub programs reach out to the youngest residents of the barrios. To foster an entrepreneurial spirit, Barrios Unidos started a silk-screening business run by teens. The proceeds of the business help fund their initiatives.

One of their most exciting projects is the Cesar Chavez School for Social Change in Santa Cruz, near where Cesar organized in the fields of Pajaro Valley. Here, future community leaders are raised in the tradition of Cesar Chavez, Martin Luther King, and Mahatma Gandhi. Nineteen-year-old Miriam Garcia is grateful to Nane and others at Barrios Unidos for making it possible for her to attend the school. "I look forward to becoming a creator of positive change in my community," she says.

Of course there is still much to do. Some days, Barrios Unidos may seem to be losing the battle. Youth crime in our country is projected to more than double over the next decade, fueled in large part by gang activity. The FBI reports nearly 1.5 million young people are now involved in gangs. For Nane, and Barrios Unidos, that means more lives to turn around, more young people who need more choices for the future. Nane finds hope in young people like Alejandro Vilchez, who is a young father and a warrior for peace. "My father taught me to be a man," says Alejandro. "Nane taught me to be a warrior for change."

At fifty-one, Nane is still the guiding spirit of his organization. He works in the office, travels across the country giving speeches and raising funds, and meets with children of the barrios. And he always takes time to pray, honoring the Creator.

In the kitchen of his modest home, Nane snuggles his ten-year-old grandson close and talks of his hopes for peace. "Not for me," he says, "maybe not for my children. But if we all keep working toward it, maybe for my grandson's children."

Nane continues to struggle for the unity of all people and challenges people from all walks of life to help us save our children. To get involved with **Barrios Unidos,** visit their Web site, www.barriosunidos.net.

BY GIVING OUR LIVES, WE FIND LIFE
Told by Marc Grossman

For the migrant farm worker, each day felt virtually endless; each night he was exhausted and often hungry. His life stood in stunning contrast to the lives of the comfortable families who savored the fruits of his labor. In a land that promised plenty, migrant farm workers in the 1960s had basically no voice, no rights or protections. But how could they possibly appeal to an America that, for the most part, didn't know they existed?

Cesar Chavez knew their troubles firsthand. As a poor, disenfranchised, foreign-born, itinerant farm worker, he was an unlikely national hero. He was small, soft-spoken, and low-key, a guy you could easily lose in a crowd. But this gentle person woke up the drowsy conscience of the most powerful country in the world when he showed ordinary Americans the power of their everyday consumer choices.

For years, Americans shopped the grocery aisles guided by nutritional facts, personal budgets, or culinary whim. They brought home sweet, plump clusters of green and red table grapes without a second thought until, in the late 1960s, deciding whether or not to buy grapes became a powerful political act.

Of all the agricultural laborers, grape pickers may have had it the worst. Farm workers had been trying to organize a union for more than one hundred years. In 1965 they went on strike against grape growers around Delano, California. Two and a half years later, in the hungry winter of 1968, with no resolution in sight, they were tired, bitter, and increasingly frustrated.

Concerned for his people's future, Cesar decided to ask for help. He believed in people's ability to find their common ground, no matter how different they appeared. He thought that if people in communities throughout the nation knew about the needless suffering of farm workers, they would step up and do what they could to help.

Taking a bold leap of faith, Cesar invited consumers across North America to join in solidarity with his union, the United Farm Workers. He asked them to send a message to the grape growers by boycotting California table grapes. The boycott began slowly, but it built steadily over the next couple of years. First California, then the rest of the nation and even Canada joined in support of the strikers.

In the meantime, some of the strikers had become understandably impatient for results. They had already waited so long, and to some of them, particularly some of the young men, the boycott must have seemed too little, too late. Mur-

murings of violence began; some workers wanted to strike back at the powers who had abused them and their families. By fighting back, they thought they could prove their manhood. But Cesar rejected that part of Hispanic culture "that tells our young men that you're not a man if you don't fight back." He had conceived the boycott in the nonviolent tradition of his hero, Mahatma Gandhi. From Gandhi, Cesar had learned how fasting could draw attention to injustice in the world. As the protest threatened to explode, he announced that he was undertaking a fast, as a profound admonishment and an example of self-control and sacrifice for his people.

The fast divided the UFW. Many didn't understand why Cesar was doing it. Others worried about his health. But those farm workers who understood held a mass nightly near where Cesar was fasting at the Forty Acres, the UFW's head-quarters in Delano. Hundreds came, then thousands. People pitched tents nearby. They brought religious offerings—pictures and small statues. Farm workers waited in line for hours to speak with Cesar in his tiny room, while he refused interviews with reporters.

After twenty-five days, Cesar was carried to a nearby park, where he ended his fast during a mass with thousands of farm workers. He had lost thirty-five pounds, and there was no more talk of violence among the farm workers. Cesar's message had gotten through. Senator Robert Kennedy came to the mass, he said, "out of respect for one of the heroic figures of our time."

Cesar was too weak to speak, so others read his statement in both English and Spanish, on his behalf: "It is my deepest belief that only by giving our lives do we find life. The truest act of courage, the strongest act of manliness, is to sacrifice ourselves for others in a totally nonviolent struggle for justice. To be a man is to suffer for others. God help us to be men."

What followed was truly amazing. Through Cesar's efforts, middle-class families in Northeastern cities and Midwestern suburbs connected with poor families in the hot California vineyards. Motivated by compassion, millions of people across North America stopped eating the grapes they had loved so much, and thousands of dinner tables became a forum for parents to teach their children a simple, powerful lesson in social justice. By 1970, bowing to pressure from the boycott, grape growers at long last signed union contracts, respecting workers' human dignity and granting a more livable wage.

In the years that followed, Cesar continued to use boycotts and fasts to galvanize farm workers in their pursuit of a better life, and to gather ordinary Americans' support for their efforts. Though they won the first and biggest battle in 1970, there were others. In 1988, at the age of sixty-one, Cesar undertook his last public fast, this time for thirty-six days, to draw attention to the pesticide poisoning of farm workers and their children. His whole life long, he was devoted to bettering the lives of farm workers, a cause he never gave up.

By some standards, Cesar Chavez was not very successful. He quit school after the eighth grade to help his family earn a living. He never owned a house and he never earned more than six thousand dollars a year. When he died in 1993, at sixty-six, he left no money for his family. Yet more than forty thousand people marched behind the plain pine casket at his funeral, and at an all-night vigil under a giant tent, thousands filed by his open casket until the morning. Parents carried newborn babies and sleeping toddlers in their arms. One farm worker explained, "I wanted to tell my children how they had once been in the presence of this great man."

A reporter once asked Cesar, "What accounts for all the affection and respect so many farm workers show you in public?" Cesar just looked down and smiled his easy smile. "The feeling is mutual" was his simple reply.

California is the first state to honor Cesar Chavez by creating a Day of Service and Learning for his birthday. On March 31, join with people who are carrying on his legacy with conservation, human service, culture and arts, and community-improvement projects. Support the **United Farm Workers of America** and their nonviolent work to carry on Cesar Chavez's dream of dignity for farm workers across America by calling 661-823-6105, or visit their Web site, www.ufw.org.

OUR TOUCHSTONE

Told by Joseph Rodriguez

When Joe Rodriguez was growing up, every Saturday night his family in New Jersey joined millions of other Latino families from Alaska to Argentina in learning, laughing, and feeding their souls. He remembers how they'd all sit around after dinner eating the best Cuban desserts, made by his mother, watching *Sabado Gigante Internacional*—waiting to see what extraordinary show Don Francisco would pull off that week.

For thirty-five years, Don Francisco has hosted a unique four-hour TV show that unites 100 million Spanish-speaking viewers in twenty-eight countries. At a time when it seems that so many TV shows prosper by exploiting human frailties, Don Francisco has made a living by uplifting people's spirits, teaching his viewers the values of giving and helping others, and the joy of compassion, family unity, and Latino community.

Joe remembers when he first saw Jose Reyes on the *Sabado Gigante Internacional.* "Jose was like a member of our family; he was the man who reupholstered all of our old furniture pieces because we couldn't afford to buy new ones. Yet he always treated us special when we'd come to his shop, and his work was always flawless—full of pride and craftsmanship. Suddenly, one night, there he was on TV—the same man who upholstered all our furniture!" Jose had lost his right arm and leg during the civil violence in his native El Salvador, when he was fifteen years old. Despite these physical limitations, he had mastered a craft requiring great physical skill. Now he was being celebrated and honored by Don Francisco—and he demonstrated his skill, handling fabric with the precision and balance of an athlete. Joe himself was a young teenager when Jose was on TV,

" 'too cool' to reveal my sense of awe in front of my parents." But it made a lasting impression on him.

One week, Don Francisco might host Jose Reyes or others like him, who had overcome hardship and adversity. People who, by sharing their experiences, "expressed their dreams and taught us important lessons about being human," Joe reflects. Another time, it might be the story of a man who was reunited with three sons he had not seen in twenty years. But in the end, all of Don Francisco's stories have a common effect: "They open a window on the entire Latino community, unifying us through our culture and inspiring us to reweave our social fabric, a fabric woven from the strong family roots that lend stability to our lives."

Perhaps the most amazing thing about Don Francisco (besides the fact that he is listed in the *Guinness Book of Records* as having the longest-lasting TV show) is his endless selflessness in spite of personal hardships; a lesson all too important for the Latino community. Born in 1940 to German Jews who emigrated to Chile to escape the tragedy of the Holocaust, he overcame linguistic and cultural barriers to become one of the most successful businessmen in the Latino community.

In spite of his hectic schedule, Don Francisco serves as a major figure at UNESCO, and heads the Institute for Paraplegic Children in Chile, which he founded over thirty years ago. In 1978, Don Francisco organized Chile's first telethon, inspired by Jerry Lewis's efforts on behalf of the March of Dimes. "I spoke to Jerry Lewis and got his advice," Don Francisco says. "I wanted to give back to the people what the public has given to me." In turn, he has inspired other telethons in Latin America while conducting Chile's for the past twenty years.

Joe has a young family of his own, so he no longer sits around the TV with his parents, waiting for Don Francisco to come on. But, although he's now thousands of miles away, he knows that this show still connects his family. And each time Joe is confronted with a seemingly insoluble problem, he thinks about Don Francisco and Jose Reyes. He reminds himself that if they could overcome the obstacles they did, he should be able to overcome his own.

Recently, Joe asked his parents if they had heard anything else about Jose. They told him that he had successfully expanded his business, and that he was in the process of starting an upholstery school to teach the local inner-city Paterson kids his trade. Many of his current employees are students he taught for free, former street kids who were lost, without direction. Today his biggest challenge is recruiting enough volunteer craftsmen and funds to keep his dream going. However, the road behind him is littered with the obstacles that have tried to keep him back—and that is one of the most important lessons he can teach his students.

Joe remarked to his parents that Jose's perseverance was the root of his success. To his surprise, his father replied, "Not exactly. The love and support he received from his family and friends was as much a factor as his personal determination."

Reflecting on his father's comments, Joe realized that, as a teenager, he had only seen the obvious—a man with one leg and one arm skillfully working his trade. He had completely missed the more important and subtler message. He now remembered Jose talking about those around him who had loved him so much that they hadn't allowed him to be lost in his limitations; they had carried and nurtured him, and helped him discover that his true potential didn't depend upon having two arms and two legs, but on the freedom to learn how to live differently with what he had. "A man's greatest victory is not in never failing, but in rising every time he does," Jose had said. "His words, lost on me at the time, now came back to me full force."

Touchstones were once used to test the purity of precious metals: when a high-grade metal was rubbed against such a stone, a distinctive mark would be left on the stone. Joe believes that we all have touchstones in our lives—images, comforting words, favorite pictures, quotes or stories—by which we measure the purity of our own thoughts and actions. Don Francisco and the everyday heroes he presents week after week are touchstones for millions of Latinos around the world.

Watch Don Francisco on Univision's *Sabado Gigante Internacional* every Saturday from 7:00 to 10:00 P.M.; visit its Web site, www.sabadogigante.com. Call talk-show hosts and encourage them to invite Stone Soup "community heroes" to share their ideas about what we can do to build a better world.

HOPE FOR "LOS CHAVALITOS"

Told by Dick Russell

Inside a classroom on New York City's Upper East Side, affluent teen-agers more used to sarcastic repartee listen in awe to their Spanish teacher, Ale-jandro Obando. In a slide show, they see the grateful faces of three hundred Nicaraguan families who now have running water, thanks to a project organized by their teacher with their New York neighbors. Modeled after the teachings of Dr. Martin Luther King Jr., the Manhattan Country School sister-city program offers students opportunities to make a difference in the world.

One student, Daniel Eddy, listens attentively as his teacher shares his dream. After teaching Spanish in New York for seven years, Alejandro is going home. His heart is aching for *los chavalitos*, the homeless children who live on the streets of Nicaragua, hustling trinkets and stolen goods. They sit together in alleyways, sniffing glue. Sometimes they sell their own bodies just to live.

This is what twelve long years of war will do to a country's children. More than six thousand Nicaraguan children are orphaned and homeless. Thousands more, lucky enough not to have lost their parents, work long hours at menial jobs to help support their families. Eighty-five percent of Nicaragua's children under the age of fifteen live in poverty.

Alejandro, too, grew up destitute in central Nicaragua. He, too, sold fake watches and shined shoes to survive. His parents divorced when he was a baby, and placed him in the care of his grandmother Celia, who scraped out a meager living selling fried bananas. But she hoped for something better for her grandson, and insisted that he read books instead of hanging out at the pool hall.

Under the Somoza dictatorship, Alejandro and the other children in little towns like Camoapa were denied education after grade school. So the boy and his grandmother made their way to Managua, looking for jobs and an education. The little money he made selling lottery tickets was enough to pay his tuition at night school. One day a doctor from his hometown found him on the streets; if Alejandro would sweep the school, he said, he could be among its first nineteen high-school students. Alejandro happily accepted the offer.

After he graduated, Alejandro was fortunate enough to receive a baseball scholarship to a Managua university. Working part-time, he made enough money to travel to New York with his baseball teammates, but more than playing ball, he wanted to teach. He left Nicaragua to study at Columbia University, but he never forgot his people and he looked for ways to help those in need in his homeland.

Alejandro is now an American citizen with big dreams—and the Manhattan Country School is helping him make his dreams come true. Alejandro asked his students if they would help him create a farm-school for abandoned children. He wanted to bring some hope to a poor town and give its children the second chance he was once given. "This was a ray of light in a war-torn land," Daniel recalls. "There was no way to hear him speak without wanting to help him."

School administrators arranged donations of clothing and school supplies. Friends of the school and cultural organizations raised funds. Several alumni traveled to Nicaragua during the summer to help build dormitories and classrooms. One of Alejandro's first Spanish students volunteered to spend an entire year there to help set up the curriculum. A baseball field built by Alejandro and a group of American volunteers awaits the debut of its first team. The school opened in the town where Alejandro was born.

"Over the next five years, I want to create a rich life for fifty homeless Nicaraguan children," he says. "Together we will live on a three-hundred-acre countryside farm with a clear-running stream and wildlife like monkeys and deer. Here children will learn how to read and write, how to grow their own food, and how to be leaders. The older children will teach the younger ones."

Back in New York City, Alejandro's students write him letters. "What you are doing is hard. We miss you, but we're proud of you. I want to come help you during my summer vacation," one wrote.

"I cried when I received their letters—offering to organize raffles and bake sales to buy the children pencils and supplies," says Alejandro. "The human heart knows no geographic boundaries."

At the school's opening ceremony, some twenty children stood together in a large circle. Their eyes brimming with hope, each one planted a small tree. "I want to teach the children to preserve the beauty of this land," Alejandro says. "I hope to accomplish what my grandmother always told me," he says. "Be a good citizen, get your education, and help other people."

> *Education makes people easy to lead, but difficult to drive; easy to govern, but impossible to enslave.*
>
> HENRY BROGHAM

Bring hope to the **Los Chavalitos School** in Nicaragua by volunteering; call Ginny Scheer at the Manhattan Country School Farm, 607-326-7049. Send tax-deductible donations to Friends of Los Chavalitos, c/o Boyda Law Office, P.O. Box 207, Marysville, KS 66508; e-mail bayardgonzalez@yahoo.com, or visit the Los Chavalitos Web site, www.guegue.net/chavalitos.

DEMOCRACY IN ACTION

Told by Marion Silverbear

Ada Deer has a deep commitment to serving her Native American tribe and her country. She grew up living with her parents and four siblings in a log cabin on the Menominee Reservation in Wisconsin. They had no electricity, running water, or telephones. They were poor, but so was everyone else she knew. Her tribe nurtured in her a healthy respect for the land, and the belief that members of the tribe should work together for the good of all.

Ada's mother, Connie, had come to the Menominee Reservation as a public-health nurse. She met and married Joe Deer, a nearly full-blooded Menominee, who kept alive many of the old tribal ways. "Mom" Deer was active in tribal council meetings. She taught her daughter to be a spirited student of tribal life, to commit herself to public service and social justice.

"Ada Deer, you were not put on this planet to indulge yourself," her mother would say. "You are here to help people." After she had completed high school, Ada's tribe awarded her a scholarship to attend college. In gratitude, she committed her life to helping the tribe.

Ada's path to leadership was shaped by many experiences, one of the most important of which was the Encampment for Citizenship, a six-week summer camp she attended when she was nineteen years old—along with more than one hundred other young people. "It was two years after the Supreme Court decision *Brown v. Board of Education*," she recalls. "I didn't know anything about race relations or this important piece of U.S. history.

"I participated in a workshop on segregation, led by a Southern African-American schoolteacher. She gave me a much greater understanding of racism's impact on individuals, and the power of the federal government to effect positive change." As part of that summer's Encampment, Ada's group visited for several hours with Eleanor Roosevelt at her Hyde Park, New York, home.

"I was impressed that the former first lady would spend so much time in discussion with us. She told us about how she had helped to create the United Nations Commission on Human Rights and the charter supporting peace and the brotherhood of man. I challenged her," Ada remembers. "I asked her, 'What about South Africa oppressing black people? Why doesn't the UN do something?'

"Mrs. Roosevelt replied, 'We have to understand that it takes time. We need to educate people that violence is not the answer. We have to have faith in humans.

Eventually, justice will prevail.' Of course, she was right. Forty years later, apartheid is over and Nelson Mandela is the president of South Africa.

"On another occasion, Dr. Kenneth Clark, the African-American psychologist, spoke to us about his work with school desegregation. I thought to myself, 'I want to make the kind of difference in the lives of my people that he has made for his.' Little did I realize where that desire would lead me."

Years later, Ada saw an opportunity to use her experience to help her tribe. Back in the early 1950s, Congress had "terminated" the Menominee Tribe, along with many others. Through an act of Congress, the government broke its treaty relationships in an attempt to force Indian tribes to assimilate into mainstream culture, to live like non-Indian people.

By the 1970s, Ada's tribe had sunk deeper into poverty, and they nearly lost their tribal identity and culture. They sold their beautiful hunting and fishing grounds to pay taxes, the local hospital was closed, and there were very few jobs. One senator described the reservation as "teetering on the brink of collapse." As a social worker and a teacher, Ada experienced firsthand the harm this policy was doing to her people. Although she had no formal training in politics, she just couldn't stand by while Congress wiped out her tribe's age-old history. She joined her mother and the other women elders to oppose the government with an organization they called DRUMS, which stood for Determination of Rights and Unity for Menominee Shareholders.

No one thought they would succeed against Goliath. Earlier attempts to reverse the law had failed, but Ada was fiercely determined. She went from home to home, driving her creaky old car along the dirt roads of the reservation. She spoke with each tribe member to explain what termination meant to the tribe, and what they could do to change it.

Then she headed to Washington, D.C., where she again went from door to door, engaging everyone she could—congressional-committee chairs, members, aides, secretaries, doormen, and even parking attendants. She worked day and night to persuade members of Congress to reverse what had been law for nearly twenty years.

One non-Indian volunteer who was deeply impressed by Ada's indefatigable energy recalled, "Ada led groups of people by the busload to Washington. We helped her set up a makeshift office with no money and little support. She didn't seem to need to eat or sleep. She just kept going, and always kept her sense of humor. She made all of us feel included and valuable."

Meanwhile, back in Wisconsin, members of DRUMS marched 150 miles from the Menominee Reservation to Madison, the capital city. The march drew widespread media attention to the plight of the tribe.

On October 16, 1973, the moment of truth arrived. Ada and her associates had persuaded enough members of Congress to hold a vote on the Menominee tribal status. It was an historic occasion. Were the tribe to regain its rights, it would be the first time the government's Indian policy had been reversed by Indian people. If they succeeded, many other tribes would be able to use this victory as a precedent to regain their rights, too. On the day of the vote, Ada, the volunteers, and other members of DRUMS attended the congressional session, and watched with excitement.

By the vote's conclusion, the Menominee Tribe had been reinstated by a landslide: 404 to 3! Ada was ecstatic. "This is democracy in action!" she cried. "This is how we, the citizens, can make a change. We can do it! We *have* done it!" Her brother Bob, who had worked alongside Ada in the struggle, remarked that the Menominee chiefs—Grizzly Bear, Great Cloud, and Oshkosh—who'd signed the first treaty would be proud.

Ada Deer is now the assistant secretary for Indian Affairs in the U.S. Department of the Interior. By working to restore the rights of Native American tribes, she has helped to preserve the richness of their culture—and of our country's history. When she participated in the dedication of a new tribal health clinic on the Menominee Reservation she reflected, "In the last two generations, I've seen my tribe come back from near collapse to restored physical and cultural well-being," and adds, "Our tribe has a saying that 'the hard work and determination of our people will benefit the next seven generations to come.'"

To get involved in Native American issues, contact Honor Our Neighbors

Origins and Rights, www.honoradvocacy.org, or the National Indian Education
Association, www.niea.org. **Encampment for Citizenship** promoted "Democracy in Action" for fifty years (1946–96); to learn more about EFC's history,
e-mail its former executive director, Margot Gibney, at laud@aol.com.

FREEDOM FROM THE MADNESS
Told by Arun Gandhi

Souren Bannerji had always thought of himself as a peaceful man. But
when his wife, son, and daughter were raped and murdered by a hate-filled
crowd of Muslims in Calcutta, Souren found himself thinking, then doing, the
unthinkable. He joined violent Hindu mobs, seeking revenge. He was involved
in the massacre of a Muslim family. Having killed a child, Souren knew he'd be
haunted forever.

Souren knew of only one man who could return him to a path of peace. His
name was Mohandas Karamchand Gandhi, but people called him *Mahatma*,
which means "Great Soul." At the same time, Gandhi was trying to teach total
nonviolence to the people of India, and in some ways it was working. His active
nonviolence freed India from British imperialism in 1947; like Souren, many
needed to believe that the Mahatma had at least one more miracle.

Gandhi knew all too well that anger, unchecked and uncontrolled, turned
people toward mindless violence. He described anger as an energy as potent as
electricity itself, and warned that if anger was abused, it could destroy and kill.
But, used intelligently, that same energy could enlighten human lives.

Gandhi had had to face his own anger when, as a young lawyer, he met
with racial prejudice in South Africa. One fateful day, a white man refused to

share a railroad compartment with a "blackie." Railroad officials physically threw Gandhi off the train. His humiliation burned, but he maintained his self-control and with deep, meditative breaths and some chanting, peace descended upon him. As he calmed himself, he concluded that justice was not revenge but enlightenment, and enlightenment could not be beaten into people, it could only be revealed through active nonviolence. Throughout his life, Gandhi came to see nonviolence as more than just a means toward conflict resolution. It was the basis of his spirituality, the sacred oneness of humanity.

However, just because his soul was great didn't mean things came easily to him. In 1946, when the British left, and the country was divided—India for Hindus and Pakistan for Muslims—hundreds of thousands of people were uprooted from the homes and lands they had occupied for generations, and in their anger, murder, mayhem, and rape prevailed. Gandhi was profoundly discouraged. His efforts to teach people to live as one family, peacefully, to put religious and personal prejudices behind them, seemed forgotten.

"If inhumanity is what my countrymen want, I have no desire to live," the anguished leader said. He embarked on a fast unto death. "I tried to teach people humanity, but they prefer bestiality," he lamented. "It is better that I die than live to see this carnage." Although he was a Hindu, the Mahatma chose to fast in a little hut in the poorest Muslim ghetto of Calcutta.

If the people did not stop fighting, Gandhi would most certainly die. At seventy-eight, he no longer had the strength or the stamina to sustain starvation for a prolonged period. Hindus and Muslims alike realized that if Gandhi should die, they would carry a burden of guilt. As much as he had cared for them through the years, now each Hindu and Muslim felt as though his or her own father were about to die for the wrongs they had done.

Souren Bannerji, for one, knew he could not let the Mahatma die. In his heart, he knew his own worst act of violence had been committed just the day before Gandhi announced his fast. Now this news about his hero was exactly the motivation he needed to detach himself from the mob. After about a week of soul-searching, he summoned up the courage to approach Gandhi face to face.

Souren hiked to the hut where Gandhi barely hung on to life. Quietly, reverentially, he entered the room where a medical doctor, an old friend, was patiently rubbing the Mahatma's forehead. Souren placed his head on Gandhi's feet and sobbed uncontrollably, asking forgiveness. "*Bapu* [father], forgive me. I am a sinner and deserve to die, but you must live," Souren pleaded.

"We are all sinners, my son," Gandhi answered, his voice barely audible. "Come close and tell me about your sin."

Souren let the words tumble out in a torrent. "I have committed a heinous crime. I murdered a Muslim family after my family was killed. My life has become a living hell. I can't accept the additional burden of your death on my conscience, *Bapu*. Please give up your fast."

"If you want to save my life, go and work for peace and harmony. And if you want to atone for your sin, I have a suggestion," Gandhi said.

"Tell me, *Bapu*," Souren said. "I will do anything you say. I want peace and I want you to give up your fast."

"First, for yourself. Go and find an orphan Muslim baby and nurture the baby as your own. You must allow the baby to grow up in its own faith." Gandhi was finding speech exhausting. He lapsed into silence, then added, "We are one human race. Religion must unify us, not divide us." With these words, Souren went away, thinking about the great man's counsel.

Word spread of Gandhi's fast and his appeal for unity and harmony. Whether the people stopped fighting because they understood his message of oneness, or simply because they wished to save his life, it is difficult to say. In any case, peace came quickly.

Souren did not forget the promise he had made to Gandhi. In his search for an orphaned Muslim child, he found a young Muslim mother with an infant baby who had miraculously escaped death. Her husband and family had been killed, she had been repeatedly raped, and now she was an outcast.

As they told each other of their suffering, Souren and Miriam found they had much in common. Slowly they came to trust, then love, each other. One day Souren shared with Miriam the last words he had heard from Gandhi: "We are one human race. Don't let religion divide us."

Souren and Miriam were married. In the spirit of Gandhi, they decided they would study both of their religions and absorb the good each had to offer.

I met Souren in Bombay several years later. He and Miriam had two children: Miriam's son, whom Souren had adopted, and a daughter. They never forgot my grandfather's role in bringing them together, in making love and new life triumph over a past scarred by hatred and violence. Before we parted that day, they told me how they had learned an important lesson from Mahatma. Looking at each other, and at their two precious children, they confided, "We understand what Gandhi meant when he said, "Change can come only one life at a time."

Experience the power of nonviolence as a proactive tool to build and maintain human relationships and avoid conflict. Call the **M. K. Gandhi Institute for Nonviolence** at 901-452-2824; e-mail gandhi@cbu.edu; or visit the institute's Web site, www.gandhiinstitute.org.

MAD DADS, CARING FATHERS

Told by Kimberly Ridley

Adapted from an article in *Hope* magazine

Ever since he was a baby, people always liked Wendell Grixby. He had a warm smile and a soft side that made him irresistible. As a guard on his school's basketball team, he was a real team player. But Wendell was having troubles in school—and eventually he dropped out. Without his teammates, Wendell was lonely and lost—looking for direction in his life. While gangs weren't really his style, there weren't a lot of other options in his neighborhood.

One day Wendell had an argument with a fourteen-year-old boy from a local gang, no one really knows over what. But later that day, when Wendell went to the local park in downtown Omaha, the other boy shot and killed him. Wendell was only nineteen years old.

At his funeral, everyone talked of being fed up with the gangs, and with the violence that was taking over their neighborhoods. Wendell's stepfather, John Gatus, says, "Wendell was a good kid with a few problems. But he didn't have to die."

"A group of us are getting together next week to see what we can do to stop the violence," Tariq Almin, a family friend and police officer, told John. "Why don't you join us?" John knew he couldn't just sit back any longer, watching young African-American men killing each other; he had to do something. So he joined six other African-American fathers who had decided to take back their community. They called themselves MAD DADS, or Men Against Destruction—Defending Against Drugs and Social Disorder.

First the men started painting over the graffiti the gangs had covered their streets with. For a while this made things look a little better, but it didn't really address the problem. However, Eddie Staton, a father of six and grandfather of eleven, knew that strong bonds between men and boys could make a world of difference. He thought it could help free kids from the cycle of violence plaguing the nation's neighborhoods. So he got these men to start walking the streets and talking to young people.

"We mobilize strong, drug-free fathers to get their parenting skills off the couch and out into the streets," Eddie says. "I tell them, 'You're not just raising your own children. You're raising everyone's children. And raising a child is about being there, over and over again.'"

"We'd talk to anyone who would listen—especially the younger ones, before they became hard-core," John explains. "We'd ask them to stop their gang activities—the drive-by shootings, the drug selling, and the violence. At first they weren't very interested in what we had to say. But eventually they started listening and telling us their troubles." It soon became clear that most were just looking for attention and affection from a strong father figure.

MAD DADS gives young people an opportunity to get the right kind of attention. Most often, trouble starts with a misunderstanding with one of the adults in their lives. A Mad Dad will offer to meet with the parents, a teacher or school counselor, and the student, and help them resolve their misunderstandings. "When you're on the outside looking in, you can see both sides—you can be objective," John says.

John and other Mad Dads try to help create a loving atmosphere—and to rebuild the family unit with understanding and compassion. "We get them to work together as a family—to see that they need each other to make the relationship work," John says. "We do whatever it takes to get them out of the gang and into a healthy relationship with their family." They also patrol some of Omaha's most volatile street corners and serve as chaperons at parties on Friday and Saturday nights. Sometimes their presence can help to defuse potentially violent situations. And it's a great way to connect with kids in need of some extra attention.

MAD DADS started in 1989 with Eddie, John, and sixteen other African-American men. Today, they and 35,000 other men serve as surrogate fathers to young boys in fifty cities in fourteen states around the country. Together, these volunteer fathers have given more than 200,000 hours counseling kids on some of the nation's meanest streets. They provide a powerful model of how human contact and caring can help stop the cycle of violence that is plaguing our nation's neighborhoods.

They have organized a gun buy-back program with local banks, businesses, and chambers of commerce. So far, they've bought back 2,600 guns and melted them down so they are off the streets for good. They've also created a rites-of-passage program to give young African-American men between the ages of six and twenty-one years the living and learning skills they need to survive in the world, as well as to expose them to the richness of black history, instilling in them a special pride in their culture and themselves.

"Helping kids in impoverished neighborhoods stay away from the lures of the drug trade and gangs is an ongoing and complex challenge," Eddie Staton says. He tells the story of the day one disillusioned young man walked into his office to tell him he was wrong. The youth had been a high-school student when he heard Eddie speak at a school assembly. Although his family sold drugs, the young man didn't, and he dutifully followed MAD DADS' advice, graduating from high school and finding a job in a local business. But he didn't have enough money to support his young daughter. He told Eddie he needed to sell drugs in order to survive.

"I told this kid, 'Living right doesn't mean everything will be easy. But I can show you how to live to be my age rather than being in prison or in a grave. What I'm showing you is a formula for life.' I asked him, 'What's going to happen to your daughter if you get yourself killed or end up in prison?' That made him think. 'Do you know what will happen when she gets to be ten or eleven and nobody's told her about sex, and a drug dealer gets after her?' 'I'd kill him,' he said. I said, 'You'd have to be around to do that. More important, you need to be there for her in the first place!' "

In conversations like these between surrogate fathers and young men looking for answers, MAD DADS is making a difference in hundreds of lives and communities. Gang activity in Omaha has dropped by half; there are fewer gang "wannabes," and a growing number of the younger kids are beginning to reject the notion of gangs.

"It's so beautiful to hear kids say, 'I'm not proud of my life, and I want to turn it around.' It makes all our efforts worthwhile," John says. "But," he adds, "it breaks your heart to see a child reaching out, asking for help, for guidance—knowing there aren't enough mentors.

"People today just don't take the time to get to know these kids. Each one of them needs the kind of special attention that comes from one caring adult. If we get to know one another, we can resolve most of our problems.

"Every state in the country is building either a prison or a jail," he adds. "If every man patrolled the streets in their community, there wouldn't be a need for most of these prisons. And, we could create a nation of caring fathers."

"Men like John are taking their anger and their pain and using it to help other kids," says Eddie. "If black men in every community were to stand up, and say, 'Let's start voting, let's work together and build community,' we could change who gets into political office. We would start having voting power instead of bullet power. We could build a future with our young people, one that we'd all be proud of."

The only solution is love.

DOROTHY DAY

To learn how you can mobilize drug-free men and women to make a difference in the lives of young people at risk of drugs, gangs, or violence, call MAD DADS at 904-721-9469, extension 218; or visit their Web site, www.maddads national.com.

WALKING SHIELD
Told by Jane Harvey

His Lakota name is Walking Shield. Outside the Sioux nation, he's known as Phil Stevens. For those on the Pine Ridge Reservation, he is the right man in the right place at the right time. Phil has brought together his Native American heritage, his engineering expertise, and his federal and military contacts to bring hope to his people. He is helping to renew a spirit of community where there has long been none. And he is rebuilding his nation's homeland and his people's trust in the United States government.

Phil grew up in a tough East Los Angeles neighborhood, with only the stories told by his dad to connect him to his Sioux roots. As the great-grandson of a Lakota chief who'd fought at the Battle of the Little Big Horn, being a leader was in his blood. He worked hard in school, went on to college, and earned two engineering degrees. Eventually he became TRW's technical director, managing a major national defense project. Then he built his own multimillion-dollar engineering business.

Phil didn't think much about his heritage until a group of Native Americans took over Alcatraz Island in 1969, protesting generations of injustice. As he read about it in the newspaper, he wondered if there was anything he could do to help. He felt a sense of responsibility toward his people that might be compatible with his other responsibilities. Later he would recall, "I wanted to help them — but from within the existing system of government."

For the next twenty years, Phil volunteered his time with various Indian tribes throughout the country. He worked with American Indians who were struggling to survive in the business world. He helped negotiate various land disputes between tribes and the federal government. In 1986 he was invited by tribal leaders to visit his homeland, the Pine Ridge Indian Reservation in South Dakota. What he saw there changed the course of Phil's life.

He was heartbroken to see people living in unheated one-room shacks. In forty-degrees-below-zero weather, they slept practically on top of one another. Entire families were living in old cars. Some people even lived in caves. For many there were no toilets, and water was a quarter-mile away. Phil was especially concerned for the children when he saw the poorly outfitted schools and grossly inadequate health care. The shockingly high rates of alcoholism and domestic abuse suggested a people in despair. An oppressive sense of hopelessness hovered like a cloud over the reservation, as it had for generations.

Phil went back home and told his family, "Our people are refugees in their own land." He made a decision that day to do whatever he could to help the

Sioux people become a strong, self-sustaining community once more. He sold his business and poured all his energy and expertise into helping his people rebuild their hopes, dreams, and dignity. "It was a tough decision," he says, "but I figured that the needs of Native Americans were greater than the needs of my company."

But, as he would soon discover, helping people help themselves is easier said than done.

"When you beat down a society of people for hundreds of years, it is very difficult to bring them back and help them to be self-sufficient," Phil says. "And the more beaten down they are, the more difficult it is to bring them back."

Phil wanted the Sioux to be the strong, proud people they had once been. And he wanted them to enjoy the same benefits enjoyed by everyone else in America. "In order to succeed, people must first believe that they can," he said. "But self-esteem is scarce on the reservation. And without hope, all is lost.

"What happened a hundred years ago is still current in the minds of our children," he says. "But despite the injustices done to my people, this is a great land, truly a land of opportunity." Without glossing over the tragic history of the Sioux, Phil wants to help them get over the past, and get on with building their future. "I grew up with very little material wealth, but I learned that if you work very hard and you have certain abilities, you can be blessed in our society," he says. "I want to give other Native Americans a chance."

Phil began by working with tribal leaders, asking them what the people wanted and needed, and how they might work together to achieve those goals. They came up with a long list of their needs—food, clothing and building supplies, better health care and education. The Sioux people were willing to work hard to rebuild their lives and their reservation, if Phil could help them.

From his work with government agencies, Phil knew that military bases often discarded their outdated or unused materials and supplies. He developed a unique strategy to get those bases to recycle and donate their supplies to the reservations. Then he founded the Walking Shield American Indian Society to coordinate all the logistics of getting these things to the people.

The society started by gathering food and clothing for reservation families. They collected books and computers for reservation schools, and prepared students for college. "We focus heavily on education so the children can have a choice of looking to the future," Phil says. "I tell the young people they need to learn how to live in both cultures—with a moccasin on one foot and a tennis shoe on the other."

To help people on the reservation rebuild their homes so they could be warm for the winter, the society took on its most ambitious undertaking, calling it Operation Walking Shield. By cooperating with the government and involving all services of the armed forces, they have helped improve reservation housing for hundreds of people.

Phil learned that because of post–Cold War military cutbacks, 463 newly refurbished houses at the Grand Forks Air Force Base in North Dakota were scheduled to be demolished. He called the base and a few senators from North and South Dakota. "These homes are just going to be bulldozed," he told them. "We need them for the reservations." In a unique deal with the Department of Defense, he arranged for these houses to be taken to seven Sioux reservations. He even got military personnel to install the foundations for the three-bedroom, two-bathroom homes as part of their military training exercises.

Through the Internet, Phil located extra construction supplies. When he found them at various military bases, he asked the air force if it could deliver them to the reservation—free of charge. Now, instead of flying circles above their bases to log training flight time, military pilots are moving these supplies from bases throughout the nation to the Indian reservations in South Dakota.

Since 1995, Operation Walking Shield has provided 967 housing units for more than six thousand needy American Indian families on fourteen reservations. In partnership with the U.S. military services, it has provided medical and health-care support to twenty thousand people, and has helped build and repair more than seven hundred miles of roads on Indian reservations. The Walking Shield Society's five hundred volunteers have helped nearly 250,000 Native

Americans from fifty of the nation's 557 tribes who live on our nation's Indian reservations.

Homer Whirlwind Soldier, a descendant of a Sioux chief, has watched cooperation build on Phil's magic. "There are four types of people in the world," he says. "The first two, poor-rich and poor-poor, have a miserly view of life and people," he explains. "Then there are the rich-poor and the rich-rich. They are full of spirit. They do things for others. Phil is one of those."

For his work with the tribe, Phil was the first person named Special Chief of the Great Sioux Nation. It is an extraordinary honor that many equate with the honor accorded Sitting Bull, who helped unite the Sioux people more than a century ago. But for Phil, the reward isn't in the honor, or even in the improved standard of living on the reservations. "It's not the clothing, the medical equipment, or the houses that are really significant," he says. "The most important thing we are doing is providing hope for our people."

Let us put our minds together and see what life we can make for our children.

SITTING BULL, LAKOTA SIOUX, 1877

Help the **Walking Shield American Indian Society** provide food to the hungry, shelter to the homeless, medical assistance to the sick, and educational support for Native Americans. To volunteer, call 714-258-7025 or e-mail walkshield@ aol.com.

A MESSENGER OF HOPE
Told by Nancy Berg

People thought he had lost his mind when he chose to film *American Me* on East L.A.'s most dangerous streets. But growing up in the barrio of Boyle

Heights, Edward James Olmos never did follow the rules; he was more likely to create them. Early on, the Latino actor and activist used his head, heart, and talent to find ways to succeed so others could one day follow. He chose his acting roles carefully so he could set an example. As the firm but fair Lieutenant Martin Castillo in *Miami Vice*, he earned great respect. Then, with the film *Stand and Deliver*, he was nominated for an Academy Award for his portrayal of Jaime Escalante, the tough math teacher who taught the lost youth of East L.A. how to earn respect.

When he was ready to direct his first film, he wanted to deliver a strong anti-drug and anti-gang message to kids in the barrios—so he went right back to East L.A. Using real gang members as extras and crew, Olmos showed the world the painfully honest reality of their brief, violent lives. For many of these kids, their only ambition was one day to go to San Quentin or Folsom Prison. "They go from being streetwise gang members into prison. When they get out, they think they can start their lives," Olmos says. "They don't see alternatives to the gang life. Without skills, and with jobs hard to come by, kids start dealing to make a buck—and gangs control that world."

Olmos gave those young people real jobs, with a real future—and an opportunity to break out of the gang-banger world. He also wanted to show the little ones—the ones who see everything—that people who look just like them can succeed and make their good dreams come true. "Kids in East L.A., like any kids, need hope. You get hope by having opportunity to see a future, and right now it looks pretty dark," he says, adding, "I think that role models are the most important thing in these kids' lives now."

Olmos has been blessed by role models who showed him that helping others is a way of life—and he carries this tradition on within his own family. His mother, Eleanor, worked for fifteen years in the Los Angeles County General Hospital AIDS ward, and his father, Pedro, helped coordinate Little League baseball in East L.A. His actress wife, Lorraine Bracco, volunteers for a group that provides housing for disabled adults, and their six children helped paint murals in L.A.'s inner-city schools. "It's all a labor of love," Olmos says.

Known for his big heart, Olmos often challenges others to share theirs. After the L.A. riots in 1992, he galvanized people from across the city to help clean up the horrific rubble. With the simple gesture of a broom and a dustpan held up on TV, he invited all who were watching to join him, in the streets, day after day, for as long as it took. Then, at the 1994 Democratic National Convention, he challenged the entire nation: "It is the task of all caring adults to be messengers of hope to these disenfranchised youth."

Olmos is a messenger of hope for thousands of Latino teens like George Sarabia. Before he met Olmos, George had only one goal in life: to come back from prison a hero, having earned his "stripes." At the young age of twenty-one, he'd been in a gang for seven years, had been shot, and had lost his brother to gang violence. At first, when he was offered a small part in *American Me*, he refused—afraid of betraying his brother's memory. But then he thought of his four younger brothers, all living in jail. "If I'm not able to forgive, when will it ever stop?" he asked himself. His decision to work with Eddie and his team was the turning point in his life.

"Eddie helped turn our community upside down," George says. "He treated me like a human being, and gave me an opportunity to help, and responsibility—for cleaning up the graffiti." Working with Olmos's team on *Lives in Hazard* inspired George to begin a new career producing educational videos. "It was as if he took me by the hand and showed me a different life," he says.

By filming scenes from *American Me* right in East L.A.'s streets and at Folsom Prison, Olmos helped deglamourize the gang world. While he got his message across to the young actors, it wasn't enough. Even before *American Me* was released, two of the young men from the film crew were killed by rival gangs. When the 1992 L.A. riots nearly destroyed South Central L.A., Eddie decided he had to do something more. Olmos thought that if other young people could see what they'd learned from the gang members who helped make *American Me*, they might decide to change their ways. After persuading the U.S. Department of Justice to fund an educational documentary, Olmos and his team created a real-life drama that showed how the movie was made. Named after the Hazard

Grande barrio and the Big Hazard gang, they called the film *Lives in Hazard*. It depicts the strange and tragic choices these young people are forced to make. They also created a study guide and a national resource guide of organizations, to give teachers, counselors, and ministers the practical tools they need to help "at risk" youth. The team now travels across the country sharing the film with teenagers, giving them a chance to talk about the social power of gangs. "These young people just want to make a mark on the world. They're in search of identity, a sense of belonging," Olmos says. "We each have the need to belong. It's an instinctual part of being human."

Whether speaking at schools, churches, jails, or juvenile halls, Eddie's message is the same: "My hope is that after watching *Lives in Hazard*, each of you will be inspired to move beyond what you think is possible for your communities by helping each other take ownership of your lives and your futures."

Gil Espinozo is another young man who now has a more hopeful future, thanks to his experience with *Lives in Hazard*. After working as a production assistant on the film, he got a job working for a casting director for a film company. His experience gave him more than just on-the-job training; it provided him with a healthy place to be. " I spend a lot of time at the theater," he says. "They are like a family to me, they accept me for what I am, and I like that."

When Eddie is praised for his work, he always gives credit to the "real heroes" like Father Gregory Boyle, a Jesuit priest who works with young people in East L.A.'s Dolores Mission Church. "I've had to bury and say good-bye to thirty-one young men and women, all killed in this madness called gang-banging," Father Boyle says. "These were kids I knew well, who were warm, unique, and full of potential. They should not have died so young."

One young woman who lost her son to gang violence told Father Boyle, "All this violence is about people who are in pain and feel disconnected from each other. We need to show up in these kids' lives," Father Boyle says. "Adults need to show up and pay loving attention to these kids. Employers need to show up with jobs for them. Health-care professionals need to show up with compassion and understanding. Leaders and legislators need to show up with a plan to remedy diminished resources in this country. What we could never accomplish alone, we will be able to do together. As a community we can help these young people imagine a better future, and then lead them into it, with confidence and hope."

Young people like George and Gil can leverage their life experiences to create better futures for themselves as well as others. At twenty-seven, George runs a nonprofit organization, Inner City Focus, which makes violence-prevention programming for TV, shown in five of L.A.'s housing developments through a local cable company. Taking a moment out of his busy life, he pauses to think about his mother, and those who never gave up on him. "Before she died of cancer last year, she got to see that I have a good life—that I'm married and have a family," he says. "She was happy to know her son had chosen to walk the other way."

Knowing that young people often listen better to someone their own age, Eddie Olmos sometimes invites George and Gil to share their stories—and their message—with other young people. "We all have choices," Gil tells them. "You can do whatever you want to do. You don't have to prove anything to anyone else, just to yourself." Then he pauses for a moment and says, with quiet intensity, "Think about it. What you could do. What you could be."

> *Whatever you can do to uplift the life of a child is a step in the right direction toward creating true civil rights for children. If you don't have children, find someone else's! Take them to the library, the theater, a picnic in the park. Use your own life to help point a young life in the right direction.*
>
> OPRAH WINFREY

Be a messenger of hope to young people in your neighborhood. Give them an opportunity for a better life. To purchase the **Lives in Hazard** study guide and video for your school, church, or community center, contact olmosproductions @hotmail.com.

COMPASSION,
THEIR PRECIOUS TREASURE
Told by Robert Thurman

Maybe it was the land itself—the largest and highest plateau on earth, ringed by the world's tallest peaks. For centuries Tibet has been known as "the rooftop of the world." Her gentle people became a symbol of inspiration because of their mystical talent for finding the sacred dimension of everyday life. The rich culture, spirituality, and language of this land of snows were uniquely and beautifully her own.

In 1950, Chinese forces invaded Tibet to gain control of what they perceived to be a strategic border area, but once there, they aimed to eradicate the Tibetan identity and make Tibet indistinguishable from China. Tibetans were not allowed to worship, and most of their monasteries and other holy sites were destroyed. The Tibetan language was forbidden, and all aspects of Tibetan culture were rigidly suppressed. Tibetans who continued to follow their own religion were tortured and killed. For more than fifty years the world has remained mostly silent as the Tibetan genocide went on and a once-thriving nation was turned into a devastated economic wasteland.

Tibet's leader, the Fourteenth Dalai Lama, born Tenzin Gyatso, was forced to flee the country in 1959 along with thousands of his followers. He established a Tibetan government-in-exile in Dharamsala, India, and has worked diligently since then to preserve Tibetan arts, scriptures, and medicine. His wisdom and compassion in leading a nonviolent struggle to regain his homeland have made him an inspiration to millions of people of various faiths from all over the world.

In 1985, 200,000 Tibetans risked the arduous journey over the mountains to Bodhgaya, India, the place that Tibetan Buddhists venerate as the spot where the Buddha attained Enlightenment, and where they celebrate one of their most sacred ceremonies, the Kalachakra initiation. To ensure their prompt return, the Chinese government held the families of the pilgrims virtually hostage.

For many it would be the first time they would see His Holiness the Dalai Lama, a moment they had anticipated their entire lives. Yak herders, shoe-makers, people who couldn't read or write, were nonetheless united in keeping this sacred commitment. They had lived through countless examples of unspeak-able horror and violence—suffering that was locked away in their own souls as they crowded onto buses and braved treacherous roads, and Nepalese and Indian police along the way extorted unlawful tolls.

The task now before Tenzin Gyatso seemed insurmountable. He knew he must speak to his people about the Buddhist principles of tolerance and com-passion. Yet he was acutely aware that he was addressing individuals who had been tortured, who had seen their families raped and mutilated, who had spent wretched years in prison.

You could almost feel the Dalai Lama's own heart break wide open as he sat close to his people. He implored them to respond to their enemies without vio-lence or hatred. He asked them to find compassion for their oppressors and to overcome their instinct to strike back.

He acknowledged that their families had been destroyed, their land, their life, their country, and their religion robbed from them. Yet he beseeched them to take all their suffering as a spur to conquer any vindictive, hateful, or destructive tendencies within themselves:

"This is war, but it is an internal war. It may seem the world has forgotten us, allowing the Chinese to do this to us. But we can win the war by completely con-quering our inner enemy. If we wage this war against our natural instinct for revenge, and conquer the vengeful egotism we have within ourselves, then we will have done something very special. Then the world will have to recognize our stand against the endless cycle of violence. The world will then see to it that there will be justice. But it must be done without vengeance against the Chinese."

As he spoke, the Dalai Lama, usually composed and stoic, was openly weeping. So were the majority of the 200,000 assembled before him. You could see the struggle in the faces of the children and teenagers. They did not know whether to believe this man or not. Over the years the Chinese had worked hard to turn them against him and his teachings. But the Dalai Lama reached them with his tenderness, and after some moments in silence, they accepted the wisdom of his message and respected his open heart. In turn, they took his high aspirations with them back to Tibet.

Four years after this amazing scene, the Dalai Lama received the Nobel Prize for Peace. In his acceptance speech he reaffirmed his belief in the path of tolerance and compassion:

"I accept the prize with profound gratitude on behalf of the oppressed everywhere and for all those who struggle for freedom and work for world peace. I accept it as a tribute to the man who founded the modern tradition of nonviolent action for change, Mahatma Gandhi, whose life taught and inspired me. And, of course, I accept it on behalf of the six million Tibetan people, my brave countrymen and women inside Tibet, who have suffered and continue to suffer so much.

"They confront a calculated and systematic strategy aimed at the destruction of their national and cultural identities. The prize reaffirms our conviction that with truth, courage, and determination as our weapons, Tibet will be liberated."

The Tibetans' struggle is gaining recognition and support. In May 2000, the Dalai Lama traveled across the United States, addressing more than 160,000 people, inviting each of us to put compassion into action to transcend violence, heal spirits, and help the world.

Love and compassion are the basis of hope and determination.

HIS HOLINESS THE DALAI LAMA

Pray for peace and develop compassion in your heart. If you want to help the Tibetan people and preserve Tibet's precious civilization, contact **Tibet House,** the Dalai Lama's official cultural organization in America. Write to them at 22 West 15th Street, New York, NY 10011 for their membership materials, or visit these Web sites: www.tibethouse.org or www.bobthurman.com.

III

COMMUNITY
COOPERATION

Imagine, if you can, a society formed of all the nations of the world.

People having different languages, beliefs, opinions;

in a word, a society without roots, without memories, without prejudices,

without routines, without common ideas, without a national character,

yet a hundred times happier than our own.

ALEXIS DE TOCQUEVILLE, *Democracy in America,* 1835

When you get together with your family and friends, do you often find yourselves talking about what's not working—in your school, your job, your neighborhood? Do you throw up your hands in frustration, thinking the problem is just too confusing, complex, or big? Do you think you're too busy, too tired, or too unimportant to make a difference?

Many of the people you will meet in this chapter faced challenges similar to yours. Instead of giving up, they rallied others to help them make things better. Through their stories, we learn that when we work together we can tackle some of the toughest challenges facing our communities. "Never doubt that a small group of thoughtful committed citizens can change the world; indeed, it's the only thing that ever has," said Margaret Mead.

The world community spontaneously responded to the events of September 11 in amazing and inspiring ways. The ten thousand people of the small town of Gander, Newfoundland, did what came naturally. After the attacks, thirty-eight airliners were forced to land immediately on their tiny runway, and 6,579 frightened passengers and crew were stranded there. This town immediately went into action—organizing a massive relief effort to provide them with housing, food, and care. Their generosity deeply touched the travelers, and lasting friendships were forged. The onetime strangers responded with gifts, invitations, and generous donations: new lighting for the local church and a scholarship fund for the children of Gander. Referring to the harsh weather, rough seas, and uncertain economy characteristic of the region, the mayor said, matter-of-factly, "We're used to helping people."

Nowhere in the world was the sense of community stronger after September 11 than in New York City. People reached out to each other in pain, in hope, and in love. This city of eight million people felt as close as a small village. During the attack, New Yorkers helped one another survive. Then they dusted themselves off and started rebuilding their morale and their city. Their resolve to go ahead with life even as they grieved reminded us of the true character of Americans. As we waved flags and sang "God Bless America," we felt we were one. "New York is the greatest city in the world," said actor Billy Crystal. "We will make this an even greater city and country."

Since September 11, our local communities are being asked to do even more with even less to take care of themselves. At times like these, we need to take care of one another, and, while we're putting things back together, make sure no one falls through the cracks.

Alexis de Tocqueville had great faith in the power of the American people. In 1831, when he was just twenty-one years old, he came from France to study the United States. As he traveled across the country, he was impressed with the helpful, inventive, and energetic people he met, gathering in small groups to solve local problems. "In France, decisions are made by professors, elected officials, professionals and managers," he wrote. "In the United States, it's the common people who are making these decisions." In his book *Democracy in America*, he told how these small groups were the building blocks of a strong society. A century and a half later, his book is still a valuable blueprint for a healthy country, which depends on the spirit and cooperation of "ordinary" people.

There is an exciting renaissance of communities across the country. From Boston's Dudley Street Neighborhood Initiative to Chicago's Bethel New Life Church, from the New York Restoration Project to Los Angeles's TreePeople, these stories give us tremendous hope, especially for our inner cities.

These heroes have different stories about how they got started and how their lives have been transformed along with others'. These heroes have worked together to plant a million trees, build a community playground, or clean up an entire city park. They have built partnerships with schools and churches, hospitals and civic organizations, and transformed toxic-waste dumps into vibrant neighborhoods and struggling economies into economic miracles. Just as there is no one right way for a community to solve its problems, there's never just one community hero. Each person gives what he or she can, and shares the results, enjoying the feeling of togetherness.

These stories give us lots of new ideas and offer valuable life lessons. They remind us how lucky we are to be American citizens, to have the power to change things with our votes or our voices, our time or our money. They show us that while each one of us can make a difference, when we work together, we make history.

The next time you get together with your family and friends,

try talking about what *you* could do to improve things in your world.

Where would you begin?

Who would you ask to join you?

And, most important, how would you celebrate when you got the job done?

Just think, if we all work together, we can make things better for everyone!

NOT SUCH A SILLY GOOSE

When you see geese heading south this winter, flying along in a V formation, think about what science has discovered about why geese fly this way. As each bird flaps its wings, it creates an uplift for the one following behind. By flying in V formation, the whole flock adds at least 71 percent greater flying range than if each bird flew on its own.

If a goose falls out of formation, it feels the drag and resistance of trying to go it alone. By connecting with the lifting power of the bird in front, it quickly gets back into formation. When the leading goose gets tired, it rotates back in the formation, and another goose takes the lead. Geese honk from behind to encourage those up front to keep up their speed. When a goose gets sick or is injured and falls out of formation, two other geese follow it to a safe haven to lend protection and help it heal. They stay with the fallen goose until it is able to fly or it dies. Only then do they fly again, joining another formation to catch up with their group.

If we have as much sense as a goose, we will travel with those who share a common vision. We will work together with those who are headed in the same direction. We will join a supportive community. We will take turns as leaders. We will stand by one another.

ASHLEY'S BIG PLANS

Told by Dawn M. Hutchison

Seven-year-old Ashley looked out from her bedroom window. A tall white man, wearing a baseball cap, was measuring the vacant lot in front of her apartment, and she thought she'd better have a talk with him. He probably didn't know it, but she had big plans for this space. Ashley pulled on her red-and-blue jumper and scampered down the stairs, braids bobbing. She darted past her mother and little brother, and ran outside.

People in the neighborhood had been watching Darell Hammond all morning from their apartment windows. Some had even walked by for a closer look at what he was doing. But Ashley was the first to speak to him. "Have you come to build the playground?" she asked. "A playground, what a great idea!" said Darell, with a smile. *How could she know that?* he thought to himself.

"I'm Ashley," she said. "I've been praying for a playground, and I have big plans for it!" "What exactly are your plans?" Darell asked. Ashley dashed back into her apartment, returning with a handful of drawings. By then, other kids had started to gather. Darell looked at Ashley's drawings and listened to the neighborhood kids. It seemed they all had big plans. "A dinosaur you can climb on," said one. "A big ship," said another.

Darell looked around at the dry, dusty, grassless area. He could just imagine what the area was used for at night. He was right. The Southeast Washington, D.C., housing complex was poorly maintained. The neighborhood was known mostly for its poverty and crime. The lot was a breeding ground after dark for illegal activity: drugs, gangs, and violence.

Darell immediately liked Ashley. She reminded him of himself when he was her age. He was a dreamer too, always coming up with ways to build a better world for children like himself. Now, twenty-four-year-old Darell had an idea to turn this place around, and he could use her help.

As the co-founder of KaBOOM!, Darell rallies inner-city residents to rebuild community spirit by building playgrounds. He gets local people to pool their money and volunteer their time, church organizations to cook food, and businesses to donate construction materials and tools. Darell wanted to make sure Ashley's neighborhood had a playground. There was much to do, so he got started, telling Ashley he would be back soon.

A week later he returned. This time Ashley's mother and her neighbors, Ms. Marshal and Ms. Law, came out to talk with him. He told the women about the children's dream, and how he wanted to help them make it come true. "But, it's going to take a lot more than imagination," he said. That was an understatement. What it would take was one hundred volunteers and about forty thousand dollars, Darell told them, as Ashley's mother stared in disbelief.

There weren't many more than one hundred adults living in the entire complex, and many of them were single mothers who had little spare time. As for the forty thousand dollars, well, that was simply going to take a miracle. Darell understood Ashley's mother's concerns, having heard them from other parents in other housing projects. But he knew they could do it. He told stories of how other neighborhoods had come together and accomplished the impossible.

The mothers weren't sure how they were going to make it happen, but for the children, they wanted to try. Even the kids wanted to do their part. "I'll help out, Darell!" Ashley yelled, as she disappeared down the sidewalk with a trail of children following her, in search of one hundred adults.

And her work paid off. A week later the community meeting was so packed, the kids had to gather outside. With paper and crayons, the youngsters drew more of their playground ideas. Inside, the adults talked excitedly. Before long, churches, grocery stores, and even the local gas stations had posters advertising the community playground project. Ashley and the other kids led a penny drive to raise money.

But as the time to build the playground neared, they were desperately short of the funds. Many people were convinced the project would never happen. "Not in that neighborhood," they said. "You'll never raise that kind of money or get enough volunteers." After a while, even Darell became disheartened.

One day when he was almost ready to give up, Ashley ran up to him, out of breath. "Darell, we raised $9.97 in pennies this week! Isn't that great?" she asked. "That can buy something, right? A sliding board, maybe?" In that moment, Darell knew Ashley would never give up. "Yes, Ashley," he said, "that will buy something wonderful," as he put his baseball cap onto her little head. If this little dreamer wouldn't quit, neither would he.

That's when fate stepped in to lend a hand. Later that day, Darell got a call from the local lumber yard. They wanted to donate a semi trailer full of wood, and five truckloads of wood mulch to spread around the playground! The next day someone else called, donating some old tires. The paint store contributed paint and brushes. The church offered to make breakfast for volunteers and send their youth group to help. The miracle Ashley's mother had asked for began to materialize.

Before long, the empty lot was filled with piles of donated supplies and swarms of people! These volunteers worked tirelessly for four straight days. On the second day it rained, but that didn't dampen their spirits. They just kept building.

The whole apartment complex was filled with the echoes of hammers and saws, and clouds of sawdust. It was a beautiful sight to see. On the last day of construction there were nearly five hundred volunteers! Even the children helped. They filled wheelbarrows and buckets with mulch, spreading it across the enormous playground. They screwed the last bolts into the tire dinosaur, and hung the tire swings.

When the work was done, Ashley's mom and the other neighbors stood back, amazed. Their community playground was finally finished. Ms. Marshall just shook her head, saying softly, "I never would have imagined . . ." But Ashley wasn't surprised. "Darell and I, we always knew," she said with confidence, as she stared at the twenty-four-foot sliding board. "We had big plans."

> *Adults need children in their lives to keep their imagination fresh and their hearts young and to make the future a reality for which they are willing to work.*
>
> MARGARET MEAD

This was the first playground built out of a partnership between Darell Hammond and Dawn Hutchison, who went on to co-found KaBOOM!, a national nonprofit organization that has since constructed more than one thousand community playgrounds. KaBOOM! gets individuals, organizations, and businesses together to create safe and accessible places for children to play. In the process, KaBOOM! helps communities establish partnerships for making further improvements. For more information on the know-how, resources, and training available from KaBOOM!, visit their Web site, www.kaboom.org; or phone 202-659-0215.

TREEPEOPLE

Told by Skye Trimble

Camp was great fun, that summer of 1970. The roasting of marshmallows and the woodsy smell of the fire made fifteen-year-old Andy Lipkis fall in love with the outdoors. But as he looked out over the forested mountains above the city of Los Angeles, his heart sank. He knew that pollution was weakening the trees, and bark beetles were killing them at a rapid rate.

Andy couldn't just stand by and watch them die. So, he rallied his fellow campers in an amazing tree-saving adventure. First they planted smog-tolerant trees in an old parking lot at the camp. As they swung their picks and sowed seedlings, they brought life back into that piece of earth. They were proud of the work they had done together. When camp was over, one fellow camper put his hand on Andy's shoulder and said, "Let's visit the trees when we're old." Andy knew they would.

But Andy couldn't just leave it at that and wait until he got old. *We need to spread this work to more land and more people,* he thought, with a twinge of fear—not of failure, he realized, but of success. He knew if he got people to join him, he would be responsible for what happened next. It might mean he would be planting trees for the rest of his life. Still, he decided to follow his heart, wherever it might lead him.

A few years later, Andy heard that the California Department of Forestry was going to destroy twenty thousand surplus seedlings. He asked if he could have them for another tree-planting project. "That would be considered a gift of public funds," the department told him. "We're prohibited by law from giving them to you."

Andy didn't give up easily. He called newspapers, senators, and anyone else who could pull some strings. He told them what was about to happen, and begged them to do something, and they did. When the *Los Angeles Times* called the governor's office to confirm a story they were planning to run, the governor's office decided it was time to act. They called the Department of Forestry and ordered the bulldozing to stop, just as the seedlings were being plowed under.

Finally, Andy was granted permission to adopt the remaining seedlings, but that's not the end of this story. Next he brought together the kids and counselors from twenty summer camps for a major replanting project. Newspaper coverage led to more donations, more volunteers, and a new law requiring the government to give surplus trees to nonprofit groups who wanted them. People from all backgrounds joined Andy and his growing pack of citizen foresters. The group's nickname, TreePeople, took root.

In 1980 the mayor of Los Angeles, Tom Bradley, heard about TreePeople's success. He'd read that massive city tree planting could reduce pollution, and wondered if planting a million trees in L.A. could breathe life back into his city. The official estimate was twenty years and $200 million to complete the project. But the city couldn't wait twenty years, Mayor Bradley could see that. So he called TreePeople.

"L.A. had just been selected as the city to host the 1984 Olympics," says Andy. "I saw this as a perfect opportunity to demonstrate the power of cooperative action to a global audience. I told the mayor I was sure the people of L.A. could do it, at virtually no cost to government."

Response to the Million Tree Campaign was enthusiastic from the beginning. One nursery on the other side of Los Angeles offered to donate 100,000 surplus trees to get it started, if TreePeople could find a way to move them. The air force had helped TreePeople before, transporting trees in their trucks. Though it had taken nearly two years for someone to get back to him the first time, the letter he had finally received from air force officer Andy Drysdale left a lasting impression: "Maybe we can help you," it had said. When Andy asked for their help again, the air force came through quickly, donating eight mega-transports and troops to help move and prepare the 100,000 seedlings.

Early one morning in November 1981, eight massive army trucks arrived in a convoy that stretched a quarter-mile on the freeway, to move the seedlings across the L.A. basin. Three hundred volunteers and soldiers worked side by side all day long to move the seedlings. They began friendships and shared stories that made the day go by quickly.

As the soldiers drove out of the canyon at day's end, they were stopped by a beautiful sight. A group of volunteers stood in a circle holding hands, the sunset's glow bathing them in warm light. The troops were so moved that they stopped and joined the circle, making it twice as big. Hand in hand, they celebrated not just the day's achievement, but also their power to contribute to life—a different way to use their force.

With this auspicious beginning, Andy and the TreePeople incited hundreds more volunteers to plant the millionth tree by the 1984 Summer Olympics. In the next three years, people from all over Los Angeles became TreePeople. Billboards exhorted TURN OVER A NEW LEAF, LOS ANGELES. Bumper stickers boasted ROOTING FOR THE FUTURE. People came together among the trees, and in the hope that they could help heal their home and the planet, too.

Four days before the Olympic flame was lit, the millionth tree was snug in the ground. The people of Los Angeles felt profoundly satisfied by what they had done with their own hands. To celebrate, volunteers gathered in the mountains overlooking the city. Old and young, men and women, leaders from corporations, government agencies, and gangs beamed with the sun and danced on the mountain together.

Since the Million Tree Campaign, TreePeople has been training young people to become "managers of the environment." They teach kids that the city is a living ecosystem that can be healed and nurtured by the informed acts of caring citizens. They even deliver fruit trees to low-income families across the city so they can grow their own fresh fruit. On Martin Luther King Day, 1990, they got thousands of Angelenos to plant the largest living memorial to Dr. King ever created. Today five hundred trees line the entire seven miles of King Boulevard. TreePeople Citizen Foresters organize neighborhoods to plant and care for trees throughout Los Angeles.

Andy's summer-camp dream is alive, the gift of a lifetime, the gift of life. He tells city kids across the country, "Believe in your dreams. That's what made mine grow."

We have a responsibility to the largest population of all, the hundreds of billions of people who have not yet been born, who have a right to be, who deserve a world at least as beautiful as ours.

DAVID R. BROWER

Plant a tree and take care of it. Learn how you can help rebuild the forests in your community by calling your local forest ranger. Join the **National Association of Service and Conservation Corps** by calling 202-737-6272. If you live in Los Angeles and want to help Andy rebuild the forests, clean the air, and strengthen the economy, call TreePeople at 818-753-4600, or visit their Web site, www.treepeople.org.

THE GREAT MARTHA'S VINEYARD BARN RAISING

Told by Rick Glassberg and Susan Spence

When islanders and summer people heard that the Agricultural Society was selling their beloved old Ag Hall, they were sick at heart. The charming building, with its gingerbread eaves, had been the center of social goings-on since it was built 139 years ago. More than just a building, it represented a cherished old-fashioned way of life. For as long as anyone could remember, it had been home to the society's annual fair and the weekly farmers' markets. Losing it would be like saying good-bye to a dear family friend.

Unfortunately, it had become too small for the society's needs and this growing island community. When the drawings for the new steel-framed hall were unveiled in 1994, there were lots of rumblings, for such a break with tradition was a bitter pill for many in the community to swallow. One society trustee, Andrew "Woody" Woodruff, quietly observed that the plan was "a very low moment for the Agricultural Society." As it was for every other island kid, the hall had been the center of his universe, a castle of memories. He still remembers his first ride on the old Ferris wheel, the games and the tasty foods that wouldn't be as tasty without the old building to go with them.

The community spirit on Martha's Vineyard is legendary. There on a little patch of land just off Cape Cod, goodwill is a way of life. Having weathered storms together, even young children know that when there is a problem, islanders get together and try to solve it. There's an unwritten code that when something needs doing, neighbors help each other out. Over the years, some people had forgotten what makes the Vineyard special, but when Woody spoke up, he reawakened many islanders to their common values and traditions, and rekindled the community's spirit.

The wiry young farmer knew he had to act quickly. He turned to Rick Anderson, a respected contractor, lover of turn-of-the-century architecture, and recycler of old barns. Rick's expertise and relaxed, patient manner were a perfect complement to the intense energy of "Hurricane Andrew," as Woody was known locally. Rick soon located a three-story, ninety-year-old dairy barn for sale in New Hampshire and immediately knew it would be a perfect replacement for the old hall. When Woody saw it, he agreed. The barn had that loving feeling.

The society leadership wasn't convinced. They balked at the expense of moving the wooden barn. But Woody and Rick were determined. They knew the island spirit could be resurrected for such a noble cause, and they predicted that the cause would in turn revive their spirit. So they lobbied sympathetic trustees and reached out to builder friends for pledges of labor, materials, and equipment.

The local newspapers joined the struggle and printed eloquent letters of support in their pages. "This may be the last old-style barn erected on the Vineyard. I want my grandchildren to see it," declared one. "It should be a place for people to feel the goodness of the earth and faith in our ability to wrest life, sustenance, and shelter from the land," said another. A petition generated seven hundred signatures in the first week alone. Donations piled up, volunteers came out of the woodwork, and the voice of the community steadily rose. A key member of the building committee who visited the snow-covered hilltop in New Hampshire to inspect the barn returned a believer, adding an exclamation point.

Woody and Rick quickly organized thirty-five volunteers of all ages, the Vineyard Barn Busters as they came to be called, who traveled to New Hampshire to take down the barn. For five frigid November days, under Rick's direction, they disassembled the massive barn, tagging every piece before they packed them onto several huge trucks loaned by island businesses. Finally the weary workers returned to the island. John Keene will never forget the trip back in the dead of night, hauling that great load of history that was also their future: "We had the road to ourselves and shared a sense of history," he says. "We were bringing this barn home, where we'll be looking at it for the rest of our lives."

As if paying their respects for all the hard work, the weather gods blessed the day they raised the barn. It was early November and sixty degrees with cloudless skies. Scores of skilled and unskilled workers volunteered with the Barn Busters to do whatever needed to be done. A large crowd gathered around the historic event, and picnic tables groaned under an endless supply of donated food, coffee, and cold drinks. Woody sat for a moment thirty-three feet up on a roof timber, thoughtfully taking in the glorious morning. "It was the most relaxing day of my life," he recalls. "Looking down on the culmination of so much work was a real high."

Under Rick's precise orchestration, willing hands and strong hearts raised the 150-by-45-foot frame within several hours. Fittingly, Woody and Rick rode up on the final massive piece of framework as it was hoisted to its resting place. Throughout the night, visitors and photographers came to pay homage to the magnificent, floodlit skeleton glowing in the middle of a twenty-two-acre field. A farmer descended from one of the island's first families commented, "It was a once-in-a-hundred-year thing, kind of a religious experience."

Building the new hall was more than a community project; it became part of a continuing communal legacy—and a new chapter of the island's colorful history. Lee Waterman, the barn's previous owner, who came to the raising, beamed at the sight of that extraordinary effort. "My husband, Asa, would have loved to be in the thick of it," she said.

The next morning, hundreds of volunteers returned to sheath the roof and sides, set the windows, and tackle the shingling. "I counted 110 people shingling, two of them five-year-old boys with their little hammers," says Woody. "It was the greatest." And the magic continued for several months as artisans and volunteer laborers worked skillfully to finish the building, adding special touches.

The new Ag Hall was christened during the 134th annual fair, exposition, and livestock show, appropriately called "The Dawn of a New Era." It was a time again to appreciate a good harvest, enjoy tasty foods, and celebrate with old friends. To recoup the costs of the barn raising, they held a musical fund-raiser, dubbed Livestock '95. Like the blue-ribbon vegetables and preserves, the acts were home-grown. Two Vineyard summer kids, James Taylor and Carly Simon, reunited for a spectacular "barn-raising thank-you concert for all those who helped support an island institution." It was the first time the two had shared a stage since the "No Nukes" concert in New York City sixteen years before. Ten thousand people shared in the glow of one late-summer evening, next to the new barn.

Today the Ag Hall stands proudly, built nail by nail and board by board with the love of its community. Most days you'll find it full of new memories in the making—a meeting, a party, or a wedding. And you are always invited to the Ag Hall Fair in August. It's the highlight of many people's summer.

Woody and Rick succeeded beyond their expectations: The Society has a magnificent new home, Vineyarders have a new community resource, and the island has a new legend. But most important, the community was reminded that while individuals can make a difference, when they work together, they can make history.

Visit the Vineyard in mid-August and you'll be truly inspired by the community spirit radiating from the Agricultural Society's magnificent barn and its renowned **Annual Livestock Show and Fair.** Contact the Martha's Vineyard Chamber of Commerce by visiting their Web site, www.mvy.com.

FOOD FROM THE 'HOOD

Told by Jeffrey Madison

When the 1992 Los Angeles riots broke out, fifteen-year-old Karla Becerra was on the bus heading home from school. She could smell the smoke and see the fires. As she looked out her window, she saw people running down the street, wheeling strollers packed with things stolen from vandalized stores. But it wasn't until a week later, when she finally got the courage to leave her house, that Karla saw the true extent of the damage.

Everywhere she looked, everything was burned to the ground. The national guard patrolled the streets. To Karla, it no longer looked like the Los Angeles she knew, but like her native El Salvador. The city and its people were lost. "Everyone at our high school was talking about what needed to be done," she remembers. "But we all felt there was nothing we could do. We were afraid even to go outside."

Karla's biology teacher, Tammy Bird, was deeply upset about her Crenshaw High School students and how they had suffered during the riots. She wanted to empower Karla and the others, and to help them regain their sense of community. Before the riots, they had peacefully crossed racial and ethnic boundaries. She wanted to let her students know they could do so again.

She had an idea. Directly behind their classroom was a cluttered, weed-infested lot. Tammy invited her students to clear this quarter-acre plot of land and plant a community garden. The students pulled weeds one by one, making room for the new life to come. They planted herbs and tomatoes. Next came cabbage, lettuce, and carrots. "When we first started, I knew nothing about gardens or plants," says Karla. But she learned quickly enough to be put in charge of the watering, weeding, and harvesting operations.

The once-vacant lot soon blossomed with colorful and delicious vegetables. The student gardeners had transformed a wasteland into a wonderland, and they all thought it was wonderful indeed to see their damaged community coming back to life. Ms. Bird and her adventurous crew next formed a company, claiming a vacant classroom as an office. The students would own and operate the business; they named it Food from the 'Hood. Ms. Bird invited Melinda McMullen, a public relations expert, to teach the students how to launch and promote it.

The students were all very proud when they shared 25 percent of their first harvest with the homeless at Crenshaw's community outreach centers. "We all fell in love with the garden because we were growing happiness there," Karla recalls. "Knowing that people in our community were fed by our food, and that Thanksgiving or Christmas dinners would be extra special for our neighbors, made me grateful to be a part of this."

They sold the rest of the crop at local farmers' markets. The student-owners were happy to provide fresh vegetables to the community and make money in the process! As the business thrived, they took it one step further, investing the profits in their own future, in the form of college scholarships for graduating seniors in their school.

The proceeds would support a few scholarships, but they wanted to create something that might help all of them pay for college. Looking at the wide variety of vegetables they had growing outside, they listed all the ingredients for a salad—the only thing missing was the dressing. So the students made up their own, "Straight Out of the Garden Creamy Italian Salad Dressing," and sold it.

The student-owners had to learn a lot about accounting, as well as making, marketing, and distributing a new product. They had to learn the distinct language of business in order to meet with grocery executives to talk about their salad dressing. "In the beginning, I was very shy—a little girl stuck in the corner with nothing to say," says Karla. "The first time I had to give a presentation, I cried. I didn't want to face those businesspeople." But over time, with the support of her fellow students, Karla found the confidence to speak with ease and let her conviction come through.

In November 1994, Prince Charles of England accepted an invitation to visit the Food from the 'Hood garden. The students voted to select one student to give the prince the tour of the garden. They chose Karla. The girl who was once too shy to speak out in the classroom braved a crowd of more than two hundred reporters armed with cameras and microphones in order to escort the prince.

"Karla was never one of those kids in danger of being involved with crime; what she was in danger of was never realizing her potential," says Tammy. "Food from the 'Hood changed all that. Just as our garden blossomed, so did she, into a confident, supportive, and outgoing person."

"We had a goal of doing something that would help everyone—all races—come together," Karla says. "And we did it. We showed the world that with hard work and a dream, anything is possible."

Today, Food from the 'Hood's salad dressings are sold in more than two thousand grocery and whole-food stores nationwide. The students' business has grown just as their vegetables did. Thanks to the scholarship fund, graduating seniors go straight out of high school into college. It all began with a few seeds in a vacant lot—and a teacher's desire to bring out the best in her students.

You can buy **Food from the 'Hood** salad dressings (Creamy Italian, Honey Mustard, Ranch, and 2,000 Island) and help graduating Crenshaw High seniors go straight into college. Ask your grocery store to join the more than two thousand grocery and whole-food stores nationwide that carry it. To learn more, visit www.foodfromthehood.com.

IT WILL TAKE A MIRACLE
Told by Patricia Broughton

"It's like a war zone." That's not a very nice thing to say about the neighborhood you call home. But for Porter Billingsley of Chicago's West Garfield Park, that is simply the way it is. The area has the highest murder rate in Chicago's seventy-seven districts. He has lived here for twelve years, and can hardly recall a day when somebody hasn't been shot, stabbed, or beaten, and often killed. "On every corner we've got kids selling drugs," he says. "As a black man, I see our race going down the drain. Somebody has to do something."

And so he has, he and hundreds like him. They've joined with the African-American congregation of Bethel Lutheran Church and its community outreach program, Bethel New Life. Their mission, Take Back the Streets, is to reclaim their neighborhood from drug dealers and gang-bangers through intensive street action combined with other community policing strategies against the core cause of the murders: a thriving, open-air drug trade that makes a mockery of law and order.

Recently, one hundred men from Bethel took to the streets. Their enemies carry automatic weapons and a chilling disregard for human life, but these peaceful warriors armed themselves with only flashlights and black T-shirts insisting on a "Cease Fire." Porter marched that Saturday night, as he has marched on countless other nights. He says of the marches, "Maybe they don't do much, but they're something. They show the gangs there are people out there who are not going to take it anymore. As men, we must set the tone for the young ones. We're supposed to be examples."

Reflecting on Saturday's march, Mary Nelson, president of Bethel New Life, talks of the biblical story of the persistent widow: "'Won't God protect His chosen ones who pray to Him day and night? Won't He be concerned for them? He will surely hurry and help them.' We must continue to be faithful," Mary exhorts her staff. "God will make a way, out of no way." She has staked her life on this promise. Together with a strong and committed staff and board, she brings new life to this struggling community on Chicago's West Side.

Mary came here in 1965 to help her brother David move from his comfortable pastorate in Country Club Hills, Illinois, to a new congregation in West Garfield Park. She was planning to return home afterward, but when she saw the amount of work to be done, she had a change of heart. "I couldn't leave my brother here by himself. I had to stay," she says. Three days after they arrived, they were pelted with rocks and stones, caught in the first of five riots that nearly destroyed Chicago's West Side. "In the beginning, we moved quickly. There wasn't a lot of time for committee meetings and long-range planning," Mary recalls. "If the church was going to do anything, it had to be out in the streets. That's where the hurt and agony is. So that is where we've been for over thirty years."

She helped David turn a dying church into a robust spiritual community of more than six hundred active members. Their community outreach program began in 1979, with the purchase of a crumbling three-flat apartment building, borrowing money from personal credit cards to pay for renovations. They started taking risks early on, and now those risks are paying off.

A deep and abiding faith sustains David, Mary, and the members of Bethel, enough for the church to offer its property as collateral, time and again, when banks refuse to make a loan. It is this faith that supports Bethel's community-based board of directors in taking on massive projects like the Beth-Anne Life Center.

In 1988 St. Anne's Hospital closed its doors to the community. Shirley McDonald lived across the street from the hospital. She noted, simply, "When the hospital closed down, the crime rate went up." A headline in *Crain's* business newspaper declared that it would take a miracle to resurrect the facility.

It hadn't counted on the people of Bethel. Together they bought the 9.2-acre site, adapting it for community use. It now boasts a state-of-the-art child-development center and a small business center for local entrepreneurs. It is also home to the area's only bank and drug store, with senior housing and a cultural center to come.

Local residents like Shirley are delighted. She was especially glad to see construction of the day-care center. At the time, she was pregnant with her sixth child, a daughter, who has just started attending the center.

The Beth-Anne Center is only one example of the miraculous work of this congregation. In 1993, when the Chicago Transit Authority seemed determined to close down the West Side elevated transit line, Bethel helped rally community and suburban leaders. The coalition persuaded the CTA not only to not close the line, but to invest $350 million to completely renovate it, and to construct a three-story commercial "superstation" at a key stop in West Garfield Park.

The Bethel success stories go on and on. They helped unemployed residents found a recycling buy-back center, on garbage-strewn vacant lots, which put more than $1 million into the hands of local residents. A Senior Services program employs more than two hundred formerly out-of-work residents, and keeps some 750 seniors out of nursing homes by providing in-home care. Twenty-five women got off welfare when Bethel helped them start day-care programs in their homes. "There truly has been a miracle worked in my life," said Nora Bryant, who lived in a roach- and rat-infested basement apartment not so long ago. She put some 750 hours of hard labor into building her home, enough "sweat equity" to earn the down payment.

Bethel New Life serves as a model for, and gives hope to, the entire nation. Through their efforts, twenty thousand people are participating in the political, economic, and spiritual reconstruction of their community. Reflecting on the many miracles brought to West Garfield Park through this church, Pastor Nelson says, "Even though we didn't know what was ahead, God did. He brought together committed people who have labored hard to produce far more than we ever imagined. We thank God for His spirit moving in these people."

If you are able to see problems as possibilities, can hang in for the long haul, and want to partner with a community rebuilding itself from the inside out, call **Bethel New Life, Inc.,** at 773-473-7870, or visit their Web site, www.bethelnew life.org.

REBUILDING L.A. IN A DAY
Told by Tom Dellner

"Today," **said** **organizer** Marianne Tyler with confidence, "we will change our city forever." It was the first L.A. Works Day, and several busloads of nervous yet excited volunteers were heading for projects all over Los Angeles. Known worldwide for its bright sun, beautiful scenery, and Hollywood stars, L.A. has also gained a reputation for violence, poverty, and racial tension. And the L.A. riots of 1991 were another black eye on the face of this high-profile city, a broken back, a last straw that called many to the rescue. The actor Richard Dreyfuss was one of them. "This is our city and we should help make it better," he thought. He knew the answers to many of the city's problems were in the hands and hearts of its people. "I sensed an enormous untapped resource in our community," he said. "People wanted to help, but didn't know what needed to be done or how to get involved." One day he joined a group of up-and-coming professionals, mostly from the entertainment community, who wanted to pool their resources for the community. Richard wrote a check to get it started—and L.A. Works was born.

On the first L.A. Works Day, in 1993, a thousand volunteers traveled to work sites in South Central from the San Fernando Valley. They brought shovels, paint and paintbrushes, trees and flowers. They painted murals, restored playgrounds, removed graffiti, beautified schools, and planted trees. And each year since then, people from all over Los Angeles collaborate, one day a year, to renew this tradition and repair their city. A lot of work gets done in one day, but perhaps even more important is the boost in the city's morale.

Volunteers working with members of local neighborhoods share stories about their lives and their families, and talk about the city's problems. "When you're working together side by side, splattered in paint, barriers that might otherwise exist tend to go away," says Dreyfuss. "It's very simple," he explains. "A school needs a sandbox. So people help build one—the teachers and students from the school as well as people from the neighborhood."

"Maybe it sounds a little superficial, cleaning up school grounds when there are so many deeper and more complicated social problems in Los Angeles," says site coordinator Bill Schwaab. "But you've got to start somewhere." And once you do, the magic spreads.

"Caring becomes contagious," he continues. "The attitudes of entire neighborhoods change. People take more pride in their community. Now when they see graffiti being painted, they call the police. This didn't happen before. It can all be traced to one day's work." Even some gang members show respect, by not repainting the graffiti.

Marianne notes, "People in Los Angeles see all the problems and say, 'Someone needs to do something.' But they're afraid to lead the charge." She and thousands like her have discovered that L.A. Works Day makes it easy to volunteer. "You make a minimal time commitment in an absolutely safe environment," she says. "You're with thousands of other people on a Sunday afternoon. You need no special skills, and they provide all the supplies."

During the rest of the year, L.A. Works guides many people toward giving more of their time to other organizations. Volunteers tutor children in reading, care for women and children living with HIV/AIDS, and work with runaway teens from Angel's Flight Shelter. And L.A. Works' three thousand volunteers are as diverse as the projects they undertake.

"Los Angeles is celebrated for its wealth of talented people in different fields, but these groups never interact—the downtown business society and the aerospace engineers, the west side money and east side academics, the artists and

Hollywood people and the black, Hispanic, Asian, white, and Jewish communities," Dreyfuss says. "The irony is that our strength as a city and a country is not in our commonalities, but in our differences. We are not linked together by ancestry, religion, or experience, but by a set of ideals that are uniquely American." And, as Dreyfuss puts it, "L.A. Works manifests those ideals."

When L.A.'s diverse peoples come together, synergy happens. "There is excitement in the air," says Dreyfuss. "To see thousands and thousands of people, who don't have to be there, turn out to paint, plant, and help rebuild the city, it's enormously moving."

As a result of his experience with L.A. Works, Dreyfuss believes that everyone should give a year of service to their country before graduating from high school. "The military, hospitals, agriculture, or community service—it's their choice," he says. "It would help our young people feel connected to their country and to the world.

"People see the problems in our society and say they can't be solved. This isn't really true. At L.A. Works, we solve small problems each day. This means more to people than all the good work that is done. It means that together we can solve the larger problems, too."

Florencia Lopez agrees. As the president of the Resident Advisory Council for the Ramona Garden Development, she saw what happened when L.A. Works Day came to her neighborhood. "It was a very special day," she says. "Everyone was really motivated with a spirit of harmony and cooperation to do something positive for our community. Thank you, L.A. Works, for this opportunity. It was especially good for our young people. Working together, we can accomplish more than we ever could alone."

Join the three thousand volunteers who contribute more than 25,000 hours each year to help the greater Los Angeles metropolitan area. Contact **L.A. Works** at its Web site, www.la-volunteer.org.

MOUNTAIN HEALING

Told by Suki Munsell

Mount Tamalpais, home of Northern California's magnificent giant red-woods, is a magical place. From my backyard you can see the mountain's crest form the reclining profile of the sleeping Indian princess Tamalpais, her face lifted upward to the sky.

Legend tells that this Miwok Indian maiden was cast under the spell of her shaman mother, who feared the girl's betrothal to a warrior of a neighboring tribe. The princess will awaken, the story goes, when peace reigns among all people.

For those of us living nearby, the beautiful mountain offers a reprieve from our overcrowded and overly busy lives. We walk through the fragrant forests, camp in the lush green valleys, and celebrate marriages on the sunny slopes over the vast panorama of the Pacific Ocean. But, in a heartbeat, our mountain was violated and our cherished serenity stolen.

In 1980 a killer stalked the trails. Over the next few months he murdered four women one by one as they were climbing in the quiet hills. The mountain, once a safe haven and a source of refuge for San Francisco city dwellers, became a symbol of fear, a repulsive place. Campers sought other grounds, and hikers chose other paths.

In the months that followed, frustration and rage tormented the people of the surrounding communities. Our beloved Mount Tamalpais was held hostage, and we felt powerless to set her free until one day, when Anna invited us to help heal the mountain.

Anna Halprin is an extraordinary dance teacher with a special passion for helping people heal themselves. A refugee from the traditional world of modern dance, Anna has pioneered ways of healing communities through expressive dance. "Cultures everywhere in the world have channeled their power to help bring rain, hunt, raise crops, and initiate the young," she said. "Dance is a power that can renew, inspire, create, and heal the life of a community."

In the ghettos of Watts, Anna has inspired people to heal racism's wounds. She's helped San Francisco's gay community face the AIDS crisis and mend their torn lives. In hospitals, she encourages patients to challenge their illnesses, as she herself did, to free her own body from cancer. Like many community heroes, Anna felt people's pain and wanted to make things better.

That Easter following the murders, she and her husband, Lawrence, an environmental architect, gathered members of our community together to help us discover our power to heal the mountain. We explored our feelings for the mountain, and recalled why it was special to each of us. We remembered why it was worth reclaiming. Anna and Lawrence encouraged us to face our fears and express our rage especially through dance.

Under Anna's guidance we became a thundering tribe who danced our mountain alive. Through our performance, we evoked the spirit of Princess Tamalpais and enacted the capture of the killer. In the audience, the mothers of the four slain women wept openly.

At sunrise the next morning, we gathered on the mountain to pray. Spiritual leaders from many faiths helped us strengthen our community's soul. Our "tribe" reconnected with the healing spirit of Mother Nature. Dancing and chanting as we made our way down the mountain, we stopped to pray at the trailside murder sites. Several days later the killer was caught, and peace returned to the mountain.

Anna has continued a yearly pilgrimage to "Circle the Mountain," and each year our community of healing has grown. One hundred of us train for a full week, perform on Friday and Saturday night, and return to the mountain on

Easter Sunday morning. By 1985, this celebration of peace had gained world-wide exposure.

Renamed "Circle the Earth," it was performed at the United Nations Plaza in New York City. Later it crossed the Atlantic to Europe and the Pacific to Australia. Today, simultaneously celebrated in as many as thirty-six countries, it is called "The Planetary Dance." But to us it will always be the dance for our mountain.

Each Easter morning as the sun rises, our community gathers in prayerful celebration. Families come, bringing their youngsters, who join the Children's Dance. By sunset, many of us journey down to the beach, where the mountain is kissed by the Pacific Ocean. We dance exuberantly with gratitude. The flames from the bonfire caress the shadow of Mount Tamalpais. In the fire, you can almost see the princess's spirit dancing with us.

The hikers and campers have returned to the mountain. Laughter and song once again echo throughout its valleys. The mountain has been healed, and so have we.

Hope is the thing with feathers
That perches in the soul
And sings the tune without the words
And never stops at all . . .

EMILY DICKINSON

Organize a dance, theater, or other arts group with your local church, synagogue, or community center. Come to Anna's Planetary Dance next Easter Sunday, or invite her to bring transformational healing through dance to your community. Contact the **Tamalpa Institute** at www.tamalpa.org.

FROM AN ACORN TO AN OAK
Told by Frances Moore Lappé

Phil Donahue enthusiastically introduces his next guest: "And now please welcome Elena Hanggi, just an ordinary American!" The audience roars its approval. Elena sits between a Democratic congressman from Massachusetts on one side and a Republican congressman from Texas, and a government banking official on the other.

It is the late 1980s, and Donahue is diving into the savings-and-loan crisis. In her disarmingly soft Southern accent, tinged with a slight lisp, Elena proceeds to straighten out the viewers and her distinguished co-panelists: "Every single one of us will pay at least one thousand dollars in taxes to clean up this mess created by a few high rollers," she tells us. Her indignation is palpable.

Elena is a guest on one of TV's most-watched shows because she is an authority on an industry—banking—the intricacies of which baffle most of us. But that's only one reason she's been invited. Elena is also speaking from a moral ground—from her deeply felt sense of what's fair.

In her late forties, Elena had already become a national leader of one of the largest citizen groups in the country—ACORN, the Association of Community Organizations for Reform Now—which was built from the ground up by low-income people.

Soon after Elena's appearance on *Donahue*, ACORN succeeded in getting the voices of ordinary Americans into the law governing the fallout from the S&Ls' collapse. This crisis threw a lot of foreclosed property onto the market. The question was, who would get it? Thanks to a law conceived largely by ACORN, tens of thousands of low-income Americans had a chance to buy some of that property, including families for whom home ownership had seemed an impossible dream. Perhaps even more important, the law specifies that ordinary citizens like Elena now have an official seat on the board governing the thrift industry, through citizens' representatives who are there to make sure that S&Ls serve the needs of all Americans.

Ever since I met Elena, I had pondered that elusive question "Why her?" — and therefore why any one of us? What makes it possible for any one of us growing up within narrowly proscribed boundaries to transcend them, and to break new moral ground for our society?

Elena's early upbringing gave little indication that she would have a future as a national leader. Growing up in Little Rock, Arkansas, in the 1950s, her home was typically blue-collar: her mom was a hairdresser, her dad an army man. They didn't teach her to take a public stand for her beliefs, although she does say, laughing, that her mom sent a few signals that set her family apart. "We were the only kids on the block allowed to buy music by black artists. So all my friends came to my house to listen to Chuck Berry!"

But there was one particular moment Elena remembers, when what she had been told to believe all her life suddenly collided head-on with what she could see for herself. It was 1957 and Little Rock's Central High, Elena's school, was being forcibly integrated. One day, as she and her classmates rose to pledge allegiance to the flag, she looked out the school's big open windows.

"Standing there, hand on my heart, I could hear the roar of a crowd getting louder and louder," she told us. "I looked to my left down to Park Street in front of the school, and I saw a mob of white people chasing an elderly black man. I thought, 'Oh my God, if they catch him, they'll kill him!'

"Suddenly, everything seemed unreal. It felt like I was in a science-fiction movie or something. How could I be standing here mouthing these beautiful words about liberty and justice while that was happening right outside?" In that moment, Elena questioned everything her friends accepted.

It was a moment she never forgot. But for the most part, in the years that followed she went along quietly. She got married, had two daughters, and lived an everyday kind of life. Then, one day in the summer of 1974, there was a knock on Elena's door. A neighbor asked Elena whether she would help fight a proposed freeway threatening to cut through their neighborhood. Her neighbor was a member of ACORN, which had formed just a few years earlier. "Sure, I'll be there," she told them. "I'll fill up a chair at your meeting, but don't even think of asking me to speak in public."

"Even though I told them I would not speak in public, they didn't listen," Elena remembers. "My task was to lay out reasons ACORN was opposed to the freeway. When my turn came to speak, I was so frightened they almost had to push me to the mike. I was terrified . . . but at the same time I was grateful. Someone saw something in me I didn't see in myself."

Having experienced the power of being pushed, Elena now heads the official "pushing people" arm of ACORN, the Institute for Social Justice. This traveling training institute prepares the housekeepers, clerks, shopkeepers, secretaries, cooks, waitresses, and truck-drivers of ACORN's 100,000 member families. She's seen people so afraid of speaking out in her training that they would break down in tears when asked to introduce themselves to the group. And she's seen those same people emerge five days later as moving public presenters and confident activists.

"Looking out my window now," Elena said, "I can see city workers cutting the curbs to put in ramps for wheelchairs—another example of what we've accomplished."

The benefits to society are clear, but for Elena there are personal rewards, too. "My four daughters are not afraid like I was to speak out," Elena says with obvious satisfaction. One daughter is even hoping to buy a house soon because of the affordable, subsidized interest rate made possible by the law ACORN helped create and pass.

"You know, I never thought that acting on what I believe is right would have led me into learning all about banking," Elena says, surprised herself about the path her life has taken. "It all seemed so far out of reach, but I found out a big secret along the way—that all that stuff they want you to believe is out of reach for average working people is really understandable by any of us."

If you think you are too small to be effective,
you have never been in bed with a mosquito.

BETTE REESE

Want to uncover your potential for working with neighbors to bring change to your neighborhood, city, state, and nation? Call **ACORN** Field Director Helene O'Brien at 877-376-1335, or visit their Web site, www.acorn.org.

MAKING LEMONADE FROM LEMONS
Told by Jenny Midgaard

Joe Tysdale was the kind of volunteer everyone would love to have. Dedicated to the success of each year's Gilroy Garlic Festival, he carried out his volunteer duties enthusiastically. Even when he was battling leukemia, being kept alive with an oxygen tank strapped to his side, he would arrive on Monday with a crew of guys to construct the Festival's "Gourmet Alley" by Friday. Then he'd put in three long, hot, and tiring days on his famous pasta pots, cooking pasta *con pesto* for the thousands of annual visitors. Joe's superhuman commitment and his perseverance were not unusual, however. The Gilroy Garlic Festival inspires extraordinary dedication, since it bolstered a community in need of pride and a sense of identity.

Rudy Melone remembers coming to Gilroy in the late 1970s and being shocked. He had heard the snide remarks and the backhand jokes. He saw the self-deprecating attitude of the residents. When people visited this California town of 32,000, residents would apologize for the odor. If asked about Gilroy, few townsfolk would mention the beautiful garlic fields—which stretched for many miles—or the huge garlic-processing plants. They figured it was better to just ignore the garlic. Lots of people hated the smell and the taste, anyway.

"There was a general embarrassment about the garlic," says Melone, who had been hired as president of the local community college. "But as I saw it, it was something to be proud of." An Italian American who had been raised eating lots of garlic, he set out to remedy the problem of the town's low self-esteem, with his own version of making lemonade from lemons.

Melone had heard of a small town in France, Arleux, which hosted eighty thousand people at its annual garlic festival. In fact, Arleux was claiming to be "the garlic capital of the world." Melone knew Gilroy's garlic production and processing far surpassed that of any other area. He needed a way to convince Gilroyans that they should have a garlic festival of their own.

Volunteerism had always been strong and vital to the town's character. Community groups were big in Gilroy—so were bake sales, car washes, door-to-door magazine peddling, and lots of little sales to raise money for good causes. Appointed as the local Rotary's fund-raising chairman, Melone was charged with raising money for their projects and for the Chamber of Commerce. If he could present a garlic festival as a fund-raising effort, he might just get the town's support, he thought.

His first step was to sell the idea to his Rotary Club. He copied reams of documents about the healthful effects of garlic, located an abundance of garlic recipes, found articles on the love of garlic in Arleux, and pasted them around the room at the next meeting. Interesting stuff, said the members, but so what? Undeterred, Melone drove down to the local café and had coffee with the garlic growers who gathered there every morning.

"Couldn't we get all the growers together, put on a nice lunch, and really show the Rotary people the value of garlic?" he asked them. Don Christopher, now one of the world's largest garlic shippers, agreed to co-host, with Melone, a lunch prepared by chef Val Filice.

They invited both local and national media to the garlic meal, which was judged "incredible." The Gilroy community leaders stood around chatting with the visiting journalists. Betsy Bosley of the *Los Angeles Times* took Christopher aside and urged him to run with the idea of a garlic festival. "This is going so well, we should do it every year," Melone said casually to Harvey Steinem of the *San Francisco Chronicle*. The next week, Steinem wrote about the luncheon and the festival idea in his column, and the bulb was rolling.

Of course there were skeptics. In fact, several of the town's big shots laughed out loud when Melone suggested the First Annual Gilroy Garlic Festival. But he kept asking. And when planning started, they were all there to help. Seven months later, the first Garlic Festival arrived, funded on borrowed money and planned by a small committee, with big hopes and more than a few doubts.

Melone remembers the quiet on the first morning of the festival—the stillness, light traffic, and slight fog. "We wondered if anyone would come to our party," he says. But after a while the sun popped through, bringing with it hordes of garlic lovers. The crowd was overwhelming. The fifteen thousand tickets printed for the event ran out, so volunteers went out to collect them, and brought them back to the ticket booth to recycle them.

Meanwhile, local women were frantically cooking pasta in a house on Bloomfield Road. In his booming voice, Filice, head chef of Gourmet Alley, ordered several men to drive to Monterey for more prawns and squid. Halfway through the first day, the beer-committee chairman called Budweiser: "Heck, forget the kegs. Start sending us the trucks!"

That first festival netted nineteen thousand dollars. In the eighteen years since then, the festival has brought over $4 million to the community. More than four thousand volunteers from all parts of Gilroy have worked hundreds of jobs, earning an hourly wage to donate to their favorite charity. Collectively, they make big contributions to the community they now care so much about.

In 1995 the local Elks Lodge raised more than ten thousand dollars to buy eyeglasses for poor children, aid a family who had lost their home in a fire, and build a flag-lined walk to honor veterans. Hope Rehabilitation, which teaches disabled people to work, earned more than three thousand dollars. Melone's idea of getting the town to celebrate garlic rather than being ashamed of it has clearly been more than successful. But there were other benefits as well.

"What I'm most proud of is how the festival has brought the people of Gilroy together," says Melone, now seventy-one. Gilroy's multicultural community— Hispanic, Caucasian, and Asian as well as the original Italian families—all pitch in. Festival volunteers often find themselves working elbow-to-elbow with someone they might never have met. School parents work with Gilroy Hispanic Chamber of Commerce members. Boy Scouts sell programs alongside 4-H members. High-school football players dish up pasta next to choir members.

Melone asks, "How often can you raise dollars for your favorite cause, but also have fun yourself?" Enjoyable as it is, the festival is only half of the event for the volunteers. Each year they're rewarded for their hard work at the volunteers' barbecue, hosted by the festival on Labor Day weekend. At the barbecue, volunteers share stories and greet the people they now know so well after working together.

Sadly, Joe Tysdale didn't make it to the 1996 volunteers' barbecue. He'd been too ill to come to the festival as well. But he did send his son and his daughter-in-law, and even several relatives from out of state, to work his shifts.

As the exhausted crew began to close down Gourmet Alley on Sunday night, they received word that Joe was dying. Steve Morrow, his friend and fellow Elks member, says, "We were closing down shop at roughly the same time Joe was dying. Exhausted as we were, we felt as though he was there, watching over the last detail, holding on just long enough to be sure we had done a good job."

Joe died that night. But his spirit lives on in the hearts of all the dedicated volunteers who make Gilroy a pretty special place to visit, and a very proud community in which to live.

Volunteering is good for the soul.

STEVE ALLEN

Work with your local **Rotary Club** to turn your community's problems into win-win situations. Call 847-866-3245 for the Rotary Club closest to you. Come to the annual Gilroy Garlic Festival, held the last full weekend in July. For information, visit www.gilroygarlicfestival.com.

STREETS OF HOPE
Told by Holly Sklar

Che' Madyun remembers the stench of smoke and garbage. She remembers the piercing wail of sirens, day and night. She remembers lying awake, heart pounding, afraid her home would be the next to burn.

In 1976, Boston's Dudley neighborhood looked like an earthquake had hit it. There were blocks and blocks of vacant land where homes and stores used to be. As the neighborhood became more racially diverse, government, banks, businesses, and landlords abandoned it. Some landlords burned down apartment buildings to collect insurance money.

By the time the smoke cleared, one-third of Dudley was wasteland. People and businesses from outside the neighborhood used the vacant land as an illegal dumping ground for all kinds of garbage—from old refrigerators to toxic chemicals. Kids vomited from the stench.

Che' and her neighbors were not about to let their children's futures be thrown away. That's how the "Don't Dump on Us" campaign was born. Organized by a group called the Dudley Street Neighborhood Initiative (DSNI), hundreds of neighborhood residents held meetings and marches and actually persuaded a new mayor to help clean up the dumps and enforce the laws against illegal dumping. After that, Dudley people felt a new kind of fire. They believed if they could clean up the dumps, they could do anything.

Working together in DSNI, Che' and her neighbors became powerful visionaries. They turned the usual top-down urban planning process upside down. They made it "bottom up," so the people who actually lived there would have the greatest say in what happened to their own neighborhood. With support from the local Riley Foundation, hundreds of residents participated in planning an "urban village." They dreamed of a livable place with affordable housing, community centers, gardens, playgrounds, small businesses, and a town common. Together they moved the city of Boston to endorse the plan in 1987, and become a partner in rebuilding the neighborhood.

Dudley residents then made history when they became the nation's first community group to win eminent domain authority. That gave the community the right to buy and develop thirty acres of vacant land in the most burnt-out part of the neighborhood. A decade later, the area that once looked devastated is alive with families living in new homes.

Yet Dudley would need a lot more than new housing to really transform the neighborhood. "You can build all the doggone houses you want," says Che', who served as DSNI's president from 1986 until 1995. "But if you're not trying to touch people's lives, you're just putting up bricks and mortar." So DSNI restored a local park and started a summer camp. It continues to sponsor annual festivals and neighborhood clean-ups. The group organizes tenants, works with employment programs, and much more. It encourages local nonprofit service agencies to be responsive to residents' needs and priorities. In 1992, when Los Angeles exploded with the fury of urban America's crushed dreams, Dudley was surging with the power of dreams unfolding. As Che' says, "Hope is the great ally of organizing."

An African proverb teaches "Together, we find the way." DSNI's Declaration of Community Rights reads:

We—the youth, adults, seniors of African, Latin American, Caribbean, Native American, Asian and European ancestry—are the Dudley community. [Once] we were Boston's dumping ground and forgotten neighborhood. Today, we are on the rise! We are reclaiming our dignity, rebuilding housing and reknitting the fabric of our communities. Tomorrow, we realize our vision of a vibrant, culturally diverse neighborhood, where everyone is valued for their talents and contributions to the larger community.

A beautiful town common provides a welcoming gateway to Dudley. People come from other states, and even other countries, to exchange ideas about community building with Dudley residents. In 1996, DSNI launched a new series of community "visioning meetings" where residents dream aloud, and plan how to make those dreams come true over the next ten to twenty years. "Our village is a culturally vibrant, active, people-centered, mutually supportive community with a sense of can-do optimism," they wrote. Their vision of the future includes lifelong learning at schools and community centers, thriving businesses and organic farming, and a safe and healthy environment.

Of course, Che' Madyun is not the only hero in this story of community. "People worked like a family," she says. DSNI, in fact, is an extended family, with over 2,500 neighborhood members and thousands of outside supporters. Hundreds of residents have actively served on DSNI's board and committees over the years. Young people are encouraged to serve on the DSNI board and its varied committees, as well as their own Youth Committee. To illustrate their theme of "unity through diversity" DSNI created a beautiful mural, featuring neighborhood children, teenagers, and elders. Che' is pictured dancing in it.

Now Dudley's youth help run summer programs. They grow food on neighborhood land and lead a mentoring program for younger children, and during Dudley's Young Architects and Planners Project they made plans for a community center. The success of the project, as Che' says, is "based on the dreams and creativity of youngsters too often written off by others as worthless." Youth leader Caroline Dorcena remembers the words of former DSNI Director Gus Newport: "The seed you plant on the first day of spring—it's going to grow and keep on growing."

The attitude of its youth is a measure of this once devastated community's extraordinary progress. Caroline Dorcena, a child of Haitian immigrants who knows prejudice firsthand, is always trying to build bridges where other people put walls. Now in college, Caroline hasn't decided yet what career she will choose. But whatever it is, she plans to use her education to improve life in Dudley. "Whatever I am—be it a lawyer, an educator, a philosopher, a corporate psychologist, or an international businesswoman—I want to come back to our community," she says. She's definitely proud of her neighborhood. "People can look at you and say, 'I respect you because you're from Dudley and I know you're trying to do something.' "

> *The vision of a new Boston must extend into the heart of Roxbury and into the mind of every child.*
>
> DR. MARTIN LUTHER KING JR., 1968

Reclaim a vacant lot in an inner-city neighborhood. To learn from the **Dudley Street Neighborhood Initiative** and its dynamic community work-in-progress, visit its Web site at www.dsni.org; or call 800-533-8478 to order the book *Streets of Hope*, or 888-367-9154 to order the film *Holding Ground*.

LET'S TALK

Every May, the city of Cincinnati comes alive with the Appalachian Festival. People dance in bright colors to bluegrass music, eat great food, and celebrate the best that Appalachian traditions have to offer. The celebration has become a tradition in its own right, since they've been doing it for thirty-two years.

Appalachians are proud of their heritage and their people: actors George Clooney and Charles Bronson, President Grant, Jesse Jackson, Tommy Dorsey and his Big Band, *Roots* author Alex Haley. There are 26 million people of Appalachian descent living in thirteen Appalachian states—and another 15 million across the country.

Like Cincinnati's other immigrants—German, Irish, and Italian—Appalachians had high hopes and dreams when they arrived here. Hundreds of thousands of families moved to Northern cities like Cincinnati after World War II in search of jobs and a better life. Cincinnati has the most: 250,000 citizens. They settled in Over-the-Rhine, where they formed a community whose people watch out for one another.

Some people think of Appalachians as "hillbillies" or "poor white trash," continuing a tradition of bigotry, as old as the culture it's set against. Ironically, Americans too ignorant to know better read an Appalachian accent as a sign of ignorance. Larry Redden has learned a lot about stereotypes and how hurtful they can be.

Having grown up in a poor family, Larry left home when he was just eleven years old, since his mother didn't have enough to feed him and his eleven siblings. He worked at odd jobs, and lived on the streets: the corner of 13th and Vine was his turf. After serving in Vietnam, Larry enrolled in a truckdrivers' training school in Cleveland, Ohio. The only white person in the class of one hundred students, his classmates nicknamed him "the Godfather."

One student, James, picked on Larry and called him names. Larry tried to ignore him. But one day, when James jumped in front of him and wouldn't let Larry get in his truck, he lost it. They had a knock-down, drag-out fight. The instructor told them to talk things over and work it out, or they'd both be kicked out of school.

Reluctantly, they did talk. James felt that Larry had usurped the place of a black person more deserving than he. "Everyone knew that white people weren't poor and didn't need any help," Larry remembers James saying. "If white people were poor, it was their own fault and they should get themselves out of trouble. It was white people that kept black people down."

When Larry shared his story, James saw how much they had in common. The only difference really was the color of their skin. After that, the two became friends.

Larry admits that he had grown up resenting blacks, too. While his people had faced the same challenges as minorities, they'd received little or no support. They'd had to fend for themselves. Some had tried going back home, but with no work there, they'd soon returned to the city. In the 1970s, racial tensions deepened when the federal War on Poverty program forced many Appalachians from their homes, to make way for new public-housing projects for the African-American community.

"It took nothing short of a miracle to help me change my mind about blacks," Larry says. "But my mentor, Ernie Mynatt, helped me understand who I was, and then who others might be, too."

Ernie had moved from Harlan County, Kentucky, to Cincinnati in 1959, and started helping Appalachians learn to cope with the big city. He talked with pride about living in the Appalachian Mountains, about the people and their heritage, religion, and education, as well as their hardships and dreams. "The way he talked about our roots, you wanted to be a part of it," says Larry. "I no longer felt like I had to compete, or make excuses for myself and others."

Ernie took Larry under his wing and helped him find a home in a residential program for teenage boys. He also taught him about the importance of talking things out. No matter where Ernie was or whom he was with, this big, powerful man always welcomed young people, saying, "Come in. Sit down. Let's talk."

By the 1970s, Ernie's Urban Appalachian Council provided a broad range of social service and cultural programs to the city's Appalachian citizens. He's known as "papa to his people" by hundreds of "Ernie's kids," who are now middle-aged, middle-class Cincinnati residents, some of whom become social workers in turn, to serve the next generation in the inner city.

As director of the council's AmeriCorps program, Larry supervises twenty-seven members from all over the city who work with GED programs and the After-School Homework Clubs. By sharing their life experiences, they build bridges of understanding. The "Rap Groups" are a big hit—their open, candid style helps people overcome their negative stereotypes. "We need to sit down and talk with each other," Larry tells the young people he now mentors. "Don't blame the whole for what a few do. "

Appalachians have the highest illiteracy and high-school-dropout rates in Cincinnati. The Urban Appalachian Council has been working hard to change this. Their extensive education services include community-based schools and GED programs as well as advocacy and emergency services, and cultural programs like the Appalachian Festival. Allison Raser, the festival's only paid staff person, is a UAC success story. After dropping out of school at sixteen, she was mentored by Larry, got her GED through the council, and became first a receptionist, then Larry's secretary.

In 2001, the riots in Cincinnati were national news. For days they threatened to tear the city apart. Larry explains how the riots started with the death of an unarmed black youth. "When he ran from police, then turned and pulled up his baggy pants, the police thought he was going for a gun." In the wake of this tragedy, the mayor and the community vowed to work together to make things better.

Larry knows how important it is to deal with people's prejudices and fears. "Blacks are afraid they will get beat up by the police. The police are afraid of getting shot for doing their job," he says. "And Appalachians are afraid that they won't get a fair shake.

"One of the great things that came out of this racial strife is the Study Circle Project, sponsored by the Cincinnati Human Relations Commission," says Larry. "Much like the council, they are training people in small groups of twelve to fourteen how to talk with each other. People from all walks of life, talking along with one policeperson, learn about each other, about their hopes and dreams as well as their fears and ideas for what can be done to make things better for everyone."

These community dialogues give Larry hope. People all over the city are talking, developing a better understanding of one another, and building trust. "Now, when incidents arise, we will be better able to handle them, instead of exploding," Larry says. Passing on Ernie's greatest lesson, he adds, "The only thing that will ever make a difference is helping others to develop positive identities for themselves and then for others," says Larry.

The Urban Appalachian Council carries on Ernie's legacy by helping Appalachian youth build a better future. They are also building bridges. By hiring blacks and whites to work together to improve their communities, the UAC is helping them get past prejudices and get to know each other as people. It's the most integrated nonprofit organization in Cincinnati. "Mixing people together creates a natural curiosity. There is a learning that happens when people share parts of their lives with each other," Larry says. "I wish there were more of us out there."

I shall pass through this world but once. Any good that I can do or any kindness that I can show to any human being, let me do it now. Let me not defer or neglect it, for I shall not pass this way again.

GANDHI

Talk with people who are different from yourself. Build bridges between different cultures in your community. Study the Appalachian traditions in our country, and encourage greater support for Appalachian communities to strengthen families, develop community resources, and reform the systems that influence their lives. Contact the Urban Appalachian Council at larryr@one.net or visit www.uacvoice.org.

GIVING KIDS A FIGHTING CHANCE

Told by Robert Marra

Judith Kurland wasn't easily shaken, but this time she was furious. It was her first walk through the Boston City Hospital nurseries, and she was outraged by the conditions she found there. So many tiny, underdeveloped babies, much too small to live, and rows and rows of sick and injured children without the care and attention they needed. All of these little people deserved much more than what the hospital was providing.

When Judith met those children, she kept flashing back to the lavish conditions at some of the health-care facilities that served Boston's wealthier neighborhoods. Did somebody think these kids were disposable, just because they were born in the wrong place at the wrong time? The more she thought about it, the more enraged she became.

It was 1988, and the mayor of Boston had just appointed Judith health commissioner of Boston City Hospital and director of the city's public health department, the first woman to be given this job. To Judith, it seemed all the male leaders of the other thirteen Boston teaching hospitals were engaged in a "medical arms race" to see who could build the biggest and best buildings. Boston had already spent far more money on hospitals than any other city in the country.

Yet within sight of these well-equipped hospitals were "death zones" where, in the middle of Boston's harsh winters, poor families had to choose each day between food and heat. Babies here were getting sick and dying at higher rates than in many third-world countries. Judith would change that if she could help it, and in her new position it seemed that maybe she could. "Given the wealth of this city," she said, "there are enough resources to make sure that every child in Boston is given a fighting chance to live a happy, healthy, and productive life."

Every day for the next five years, Judith used her savvy, chutzpah, and clout in every way she could—regardless of the personal costs. She shared her vision with legislators, philanthropists, policy-makers, and foundations. She made history by actually getting them to donate money, and lots of it. Then she used that money to expand public-health programs that empowered mothers, their children, and others in need. And she built a new $180-million hospital for Boston's most desperate citizens—"a yardstick of excellence" against which to measure other hospitals' services to the poor.

Still, Judith never believed that just "throwing money at a problem" was enough to make a lasting difference. In her earlier life as a working mother whose child was in a community day-care center, she'd seen mothers on welfare lose their already fragile self-esteem when a confused bureaucracy prevented them, willing and able people, from helping at the center.

"While visiting community health centers and public hospitals in South Africa, I had exactly the opposite experience," says Judith. "There was little help from the government, and even the poorest of the poor were expected to help provide health education and health care for themselves and their families. They did so with remarkable creativity and enthusiasm—healing themselves in body and spirit as they helped others."

Judith determined that the considerable untapped human resources of Boston's inner city would no longer go to waste. She'd tap these resources for solutions to the complex problems of infant mortality and urban poverty, with a unique mix of public and private support. She gathered 250 health and community development leaders from Boston and around the world. Their conclusion was straightforward: If you want to improve the health of a child, then you must raise the educational level of its mother.

Judith took the recommendation very seriously, and with it she mapped the highest goals as well as the bottom line of the new Healthy Boston initiative, which would involve people from all parts of the community to create good health out of good jobs, schools, housing, and medical care. Through Healthy Boston, people from Boston's richest and poorest neighborhoods collaborated, some for the first time in their lives. Both groups were amazed to discover such goodness in people they'd been trained to distrust for as long as they could remember.

She was also determined to make Boston's wealthy hospitals responsible. After three years of politely urging hospital leaders to share more of their wealth with the community, she decided they needed a push. She commissioned a report that the *Boston Globe* ran as a three-day front-page series. It contrasted the high infant mortality rate with the wealth of Boston's hospitals. Finally, even the most recalcitrant hospital administrators loosened their grip on their wallets.

Challenging those powerful men made Judith a lot of powerful enemies. Many of the Boston bluebloods had no idea how to deal with a small Jewish ball of fire transplanted from New Jersey. And being the outsider was not always easy for Judith. Fortunately, Judith had the strong support of her husband, Benny, the father of their three children. He would help her through the hard times by lovingly reminding her of why she had taken on this momentous work—in Gandhi's words—"of making injustice visible."

Tragically, without any warning, Benny had a fatal heart attack at age forty-six. Judith's greatest friend, supporter, and partner was gone. She wrestled with how to go on—raising her children and finishing out her term. As a result of her persistence, health support for Boston's children improved dramatically. During her tenure, black infant mortality and teenage pregnancy rates decreased significantly.

When people look at Judith's accomplishments, they sometimes think she has conquered the unthinkable. As she sees it, she took those bold and brave steps only because it was unthinkable not to. Those of us who have worked with Judith say she reminds us of the Wizard of Oz. With tornado-like force and Glinda-like magic, she turned Boston upside-down and shook it mightily until rich and poor alike rediscovered the good within themselves.

Get your hospital and community organizations to work together to build a healthier community. To learn about the growing community movement across the nation, visit **The Coalition for Healthier Cities and Communities** at their Web site, www.hospitalconnect.com/healthycommunities/usa/index.htm.

POLISHING THE BIG APPLE

Told by Nancy Berg

Annette Williams had been on welfare for ten years when Joseph Pupello offered her a job at the New York Restoration Project (NYRP). After volunteering as a reading tutor and as a garden helper in the New York City public schools for the preceding five years, she'd become known as a dependable, hard worker who was exceptionally good with people. For seven summers she worked with Joseph at Success Gardens, a nonprofit organization that turned vacant lots into little community Edens.

Annette remembers her first NYRP meeting with Joseph; it was in an abandoned park that she says "looked more like a jungle." Seeing the overgrown area and the temporary homeless shelter behind the playground, she wondered if this sad patch of land could ever be turned into a park again. But just one month later, she had a fairy tale to tell. "People started coming back," Annette said. "The kids came first, asking questions about what we were doing. 'We are giving you back your park' was all we said." Before long, the whole neighborhood began to show signs of transformation. "When children see people giving back, they see something wonderful," Annette says. "It gives them an idea about how they too can help."

As a mother raising six children in an economically troubled area, Annette knows the importance of having safe places for children to play. "Kids nowadays don't have places to play," she says. "Our cities are full of concrete and our parks with drug addicts, homeless people, and unleashed dogs. The kids say, 'We have nothing to do.' No wonder they get in trouble." Thanks to Annette and her team, they now have a safe place to go.

After a year at the New York Restoration Project, Annette was promoted to field director, managing a team of four employees and twenty AmeriCorps volunteers, supervising thirty-four members of the Work Experience Program (WEP). Together they are responsible for restoring six of New York City's parks to their natural beauty. "The AmeriCorps volunteers are like my kids," she says. "I become their mother, sister, brother, and friend. I'm there for them. We're like a family."

By working with Annette, the WEP members learn job skills and build self-esteem. By getting up each morning and doing something positive for themselves and others, they gain confidence that they can get a real job. "I know what it's like to be on welfare," Annette says. "It's easy to get stuck in the cycle." She encourages people to start moving away from welfare by volunteering "so people can see you as more than a mother on welfare." After two years, she has seen five of her Welfare To Work people get good jobs. "One just got married and drives a Lexus!" she says happily.

Most people would be surprised to learn that Annette Williams has a good friend and partner named Bette Midler who founded the New York Restoration Project. They have more in common than first meets the eye: both women had to work their own way out of poverty, but while Annette spent her childhood in the concrete maze of New York, Bette grew up surrounded by the lush beauty of Hawaii.

Growing up in Halawa, one of the poorest neighborhoods on Hawaii, Bette Midler and her family were the only non-Hawaiian family for miles around. Treated as an outcast as a young child, she found solace in the awesome natural beauty around her. In the crystal-clear aquamarine sea, the little girl swam alongside bright magenta *kuma* and dazzling indigo parrotfish. Words like "smog" and "pollution" held no meaning for her in those early tropical days. She thought the whole world was as beautiful as Hawaii. When she grew up, she made her first journey to the mainland. It was as if she had just stepped off a time machine from some pre-industrial age. She was shocked by the way people carelessly treated her beloved earth, though she could barely recognize it.

For years, she lived in Southern California, developing her career. Later, she and her husband, Martin, moved to New York to raise their daughter Sophie. In a sense, the entertainer found a spiritual home there. "I love New Yorkers, and I'm like them," she says. "I'm noisy. I have my opinions." Bette exudes an energy and drive that have led most Americans to assume she was a New Yorker all along.

But the extent of careless waste and filth in New York took her by surprise. People were throwing their garbage out the windows. The city's once-majestic parks were marred by refuse, old furniture, and abandoned toilet bowls. "We love the city. This degradation is heartbreaking and unacceptable," says Midler. "I realized I had to do something. Even if it meant I had to go out and pick up all that stuff with my own two hands."

The city once had eighty thousand park workers to care for its natural land—more than thirty thousand acres of playground, woodlands, recreation centers, trails, gardens, and miles of protected waterfront. Cuts in public funding eliminated a staggering 77,600 of those jobs. With only 2,400 workers, there's too much litter, illegal dumping, and vandalism for the Parks Department to keep up with. It quickly became obvious to anyone who walked in New York City's parks that a volunteer effort was needed.

Bette decided to call her friend Scott Mathes at the California Environmental Project, an organization that had removed more than 3.5 million pounds of debris since 1989. Bette enlisted Mathes's help to set up a similar project in New York. The New York Restoration Project was born, funded by a special benefit premiere for her film *The First Wives Club* and $250,000 from Bette's own pocket.

Joseph Pupello remembers his first day as NYRP's director, at the Little Red Lighthouse under the George Washington Bridge. He joined Midler and Mayor Rudolph Giuliani, volunteers, and sixty schoolchildren from Upper Manhattan to clear away dump sites, plant trees, and remove rusted cars in a massive effort to reclaim Fort Tryon and Fort Washington parks and restore beauty to seven miles of the Hudson River waterfront. Since then, with the help of AmeriCorps volunteers, the U.S. Army Corps of Engineers, and Welfare To Work partici- pants, they've carted away more than fifty thousand pounds of refuse from the city's parks. "The Divine Miss M. brings style to the project, and she really gets her hands dirty," Joseph says. "She shows New Yorkers that they can be involved."

When people ask Annette Williams about her job, she says proudly, "I pick up garbage." She finds working with Bette a real joy. "Bette is part of our extended family," she says. "She's very down to earth—and just does her job. In her over- alls and sneakers, she picks up trash, showing others there's a cleaner way to live." People walk by and say hi to her, without recognizing who she is. She just goes on about her business. That *is* who she is.

Yet Bette's willing to use her celebrity status if it gets results, particularly with kids. "As long as I can remember, there have been anti-littering campaigns, but nobody pays attention to them," Midler says to a group of children, who burst out laughing as she slips into her famous flamboyant persona. "They drop their lunch on the ground and that's the end of it. And I have to come along and sweep it up and I mean, kids, I'm pooped, I'm exhausted! There's more trash out there than even I can handle, and if we keep this up there won't be any place left to walk; we'll be picking our way over mounds of cans and bottles, acres of egg cartons and oceans of shrink-wrap. So please, please let's stop treating the earth like it was an ashtray. Tell your friends, tell your moms, tell your kids, we just have to stop! I really feel that if everybody did their part it would be a beautiful world."

Organize a clean-up day in your community. If you want to help beautify New York City's parks and rivers, contact the **New York Restoration Project** at 212- 258-2333 or visit their Web site, www.nyrp.org.

IV

GROWING
NATIONALLY

Johnny Appleseed was one of the first American heroes. Born John Chapman in Boston, in 1774, on the eve of the American Revolution, he found his joy in caring for the land. As a young man he was inspired by a vision of a shimmering, heavenly community surrounded by beautiful apple trees. Pleasant as it was, he wasn't satisfied with mere contemplation. His vision became his mission, and he took it on the road. All the way across America, he planted apple seeds wherever he went, so that families moving west would feel more at home. Like the traveler in the Stone Soup folktale, Johnny Appleseed sparked a spirit of community with a simple act. For forty years he visited his apple orchards tirelessly, pruning and caring for them and teaching hundreds of settlers how to grow their own. When de Tocqueville toured the country in 1831, he probably enjoyed the blossoming, fragrant flowers and delicious fruit of the fully grown trees as much as he appreciated the people's community spirit.

Like Johnny Appleseed, the heroes featured in this chapter have been planting seeds of hope and teaching others how to care for their communities, for many years. Today there are more than 600,000 nonprofit organizations, with 14 million employees and over 100 million volunteers, that serve America's people. No other country in the world has such a richly developed public sector. Every day we benefit from the fruits of their labor. Their service is invaluable, the life-force of our democracy.

The stories in this chapter honor just a few of the many Americans who have dedicated their lives to service. They work to help others less fortunate who are struggling to realize the American dream. Their stories show that the path of service is never predictable. While some community heroes started with a dramatic turn in the road, for many others it was a gradually evolving commitment—one step leading to another, and then another. Marian Wright Edelman's son Jonah tells us about the inspiration behind his mother's lifelong commitment to making the world a better place for all children. Harris Wofford shares the experience of working with John F. Kennedy in the founding of the Peace Corps.

Some stories show how national heroes, like Bill Shore at Share Our Strength and Patty Johnson at Christmas in April, are building public-private partnerships with companies to more effectively realize their organizations' goals. Other national heroes, like Dorothy Stoneman, have built a coalition among hundreds of youth organizations and partnerships with government agencies to use federal funds more effectively to meet community needs.

Some of these stories show how young people have carried out the legacy of their heroes. For Alan Khazei and Michael Brown, it was President Kennedy who inspired them to found City Year. Gandhi's ability to mobilize millions of people with the simple act of fasting led Nathan Gray to found Oxfam America's Fast for a World Harvest.

Sometimes as the work grows, from one small office to a sprawling national organization, we get tired. Years of writing grants, working with bureaucracies, and dealing with politics can distance us from the ultimate goal. The stories of birth and inspiration in this chapter can plug us back into the power and the promise of service; their heroes' hands-on experience and wealth of knowledge are among our country's greatest resources. Not everyone dedicates his or her life to service, yet we can all learn from those who have done so and discover how we, too, can help with this important work.

Every one of these people and their organizations could use your help, your special gifts, skills, and resources. Give them a call and learn how you could change your life and the world, one day at a time.

STAND FOR CHILDREN

Told by Jonah Edelman

In 1967, Mississippi was a dangerous place to be if you were black. Cora Bell Shade knew that all too well. Still, life had given her Efrem Douglas, her five-year-old son, and his birth had renewed her hope for a better future.

Cora Bell gave Efrem everything in her power, and he was generally as happy as you could expect a little boy to be. Then one day they went into town in their beat-up green pickup truck. As they reached the main intersection, she pointed out a group of black children playing on the elementary school grounds nearby and told him, "When you go to school next year, Efrem, you'll be playing over there."

Efrem looked at the playground she was pointing at, and then he looked across the road. "But I don't want to go to school there, Mama," he replied. "I want to go over here." Cora Bell's heart sank as her eyes followed Efrem's finger to the all-white elementary school across the street from the black one.

"Oh, you can't go there, Sugar," Cora Bell was forced to tell her son. "That school is for white children." Efrem's small face crumpled. The sight of her son's tears tore Cora Bell up inside. She thought about how she had always told Efrem he could be whatever he wanted to be in life if he had an education, even if he was black and poor.

In that moment, something in Cora Bell changed, and her resolve strengthened. She couldn't let her son compromise his dreams. Before she knew what she was doing, she found herself pointing to the white school and saying, "When it's time for you to go to school, you'll go there."

She heard those words come out of her own mouth as if someone else were saying them. Then she just shook her head and sighed. Cora Bell Shade had absolutely no idea how she would keep her promise.

Not long after that, a friend told her about Marian Wright Edelman, who was working as an NAACP Legal Defense Fund lawyer. Cora told Marian her story, and Marian leaped into action. First she detailed the legal and political ramifications of enrolling a black child in the white school. Then she arranged tutoring for Efrem so he would be prepared to attend the white school, if and when they won their case. They did win, and because Efrem had gone to Head Start, he was ready to go. That fall, he went to the formerly segregated school, and forward into his life.

Marian continued her work as she moved from Mississippi to Washington, D.C., and left a rich legacy. With the NAACP she opened the doors for hundreds of children like Efrem to attend formerly segregated schools. By bringing Head Start to Mississippi, she gave thousands of poor children the chance to learn. Because of national nutritional programs she helped to expand, tens of thousands of children and families no longer went hungry. And hundreds of children whose lives she had touched personally came to believe in themselves. Where did she get the courage to serve so well, for so long? Part of the answer is in a story Marian often told *her* son, Jonah, when he was growing up.

On the night her father, Arthur Jerome Wright, died of a heart attack in 1954, he asked Marian to ride with him to the hospital in the ambulance. He knew he had precious little time left, and he didn't want to lose his last chance to counsel his youngest child.

Marian climbed in, next to where her daddy lay on a stretcher. By this time his feet were itching terribly from poor circulation, and he asked her to scratch them for him. As she began to untie his shoes, she was dumbstruck by what she saw. Her father was a minister, and one of the most respected Negro leaders in the segregated town of Bennettsville, South Carolina. He had built a new church, a parsonage, a Sunday-school building, and a home for the aged. He had put three of his children through college and had taken in his deceased sister's children and other orphans. And this man who had done so much, for so many, had holes in the bottoms of his shoes!

Those beat-up soles left a lifelong impression on Marian. Her mother and father had told her time and again that material things were not the measure of our success. The true measure, they said, was our service to others. "If you see a need, don't sit by and think someone else will do something about it," Daddy Wright always said. "Stand up and address the need yourself, and don't worry about getting money or credit for it." The sight of her father's beat-up shoes drove that advice home in a lasting way.

As the ambulance wove its way through Bennettsville's sleepy streets toward the "black" hospital ward, Grandpa Wright grabbed his daughter's hand and shared with her a final lesson. "People will tell you that because you are black and a woman, you can't do what you want to do in life," he said, looking intently into her eyes. "But don't you ever believe that. If you get an education, you can accomplish anything you want to." With tears rolling down her face, Marian drank up her father's words. A few hours later he was gone.

Marian never had holes in her shoes, but she followed directly in her father's footsteps and has spent her life standing up for people who need help.

When her son Jonah was growing up, Marian was extremely busy with her work. Yet even though she traveled a lot, he and his brothers always knew that they came first. Most mornings his mother somehow managed to make them the best French toast in the world. She attended all of their parent-teacher nights and cheered them on at important games. And as her parents had done for her, she was always bringing them along with her on trips, taking them to hear speakers, introducing them to interesting people. She wanted to be sure they were never lost in her shadow. "Have you met my son?" were always her first words when they went to a new place. "It means everything, having your parents always put you first like that," says Jonah. "It gives you the feeling that you can do anything."

So when she asked Jonah to help her jump-start a powerful movement for children in this country, he gladly stood by her side. Together, they called for a day to Stand for Children.

Although many said they had too little time and too little money, they took a lesson from Daddy Wright and paid the "can't do" critics no mind. They booked the Lincoln Memorial in Washington, D.C., for June 1, 1996, and secured office space for their headquarters. In January, they hoped forty or fifty organizations would join the Children's Defense Fund's call to action. By May, more than 3,700 organizations had endorsed Stand for Children Day.

Soon thousands of people from every walk of life were spreading the word about the rally. Henry Bird, a grandfather in Maine who had never considered himself an activist, organized a busload of marchers. The Jacobsens, a family whose members were scattered around the Midwest, made Stand for Children into a family reunion, picking up three generations of family members along the route from Wisconsin to Washington. Cory Fischer-Hoffman, a twelve-year-old Philadelphia girl, organized a bus from her synagogue for her bat mitzvah project.

"In all, well over a quarter of a million people answered my mother's call for Americans to recommit themselves to our children," Jonah says. They came from every state to the Lincoln Memorial on June 1 to Stand for Children. Those who attended heard the same simple message that Grandpa Wright had passed on to his daughter, that Cora Bell Shade had passed on to her son Efrem, and that Marian has passed on to her sons: that caring, concerned people standing for children enable them eventually to stand for themselves.

In our struggles, if we are to bring about the kind of changes that will cause the world to stand up and take notice, we must be committed. There is so much work that needs to be done. It is a big job, but there is no one better to do it than those who live here. . . . We could show the world how it should be done and how to do it with dignity.

DR. MARTIN LUTHER KING JR.

To build a better life for children in your community, join **Stand for Children**, a network of local children's activists who are developing direct-service and advocacy initiatives. To form or join a local Children's Action Team, call 800-663-4032, or visit www.stand.org.

SHARE YOUR STRENGTH
Told by Bill Shore

Battles are won or lost, and the future is decided, inside one room. In a presidential campaign it's called the War Room. In the White House it's called the Situation Room. At Boston City Hospital's Growth and Nutrition Clinic, the doctors call it what it is: a coat room. It's the only place they could find. But don't let the name fool you. The work done here is often a matter of life or death.

This is where Dr. Deborah Frank and her team—a doctor, a social worker, a nutritionist, a community worker, and a psychologist—meet every Wednesday. They ask themselves what can be done for Boston's malnourished babies, born into the poorest of families. Every day, Dr. Frank and this dedicated team face medical problems that medicine can't cure. They look for symptoms, not with a stethoscope, but by examining a family's lifestyle, parent-child dynamics, and household budgets.

From this coat room, Dr. Frank has helped nourish "at risk" babies for nearly two decades. She and her team sit on lopsided swivel chairs, crowded around a small table, reviewing cases and choosing strategies. All around them are supplies to meet the needs of their patients—coats, shoes, secondhand clothing, and a makeshift food pantry.

Today the team is working on a case that has everyone stumped. Rosie Smith, twenty-six months old, has not gained an ounce in four months. The doctors classify her as "failing to thrive." With her height and weight far below normal for her age, the tiny girl faces the likelihood of lifelong health problems and learning difficulties. Rosie's worried parents insist that they always give her enough food, even though their income is below the federal poverty line. Dr. Frank hunts for clues to why the markers on Rosie's growth chart won't budge.

This five-foot-tall dynamo doctor is passionate about kids. She will be the first to tell you it takes more than food to fight hunger. She knows that in America, childhood hunger masquerades as a sleepy kindergartener, a toddler with an earache that won't go away, or a seemingly healthy two-year-old who is really an undernourished four-year-old.

She reaches beyond the limits of traditional medicine, investigating the homes of families in need. Low test scores, underactive learning behavior, and underdeveloped bodies and brains are some of the clues she looks for. For some, she prescribes enrollment in federal nutrition programs; for others, adequate housing. She stocks peanut butter and raisins right next to the cotton swabs and bandages in her tiny office.

She also coaches thousands of parents through the daily dilemmas of raising children under less-than-ideal conditions. Many parents must make painful choices: heating their homes or eating; giving an infant all the milk or watering it down so the other kids get some; filling growling tummies with water until the next meal or distracting the kids until the hunger passes.

Dr. Frank must be doing something right: Eighty-five percent of the children from her clinic have reversed their malnutrition and are growing normally.

Back in the coat room, Dr. Frank has a winning idea. She shouts out, "A high chair! Do Rosie's parents have a high chair?" That was it! Evidently, Rosie was eating while walking around the house and never stopped long enough to digest her food. The clinic team will get a high chair for Rosie, and Dr. Frank will make certain that the family receives extra support, as well as a follow-up home visit.

"Hungry children need more than a high-calorie, high-protein diet," Dr. Frank says. "They need medical care to address the serious complications of malnutrition. They need teachers who have the time to give individualized attention to their learning style. They need their parents' workplace to offer health insurance, and, of course, they need love."

Dr. Frank is one of the thousands of extraordinary people involved with Share Our Strength, the anti-hunger organization that meets immediate demands for food while investing in organizations that have a proven track record of success and whose work actually attacks the root of the hunger problem. Since 1984, Share Our Strength has mobilized thousands of people nationwide—chefs, writers, business leaders, and artists—to lend their skills and talents, raising more than $65 million in the fight to end hunger.

Through unique partnerships with American Express, Tyson Foods, Inc., and other corporations, Share Our Strength is able to help people like Dr. Frank and her team bring kids like Rosie back to health. Each year, Share Our Strength hosts gourmet "Taste of the Nation" events across the country, where 100 percent of ticket sales benefit the fight to end hunger. Tyson Foods has donated millions of pounds of their products to food banks across the country.

Share Our Strength measures its success not by the number of meals they've served, but by the families they've helped for the long run—families like Rosie's, who no longer go to a food pantry at the end of the month. With a healthy start in life, Rosie takes her rambling spirit into a brighter future. Her strength will help her learn better and live better, and help the world thrive.

There's a country at the end of the world
where no child is born, but to outlive the moon.

WILLIAM BUTLER YEATS

Buy extra food, volunteer, and encourage your favorite restaurant to donate excess food to your local food bank. Donate to national and local organizations fighting to end hunger. Educate yourself on the issues of hunger and poverty so that you can take action. To learn more about how you can make a difference in the fight to end hunger, call 800-969-4767, or visit www.strength.org.

SOMETHING GREATER
THAN THEMSELVES

Told by Rosabeth Moss Kanter

As a young boy growing up in Boston, Herman didn't have much hope. Living in a broken and abusive home, he was short on love or support. His backyard was a vacant lot where he played with his friends amid broken bottles and trash. He hadn't yet imagined that one day he'd be one in a chain of people linking hope for young people through cities across America.

It all started one afternoon when Herman was playing outside with his friends. A dozen young people wearing bright red jackets suddenly appeared, and to his surprise, they began to clean up the vacant lot. They were still hard at work that evening when he went home, wondering why they all had "City Year" written across their backs.

When Herman returned the next day, he was amazed. He had never seen anything so wonderful happen in his neighborhood before. Not only was the lot completely clean, but the young people were building a playground! For Herman, it was a magical day.

Several years later, City Year brought more magic to Herman's life. It was his first day of middle school, and he was nervous, wondering whether or not he'd fit in. As he turned the corner to enter his classroom, one of those familiar red jackets flashed in front of him. Khary, a City Year corps member, was there to assist Herman's teacher.

When Khary smiled at him, Herman knew things would be just fine. And for a while they were. Khary was funny and warm and gave Herman lots of one-on-one attention. And when Herman decided to enter the Boston public schools' oratorical competition, an entire City Year team coached him. They were as proud as he was when he actually won!

However, through the years, the encouragement Herman received from City Year volunteers wasn't enough to combat all the things working against him. He fell behind in school, failed the eleventh grade, and eventually dropped out. He was near despair when a guidance counselor suggested that he join the Boston corps. City Year, he was told, took committed young people of all backgrounds, even high-school dropouts, as long as they agreed to try to get their GEDs. He was thrilled when he was accepted into the program, and so began to turn his life around.

City Year hatched in 1978 in a dorm room shared by two Harvard freshmen, Michael Brown and Alan Khazei. The roommates soon became best friends, and each night they would stay up late, making passionate plans to solve their country's problems. In school, they learned how President Roosevelt's Civilian Conservation Corps helped pull America out of the Depression of the 1930s. They studied the Civil Rights Movement and the Peace Corps, which had brought people together in the 1960s. They worried especially about the lives of inner-city kids.

Michael and Alan wanted to change the world as their heroes—Gandhi, Martin Luther King Jr., and President Kennedy, had done. Like them, young Michael and Alan dreamed of leading people, especially young ones, into service, into something greater than themselves. In the summer of 1988, their formal education complete, they started City Year with thirty young people and a long list of community projects.

Today, clad in uniforms of khaki pants, white shirts, and those bright red jackets, more than seven hundred City Year graduates from all walks of life continue to live City Year's motto around the country, "putting idealism to work," serving inner-city neighborhoods, boosting the lives of kids like Herman with a little more love and support. Since its inception in 1988, City Year corps members have charged and recharged with the love and support they get back.

In 1993, President Clinton used City Year as a model for his national service program, AmeriCorps. Every year, thousands of adults join these dedicated young people in Serve-a-Thons, giving a day of their own time to work on special community projects.

With his City Year team, Herman worked with handicapped children at an elementary school in Boston. He became another of the multiplying links in the chain of national service, from Franklin Roosevelt, John F. Kennedy, and Martin Luther King Jr. to Michael, Khary, and now Herman. He learned that what might seem small steps to others are leaps and bounds for "his" kids. Helping them learn to read, paint, and accomplish other new things makes him happy, and happiness charged his life. He earned his GED and received financial aid to go to college. Like the ripple effect when a pebble drops into a pool of water, City Year's work goes far beyond good deeds done today. City Year workers help the Hermans of this world, so that they too expand to something greater than themselves.

Each time a man stands up for an ideal, or acts to improve the life of others, or strikes out against injustice, he sends a tiny ripple of hope, and those ripples, crossing each other from a million different centers of energy, build a current which can sweep down the mightiest walls of oppression and resistance.

ROBERT F. KENNEDY

If you're between seventeen and twenty-four years of age, and want to give a year of your life to help public schools and urban neighborhoods, or if your company is looking for ways to change communities by producing leaders to engage in service projects, call City Year at 617-927-2500, or visit its Web site, www.cityyear.org.

READ BABY READ

Told by Jennifer Pooley

At 11:00 A.M. on a Saturday morning, cheers erupt, as in the final seconds of a Houston Rockets game. "What room is this?" Mike Feinberg asks. "This is the room . . . that has the kids . . . who want to learn . . . to read books . . . to build a better tomorrow," his fifth-graders chant, drumming their hands on their desks. Their enthusiastic voices also sing the continents, harmonize fractions, and hip-hop long division.

Teachers Dave Levin and Mike Feinberg clap encouragement, chant with the students, and constantly invent new challenges. The fifth-graders can't take their eyes off them as they fire off questions and explain problems. With fourth-quarter do-or-die urgency, they seize every minute to learn. Hands wave. Volunteers read. Every student contributes. Motivation flows around the room, student to student. They all pull for each other. They succeed as a team. Learning is winning.

Outside Mike and Dave's classroom in Houston, there are more than enough obstacles for a grueling obstacle course. Poverty, deficient school systems, and street violence have shadowed the students' young lives. In most inner-city schools, apathy reigns, gangs organize, and academic performance falls. Mike and Dave's alternative middle school, and their Knowledge Is Power Program (KIPP), offer students a choice, and the way they put it, the students choose to learn. Theirs is the winning team: Drug users, gangs, and dropouts are losing.

Students at the KIPP Academy attend school nine and a half hours a day, Monday through Friday, and four hours on Saturdays. Even though they attend school year-round, they rarely miss a day or take a vacation. In fact they boast an impressive 99-percent attendance rate.

For Mike and Dave, KIPP is a twenty-four-hour effort. To stay connected, they have an 800 number, a work number, and a cell phone. They even buy alarm clocks for the students so that they can take charge of being on time. Anxious students can call from local pay phones when they need to talk about their homework, or just talk. Every day, Mike and Dave invigorate students by sitting with them at lunch tables, showing them new dance steps, or shooting baskets with them. They are ready to do whatever it takes to get these kids to college: University banners hang alongside the posters with positive slogans, colorful decorations, and math problems on the blackboards.

"There are no shortcuts. There is no margin for error," says Mike. "We must play a perfect game." In KIPP classrooms, students must learn to take responsibility for themselves and their education. Self-sufficiency and self-esteem are daily subjects, skills as important as good spelling. The kids know the odds are against them, but more important, they believe they can win.

As a senior at Princeton, Wendy Kopp started Teach For America (TFA), the national teacher corps that has mobilized some of the nation's outstanding college seniors to improve our schools. Each TFA teacher gets real-life experience by committing to work for two years in some of America's most under-resourced urban and rural public schools.

When Dave and Mike joined TFA, they were both rookies with nothing more to give than their promise and natural talent. A few years later they opened their own school, the KIPP Academy, in Houston. Their energy, innovation, and impressive results caught the attention of school administrators in New York. Dave is now in the South Bronx, operating the second KIPP Academy, for grades five through eight.

After completing his two years in TFA, before moving to New York City, Dave joined Mike and the Houston students on a trip to celebrate the end of the 1995 school year. They raised enough money to travel all the way to Washington, D.C. When they arrived, they made the city their open classroom. Naturally, in the nation's capital, U.S. history took center stage, generating fascinating discussions. Questions and answers were electric.

During a tour of the Supreme Court, the students met Justice Stephen Breyer. Mike introduced the fifth-graders to the justice as the hardest-working kids in the country. "Are you enjoying your trip?" the justice asked the kids. One small hand started waving frantically. "Excuse me, sir," asked Ruben Garcia, "but were you here when *Miranda v. Arizona* was decided?" "No, that was before my time," replied the astonished justice. "Well, then, how would you have decided?" pressed the confident eleven-year-old. "You *go*, Ruben!" his classmates cheered. The justice thoughtfully replied, "I would have agreed. The Constitution was designed to safeguard the rights of all our citizens." Ruben listened carefully: It's not often that a fifth-grader's question of law is answered by a Supreme Court justice.

On their last night in Washington, excitement and wonder overflowed these eleven-year-olds. Dave and Mike had arranged for a trip to the White House the next day. Who knows what secret dreams and ambitions danced through the minds of these youngsters? As they stood on the front lawn, they chanted, "We want Bill!" and followed this chant with their own original "School House Rock": "This is KIPP in the house! Give me a beat! You gotta read, baby, read!"

A large crowd gathered around the students and listened as they serenaded the president. They sang the preamble to the Constitution and belted out the Declaration of Independence. From the rooftops, quite spontaneously, Secret Service agents waved their arms in time, joining in as if they were conducting.

When out came President Clinton, excitement overcame the group. They hugged each other, cheered, and crushed their teachers in their enthusiasm. Their radiant faces exuded the joy of their big day, and all the hope for *their* bright futures.

I dwell in possibility.

EMILY DICKINSON

With the support of Doris and Don Fisher, the founders of the Gap, KIPP has begun to train educators to plan, open, and run their own KIPP-like school to ensure that more children from more communities have an opportunity to receive the best possible education. To learn about their Fellowship and training program for people to open up their own great schools, visit www.kipp.org. Join **Teach For America** and other outstanding recent college graduates who commit two years to teach in America's under-resourced urban and rural public schools. Call 800-832-1230, or visit their Web site, www.teachforamerica.org.

YOUTHBUILD
Told by John Bell

Chantay Henderson Jones was just fourteen years old when Dorothy Stoneman asked her and her teenage East Harlem friends a question that would change their lives: "What would you do to improve your neighborhood if you knew I would do everything in my power to help you succeed? If I helped you think through the project, got other adults to support you, and helped you raise money? What would you really like to do?"

It was as if Chantay and her friends had been just waiting for someone to ask them. "I would fix up the broken-down buildings so homeless people could live in them," said one student enthusiastically. "I would fix the elevators in the projects so old people wouldn't have to walk up the stairs," said another. "I would make a place for us to go, so we wouldn't have to hang out on street corners." "I'd eliminate crime!" "I'd make beautiful parks for little children to play in," others chimed in. When Chantay shared her idea, they all nodded approvingly. "What about hiring unemployed young people like us to rebuild the abandoned buildings and make housing for the homeless?"

They all agreed that, if given a chance, they would make permanent improvements such as fixing buildings instead of cleaning the streets and parks, since the latter would just get dirty again the next day. "We would do something we could show to our grandchildren," they said.

It was 1978, and Dorothy had been teaching and working in the community for fourteen years. She'd taught Chantay and many of these students when they were in the first grade. Deeply troubled that some of her favorite students had died as teenagers in the tough city streets, she thought that the waste of their brilliance and goodness was a national shame that could and should be reversed. She also thought these youngsters might know best how to help her do just that.

So Dorothy listened carefully as Chantay and her friends shared their ideas with her. She was impressed with their ability to see what was needed in their community—and their energy and desire to do something about it. They reaffirmed Dorothy's belief that young people could be a vital force for improving their communities. And they confirmed her desire to build a national movement of young people as leaders for positive social change. Dorothy asked Chantay and her friends to join her in taking the first steps.

At the time, there were tens of thousands of unemployed young people in New York City. Dorothy had also discovered that there were ten thousand abandoned city-owned buildings and fifty thousand homeless people living on New York's streets and in its subway tunnels. If these kids were given real jobs, Dorothy knew they could contribute to their families' income as well as their communities' well-being.

Dorothy invited me, her longtime work partner—and husband—as well as other teachers and parents, and Chantay and her friends, to start with an abandoned building on 107th Street between Lexington and Third Avenues. When we began, all we had were garbage bags, a couple of shovels, and gritty determination. During the days, we'd all work together. The neighbors pitched in, bringing us refreshments and organizing bake sales to buy tools and supplies.

But at night the building belonged to the winos who drank and slept there. So we bought cinder blocks and cement and boarded up the windows. One night, by the light of the streetlights, we spent five hours laying fourteen bricks. We used the water from the fire hydrant two blocks away to mix the cement in a little bucket. But the nighttime "tenants" just knocked in the bricks and took over again. While we were forced to abandon that building, we carried on—chalking it up as a "learning experience."

For the next six months, Dorothy went about rallying support from different community leaders and organized various volunteer projects. We got the East Harlem Block Schools, a parent-controlled school where we'd been working for many years, to agree to house us and our Youth Action Program (YAP). We put our ideas into a proposal and received a start-up grant from the federal government. Our first official project was to rehabilitate a six-story tenement building on Second Avenue and 119th Street.

It was a big job—and it took us five years to finish. We had to tear out the old before we could build the new. Day after day, young people volunteered their time and energy. It was hard work, but fulfilling. At the end of each day, these teens felt proud of the contribution they'd made to the neighborhood. And in the process of renovating the building, many of them rebuilt their own lives. For the homeless youth who worked on the project, the building became their new home. Others felt empowered to help. As one young man put it, "The building was like me, messed up on the inside. But we cleaned it out, fixed it up, and now it's new, just like me!"

Over the years, Chantay and her friends also worked on their other dreams. In addition to rehabilitating the tenement building, they built a park, organized a crime-prevention patrol, created a "Home Away from Home" for homeless teenagers and a child-care center for children of working single mothers. They started a leadership school and organized the East Harlem Youth Congress.

It wasn't long before YAP became famous. Teenagers ascended in their own neighborhoods as they turned their ideas into action plans, and plans into action—with guidance from experienced adults. They helped make all the decisions—hiring the staff, managing the program, and even helping Dorothy make policy decisions. In the process, they showed what a powerful force for social change teens could be—if given the chance.

I guess all this success went to their heads, because then they started thinking *really* big. If they could make things better in East Harlem, why not all over New York City? Their East Harlem Youth Congress set up a network of community organizations, called the Coalition for $10 Million, to persuade the New York City Council to fund programs like YAP throughout the city. Hundreds of young people testified in City Hall, calling for the resources to rebuild their crumbling neighborhoods. Council members were impressed with their sincerity as well as with their track record.

By 1988, calls were coming from people in fixer-upper neighborhoods all over the country. So we launched our model nationally and named it YouthBuild. There now are two hundred YouthBuild programs in forty-four states, putting 7,500 young people to work each year. Our network has grown to 650 organizations in forty-nine states—advocating for federal funds of which, over the years, the YouthBuild Coalition has raised $350 million to employ and train tens of thousands of young people in housing rehabilitation projects who have built seven thousand units of housing. One student in that first East Harlem project predicted our future when he said, "There's a lot of love in the Youth Action Program, and someday we're going to spread it around the world."

Chantay is now the program coordinator for a drug-rehabilitation program in Brooklyn. She uses many of the leadership skills she learned during her years in the Youth Action Program: writing, negotiating, challenging people to think, and mobilizing communities. Standing on 119th Street and Second Avenue, looking at that first building she helped to rebuild almost twenty years ago, she says, "There's an old African proverb: It takes a village to raise a child. Well, it also takes a child to raise a village," she says. "Everyone, no matter how young or how old, has a responsibility to help their community. Young people can take the lead."

When I dare to be powerful—to use my strength in the service of my vision—then it becomes less and less important whether I am afraid.

AUDRE LORDE

To join the **YouthBuild** movement of young adults who are rebuilding housing for low-income and homeless people, achieving higher academic skills, and taking leadership to improve their lives and their communities, call YouthBuild USA at 617-623-9900, or visit their Web site, www.youthbuild.org.

REBUILDING TOGETHER
Told by Skye Trimble

It was three-thirty in the morning, and Frances Vaughn had just finished her shift at the *Washington Post*. Her hands were ink-stained from hours of sorting papers. By moonlight, she hurried to make the last bus of the night. Holding tight to the driver's hand, Frances climbed aboard. She sat in the first empty seat and closed her tired eyes. To pass the time, she began to hum a tune quietly. Soon the engine's roar shifted. The weary woman knew her stop was next. After the driver helped her down, Frances thanked him with her dark eyes.

She followed the streetlights to her house and gazed up at her stairs. Those darn steps. With two artificial knees, it was a real struggle for Frances. She'd done it before and she would do it again. But at seventy-two years old, it wasn't easy.

Frances went to bed that night thinking about her future. She lay on her old mattress, looking around the dilapidated room. Over the years, her house had fallen apart around her. She wished she could take care of it as she used to, before she got sick. She hated to think of moving to a nursing home or even living on the streets. Tonight, as she did every night, Frances prayed with a hopeful heart.

She awakened to a surprising phone call from Patty Johnson, the co-founder of Rebuilding Together. For fourteen years, its more than 255 chapters across the country have been organizing volunteers, rekindling the tradition of neighbors helping neighbors. Their specialty happened to be repairing low-income homes.

Frances stood awestruck, wrapped in her flannel nightgown, listening to Patty's enthusiasm pour out over the phone: "One Saturday in April each year, we send our crew to homes all over the country," she explained. "By dinnertime, neighbors like you have a little comfort and security back in their lives. This year we'd like to visit your house!"

Frances was quiet for a moment. She searched her memory and finally had to admit that, in all her years, nobody had ever helped her with her home. Patty Johnson's news was welcome indeed. "This is an extraordinary day!" Frances exclaimed to Patty. As she hung up the phone, her heart raced and she was already quite excited, just thinking about fixing things up.

On the last Saturday in April, thirty eager volunteers arrived at Frances's door. They carried supplies donated from corporate sponsors like Home Depot, and under Patty Johnson's guidance, as Frances puts it, "they tore my house up and put it back together again, like it was brand-new!" Frances perched nearby, beaming, especially when they fixed the stairs. They built the strongest banister possible, so Frances could get up and down the steps more easily. If that were all the Rebuilding Together crew did, she would have been happy. But these kind folks had more in store for Frances. While some patched her leaky roof, others laid down tile and carpet, secured her front door with a new lock, and installed a safer stove and a smoke detector. They laid down sod for the lawn and a shade tree.

That day, every corner of Frances's home had smiles and stories. Anyone passing by the "neighborhood family" would have seen various members of the community pitching in. Street kids worked side by side with the ladies of the Junior League, who "turn their white gloves to white paint," as Patty puts it. "It all comes from caring people," Patty reflects. "There are no suits, no white or blue collars, just people. That's the way it should be." Even President Reagan sent some of his staff to chip away the old paint and slap on a fresh coat of white.

One teenage boy sat outside with Frances, breathing the sweet smell of new grass. He told her how Patty Johnson came from a poor home and grew up determined to help people feel secure in theirs. He described her work as "building miracles, one house at a time." Frances was impressed when he explained that their energetic leader had worked overtime in her unheated cellar, just to get the program going, nearly fifteen years ago. She felt a deep sense of gratitude—and a real sisterhood with Patty's enthusiastic spirit.

That evening, everyone gathered outside Frances's beautiful new house. As she proudly walked up the stairs, holding on to the new banister, her new friends cheered, "Fran-ces! Fran-ces!" She might not have belived it if she weren't standing right on it, what Rebuilding Together had created in just one day.

The world needs friendly folks like you.
In this troubled world, it's refreshing to find someone
Who still has the time to be kind.
Someone who still has the faith to believe that
The more you give, the more you receive.
Someone who's ready by thought, word or deed
To reach out a hand, in the hour of need.

HELEN STEINER RICE

Join the quarter-million volunteers of Rebuilding Together, rehabilitating homes and renewing the lives of the elderly and disabled. Call 202-483-9083, or visit their Web site, www.rebuildingtogether.com, to connect with one of the 865 communities nationwide.

OPENING HEARTS

Told by Elaina Verveer

While most seventy-nine-year-olds have settled into retirement, Louise Jackson is much too busy even to think of slowing down. This mother of four, grandmother of eleven, and great- and great-great-grandmother of seventy-seven also takes care of the neglected children of our nation's capital. Don't look for her to stop anytime soon. She thinks her work has just begun.

Actually, it started when she was about eight years old, when Louise accompanied her great-grandmother, a midwife, to the bedsides of poor women. Often given the responsibility of cradling the newborns, she learned to care for little ones at a very young age. Over the years, she instinctively made this caring a touchstone of her life.

Now, as a volunteer with the District of Columbia's Foster Grandparent Program, Louise works with families affected by child abuse. She teaches adults parenting skills and helps them find employment. But Louise's greatest gift is her love for the children. "Every child deserves to be loved," says Louise. "If I find children whose tears are caused by neglect, I'll help open their hearts so they can love again."

In 1985, Louise did precisely that for baby twins, Phyllis and Phillip, and their single mother. During their first meeting, Louise noticed the mother's bloodshot eyes and blackened veins. She saw the children's bandaged limbs and tear-stained faces. Sensing the magnitude of her challenge, Louise dedicated the next few months to helping this troubled family.

She gave the mother cooking lessons and job-training advice. But the young woman, overwhelmed by her difficult life, continued to put her craving for drugs over her children's needs. Louise was upset to find the babies alone and unfed several nights each week, crammed into one crib, faces red from hours of crying. She knew their unchanged diapers and empty stomachs were signs of a much larger problem. When their mother was incarcerated for drug possession and child abuse, the baby twins were left with no one.

Every time Louise saw children thrown randomly into foster homes, she suffered. *Haven't these two little ones been through enough?* she thought. Louise knew that what the baby twins needed more than anything else was a mother. Though at the time she was seventy years old, she accepted the judge's suggestion to adopt them officially. "I felt, within my soul, they were meant for me," she says. "From the start, I loved them as if they were my own."

Her brave love for these children helped Louise get through the long and difficult adoption process and remedied the worst of the twins' early life. Phyllis and Phillip are happy and healthy fifteen-year-olds, busy with school, church, and helping Louise deliver food to needy families. They are often at the Rosa Parks Institute for Self-Development, learning about their heritage, mapping the trails of the Underground Railroad across the United States, Canada, and Mexico.

Louise still knows what it's like to be a kid. "I never *make* them do anything," she says. "I teach them to do the right thing. I tell them that I may not always be around, so I want them to be well prepared to make good decisions for themselves."

What does Louise expect in return for all that she has done? "I just want them to open their hearts and be kind to everyone," she says. "Trust in the Lord and do good."

Louise is a wonderful example for all those who think they are too old, too tired, or too busy to help someone. For as long as she lives, she'll be giving it everything she's got. Often, she finds love is enough.

> *It may not make the evening news when a Foster Grandparent takes the hand of a child who has never had anyone raise a hand to her, except in violence. It may not be what most people write about when seniors*

understand that they, too, have something to give, but countless children
benefit from the action of a Foster Grandparent every single day.

SENATOR HILLARY RODHAM CLINTON

If you are age sixty or over and love children, join the Foster Grandparent Program of the National Senior Service Corps (Senior Corps) of the Corporation for National and Community Service, which also includes the Senior Companion Program. To find out where your local office is, call 800-424-8867, or visit www.seniorcorps.org.

HELPING OTHERS TO SEE
Told by Ram Dass

If you are at a point in your life where you are ready to grow, to push yourself a little, to open your heart to a deeper compassion, drop in at the Aravind Eye Hospital in Madurai, India. Offer yourself as a volunteer—for as long as you are comfortable. Even a week would work, as it did for me. Then watch with awe as Dr. V. or Thulasi, his second-in-command, finds a place just for you.

In your "free" time, don't miss 6:00 A.M. in the waiting room of the hospital, when Dr. V. walks about in the river of humanity. Hundreds of village folk stand in lines, waiting patiently for inexpensive, often free, outpatient eye care. In an adjoining wing, long lines of the blind and the near blind, guided by friends and relatives, await the ten-minute miracle of surgery that will give them back their sight.

Or join Dr. V.'s sister, a brilliant eye surgeon in her own right, as she, after six hours of surgery, leads a class of nurses in meditation and song.

After you have wandered around enough to begin to understand what this hospital is really about, ask Dr. V. if you can visit one of his Sunday-morning family sessions with his brothers, sisters, nieces, nephews, in-laws, and all the children. Each week a different child presents something: It could be one of the holy stories of India through which the Hindi people contemplate their values and incorporate them into their lives. Or a political issue, a world public-health issue, an environmental issue, a family issue. After the presentation, all three generations hang out together and discuss the way they can put into practice the values brought forth in the presentation.

Dr. V. is a hero to these people for alleviating preventable and curable blindness in the world. He is a winner of the highest honors, and "chief" of this huge, world-class eye hospital complex. A strangely arresting man—with his gnarled arthritic hands and feet, his gray rumpled suit, his seventy-odd years, and a perfect "poster man" at the same time—a brilliant mirror of compassion to all.

In the waiting-room scene at sunrise, Dr. V. is simultaneously the fellow villager that he once was, and continues to be, and the extraordinary healer he has become. For a moment his hand rests reassuringly on the arm of a frightened elderly woman. He explains a surgical procedure to a man. He nods to people and keeps the line moving. He cautions the children to be careful of others in their play. He is both village elder and hospital chief. He is also keeping an eye on the staff, insisting on their impeccability in service—guiding his superbly honed institution of compassion with a glance, a word, a silent presence, a smile. As Gandhi once said, "My life is my message." So Dr. V.'s blend of being and doing is his message. He continually seeks to be an instrument of imbuing the physical world with Living Spirit.

"India will enter the twenty-first century with 13 million of her people needlessly blind," says Dr. V. "Intelligence and capability are not enough to solve our problems. We must have the joy of doing something beautiful. If you allow the divine force to flow through you, you will accomplish things far greater than you ever imagined."

Dr. V. and his staff perform 92,000 cataract surgeries a year; nearly 850,000 outpatient treatments. That's over three hundred surgeries a day, and 2,800 outpatients registered and seen each day. At the Seva Foundation, hundreds of members help support special people like Dr. V. and their noble work in under-privileged communities around the world. The Aravind Clinic has become a factory of caring for human beings. Their tall building of cement and steel and large plate-glass windows is a shining monument to Western technology. But it is also, like Dr. V. himself, a blend of being and doing.

From Ram Dass's experiences with Dr. V. and the Aravind family, he deepened his understanding of a basic tenet of the Seva Foundation—that one need not forgo doing for being, or being for doing. In Madurai he found himself immersed in a demonstration of the successful integration of these two aspects of life—actions involving the best skills and technology balanced with caring hearts rooted in a sweet spiritual presence that is embracing of all fellow souls. It is a great teaching.

Want to help restore sight to people in India, Nepal, and Tibet? Help indigenous people in Guatemala and Chiapas, Mexico, preserve their culture and build sustainable communities? Support the development of a holistic approach to diabetes for Native Americans, or attend a retreat for social activists? Call 1-800-223-7382, or visit www.seva.org for information and a copy of Seva's beautiful Gifts of Service catalogue.

SMALL ACTS FOR BIG CHANGE: THE OXFAM FAST

Told by Sarah Bachman

Nathan Gray believed that small acts could bring about big change. He was twenty-five years old, and he had seen it work. For four years he had lived as a community organizer working with poor village people in Latin America. They took out tiny loans and built small businesses, and he had witnessed their emergence from grinding, depressing poverty into new hope and dignity, and even some prosperity.

In Guatemala he was impressed by the gentle strength and determination of one village leader, Francisco Basival. He had quietly organized the village to achieve once-impossible goals. Francisco drew on the practical wisdom of his people's Mayan ancestry by reintroducing sawgrass to stabilize hillside irrigation and thatch roofs. He introduced other modest improvements that, together, spelled the difference between life and death.

Back in the States, Nathan thought of Francisco. Although poor and uneducated, he was a genius at bringing about grassroots—literally!—change. There must be a way to help Americans appreciate what people like him are up to. Nathan had read about Mahatma Gandhi, an ordinary South African lawyer of Indian ancestry, who had dramatized the dignity of ordinary folk, with great effect. Whenever Gandhi wanted to show the British his displeasure, he would simply stop eating. The British hated Gandhi's simplicity, his mass demonstrations, and his fasts. Eventually they gave in, granting India its freedom in 1947 without a shot having been fired.

"Perhaps Americans would feel empathy for the poor if they fasted," Nathan thought. "If they shared their daily experience of hunger, even for a day." A fast could help people in the wealthy United States connect with grassroots leaders like Franscisco in the third world. If people could be persuaded to fast for a day in solidarity with people like him, they could donate the money they saved on food to fund self-help projects in poor countries. The feeling of connectedness would be good for everyone. "Let's have a big fast!" Nathan thought. "Get lots of people fasting. Make a movement out of it. Raise money and consciences."

Oxfam America, the international organization Nathan had joined in Massachusetts, had organized small fasts for years. However, the then-stodgy Oxfam board thought a big, organized fast would be too crass. As far as the board members were concerned, the idea was a dud. But Nathan was determined.

He proposed a name—Fast for a World Harvest—and set a date: a week before Thanksgiving. To pay for publicity, he sold old greeting cards and baskets made by Oxfam-supported third-world groups. Then it struck him: Every major religion advocates fasting as a way to cleanse the soul and focus thoughts on the humble essentials of life. Nathan sent a mailing to ten thousand college chaplains, inviting them to get involved. The chaplains responded immediately to count themselves—and their students—in.

To create the biggest fast in America, he needed more help getting the word out. Fearlessly, he went to New York and visited AP and UPI, the largest wire services; the *New York Times*, the most prestigious U.S. newspaper; and CBS, then home of the top-rated evening news program, hosted by America's favorite anchor, Walter Cronkite. Nathan's father, a distinguished-looking lawyer, joined with his son to lend him credibility and support.

The idea took off. Anthony Lewis, a big-hearted *New York Times* columnist, embraced the fast and promoted it in his column. The *Times* endorsed it, mentioning tiny Oxfam America alongside much larger charities. Walter Cronkite dedicated a remarkable four and a half minutes of the evening news to the fast.

Nathan really scrambled to make it happen. He had told CBS, for instance, that there would be a major event in Macon, Georgia, but when he checked with folks in Macon, no major event had been planned. "Well," he told the college chaplain there, "better make sure something big happens, because a CBS camera crew is coming in tomorrow to film it." A few phone calls later, he had a celebrity guest on his way to Macon: Dick Gregory, an African-American comedian and social activist whose fasts for peace were famous.

On the Thursday before Thanksgiving, 1974, 250,000 people joined together to give up one day's meals. The fast was a huge success, generating enormous publicity for Oxfam America and almost a million dollars in donations. From a small idea, the fast had grown into a national cause.

An annual tradition was born. The Oxfam fast continues today, a quarter-century later. It remains the largest nonreligious fast in America and is especially popular on hundreds of college campuses. It has generated many millions of dollars, which have empowered grassroots leaders like Francisco. It's a global irony that many people in the richest, most powerful societies feel powerless to help. They think, "World hunger is overwhelming. What can I do?" When they participate in the fast, however, they feel connected with real people doing real work, and they find inspiration and hope, and perhaps a kind of power that they've never felt before.

A couple of years after the first fast, Nathan felt the impact of his work first-hand. A huge earthquake had just shaken Guatemala, killing thirty thousand people in the capital, Guatemala City. He delivered some Oxfam relief supplies and worked with Francisco to distribute them. Together they dragged bodies from the rubble. They restored the roofs of houses. It was exhausting work, but they boosted each other's spirits.

After a couple of long, tiring days of emotional and physical strain, Nathan and Francisco were sitting alone together one night. They were both too tired to sleep. Suddenly Francisco, a man of few words, ventured a question. "Whose money is helping us recover and rebuild after this earthquake?" he asked.

Nathan searched for the words to explain the fast. "Well, a lot of people gave up eating for just one day. Then they took the money they would have spent on food and gave it to Oxfam to spend on people like you." Francisco still looked puzzled. "Why would people in the world's richest country give up eating?" he asked. Forgoing the logical response, Nathan spoke from his heart: "We wanted you to know how much we care about you and support you."

They hugged, tears etching lines in their dusty faces. The next day they worked together with a new strength, clearing rubble, one rock at a time.

> *Instead of thinking about: How do I earn a living? . . . how do I survive? . . . we ought to say, what is it that my experience teaches me that could bring advantage to all humanity?*
>
> R. BUCKMINSTER FULLER

Oxfam America's Fast for World Harvest is the Thursday before Thanksgiving. To organize a learning experience or event at your church, school, college, or company, call 800-597-FAST, or visit www.oxfamamerica.org/advocacy/art890.html.

KENNEDY AND THE PEACE CORPS
Told by Harris Wofford

"**Ask not what** your country can do for you; ask what you can do for your country." With these words, a young president launched what has become one of the most successful social inventions of this century: the Peace Corps.

When John Kennedy first gave voice to the idea of the Peace Corps, circumstances did not hint that history was about to be made. In the final weeks of the

1960 presidential campaign, after a television debate with his Republican opponent, Richard Nixon, Kennedy traveled to the University of Michigan. He wasn't supposed to speak, but a crowd of ten thousand students and faculty awaited his arrival—at nearly two in the morning.

Moved by the crowd, Kennedy decided to speak to them. He challenged the students to use their educational training as teachers, doctors, and engineers to help people in faraway lands. "How many of you are willing to spend five or ten years in Africa, Latin America, or Asia, working for the U.S. and working for freedom?"

Their response was an enthusiastic ovation. The next morning two graduate students, Alan and Judy Guskin, sat in their student cafeteria and wrote a letter to the college paper asking readers to join them in working for a Peace Corps. Their phone rang day and night with offers of help. Within days, one thousand students had signed a petition saying they would volunteer if a Peace Corps were formed.

News of the students' petition spread to the Kennedy campaign. Spurred by this spontaneous outpouring of support, Kennedy made a major speech in San Francisco expanding on the idea. He promised, if elected, to create a Peace Corps of talented men and women who "could work modern miracles for peace in dozens of underdeveloped nations."

On his way back to Washington, Kennedy met with the Michigan students. They presented their petitions, and Kennedy was impressed with the long list of names. When he began to put the petitions in his car, he sensed some discomfort from the Guskins. "You need them back, don't you?" he asked. Photocopying was not available in those days, and they only had one copy of the names and addresses.

As they shared their ideas about the Peace Corps with the Kennedy staffers, one of them told the students, "You'll be the first to go—that's a promise!" And some of them were—Judy and Al Guskin were among the first volunteers sent to Thailand.

Campaign promises are often forgotten, but not this one. After Kennedy was elected, the White House received more mail on the Peace Corps than on any other subject, and it was wildly popular in the polls. But support for the idea was far from universal. President Eisenhower derided it as a "juvenile experiment," and journalists called it a "Kiddie Korps."

Few expected that young people of the "silent generation" would volunteer, or that they could make a difference if they did. But Kennedy knew that young people would rise to the challenge. To a reporter's skeptical question, one of the first Peace Corps volunteers said, "Nobody asked me to do anything unselfish, patriotic, and for the common good before. Kennedy asked."

President Kennedy appointed his brother-in-law, Sargent Shriver, to organize the Peace Corps. Shriver joked that Kennedy picked him because it was easier to fire a relative than a political friend, but in truth Kennedy couldn't have made a better choice. Shriver was a man of vision and practicality, with inexhaustible energy and imagination. He knew the Peace Corps would have only one chance to work. "As with the parachute jumper, the chute had to open the first time," he used to say. He proposed a big and bold start to capture the imagination of the potential volunteers and the public.

I was lucky to be on the team Sargent Shriver assembled to turn Kennedy's idea into a living program. Shriver's guiding premise was never to accept no as an answer. When he asked the State Department experts how long it would take to get the first volunteers overseas, they estimated at least two and a half years. Shriver said, "We're going to show them. In five months we'll have five hundred volunteers in at least five countries." And that's exactly what happened.

Beating the bureaucracy became the name of the game. "You guys had a good day today," a civil service expert helping us wryly remarked one afternoon. "You broke fourteen laws." Instead of waiting for Congress to pass a law, we recommended that Kennedy create the Peace Corps by executive order, as a pilot, and then ask for legislation. He agreed, and on March 1, 1961, six weeks after he was sworn in, the Peace Corps was born. In his State of the Union address, he said, "Nothing carries the spirit of American idealism and expresses our hopes better and more effectively to the far corners of the earth than the Peace Corps."

Unfortunately, Kennedy did not live to see the Peace Corps grow to fifteen thousand volunteers. Since 1961, about 162,000 Americans have served in the Peace Corps, in more than 135 countries. Millions of people in Asia, Africa, and Latin America now enjoy better education, safer water, more productive land, and greater economic prosperity because of their service. Currently the Peace Corps is at work in the former Soviet Union, South Africa, and Communist China. It continues to provide a worldwide training for Great Citizens—volunteers who return home with the skills and determination to help solve problems in America.

Another of President Kennedy's high hopes is at long last beginning to be realized. After sending off the first Peace Corps volunteers from the White House lawn, Kennedy said, "The logic of this idea is that someday we will bring it home to America." At last that day has come.

Today, fifty thousand Americans from many walks of life, most of them young, are teaching kids, fighting crime, building homes, and cleaning the environment through service in AmeriCorps. Created by Congress and President Clinton in 1993, AmeriCorps is often called "the domestic Peace Corps." Indeed, in creating AmeriCorps, we often turned to the experience of the Peace Corps for guidance. The Peace Corps set a precedent for government playing a vital role in creating opportunities for citizens to serve—in local community programs under local leadership.

The secret to American success has always been Americans' belief that they can change things, make things better, solve our most serious problems by working together. Through the Peace Corps, we are spreading that spirit around the world. Through AmeriCorps, we are renewing that spirit here at home. As we enter a new century full of challenges, we must do everything we can to keep that spirit going and growing.

Want to help others while experiencing an unforgettable opportunity for personal and professional growth? Serve in the **Peace Corps.** Call 800-424-8580, or visit www.peacecorps.gov.

V

GLOBAL VILLAGE

t was Marshall McLuhan who first predicted that we would all one day live in a "global village." As we learn more about our neighbors in foreign lands, we become fascinated with them—and they with us. Is it their rich culture, lively music and dancing, exotic foods and colorful festivals? Is it our comfy lifestyle, our fast foods and action-packed movies, modern conveniences and money-making schemes? Or is it our shared sense of humanity, our desire to learn from one another and welcome the other into our worlds?

We hear mostly about the bad news in our global village: terrorism, war, political turmoil, and environmental disaster. This can overwhelm us, leading to "compassion fatigue" and doubt that we can effectively manage this complex world of ours. Sometimes we wonder how we can help people in other countries when we have so many problems to deal with at home. After September 11 we realized that, like it or not, the problems of the rest of the world are ours, too.

Average Americans reached outside themselves to help rehabilitate the global village. We are working with nations around the world to stop terrorism. We are learning to balance this powerful urge with the delicate process of protecting our civil liberties and preserving our precious democracy. The next step is to work with all nations to build a global economy that includes less well developed countries and redistributes wealth to the impoverished people around the world. For, while developed countries receive 80 percent of the world's income and use 50 percent of the world's oil and gas (up from 20 percent in 1975), half of the world lives on less than two dollars a day. If we want to root out terrorism in the global village, we must bring peace, health, and opportunity to people crying out in Afghanistan, the Middle East, and other countries around the world.

"Our security initiative includes military as well as human and ecological security," says Marietta Goco, director of the Sambayanihan Foundation. Working with the largest coalition of NGOs (local grassroots community organizations) in the world, she explains, "If we are to be successful, the heart of our antiterrorism strategy must be an antipoverty program—so people can meet their basic human needs—and have hope for their future."

This section of the book offers an "advanced course" of *Stone Soup for the World*—how to convince those in this country who doubt it's possible to change an entire nation and global relations. "While governments sign peace treaties, ordinary citizens still have to overcome their fears and prejudices in order to build a peace that endures," says Father Bruno Hussar, a Jew born in the Muslim land of Egypt and founder of Neve Shalom / Wahat al-Salam, a village in the Middle East where Jewish and Palestinian families live side by side, working together in harmony.

The stories in this chapter also show the positive impact new immigrants are making in America. Most of them have a Stone Soup story to tell—how each generation gives to the next, preserving family unity and creating a strong sense of community. We see how their giving inspired other Americans to join with them and pay more attention to the problems in their countries of origin. From building schools for street children in Nicaragua to bringing dances for peace to refugee children in Bosnia, they rise above the horrors of war.

Some of the stories in this chapter tell how global heroes rekindle their traditions to encourage the dignity and action of their countrymen. Filipinos call their tradition of giving back *Bayanihan:* working together for the common good. In Japan, people speak of *kyosei* to describe a vision of living together in harmony and interdependence with the world. Children all over the world are told some version of the Stone Soup fable. First-grade teachers in America use the story to teach students to share with others. In the Philippines, the story *Sopas Na Bato* is legendary. (Instead of adding carrots, potatoes, and onions to their soup, they add rice, chicken, and jalapeño peppers!) In China, the Stone Soup story illustrates the power of changing our minds about what we think we can give. While their recipes may be a little different from ours, it's the same story of the magical power of community.

As you read these stories, you will discover how much we can learn from one another. They encourage careful thinking about the term "global village" and offer ideas for how we can bring about a new era of peace and prosperity everywhere in the world.

When you travel abroad, be sure to look for the hopeful stories and bring home the good news along with your postcards and memories. By taking the time to get to know one another and share our stories, we will bring out the best in each other and discover how to live together on one planet. Our children and grandchildren can then look forward to a more hopeful, safer future.

A LONG ROAD TO FREEDOM

Told by Nelson Mandela

Adapted from his book *Long Walk to Freedom*

I awoke on the day of my release after only a few hours' sleep at 4:30 A.M. February 11 was a cloudless, end-of-summer Cape Town day. I did a shortened version of my usual exercise regimen, washed, and ate breakfast. I then telephoned a number of people to come to the cottage to prepare for my release and work on my speech. As so often happens in life, the momentousness of an occasion is lost in the welter of a thousand details. My actual release time was set for 3:00 P.M.

By three-thirty, I began to get restless. I told the members of the reception committee that my people had been waiting for me for twenty-seven years and I did not want to keep them waiting any longer. Shortly before four o'clock, we left in a small motorcade. About a quarter of a mile in front of the gate, the car slowed to a stop, and I got out and began to walk toward the prison gate.

At first I could not really make out what was going on in front of us, but when I was within 150 feet or so, I saw a tremendous commotion and a great crowd of people: hundreds of photographers and television cameras and newspeople, as well as several thousand well-wishers. I was astounded and a little bit alarmed. I had truly not expected such a scene. At most, I had imagined that there would be several dozen people, mainly the warders and their families. But this proved to be only the beginning; I realized we had not thoroughly prepared for all that was about to happen.

Within twenty feet or so of the gate, the cameras started clicking, a noise that sounded like some great herd of metallic beasts. Reporters started shouting questions. Television crews began crowding in. ANC supporters were yelling and cheering. It was a happy, if slightly disorienting, chaos. When a television crew thrust a long, dark, furry object at me, I recoiled slightly, wondering if it was some new-fangled weapon developed while I was in prison. Winnie informed me that it was a microphone.

When I was among the crowd, I raised my right fist and there was a roar. I had not been able to do that for twenty-seven years, and it gave me a surge of strength and joy. I felt—even at the age of seventy-one—that my life was beginning anew. My ten thousand days of imprisonment were over.

At my first speech, at a rally at the Grand Parade in Cape Town, I spoke from the heart. I wanted first of all to tell the people that I was not a messiah, but an ordinary man who had become a leader because of extraordinary circumstances.

> Friends, comrades, and fellow South Africans. I greet you all in the name of peace, democracy, and freedom for all! I stand here before you not as a prophet but as a humble servant of you, the people. Your tireless and heroic sacrifices have made it possible for me to be here today. I therefore place the remaining years of my life in your hands.

It was my desire for the freedom of my people to live their lives with dignity and self-respect that animated my life, that transformed a frightened young man into a bold one, that drove a law-abiding attorney to become a criminal, that turned a family-loving husband into a man without a home, that forced a life-loving man to live like a monk.

It is from my comrades in the struggle that I learned the meaning of courage. Time and again I have seen men and women risk and give their lives for an idea. I have seen men stand up to attacks and torture without breaking, showing a strength and resiliency that defies the imagination. I learned that courage was not the absence of fear, but the triumph over it. I felt fear myself more times than I can remember, but I hid it behind a mask of boldness. The brave man is not he who does not feel afraid, but he who conquers that fear.

To survive in prison, I developed ways to find satisfaction in my daily life. One can feel fulfilled by washing one's clothes so they are really clean, by sweeping a hallway so that it is empty of dust, by organizing one's cell to conserve as much space as possible. The same pride one takes in consequential tasks outside of prison, one can find doing small things.

While I have always enjoyed gardening, it was not until I was behind bars that I was able to tend my own garden. A garden was one of the few things in prison that one could control. To plant a seed, watch it grow, to tend it and then harvest it, offered a simple but enduring satisfaction. The sense of being the custodian for this small patch of earth offered a small taste of freedom.

In some ways I saw the garden as a metaphor for certain aspects of my life. A leader must also tend his garden; he, too, plants seeds and then watches, cultivates, and harvests the result. Like a gardener, he must take responsibility for what he cultivates; he must mind his work, try to repel enemies, preserve what can be preserved, and eliminate what cannot succeed.

The authorities supplied me with seeds. I initially planted tomatoes, chilies, and onions—hardy plants that did not require rich earth or constant care. The early harvests were poor, but they soon improved. I coaxed a particularly beautiful tomato plant from a tender seedling to a robust plant that produced deep red fruit. Once the garden began to flourish, I often provided the warders with some of my best tomatoes and onions.

I always knew that deep down in every human heart, there is mercy and generosity. No one is born hating another person because of the color of his skin, or his background or his religion. People must learn to hate, and if they can learn to hate, they can be taught to love, for love comes more naturally to the human heart than its opposite. Even in the grimmest times in prison, when my comrades and I were pushed to our limits, I would see a glimmer of humanity in one of the guards, perhaps just for a second, but it was enough to reassure me and keep me going. Man's goodness is a flame that can be hidden but never extinguished.

I have walked that long road to freedom. I have tried not to falter; I have made missteps along the way. But I have discovered the secret that after climbing a great hill, one only finds that there are many more hills to climb. I have taken a moment here to rest, to steal a view of the glorious vista that surrounds me, to look back on the distance I have come. But I can rest only for a moment, for with freedom comes responsibilities, and I dare not linger, for my long walk is not yet ended.

> *Freedom is indivisible; the chains on any one of my people were the chains on all of them, the chains on all of them, were the chains on me.*

NELSON MANDELA

Help build a strong, free South Africa. To invest in South Africa's democratic and equitable development, visit **Shared Interest** at www.shared interest.org. To work with **The Africa Fund** visit www.theafricafund.org.

THE COURAGE TO CARE

Told by Allan Luks

Adapted from the book *The Healing Power of Doing Good,*
by Allan Luks with Peggy Payne

"Please, may I come in?" asked the woman at the door. It was dark and she was frightened. Magda Trocme opened the door. "Come in," she said. Later she admitted, "I did not know it would be dangerous. Nobody thought of that."

The woman at the door was *Juif*—a German Jew. She had come to this village in the mountains of France to hide until the Nazi regime was over.

André Trocme, a Protestant minister, and his wife, Magda, wanted to help. "Will you hide the Jews?" André had been asked. "Is your village prepared to do that?" He had gone to the town church council, and in minutes they had agreed. Now they were tested. A German Jew was at the door seeking shelter.

Le Chambon-sur-Lignon sits on a plateau surrounded by the high mountains of south central France. During World War II and the German occupation, the community of Le Chambon made a collective decision to hide Jews who were fleeing Hitler's wrath. They refused to identify their Jewish neighbors and instead created a haven for Jewish children and families from all over the world. Not one refugee was turned in or turned away. In the end, five thousand Jews found shelter there, a number equal to the native population of the town.

In Le Chambon, Jewish children went to school with Gentiles. They played together, sometimes with a pig that they called Adolf. At night the Jewish children hid and slept in the barns and stables of farms around the town. In the morning they emerged from their hiding places to go to school. A young village boy gave the signal to let Jewish children know when the road was safe. When the shutters to his room were open, the road was open. When the shutters to his room were closed, they were to return to their hiding places.

Over and over the residents of Le Chambon were pressured to turn in the Jews, and each time they refused to cooperate with the Nazis and the occupation government. As a pacifist, André Trocme urged his parishioners and neighbors to resist violence with "weapons of the spirit." When asked to list the names of Jews in hiding, he refused, declaring, "The Jews are my brothers." He was imprisoned for his strong convictions. When the police came to take him away, Magda invited the gendarmes to sit and eat while she packed her husband's suitcase. To offer them such a kindness was nothing extraordinary, according to her. "There we were, and it was time to eat. . . . It was nothing at all."

Years after the war was over, film director Pierre Sauvage came to Le Chambon to learn more about this story. Sauvage had his own reasons for this visit: "It was in Chambon that I was born, in March 1944, a Jewish baby," he says. "I was very lucky to see the light of day in a place that was committed to my survival, at the very time when much of my family was disappearing into the abyss." Sauvage interviewed the aging survivors of World War II for his documentary *Weapons of the Spirit,* to discover why the citizens had acted as they did. What had given them the courage to care and to risk their own lives to save these Jews?

Many of the villagers were Huguenots, French Protestants whose ancestors had been persecuted by the Catholic kings of France. The stories they'd heard all their lives of what their forebears had been through helped prepare them to take a courageous stand. When the time came, they were eager to help others who were being persecuted. When many other congregations across Europe had closed their eyes to what was occurring around them, the people of this church understood the word of God to mean that they should help their brothers, the Jews. And all the townspeople, many of whom were not Huguenots, embraced their heroic example.

Sauvage asked the question again and again and often got the same response—a slight shrug of the shoulders and these simple words of explanation: "It was the right thing to do."

To learn more about Le Chambon-sur-Lignon, see Pierre Sauvage's movie *Weapons of the Spirit.* To order, visit www.chambon.org/weapons.htm.

THE OASIS OF PEACE

Told by Nina Mermey Klippel and Sharon Burde

In the heart of a land known for conflict and violence, there endures a symbol of hope. Its name is its message. In Hebrew, it is Neve Shalom. In Arabic, it is Wahat al-Salam. In English, it is the Oasis of Peace.

Located halfway between Jerusalem and Tel Aviv, the Oasis of Peace is a haven for Palestinians and Jews who choose to live and work together, in peace. Only fifty families currently live there, limited by land, and another three hundred families wait on a list until there's room, to live in this bilingual, bicultural village, but the model of coexistence inspires people everywhere.

For generations, Jews and Arabs have struggled over the biblical land of Palestine. For Jews, it is their Promised Land. For Arabs, it is the home where they have dwelt for centuries.

After World War II, thousands of Holocaust survivors arrived in Israel with hopes of a more peaceful future, but the Palestinians resisted this massive immigration into their homeland. When the Jews asked the United Nations to recognize the state of Israel, bitter fighting erupted, and a tragic cycle of violence took hold. Today the people of this land live with a fragile commitment to peace, and the fear of a continuing legacy of violence.

Against this backdrop, Neve Shalom / Wahat al-Salam is a miracle. Throughout most of Israel, Arabs and Jews live completely apart—separated by community, language, culture, and schools. But, in this unique village, Jewish and Palestinian families live and work side by side, sharing their gardens and their homes. Since both Hebrew and Arabic are taught in school, children at play call out to each other in both languages.

Neve Shalom / Wahat al-Salam started as the vision of one very gentle man with an unusual heritage. Father Bruno Hussar was born a Jew in the Muslim land of Egypt. He converted to Catholicism, became a monk, and devoted his life to building understanding among Christians, Jews, and Muslims. After working with organizations like the Vatican and the United Nations, Father Bruno wanted to make his dream of peace become reality for ordinary people.

He pictured a village where Muslims, Jews, and Christians would live together in peace, where their very diversity would be a source of enrichment rather than dissension. Living together, they would learn to break down the barriers of fear and ignorance and build bridges of trust, respect, and understanding.

Father Bruno obtained, from the abbot of the monastery at Latrun, a ninety-nine-year lease on a plot of land, a stony, brambled hillside without water or shade. It was hardly an oasis, but for him it was the Garden of Eden. He was sixty years old when he and a few friends took up residence in this desolate place, living at first in empty packing cases. Word of this extraordinary new community spread, and, gradually, a few pioneering Jewish and Arab families came and built houses. In 1972, Neve Shalom / Wahat al-Salam was born.

The soul of the village, the School for Peace, is a magnet for peace-seeking Jews, Palestinians, and others from all over the world, one of whom was an Arab boy named Ahmad Hijazi. This young Palestinian grew up in an Arab village in northern Israel. When he was sixteen, his class came to a School for Peace workshop. For the first time, he met Jewish students face-to-face in a safe, supportive environment and witnessed their Arab and Jewish teachers cooperating.

In the workshop, the young people, led by skilled facilitators, got to know each other. They talked, argued, and, in the end, told each other honestly of the mutual distrust, fear, and anger they bore. Many cried, remembering friends or family members who had been killed or injured by one side or the other. "As we envisioned steps to a more peaceful future," says Ahmad, "we saw each other with new eyes, as human beings. For the first time in our lives, we could see that peace was possible."

The experience changed Ahmad's life. After going to university, he moved to the village and joined the staff of the School for Peace. Today he is the general secretary of the village, a job similar to that of mayor, which rotates between Jewish and Palestinian citizens. He and his Jewish colleagues travel to the United States, Europe, and Japan to share their dream for peace. "Although governments sign peace treaties, ordinary citizens still have to learn to overcome their fear and prejudices in order to build a peace that endures," Ahmad says.

Since its founding in 1979, the School for Peace has trained more than twenty thousand young people in the ways of peace—Jews, Arabs, and even inner-city youth from America. Teachers from the School for Peace also serve as ambassadors, sharing their training in Northern Ireland, the barrios of Los Angeles, and other troubled places. They hope to spread their message of tolerance, mutual respect, and understanding to all war-torn areas.

Today the village has a long waiting list of families who want to move in. Children from nearby towns as well as from the village attend the primary school, the only comprehensive Arabic/Hebrew bilingual school in Israel, which has become a model for other schools in the country.

Neve Shalom / Wahat al-Salam has been nominated five times for the Nobel Peace Prize. It has been honored with prestigious awards in Italy, Japan, Germany, Austria, Sweden, and the United States. The great humanitarian Elie Wiesel said, "Neve Shalom / Wahat al-Salam deserves our warmest support. . . . For it justifies our highest hopes." The late Palestinian leader Faisal al Husseini said, "I would like to see the moment when there would be such a thing as Neve Shalom / Wahat al-Salam not only between the Palestinians and Israelis, but between all the people in the Middle East."

Father Bruno, who died recently at age eighty-four, lived to see his Oasis of Peace nourish people throughout the world. He once said, "I have just sown the seeds; others have cultivated the plants." In the village, a new crop is sprouting: The Jewish and Arab children who are growing up in Neve Shalom / Wahat al-Salam share their languages and cultures and, most important of all, a commitment to peace. With young people like these to lead the way through the twenty-first century, is it too much to hope that the Middle East itself might one day become an Oasis of Peace?

Raise your voice for tolerance and democracy in the Middle East. Become a partner for peace by contacting the **American Friends of Neve Shalom / Wahat Al-Salam,** 212-226-9246, afnswas@oasisofpeace.org, or visit www.oasisofpeace. org.

HUNGER CAN'T WAIT!

Told by Peter Mann

Herbert de Souza spoke the truth when he told his fellow Brazilians, "If we want a democratic country, we must fight poverty." Known affectionately as Betinho by his countrymen, de Souza is a frail, sixty-year-old man with gray, wavy hair and deep, luminous green eyes, and one of three brothers, all hemophiliacs who contracted the HIV virus from blood transfusions. Betinho's brothers have already died of AIDS. Betinho is often very sick from the disease, but he is a man with a cause, and the urgency of his cause keeps him going. "Hunger is in a hurry," he says. "Hunger cannot wait!"

Over the years, Brazil has become a land of paradox. Its people live in one of two worlds: a life of luxury, or one of misery. Rich in agriculture, Brazil is one of the world's largest food exporters. Nevertheless, 32 million of its people, more than one-fifth of the country, go hungry every day. Until recently, instead of dealing with the social apartheid that spread like a disease throughout their country, wealthy people armed themselves and closed their hearts to the desperate plight of their fellow countrymen.

But in 1993, through mass demonstrations, Brazilians forced a powerful, corrupt president to resign. Encouraged by their success, they were ready for Betinho's challenge. "In the past we've tolerated poverty and misery," he said. "We've tried to explain it away. But now we must fight against it—and make this a priority."

Betinho invited people to use their new democratic freedom to discover their personal power to break the cycle of poverty. He created Citizen Action: A Campaign Against Hunger and encouraged people to organize locally to fight hunger in their communities. "We'll help you, but we won't tell you what to do," he told them. The response was tremendous. All over the country, committees formed to build bridges between the wealthy and the poor.

In Rio de Janeiro, seven thousand cyclists "pedaled against hunger" and collected sixteen tons of food. In São Paolo, middle-class citizens joined their shantytown neighbors to organize food-distribution networks in the slums. The comfortable learned where the hungry were, where the food was, and how to get it to the hungry. Most of all, they got to know hungry people personally. When one committee discovered that twelve thousand of the 100,000 people in its jurisdiction were destitute, they had food and clothing donated. Wealthier families "adopted" poor families, helping them to deal with their specific problems. "We are replacing the map of hunger with the map of solidarity," Betinho says. "Poverty now has a human face."

The impact of Citizen Action has been phenomenal. Today, 3 million people are involved in campaign committees, and 30 million more support the campaign. Everyone gives what they can. The Small Farmers Union in São Paolo created a "green belt" to grow food for the hungry. Workers at one company started by donating their monthly meal vouchers to buy food for five hundred poor children at a nearby school. Then they offered training courses to help their parents get jobs. Companies with industrial kitchens created Project Our Soup, giving thirty thousand people soup each day. For many, it is their only meal. Even prisoners at a tough jail contributed to the cause by going without one meal each week. In solidarity with their poor countrymen on the outside, they sent them rice, beans, flour, and cooking oil.

The campaign crosses all social and political lines, uniting and empowering people. For the first time, instead of waiting for their political party, union, or church to do something, people are taking action as citizens, for themselves and their fellow citizens. "The committees did more than just give food to people," Betinho said. "They started breaking the cycle of poverty—by providing housing and sanitation, by educating the children and helping the elderly."

As the program takes hold, people eventually discover the connection between feeding the hungry and helping hungry people to become self-reliant. "After the first year, we realized we couldn't continue to give food away indefinitely," Betinho said. "With the slogan 'Food Against Hunger, Jobs Against Misery,' local committees responded with much-needed jobs. They created entrepreneurial projects such as bakeries, small vegetable gardens, and paper-recycling ventures. This way even the poorest people can experience their own power and dignity— and then give back to the community." Grateful for her new skills as a flower arranger, Maria, one of the poor women who has benefited from the program, is now teaching other women how to create a livelihood for themselves.

In Brazil, giant institutions like banks and the military are teaming with the government, the media, and the local committees to help get food to those in need. From the beginning, Betinho knew that the media were key to the campaign. He often appears on television. When a major São Paolo newspaper decided to back the campaign, hundreds of committees sprang up throughout the city. One television station wove the hunger campaign into the story line of a popular soap opera. PR agencies pooled their efforts to donate advertising, creating commercials that show Brazil's "two worlds." One of them, shot in stark black and white, shows a luxury car stopped at a traffic light on a busy Rio street. An elegantly dressed man looks straight ahead. Then he glances to his side and quickly pushes a button to close the car window. As the glass rises, you see the reflection of a child, begging, an empty dish in hand. The child keeps looking, hoping, but the man doesn't look back. He waits for the light to change, then drives away. No words are spoken; there is just a closing caption: "Hunger doesn't just isolate the hungry—you are a prisoner of poverty, too."

Betinho died in 1999, but his work isn't done. In areas where the campaign committees applied themselves, they've reduced hunger by as much as one-third. As for the 3 million campaign workers, through this work many of them have changed forever.

People talk of Betinho—with his tremendous inner strength and positive energy—as if he were a saint. Certainly, he was full of life and hope for the future, and yet in his typically cooperative spirit, he credited the people of Brazil: "This period will be remembered as the era when citizenship was awakened."

This nation is looking for a vision.
We had "manifest destiny."
We built the railroads, industry, won two world wars.
We're looking for something grand and good to do.
Feeding the world could be that thing.

HARRY CHAPIN, FOUNDER OF WORLD HUNGER YEAR

Learn how you can work with others to fight hunger in your community. Phone **World Hunger Year** at 800-5-HUNGRY, or visit their Web site, www.world hungeryear.org.

ADAGIO IN SARAJEVO

Told by Richard Deats

Adapted from "Adagio in Sarajevo" in *Fellowship,*
the Magazine of the Fellowship of Reconciliation

What a difference a few years can make. It's hard to believe that not too long ago, the world looked to Sarajevo as a model of religious and ethnic harmony. In 1984, when athletes came to this exquisite city to compete in the Winter Olympic games, people marveled that here Orthodox Serbian and Muslim, Catholic and Jew lived and worked side by side peacefully in a unique atmosphere of tolerance and goodwill. The ancient city of Sarajevo, with over half a million people, was for centuries a cultural haven for Croats, Serbs, and Muslims.

How could it all have changed so quickly? By 1990, Yugoslavia was disintegrating into rival ethnic states, and Sarajevo, the jewel of Bosnia, was surrounded in a siege that was slowly destroying the city. Civil war engulfed the region; its people were subjected to regular shellings and unpredictable sniper fire. Food and supplies were scarce at best.

Waiting hours on the street for a single loaf of bread became a regular routine. One day in May 1992, a long line at a Sarajevo bakery stretched outside and snaked down the block. As the people waited they spoke about the war, about hunger, about their children trapped at home, too afraid to go to school. At four o'clock in the afternoon, their conversations ended abruptly. A shell exploded directly in the middle of the line, killing twenty-two people and wounding more than one hundred.

The world was shocked, and the grief of the victims' families overwhelming. Still, people needed to eat. So the next day the bakery once again opened its doors. As four o'clock approached, people in line became tense and silent. But instead of another shell, they were surprised to be "hit" by the sounds of music. Vedran Smailovic, the principal cellist of the Sarajevo Opera, arrived at the bakery at exactly four, carrying a chair and his cello. Dressed in a formal black suit and white tie, Smailovic played the majestic yet sorrowful lines of Albinoni's *Adagio,* and the music fed the people's souls. Every day for twenty-two days he came at the same time and played again, one performance for each person killed in the attack. With his music, he honored those who had died there, affirming the indomitable spirit of life even in the midst of death. He also set into motion around the world a series of musical and artistic homages to those victims.

The place of the Breadline Massacre has become a shrine, marked by wreaths, candles, and pieces of paper holding the names of the victims who died there. Not far from where the bread line was hit is a ruined city square, remembered for being a place where a Muslim mosque, a Roman Catholic cathedral, and an Orthodox church once stood. In April 1993, Joan Baez was the first major artist to visit Sarajevo since the siege began. With Smailovic accompanying her on the cello, she sang "Amazing Grace."

How do people respond to unspeakable acts of violence? Monks pray, workers strike, and artists raise awareness by doing what they do best. Half a world away, Seattle sculptor Beliz Brother heard the story of Vedran Smailovic and created her own memorial to the massacre. On a street corner in Seattle, she built a ten-foot-high stack of bread pans, with twenty-two loaves scattered about. In front of this she placed a cello case, looking eerily like a coffin, and covered it with flour and pieces of mortar. Symbolically, her sculpture depicted "the white-out of ethnic cleansing."

In solidarity with Smailovic, Brother also arranged for Seattle cellists dressed in formal attire to perform the *Adagio* at twenty-two sites around the city. Their only props were baskets of bread and bouquets of flowers. She repeated the gesture for the 1993 inauguration of President Clinton, persuading twenty-two cellists to perform the Albinoni piece at various places around Washington, D.C. The *Adagio* cried out from federal buildings to sites of terrorist acts, from city squares to the White House, and in the midst of the inaugural festivities, the siege of an Olympic city was not forgotten.

In April 1994, cellists gathered at the International Cello Festival in Manchester, England, to hear the renowned cellist Yo-Yo Ma perform *The Cellist of Sarajevo*, a piece for unaccompanied cello written by the English composer David Wilde. When he had finished, listeners sat in stunned silence as he walked into the audience and embraced a man with long, wild hair and a huge mustache, who wore a stained and tattered leather motorcycle jacket. The man's face was old beyond his years, creased with pain and suffering. Then the audience recognized Vedran Smailovic—the cellist of Sarajevo himself!

They rose as one, in a wave of emotional release: clapping, weeping, shouting, embracing, and cheering. And in the center of it all stood those two men, embracing each other, both crying freely: Yo-Yo Ma, the suave, elegant prince of classical music worldwide, flawless in appearance and performance, and Vedran Smailovic, who had just escaped from Sarajevo, disheveled and defiant, who, with his music, had defied death itself, inspiring many to resist despair and celebrate love, life, and that spark of human spirit that can never be put out.

In 1995, to commemorate the thousandth day of the siege of Sarajevo, Smailovic performed at the Statue of Liberty, to remind the world that we should not rest until peace has come again.

To work for a world of peace and understanding, contact **Fellowship of Reconciliation,** at www.forusa.org.

AWAKENING

Told by Patrick Mendis

A. T. Ariyaratne stood before a group of villagers in Sri Lanka. They were in despair: Their irrigation system was in shambles, and the government had ignored their pleas for help. For years they had gone without enough water for their animals, their crops, and their children. Now they could wait no longer. Their village was dying, and they needed a miracle.

Ari knew that only by working together could they create one. He asked the villagers a few simple questions. "Who can feed one person by sharing his meal with another?" One by one, several hands went up. "Who can feed two, three, or four?" A few more hands went up. Gathering materials in the same way, Ari organized a work camp for the villagers to repair their own water system, save their village, and begin to make history.

In 1958, Ari had the idea of bringing his upper-caste high-school students to remote poverty-stricken villages to help rebuild them. For two weeks these privileged young people lived and worked side by side with people of the lower caste. They learned practical skills while developing compassion for their fellow countrymen and acquiring a broader perspective of the world—two weeks that made a lasting impression on both the students and the villagers.

From these *shramadanas* or work camps, Ari began a national movement, first mobilizing individuals, then local communities, then the world. He wove Gandhian and Buddhist principles together to create a powerful volunteer service and grassroots human development organization. The *shramadanas* were to be "gifts of labor"; the movement he called *Sarvodaya*, a term Gandhi used for "awakening of all."

As a child growing up in a tiny Sri Lankan village, Patrick Mendis had heard stories about this small man with a large spirit. By 1972, everyone in every village in Sri Lanka knew about the good works of the *Sarvodaya*. Since the government was ignoring the needs of small villages, the *Sarvodaya* was the only hope for the "little people" of Sri Lanka. Patrick says, "When we heard that the *Sarvodaya* was coming to our small village in Polonnaruwa, we were ecstatic! It was like Santa Claus was coming home. We'd ask ourselves, 'Is it really going to happen in *our* village?' It gave us hope, because we knew now things would get changed for the better."

Patrick was only twelve years old, one of the youngest of thirty young boys who participated in a one-day *shramadana*. Since he had been left by his parents as an infant and raised by his grandparents, he'd always felt like an outsider. Here he was the only Christian in a group of Buddhists. To his surprise, they welcomed him warmly. "Everyone called each other *mali* or 'brother,' not by the names," he says. "We lived as brothers in one big family. We shared and treated each other as equals."

Those thirty youngsters spent one whole day together planting gardens, digging latrines, connecting the village's road to the main highway. "We didn't have a plan, a design, or a blueprint," Patrick says. "After we talked about our ideas and what we'd like to see in our village, a leader emerged from among us, and we worked together until we got it right. We started the day with a Buddhist chant—a loving-kindness meditation—and finished with a meal. From early morning until late at night, everyone worked together to improve life in the village. At the end of the day, everyone was jubilant," Patrick says. "We'd built more than roads, we had built a family, a community, and a new sense of spirit in our village."

Patrick's own inner awakening started connecting him to the larger "family of man." The seeds planted that day left an indelible mark on his soul.

A few years later, on scholarship, Patrick left Sri Lanka for the United States. He was fortunate to study at the best American universities, learn from great teachers, work at the best organizations and companies, and receive many honors and awards. He became an accomplished researcher and teacher of international development and foreign affairs. He had a wonderful wife, two beautiful children, and a good life in Minnesota, but in the back of his mind, he kept thinking about that special day from his childhood.

One day he started writing about the *Sarvodaya* and couldn't stop. "What is happening to me?" he wondered. There were other books he was supposed to be writing, but memories of his experience with the *shramadana* just kept coming back to him and wouldn't let go. He published articles, then a book, about it. Finally he decided it was time to write to Ari and reintroduce himself.

By 1995 the *Sarvodaya* had become the world's largest volunteer movement. More than 7 million people, almost half of Sri Lanka's population, were working together to improve over eleven thousand villages throughout the country. They had one hundred coordinating centers, each serving the needs of twenty to thirty villages, implementing programs in education, health care, transportation, agriculture, and technologically appropriate energies like windmills and methane generators. In one year, *Sarvodaya* built three times as many roads as the government had, linking many underdeveloped villages for the first time with the outside world.

Ari was pleased to hear from Patrick and invited him to come home for a visit, as his guest. It would be Patrick's first visit to Sri Lanka in over twenty-five years. He was a bit nervous and very curious. "When I arrived at Ari's house, he bowed his head to me," Patrick said. "I was shocked. I thought I should be bowing to him. Then Ari put his hands together and called me *Mali*, or brother, and told me to call him *Ayya*, or big brother." "This is our home—it is always open to you," Ari told Patrick. "Here, we are one family." Patrick felt that same wonderful connection that he had when he was a twelve-year-old poor village boy.

One day Ari asked Patrick to join him at a *Sarvodaya* family gathering. There people would talk about their village's problems and share their ideas about how to make things better. When they arrived, Patrick was invited to come up to the podium. When he was introduced, he was nervous—and embarrassed. He hadn't spoken his native Sinhalese for many years. "You can speak any language you want," he was told. "We will translate."

"This is our guest, Dr. Patrick Mendis from the United States," Ari told the people who were gathered. "He is from Polonnaruwa. A long time ago he worked in the *Sarvodaya*." As Patrick stood to address them, he told the expectant crowd, "I really came to learn from you." He told them of his experience as a young boy at the *shramadana* and how his life had been changed by one very special day. "*Sarvodaya* awakens young people like you and me, who then awaken their families, their communities, and then the entire world," he said. "But the awakening must start first with each of us."

Everyone loved hearing Patrick speak, even though he mixed up the two languages. Some wanted to shake his hand. Others wanted to know how he got to America. "They thought I was a big shot," Patrick says. "They wondered how I could end up in the United States, coming from a tiny village in Sri Lanka. They wanted to know my secret."

Patrick told the villagers that the secret was there for them, right in their own soul and in their own village. And that coming to America wasn't the key to happiness. Smiling, he reminded them of the *Sarvodaya*, saying, "We build the road and the road builds us."

The time has come when science, technology and spiritual wisdom have to be synthesized on an international scale to build a nobler, more just and peaceful global community.

GANDHI

If you would like to create an awakening in your life, experience a *shramadana* work camp at the **Sarvodaya** in Sri Lanka. Visit *Sarvodaya* at www.sarvodaya.org; or e-mail Dr. A. T. Ariyaratne at arisar@sri.lanka.net or Dr. Richard P. Vlosky, Executive Director of Sarvodaya USA, 7934 Boone Drive, Baton Rouge, LA 70808. Phone/Fax: 225-761-0181; e-mail vlosky@lsu.edu.

TURNING LEFTOVERS INTO LIFESAVERS

Told by Carrie Caton Pillsbury

After twenty years in America, Mohamed Ahmed couldn't believe his eyes. With the violent overthrow of Ethiopia's King Haile Selassie, the military had taken over everyone's land in this stunned country. Ethiopians lost their incentive to work, production bottomed out, and starvation was epidemic. Independent businessmen like Mohamed's father, who owned a small salt factory, were labeled enemies of the state, and many were imprisoned.

In the midst of this nightmare, Mohamed's father died. One morning he awoke with acute, inexplicable pain and was rushed to the Dessie Regional Hospital, where poverty had wiped out any available medicine or supplies. Here, Ethiopian physicians were attempting to treat 100,000 refugees with nothing but tongue depressors and stethoscopes. The doctors had to send Mr. Ahmed's diagnostic tests via bus along dusty, one-lane paths to Addis Ababa, more than 250 miles away. The letter revealing his fatal diagnosis of bone cancer finally arrived back in Wollo, Mohamed's home village—ten days after his burial.

As Mohamed stood over his father's grave, he remembered the Ethiopia he had left twenty years ago. His plan then had been to get an education in the United States and return home to teach young Ethiopians at their only university. But he had soon realized that his dream was not to be. His future students were busy waging war against the dictators who wreaked havoc on his homeland. Now, beside his father's grave, Mohamed wept—for the father he had loved, for the country he had all but lost, for his dying people who could not be saved at hospitals bereft of the tools of healing.

The doctors had told his family, "We are in Ethiopia—there is nothing we could do for him." But Mohamed Ahmed didn't like feeling helpless, and in that moment he swore to do everything in his power to see that no Ethiopian family would ever have to hear those words again.

Returning to America to hunt for resources, Mohamed contacted close friends and fellow Ethiopians in his adopted home of Dallas to enlist their aid. But he quickly realized that galvanizing the forces needed to save his faraway village was more than a one-man job.

He remembered reading an article in the *Dallas Morning News* about a group of people committed to improving health care in developing countries and soon found his way to the doorstep of MEDISEND. This Dallas nonprofit organization aimed to transform America's medical surplus into lifesaving supplies for third-world countries. Mohamed was most definitely in the right place at the right time.

At MEDISEND Mohamed met Dr. Martin Lazar, a neurosurgeon who, in 1987, had witnessed firsthand the abysmal conditions of health-care facilities in developing countries. Dr. Lazar also knew firsthand of the excessive waste in American hospitals, where strict safety standards forced throwing away untouched packets of cotton gauze exposed only to air; where expensive, but outdated, orthopedic supplies—$6.5 billion worth of perfectly usable medical materials—were needlessly dumped into American landfills each year.

Dr. Lazar knew that a once life-giving heart-lung machine now gathering dust in a Texas hospital storage room could be refurbished and shipped to a hospital in Africa, Eastern Europe, or Asia to save many more lives. He also knew that rubber gloves, unused and discarded during a surgical procedure in a Washington, D.C., hospital could be resterilized and used for as many as ten operations in other countries. In 1990, Dr. Lazar founded MEDISEND to "turn leftovers into lifesavers" and become "a lifesaving force for our neighbors throughout the world."

Mohamed Ahmed and Dr. Lazar shared a common dream—extending medical care and hope to lands of poverty. They worked together to make that dream reality for the hospital in Mohamed's village. Soon the supplies that could not be used in America were being shipped to Ethiopia. "The supplies and equipment MEDISEND sent made the difference between having nothing and having a lot," says Mohamed. "They gave our hospital the chance to survive and serve its community."

It was one more humanitarian and environmental success story for MEDISEND. To date, the organization has shipped four hundred tons of medical supplies and equipment, valued at more than $7.5 million, to over 350 hospitals in sixty-seven developing countries. The value of the human lives these shipments have saved is incalculable.

As Mohamed recovered from grieving for his father, he started a family of his own, and having experienced the profound fulfillment of reaching out to others, he made sure to pass generosity and compassion on to his children. A quarter of a century after the death of the grandfather they never knew, Mohamed's twelve-year-old daughter, Sophie, and eight-year-old son, Amir, showed that they got the message. They saved their allowances and birthday gifts and donated their combined life savings of $515 to MEDISEND, explaining that they wanted to help more poor people get medical attention.

The overworked doctor or nurse in Ethiopia who opens that new parcel of post-op products with a note that reads "From Sophie and Amir with love" might not know the story of how the whole thing started. But surely they will see that love bears miracles, and maybe this will give them hope as they work to make their beloved homeland the healthy place it once was.

You start with one step and it's amazing how wonderful people will rise to the occasion.

MARTIN LAZAR

If you want to help MEDISEND "turn leftovers into life savers" and identify new sources of usable medical surplus or be part of the MEDISEND distribution channel, visit their Web site, medisendinternational.org.

STEP BY STEP
Told by Gil Friend

Karl-Henrik Robert, a Swedish doctor specializing in pediatric medicine, was tired of seeing children die of cancer. Like many of his colleagues, he had developed a certain professional detachment from the daily agony of watching young children waste away. But one day, when yet another young girl died of leukemia, something in him snapped.

"Why are so many little ones dying this way?" he wanted to know. Most of his patients were far too young to have developed the type of at-risk lifestyle often associated with cancer. There was growing evidence in the medical community about the role of the environment in disease, and as a medical researcher of some note, he had heard the endless scientific and political bantering: Was this substance the main culprit, or that one? How many parts per billion of this toxin or that were "acceptable"? Dr. Robert became impatient with the debate and decided to *do* something about it.

"Much of the debate over the environment," he later wrote, "has had the character of monkey chatter amid the withering leaves of a dying tree. In the midst of all this chatter, very few of us have been paying attention to the trunk and branches . . . if we heal the trunk and the branches, the benefits for the leaves will follow naturally."

Robert decided to study the trunk of the tree, the fundamental and inarguable principles underlying our environmental problems. He organized the basic facts and circulated a draft to leading scientists, inviting them to make corrections and add their ideas.

The scientists responded to his call. Dr. Robert revised the paper and recirculated it. Ultimately he repeated the cycle twenty-one times. He never argued for his point of view; he just asked, listened, and revised, until all the scientists agreed they had identified the trunk of the tree—and the healthy environment it would need in order to grow. They concluded that putting the laws of nature at the heart of our enterprise and into our daily lives was nonnegotiable for the sustainability of the planet.

Knowing about a problem is one thing; doing something about it is entirely different. Robert knew he must share the message in such a way that everyone in Sweden would want to get involved. He founded The Natural Step to provide ordinary people with the information they needed to help improve their country's environment.

In another creative leap, Dr. Robert approached Swedish television, asking, "If I had the participation of our leading musicians, actors, and business executives, would you broadcast an environmental message?" The answer was an enthusiastic yes. He then enrolled the country's most noted musicians and actors with a similar appeal: "If I had the television air time, and the support of leading businesses, would you appear on a show to help the environment?" Intrigued by the cause, they agreed. And so he approached business leaders and got them involved, too.

Together they created a television program that documented why every Swedish citizen was needed to help create a healthy environment. To show people how they could help, they developed a booklet and an audio tape—and mailed them to every household in the country. Step by step, the project has established itself nationally.

The Federation of Swedish Farmers took as its goal to grow the "world's cleanest agriculture." It is helping farmers to decrease their use of chemical fertilizers and pesticides and shift their production to organic farming. This shift is not only healthy, it is profitable: Sweden's agricultural exports have significantly increased.

Dozens of local governments have created ambitious environmental programs for their "eco-municipalities," forging agreements with residents, retailers, and manufacturers to help meet those goals. One town developed a plan to reduce the burden on municipal water-treatment systems. Residents of this town shop for cleaning products that generate less toxic waste, and retailers are encouraging their suppliers to come up with cleaner products. The result is a chain reaction of ecological activism, exactly what Dr. Robert wanted to inspire.

Dr. Robert has also inspired corporations to invest in redesigning their products with the environment in mind. The IKEA retail furniture chain now analyzes the environmental life cycle of all its products. It is also asking its suppliers to change their manufacturing processes and materials "to meet ecocyclical requirements." So that every employee can understand and contribute to changes and explain them to customers, the company's entire workforce is receiving basic environmental training, as are its suppliers.

By 1996, seven years after Dr. Robert began his effort, more than sixty major companies and fifty municipalities in Sweden had adopted The Natural Step as a guideline for improving the environment through their operations. The world's largest appliance manufacturer, Electrolux, didn't enter the game eagerly. One of its largest customers refused to sign a major contract, having concluded that Electrolux products did not meet the "system conditions" for sustainability. When Electrolux executives found out why they'd lost the account, company executives angrily demanded a meeting with Dr. Robert.

Dr. Robert patiently shared the basic science underlying TNS strategy. As good scientists and engineers, they had to admit that his nonnegotiable scientific principles were, well, nonnegotiable! From there they committed to aligning their company with the laws of nature.

Electrolux now designs household appliances, such as dishwashers, to conserve water and energy. Their annual report insists that Electrolux is not a "green" company; they say it is simply taking prudent steps to meet business goals and build shareholder value. The fact that those "prudent steps" serve environmental interests is beyond the imaginings of most environmental activists five years ago. Electrolux calls their billion-kroner investment in Natural Step initiatives one of the best financial investments they have ever made.

The Natural Step is simple, yet powerful. One man's idea has helped change an entire nation—by getting people to pay attention to what they can agree on, instead of how they disagree. Imagine what could happen if everyone in your community did the same. If we put the laws of nature into the heart of our enterprise and made them the business of our daily lives, we could build a healthier world for everyone to enjoy, naturally.

If the people lead, the leaders will follow.

Dwight Eisenhower

Learn more about how you can take the next step toward improving the environment in your community. Call **The Natural Step** at 415-332-9394, or visit their Web site, www.thenaturalstep.org.

PATHWAYS TO PEACE

Told by Masankho Banda

On September 11, 2001, Avon Mattison was at the United Nations, launching what was to be the first annual Culture of Peace Week. This same day, New York City became the site of the most horrific act of war ever inflicted on U.S. soil.

People were being evacuated from the UN and the surrounding area, but Avon decided to stay. She stood on the grounds of the United Nations, under the flags of all nations on the planet. On this perfectly clear day, she could hear the sounds of sirens and planes flying very low; she didn't know whether they were more attacks, or U.S. security forces protecting the city. Instead of fear, she felt an unearthly calm. "If this is my last moment on earth," she thought, "I want people to know what we stood for."

Avon was just doing her job that day: helping young voices for peace be heard. The next day she helped provide supplies to relief workers at "Ground Zero." "The spirit of love was everywhere," Avon says. "I've never seen so much courage—as in the French word *coeur*, courage comes from an unselfish and giving heart.

"War is so horrifying, so unnecessary, and so destructive of life," she thought, remembering other war zones she had witnessed. "It is always the innocent who become the victims." That day, Avon renewed her commitment: to work with others to bring forward the highest good for all beings, especially the children.

Over the years, Avon has mentored children from all over the world, like Masankho Banda, who, at eighteen, fled political persecution in Malawi, West Africa. Masankho's passion for peace through social justice was born when his father was imprisoned for speaking out for democracy. "We will lock him up until he learns to be quiet," said the president of Malawi. Masankho's father languished in a cell for twelve long years: another voice for freedom silenced.

At the time, there was little Masankho or anyone could do. For thirty years, Malawians lived in terror under the cruel dictatorship of their president. Relatively speaking, Masankho's father was one of the lucky ones. Today he is one of only three surviving members of the twenty in Malawi's first cabinet, formed in 1964. Most of the others disappeared without a trace. Their children were considered outcasts and were prohibited from going to school.

Arriving alone in the United States, Masankho carried the weight of his family's suffering. He wanted to connect with other young people whose lives had been shattered by war, but he didn't know where to go. One day a friend said to him, "Masankho, if you want to work with someone who is truly making a difference in children's lives around the world, call Avon Mattison." It turned out to be the most important telephone call of his life.

Although Avon was from America—on the other side of the world—she was a kindred spirit. When she was born in 1941, the darkness of World War II covered the whole earth. On her fourth birthday, Avon looked out her window and made a silent wish for peace.

Avon's wish was answered by a most extraordinary vision! As she stood there, she saw the planet Earth as a living being, and people of all ages and countries living harmoniously with the Earth and with one another. When she wondered what they were doing, an inner voice told her they were building pathways to peace for future generations.

Young Avon wasn't sure what her birthday message and "pathways to peace" meant. She tried to tell some grownups what she had seen and asked them for an explanation. She was told that it was just her childish imagination. While her voice was not heard, she kept trying.

As a young adult, Avon asked how people could make peace a practical reality for future generations. She met with leaders from the United Nations, corporations, and government agencies, and with military officials and scientists, and asked them all the same question. Many of them were too busy preparing for and fighting wars to answer her, but, in time, she found one or two brave souls from each walk of life who were willing to see what they could do together to build pathways to peace.

In the mid-1970s, Avon decided to bring these kindred spirits together. For the last twenty-five years, Avon's organization, Pathways to Peace (PTP), has coordinated a peace-building initiative involving two hundred global organizations and has co-sponsored several International Children's Conferences, sending young people as its official representatives to UN conferences.

Avon's greatest joy comes from working closely with young people, preparing them to become leaders of the twenty-first century. She believes that they have the greatest stake in creating peace, since they will be the ones who have to live with the decisions we all make today.

At their very first meeting, Avon began training Masankho to be a facilitator at the upcoming Children's Conference on Human Rights in Vienna. She gave him her ticket and her place at the conference, and in so doing, she passed him the torch. She was living her commitment to putting young people first. Four weeks later, Masankho was on a plane to Vienna.

In Vienna, Masankho met 140 other young people, many of whom had been traumatized by years of war. At first, some of the youth had trouble even speaking their names. But in time they came to trust each other, and their transformations were dramatic. For example, at the beginning of the conference, Liliana, a shy fifteen-year-old high-school student, could barely introduce herself. But by the fifth day she was leading workshops with strength and authority. Igor and Vladimir, Bosnian and Serbian teenagers who had each lost a close relative in the war, led a joint workshop on tolerance and forgiveness. At one point, Igor turned to Vladimir and said, "You and I are here, we are friends. Our people have done horrible things to each other. We can create something different. Instead of revenge, we need to talk about reconciliation. Instead of destroying, we can rebuild our country." When they hugged, there was not a dry eye in the room.

Each night, Masankho worked with the children from Croatian refugee camps. On the last night they gave a special presentation wherein these children who had known only war in their lives danced for peace. Everyone danced and sang together and spoke of peace, love, and reconciliation. They all knew that this was the way things should be, all the time.

After the dancing, Ivana, the Croatian children's chaperone, approached Masankho. "These children have been in the refugee camps for two years," she said. "This is the happiest I have ever seen them. Please come and dance and sing with the children we have left behind." So they designed a children's peace education project for the Croatian refugee camps. Since then, they have made three trips to the camps and have touched the lives of more than one thousand children.

Through Pathways to Peace, Masankho sees Avon's childhood vision becoming a reality. Although the pathways to peace are difficult to build, Masankho truly believes that each one of us can make a difference so that peace will prevail on earth.

> *Life is no brief candle to me; it is a sort of bright torch which I have got hold of for a moment and I want to make it burn as brightly as possible before handing it on to future generations.*

> GEORGE BERNARD SHAW

Participate in the annual Culture of Peace Week from September 11–21, including Hear the Children Day of Peace, concluding with the International Day of Peace. Participate in the We The Peoples initiative, for local-global citizen peacebuilding. To learn more, including how to support **Pathways to Peace**, write to P.O. Box 1057, Larkspur, CA 94977; e-mail pathways@peacenet.org; or visit their Web site, www.pathwaystopeace.org.

THE HEAVENS OPEN

Like many other Americans who watched the peaceful revolution in the Philippines in 1986 on CNN, I was spellbound. When "People Power" was born, many of us felt a mysterious hope for the rest of the world. Watching a housewife like Cory Aquino become a president was truly inspiring. Her courageous invitation for Americans to help her fragile country touched my heart. Before I knew it, I was on a journey that changed my life.

When I arrived in 1987, the Philippines was a magical place. Everyone was eager to share their moment in history. Each taxi ride became a history lesson, enlivened with examples of extraordinary courage, determination, and faith such as I saw everywhere I went.

For almost twenty years, Filipinos had agonized as President Marcos sold their country's soul to the highest bidder. But when Ninoy Aquino, their imprisoned hero, was assassinated, they'd had enough. Prominent Filipino women started talking with their friends and gathering facts about the corruption, greed, and deception drowning their country. They pursuaded their influential husbands to turn their economic power against Marcos. With the strength of their numbers they chipped away at the status quo. In the process, they risked their personal comfort and security, their marriages, their families, and even their lives. Every day for three years, they prayed for a better future, and in February 1986 their prayers were answered.

At first it looked as if the Philippine Revolution would be a bloodbath, with all the soldiers, guns, and tanks around. Marcos cut off communication with the outside world. The people were terrified, but a local radio announcer coaxed them to join together in Manila's streets, and for one day, these frightened souls became an army. Teenagers put their bodies in front of tanks, befriended the soldiers, and placed flowers in their guns. Singing, "All we are saying, is give peace a chance," they rekindled the spirit of the sixties, showing how to make love, not war—slowly, gently.

For nearly a year, I worked alongside these Filipinos. One of my greatest teachers was Marietta Goco. A tall, strong woman from a privileged family, she had a generous spirit, a clever mind, and a deep commitment to making the system work for those less fortunate than herself. She used her political savvy to build bridges between poor villagers and global funders.

Marietta took me under her wing and introduced me to her world. Each day we'd meet with those who were planning the country's future. We traveled together to some of the seven thousand Philippine islands—listening to business, government, and community leaders as well as farmers, educators, and laborers. Each night we shared with each other the lessons we were learning.

One of the toughest lessons was the cost of ignoring a problem. Twenty years of Marcos's greedy rule had left the country in shambles. UNICEF's report on malnutrition in the Philippines woke the international community to the country's crisis, shocking the global funders who'd thought that their millions were improving life for the poor. Their refusal to continue funding the deceptive Marcos dictatorship helped topple it, but $28 million in debt was strangling any hope for the future of the Filipinos. The gap between the haves and the have-nots had grown to an impassable chasm. Almost half of all Filipino families were destitute. Unless they resolved this inequity, it was clear that their newfound peace would be short-lived.

People told us they were euphoric about bringing down Marcos, but they were angry with the destruction left behind. Many were excited by the opportunity to rebuild their country's democracy but feared an unknown future. Some were in despair, questioning whether the revolution had been worth it. Having been united against a common enemy, some were lost without one. Through all this uncertainty, though, we heard a common refrain: People wanted a better life for their children, and a lasting peace.

One night, Marietta awoke as if from a deep sleep. "My father used to tell me about *Bayanihan*, one of our traditional Filipino values," she told me. "To help me understand, he used to tell me stories about people called Bayani, or heroes, who worked together for the common good. What made them special was their willingness to think of others instead of themselves, to perform a kind of selfless service." She remembered, "My father told me that *Bayanihan* gave people the courage to face their fears, stand up for their convictions, and make choices that bettered their family, community, and the world."

As Marietta reflected on her father's words, she said, "Over the years, we've forgotten about the importance of working together for the common good. If we're ever going to create lasting peace in the Philippines, we'd better remind our people—and teach our children—about *Bayanihan*."

Indeed, over the next ten years, I saw that the Philippine Revolution inspired others to find peaceful ways to freedom in Poland, Russia, South Africa, and Berlin.

After Cory Aquino's close friend and ally Fidel Ramos was elected president, he asked Marietta to develop a plan to decrease poverty by 10 percent in five years. She drew on *Bayanihan* to rally her countrymen to make this goal their own. Each citizen personalized a plan to meet his or her own basic needs and help rebuild the country. People quit smoking and learned how to read or be a better father. They took care of their neighbors and ran for local government.

At first it wasn't easy. As Marietta's deputy, Chukie, remembers, "Over the last twenty years, people had forgotten the basic goodness of Filipinos. But after a while, Marietta's sincerity touched people's hearts. It was like coming home. She helped you remember your own goodness." And people—six million of them in just five years—in turn helped Marietta reach her goal. Her program became the heart of the Philippines' social and economic recovery. On his last day of office, President Ramos awarded Marietta with the Order of the Golden Heart, similar to being knighted in Britain.

Today, Marietta works with the poorest Filipinos through the Sambayanihan Foundation's micro-enterprise initiatives. "Our security initiative includes military as well as human and ecological security," she explains. "If we are to be successful, the heart of our antiterrorism strategy must be an antipoverty program—so people have basic human needs—and hope for their future."

Marietta continues to open people's eyes to what can happen when we empower people to change their lives. As a true *Bayani*, Marietta muses, "It's not that I want to do this: I just can't do anything but this. It becomes a choiceless choice—a calling. And once you make the decision, the heavens open."

Bayanihan, *it's the goodness in every Filipino.*
Bayanihan, *each one helping each other.*
Bayanihan, *let's learn to give and take.*
Bayanihan, *this is the hope for our country.*

JIM PARADES

If you would like to learn more about this *Bayanihan* spirit and the Sambayani-han Foundation, e-mail Marietta Goco at <u>mariettagoco@yahoo.com</u>.

REVOLUTION OF THE SPIRIT
Told by Leslie Kean

It was August 1988, and Aung San Suu Kyi's speech to the massive rally at Rangoon's Shwedagon Pagoda began with a minute of silence. Thousands of people took a moment to honor the students who had recently lost their lives demonstrating for freedom and democracy in Burma.

On March 18 schoolchildren and college students had marched by the hundreds along the bridge on Inya Lake, singing Burma's national anthem, hoping to end the harsh military rule that had been in place since a 1962 military coup. Years of misrule had reduced the once prosperous "golden land" of Burma to one of the world's most destitute nations, whose government now wanted to remake it into the next Asian "tiger." To this end it forced more than 2 million people, many of them children, into slave labor. Human-rights abuses were rampant. On that day in March, riot police arrived in steel helmets and beat many of the protesters to death. Others escaped into the lake and drowned. In the following weeks, demonstrations intensified and thousands fled the country. British television referred to those left behind as "40 million hostages."

Aung San Suu Kyi was returning to Burma from England to nurse her dying mother and arrived in the middle of this bloody chaos. Many a person would have turned right back around and headed for safety, but she was the daughter of Aung San, the independence hero who had won Burma's freedom from the British in 1947, and she thought that she was being called to bring peace to her homeland. She accepted the mission.

As she traveled around the country, sharing her vision of freedom, democracy, personal responsibility, and compassion with huge, electrified crowds, her charisma and brilliance dazzled the world. The Burmese people rallied, challenging the military's claim to absolute power.

When Aung San Suu Kyi's popularity grew large enough to threaten the ruling junta, she was placed under house arrest along with forty other young activists who worked with her. She would not walk freely beneath the sun for six long years, but her countrymen did not forget her.

When the elections finally came, in 1990, Aung San Suu Kyi's party, the National League for Democracy, won a landslide victory. Since she was under house arrest, she wasn't officially allowed to run, but the people of Burma voted for her anyway.

The generals not only refused to honor the results of the elections; they threw most of the newly elected parliament into prison, but they couldn't capture Aung San Suu Kyi's spirit. The guards were amazed that she never once regarded them with anger. Instead, she cultivated the Buddhist practice of *metta*, or loving kindness. She sold her furniture to buy food, refusing to take anything from her captors. Following the example of Gandhi, she employed one of the most potent forms of nonviolent protest available: fasting for justice. She meditated every day, and a flame of purpose and dedication burned steadily within her.

In 1991, on International Human Rights Day, Aung San Suu Kyi was awarded the Nobel Peace Prize in absentia. Because she was still in captivity, her son traveled to Oslo and accepted the prize for her, on behalf of "all the people of Burma." He said, "I know if she were free today, my mother would, in thanking you, also ask you to pray that the oppressors and the oppressed should throw down their weapons and join together to build a nation founded on humanity in the spirit of peace."

The international press has recognized Aung San Suu Kyi as the world's most famous political prisoner since Nelson Mandela and has called the human-rights disaster in Burma "the new South Africa." After six years in detention, Aung San Suu Kyi was finally released in July of 1995. Still the indefatigable leader of

Burma's struggling democracy movement, she began to encourage dialogue and reconciliation between her country's military rulers and its populace. She believes a very different Burma will emerge within her lifetime, for she has "come to the conclusion that the human race is not divided into two opposing camps of good and evil. It is made up of those who are capable of learning and those who are not. Learning is a process of absorbing those lessons of life that enable us to increase peace and happiness in our world. As we strive to teach others, we must have the humility to acknowledge that we, too, still have much to learn. The quintessential revolution is the revolution of the spirit." For the thousands of citizens, young and old, who gather outside her home in Rangoon to learn what they can do, sitting on plastic bags and newspapers, enduring both sweltering heat and torrential downpours to hear about what she is doing and plans to do, Aung San Suu Kyi's message is simple and direct: "We're in this together. If you want freedom and democracy, you must work for it. It will not be given to you. I can only point the way." For over a decade, she has been pointing with her life, with her spirit.

She achieved a victory when her military oppressors agreed to begin a dialogue in the fall of 2000 and then freed some political prisoners. In May 2002, Aung San Suu Kyi was released from house arrest after nineteen months of confinement with no telephone. While she continues to work for political reform so desperately needed in Burma, she never loses sight of the underlying spiritual aims of the struggle. "The quintessential revolution is a revolution of the spirit," she says.

The nonviolent approach does not immediately change the heart of the oppressor. It first does something to the hearts and souls of those committed to it. It gives them a new self-respect: it calls up resources of strength and courage that they did not know they had. Finally, it reaches the opponent and so stirs his conscience that reconciliation becomes reality.

MARTIN LUTHER KING JR.

Join Aung San Suu Kyi's revolution of the spirit and help support human rights and democracy in Burma. **The Burma Project USA,** California, can be reached at burmausa@ix.netcom.com. For more information about the struggle and what you can do, visit www.freeburmacoalition.org.

THE PIED PIPER

Told by Karen Anderson

In 1995, Myron was a twenty-year-old father of five living a life of crime—drugs, guns, the works—one of Baltimore's toughest, most misguided, most troubled youth. He had met his own father only once, a few years earlier. As a kid, Myron got by on his own—with his street smarts. Myron is the kind of young man that Joe Jones helps.

For hundreds of young men struggling to make it on the streets of Baltimore, Joe Jones is role model, mentor, and moral compass. Sometimes he looks like a pied piper, causing heads to turn as he passes, with people of all ages trailing along behind. He's trying to lead kids off the streets and back into society.

Joe knows what it's like on the streets. His parents divorced when he was eleven years old, and that's when he began his career as a drug addict. He has been lucky and got help. "When my father left, our extended family stepped in," he says. "Later, it was a treatment center that helped me turn away from drugs."

Joe started helping others. First he took care of young men who were dying of AIDS in hospices. Then he helped addicted mothers and their children—initially as a substance-abuse counselor, then with the Healthy Start program. To Joe, working with some of the city's poorest unwed mothers felt like a never-ending turnstile.

When some of the fathers came in with "their women," Joe realized that there was nothing he could offer them. "There were so many maternal and child health-care programs available, but something was missing from the equation," Joe says. "If we really want to reduce infant mortality, we can't forget the young men." Joe set out to balance the equation.

In 1993, Joe developed the Men's Services program for Baltimore City Healthy Start for some 450 young men—many of whom were jobless, direction-less, and fathering a whole new generation of potentially disenfranchised children. "Too often, they care little about the mother of their children, and maybe even less about themselves, so we focus instead on the child," Joe says sadly. "The first thing I ask is, 'Do you want your child to have a real father?' Usually they answer yes."

In 1999, Joe started the Center for Fathers, Families and Workforce Development, a nonprofit human-services agency, which now operates Men's Services. The mechanism for the Men's Services program is simple. It targets the fathers—the significant others—of the many young mothers coming into Healthy Start, providing a support system, positive feedback, and sometimes a "kick in the butt." "These young adult males virtually raised themselves in the streets," Joe explains. "These guys are leaders, they have tremendous skills, but they have never been given the guidance to put those skills to work in a positive way."

Myron was meandering through Baltimore's juvenile court system when he met Joe. With Joe's vigilant encouragement, Myron concentrated on "doing the right thing, being a father to his children and a positive role model to other young men in the community." Within two years, Myron's sense of community expanded considerably, and he showed leadership qualities that prompted Joe to take him on a special trip to Kingston, Jamaica, as part of the Lessons Without Borders program at the U.S. Agency for International Development (USAID).

Lessons Without Borders was launched in June 1994, to bring home lessons in community development that the agency has learned through its work in developing countries over the last three decades. Through Lessons Without Borders, Joe visited Jamaica and saw firsthand how a country with severely limited resources was dealing with problems similar to those in his own community.

In the heart of Kingston is Gold Street—an area known as "Tel Aviv" for its burned-out buildings and dilapidated shacks. Acting as the border between two warring gangs, it is infamous for its crime and violence. Most Jamaicans shudder at the thought of venturing near there, but the past decade has seen concerted efforts to repair the neighborhood and revitalize the community.

When he visited, Myron was particularly impressed by a community policing initiative nothing like the combative, punitive relations he'd had with the police when he grew up in Baltimore. The Gold Street police station has become a focal point of the community's healing process. Kingston police walk the beat so they can talk, rebuild trust, and create friendships with young people. They offer tutoring, mentoring, and after-school programs right in the police station and dare to confront the poorest of the poor and the worst of the bad with hope and a sense of what's right, raising the standards for the next generation.

Whether he's speaking at a national forum on the role of the fathers in the family or sitting in 105 degrees in a three-sided schoolroom in Kingston, "rapping" with some of the world's most unfortunate, yet hopeful, thirteen-year-olds, Joe's lesson is often the same. "Each of us—and especially cops—can have a positive impact on the lives of young kids simply by showing that they care," he says. "Solutions don't always cost a lot of money. Sometimes all it takes is a helping hand and the moral support to make kids feel like they're really worth something." For young people like Myron, that makes a big difference.

As we look at the lessons that have been learned from our work overseas, I'm convinced that many of those lessons can be learned and applied in America.

SENATOR HILLARY RODHAM CLINTON

For more information about **CFWD** or Men's Services, contact Joe Jones, President/CEO, CFWD, 3002 Druid Park Drive, Baltimore, MD 21215-7800, 410-367-5691; or visit their Web site, www.cfwd.org.

THANK YOU, DR. COUÉ

Told by Robert Muller

Adapted from his book *Most of All They Taught Me Happiness*

As Assistant Secretary-General at the United Nations, when bad news dragged me down, I remembered a great lesson I had learned from Dr. Émile Coué when I was a student at the University of Heidelberg and a dying friend asked me to help him. It is a mystery to me. I do not understand it. But it has created miracles for me, and it saved my life during the war.

"Could you please go to the library and borrow a book by Dr. Coué?" my friend in the hospital asked. "Bring it to me as soon as possible." I went the following morning and found *Self-Mastery Through Conscious Autosuggestion.* Looking through the book, I learned that this doctor, who was from my neighboring French town, had gained worldwide fame for his healing methods, which drew on the confidence and imagination of the patient.

The essence of his work lies in this simple practice: Every morning before rising, and every evening before getting into bed, you shut your eyes and repeat several times, "Every day, in every way, I am getting better and better." One can also add one's own words. I got accustomed to saying, "I feel wonderful, I feel happier than yesterday, I have never felt so good. It is marvelous to be alive and so healthy."

I thought at first that it was a little too easy—to seek happiness by just repeat-

*Published under that title in England by George Allen and Unwin, London, and in the United States by Samuel Weiser, New York, under the title *Suggestion and Autosuggestion* by Dr. Émile Coué and C. H. Brooks.

ing to oneself that one felt happy! But after reflecting on it, I could see that we had the choice of seeing everything in light or in dark. I now start the day with the conviction to feel good, healthy, and happy to be alive. My happiness, zest for life, and attitude toward the world are affected by this internal decision, taken at the beginning of each day. Then, when difficulties arise, I revert to an innermost part of myself, switch on optimism and confidence, and return to peace of mind.

To the great surprise of the doctors, my friend recovered within a few weeks and was released from the hospital. I have never forgotten him and Dr. Coué's method. I have not always remembered to repeat the affirmation, but I have instinctively followed his philosophy of optimism and self-reliance all my life.

When I was twenty, I worked as an informant for the French Resistance. Under the false identity of Louis Parizot, I had an administrative position in a French telecommunications center that enabled me to warn my friends of impending inspections by the Germans. One evening I noticed that someone had gone through my possessions in my hotel room. I asked the hotelkeeper if anyone had entered my room. "Yes, two workers from the electrical company checked it." Had electrical workers really displaced some of my belongings, I wondered. Was it a routine inspection by the French police, or were the Germans on my trail?

The following morning I received a telephone call from the guard at the entrance of the office building. Three gentlemen wanted to see me on behalf of a friend named André Royer. My heart jumped violently when I heard his name. The news had just reached me that this good school-friend of mine had been arrested by the Germans during a raid. I suspected that the men who were on their way to my office were Germans. I told my secretary to receive them, to find out what they wanted, and to let me know by telephoning the secretary of a colleague in a nearby office, where I took refuge.

After a while the telephone rang, and I could hear my secretary say over the phone, "I am looking for Mr. Parizot. Do you know where he is? Three gentlemen from the police want to see him." This message was clear enough. To gain time, I went to the hotel attic, and I asked the secretary who had harbored me to give a message to one of my Resistance colleagues. He soon joined me and said, "You have little chance of escape, if any. There are five or six Gestapo in the building. They are systematically searching offices and appear quite relaxed, for they know that you are here. The entrance to the hotel is blocked, and a prison van is stationed at the curb. To hide here in the attic or climb on the roof will not help. You know perfectly well that they will shoot you down like a pigeon."

Then he left me, promising to return if there were any new developments. I found myself alone to consider the trap I was in. "This is the moment of all moments," I thought to myself, "to keep cool and in full command of my mental and physical capabilities." Suddenly I remembered Dr. Coué. "I must feel relaxed and even elated about this situation." Following the good doctor's advice, I repeated to myself that it was indeed an extraordinary and thrilling adventure for a twenty-year-old youth to be trapped in a hotel, pursued by the Nazis. Would it not be exciting if I could play a trick on them and slip through their fingers?

Having switched my perspective to a positive, confident frame of mind, I felt relaxed, even happy and cheerful, without any fear or thought of failure. I began to think calmly and decisively. "Nothing is hopeless in this world," I thought. "There must be at least one chance in a thousand to escape from this situation. I must find it. I must concentrate on the mentality of the Nazis. They know that I am in this building. They are convinced that they will get me and that it is only a matter of time and *Gründlichkeit* [thoroughness]. There is no rational means of escape. I must think of something that is foreign to their psychology."

I examined various options. All but one led to certain arrest and possible death. Then a little flicker of hope arose. "There are many people in the hotel. My best chance of escape is to become part of the crowd. Why not walk downstairs and go straight to the group of people who must be gathered? The Nazis certainly do not expect me to do that. The worst that would happen is I would be arrested. But this is likely to happen anyway. If I have any chance at all, it is by doing the one thing the Germans do not expect me to do: to walk straight to them."

I put my plan into action. I changed my physical appearance as best I could, wetting my hair with water from a faucet, parting it on the side. I took off my glasses and lit a cigarette to gain a relaxed posture. I seized a file from a desk and put it under my arm. When I walked down the majestic staircase, a large gathering of people had assembled. I could not see very well without my glasses, but I distinguished a group dominated by shiny spots: These must be the bald heads of the Germans, I surmised. I walked straight up to them. A split second of silence set in when my French colleagues saw me appear on the staircase. But they immediately understood what I was doing and chatted louder to create a diversion.

I walked up to the group of Germans and recognized my secretary, whom they were still interrogating. I asked her calmly, "What is all this turmoil about?" She answered very composedly, "These gentlemen are looking for Mr. Parizot." I expressed surprise: "Parizot? But I just saw him a few minutes ago on the fourth floor!" "*Schnell hinauf!*" (Quickly upstairs!) shouted one of the Germans, and the whole group ran upstairs! I hung around casually for a few more minutes, in case I was being observed by one of the smarter Nazis. My French colleagues were careful not to pay any attention to me, returning to their desks.

Then I went to a compatriot's office and asked how I could get out of the building. "The main entrance is guarded, but there may be a way of getting to the garage through the cellars. The French superintendent downstairs should be able to help you." Under his guidance, I finally reached the garage, which was full of bicycles. I took a good, sturdy one and rode to the house of a member of the Underground. I waited there for a few days until the search had abated and then proceeded to the hills.

Thirty-five years later I flew to Paris to receive UNESCO's Peace Education Prize. At the ceremony I was astonished to see my former secretary, whom I hadn't seen since that memorable day. I embraced her warmly and listened as she told me the rest of the story. She said that the Germans had been so thorough and convinced of finding me that they had even unrolled old carpets stored in the attics!

She told me that when she had seen me walking down the staircase, she had recited to herself: *"Passera, passera pas, passera . . ."* (Will pass, will not pass, will pass . . .).

After several other instances in which Dr. Coué's method saved me from danger during the war, I have become a strong advocate for the power of optimism. Now I live on the positive and sunny side of life that God has given me. Optimism, hard work, and faith are not only in our highest self-interest; they are also the affirmations of life itself. I was fortunate that one of my compatriots taught me this at an early age.

Thank you, Dr. Coué, thank you from the bottom of my heart.

Life is a true miracle and our planet a paradise, or we can make it so. To learn more about Dr. Muller's 5,000 dreams and ideas, or to share your own, visit www.robertmuller.org.

OSKAR SCHINDLER

Adapted from the *Schindler's List* Study Guide,
from *Facing History and Ourselves*

The film Schindler's List *focuses on the years of the Holocaust—a time when millions of Jews and other men, women, and children were murdered solely because of their ancestry. It is one of the darkest chapters in human history. Yet an appalling number of people, young and old, know little if anything about it. Even today the world has not yet learned the lesson of those terrible years. There are far too many places where hate, intolerance, and genocide still exist. Thus* Schindler's List *is not just a "Jewish story" or a "German story"—it is a human story. And its subject matter applies to every generation.* Schindler's List *is simply about racial hatred—which is the state of*

mind that attacks not what makes us people but what makes us different from
each other. It is my hope that Schindler's List *will awaken and sustain an*
awareness of such evil and inspire this generation and future generations to
seek an end to racial hatred.

— Steven Spielberg, Amblin Entertainment, Inc.

People were suspicious of the stories they heard of a Nazi war profiteer
who rescued Jews. Oskar Schindler came to Krakow, Poland, from his native
German town of Zwittau. Unlike most of the carpetbaggers, he took over a factory that had lain idle and in bankruptcy for many years. In the winter of
1939–40, he began operations with four thousand square meters of floor space
and a hundred workers, of whom seven were Jewish.

Production started with a rush, for Schindler was a shrewd and tireless worker.
During the first year the labor force expanded to three hundred, including 150
Jews. By the end of 1942, the factory had grown to 45,000 square meters and
employed almost eight hundred men and women. The Jewish workers, of whom
there were now 370, all came from the Krakow ghetto. "To avoid life at the
camps, it had become a tremendous advantage," says Itzhak Stern, Schindler's
Jewish bookkeeper, "to be able to leave the ghetto in the daytime and work in a
German factory."

Word spread among Krakow's Jews that Schindler's factory was the place to
work. Schindler helped his Jewish employees by falsifying the factory records.
He recorded old people as being twenty years younger and listed children as
adults. Lawyers, doctors, and engineers were registered as metalworkers, mechan-
ics, and draftsmen — all trades considered essential to war production.

From behind his high bookkeeper's table, Stern could see through the glass
door of Schindler's private office. "Almost every day, from morning until
evening, officials and other visitors came to the factory and made me nervous.
Schindler used to keep pouring them vodka and joking with them. When they

left he would ask me in, close the door, and then quietly tell me whatever they had come for. He used to tell them that he knew how to get work out of these Jews and that he wanted more brought in. That was how we managed to get in the families and relatives all the time and save them from deportation."

Then, on March 13, 1943, came the orders to close the Krakow ghetto. All Jews were moved to the forced-labor camp of Plaszow, outside the city. Conditions there, even for the graduates of the terrible Krakow ghetto, were shocking. The prisoners suffered horribly and either died by the hundreds in camp or were moved to Auschwitz.

Stern, along with Schindler's other workers, had also been moved to Plaszow from the ghetto, but like some 25,000 other inmates who inhabited the camp and had jobs on the outside, they continued spending their days in the factory. When he fell gravely ill one day, Stern sent word to Schindler pleading for help. Schindler came at once, bringing essential medicine, and continued his visits until Stern recovered. But what he had seen in Plaszow had chilled him. Nor did he like the turn things had taken in the factory.

Increasingly helpless before the frenetic Jew-haters and Jew-destroyers, Schindler found that he could no longer joke easily with the German officials who came on inspections. The double game he was playing was becoming more difficult. Troubling incidents happened more often.

The increasing frequency of unpleasant incidents in the factory and the evil his eyes had seen at the Plaszow camp probably moved Schindler into a more active role. In the spring of 1943 he began the all-out conspiring, string-pulling, bribery, and shrewd outguessing of Nazi officialdom that ultimately saved so many lives. At this point the real legend begins. For the next two years, Oskar Schindler's constant obsession was to save the greatest possible number of Jews from the Auschwitz gas chambers, only sixty kilometers from Krakow.

Plaszow seemed doomed. Other labor camps in Poland had already been shut down and their inhabitants liquidated. At the prompting of Stern and the others in the "inner office" circle, one evening Schindler managed to convince one of his drinking companions, General Schindler—no relative—that Plaszow's camp workshops would be ideally suited for serious war production. The general fell in with the idea and ordered the necessary materials, wood and metal, for the camp. As a result, Plaszow was officially transformed into a war-essential "concentration camp." And though conditions hardly improved, it came off the list of labor camps that were then being eliminated, inhabitants and all.

But by the spring of 1944, the Germans were retreating from the Eastern Front in earnest. They ordered Plaszow and all its sub-camps to be emptied. Schindler and his workers had no illusions about what a move to another concentration camp implied. The time had come for Oskar Schindler to play his trump card, and he was ready.

He went to work on all his drinking companions, and on his connections in military and industrial circles in Krakow and Warsaw. He bribed, cajoled, and pleaded, working desperately against time, fighting for what everyone assured him was a lost cause. He persisted until someone, somewhere in the hierarchy, perhaps impatient to end the seemingly trifling business, finally gave him the authorization to move a force of seven hundred men and three hundred women from the Plaszow camp into a factory at Brennec, in his native Czechoslovakia. Most of the other 25,000 men, women, and children at Plaszow were sent to Auschwitz, where they found the same end that several million other Jews had already met. But out of the vast calamity, and through the stubborn efforts of one man, a thousand half-starved, sick, and almost broken Jews were given a reprieve.

The *Schindlerjuden* by now depended on Schindler. His compassion and sacrifice were unstinting. He spent every bit of money still left in his possession and traded his wife's jewelry as well, for food, clothing, and medicine, and for schnapps with which to bribe the many SS investigators. He furnished a secret hospital with stolen and black-market medical equipment and made a three-hundred-mile trip himself carrying two enormous flasks filled with Polish vodka and bringing them back full of medicine. His wife, Emilie, cooked and cared for the sick and earned her own reputation and gratitude.

Just about the time the Nazi empire was crashing down, someone called Schindler from the railway station late one evening, asking whether he cared to accept delivery of two railway cars full of near-frozen Jews. The train had left Auschwitz ten days earlier, carrying almost a hundred sick men in cars frozen shut at five degrees Fahrenheit until some factory would take them. When informed of the condition of the prisoners, no factory manager would. Until Schindler.

The train was awesome to behold. Ice had formed on the locks, and the cars had to be opened with axes and acetylene torches. Inside, the miserable relics of human beings were stretched out, frozen stiff, so that each had to be unloaded like a carcass of frozen beef. Thirteen were unmistakably dead, but the others still breathed.

Throughout that night and for many days and nights following, Oskar and Emilie Schindler and a number of the factory men worked to revive the frozen and starved bodies in one large room of the factory that they emptied for the purpose. Three more men died, but with care, warmth, milk, and medicine, the others gradually rallied. All this had been achieved surreptitiously, with the factory guards as usual receiving bribes to dissuade them from informing the SS commandant.

Such was life at Brennec until the Russians arrived on May 9 and ended the nightmare. One early morning shortly after that, Schindler, Emilie, and several of their closest (Jewish) friends discreetly disappeared, not to be heard from until they turned up, months later, deep in Austria's U.S. Zone.

To receive a Schindler's List Study Guide, call **Facing History and Ourselves** at 617-232-1595, or visit its Web site, www. facing.org.

Steven Spielberg created **Survivors of the Shoah Visual History Foundation** to videotape and archive interviews with Holocaust survivors all over the world. For more information, visit its Web site, www.VHF.org.

PEACE, FOR THEIR GRANDCHILDREN

Told by Jimmy Carter

Adapted from his book *Talking Peace: A Vision for the Next Generation*

Shortly after my inauguration in 1977, President Anwar Sadat of Egypt came to visit me in Washington. He was interested in bringing peace to his own people and strengthening friendship between Egypt and the United States. However, he saw no chance to make real progress on resolving basic differences with Israel anytime soon. On several issues he responded, "Maybe in my lifetime."

I told him that I was prepared to use my full personal influence and that of my country in support of any effort he was willing to make. Later, during our private talks upstairs in the White House, he agreed to take major strides toward peace in the long-standing conflict between his country and Israel. This was very much in the interest of the United States.

My role as a mediator in the talks would be a challenge. To prepare, I studied thick books on the personalities of the two leaders, prepared for me by specialists. These books told me about each man's family relationships, religious beliefs, early life experiences, health, and, most important, friends. I also learned about how each had won office, how he responded to pressure, and what his hobbies and personal habits were. As I read I took notes that later proved very useful in the actual meetings. I also prepared lists of points on which the Egyptians and the Israelis were in apparent agreement, points of difference between them, questions to be asked during the negotiations, and some compromises I thought both men might accept.

President Sadat was the first to arrive for the peace talks, and I was pleased to discover that he seemed quite flexible on most questions. When Prime Minister

Begin arrived later, he and I also had a private discussion about the major issues. Yet I soon realized that he viewed our Camp David sessions as just the first in an ongoing series of negotiations. Sadat and I had hoped to settle all the major controversial issues between the two countries during the next few days, if we possibly could.

As we discussed various issues, I realized that Begin and Sadat were personally incompatible. The sometimes petty, sometimes heated arguments that arose between them when we were all in the same room convinced me it would be better if each of them spoke to me as the mediator instead of directly to each other. For the last ten days of the Camp David negotiations, the two men never spoke to or even saw each other except for one Sunday-afternoon trip. Meanwhile, their teams of advisers continued to meet face-to-face.

Toward the end of the talks, Begin's foreign minister told Sadat that Israel would never compromise on certain major issues, and Sadat decided it was time to leave. The Egyptians began packing their bags and asked for a helicopter to take them to Washington so they could return home. When I heard about this, I said a silent prayer, quickly changed into more formal clothes, and went to confront Sadat in his cabin. After an intense argument in which I reminded him of his promises to me and stressed the global importance of his role as a man of peace, Sadat agreed to give the process another chance.

In the end, something unexpected almost miraculously helped to break the deadlock. We had made some photos of the three of us, and Begin had asked me to sign one for each of his eight grandchildren. Sadat had already signed them. My secretary suggested that I personalize them, and on each photograph I wrote in the name of one grandchild above my signature. Although Begin had become quite unfriendly toward me because of the pressure I was putting on him and Sadat, I decided to take the photographs over to his cabin myself.

As he looked at the pictures and read the names aloud, he became very emotional. He was thinking, I am sure, about his responsibility to his people and about what happens to children in war. Soon both of us had tears in our eyes. I was very grateful when he promised to review the language of my latest revisions.

Shortly thereafter, Begin called me and said he would accept my compromise proposal. This was, indeed, a framework for peace, as we called it, laying the foundation for a future treaty between Israel and Egypt.

That afternoon, Begin, Sadat, and I left Camp David in my helicopter and flew to the White House for the signing ceremony. Six months later, a formal treaty was signed between the two countries—the first treaty ever between Israel and an Arab nation.

> *Cooperation is a state of mind. There is little hope of real progress until we make this discovery and act upon this knowledge.*
>
> THOMAS JEFFERSON

Find a cause that is close to your heart and support it. To learn more about and support The Carter Center, visit www.cartercenter.org.

THE BANKER WITH HEART

Told by Alex Counts

Adapted from his book *Give Us Credit: How Muhammad Yunus's Micro-Lending Revolution Is Empowering Women from Bangladesh to Chicago*

In his early twenties, Muhammad Yunus was an impatient young man brimming with self-confidence, optimism, and ambition. Before planning his trip to America, he had never heard of Vanderbilt University in Tennessee, to which he had received a Fulbright scholarship. Looking at a globe, he realized it was almost exactly halfway around the world from Bangladesh.

At Vanderbilt, he studied economics and planned to apply his lessons back in Bangladesh after he graduated. He returned just in time for the famine of 1974, a time when Henry Kissinger called Bangladesh "the world's basket case." But for Yunus, it was home. He got a job teaching economics at the university. On his way to class, he had to walk past hundreds of his countrymen dying from starvation. Yunus no longer had grand illusions about what one man could do. But he knew he had to act.

He started by talking with poor people on the street and in the villages. He immersed himself in their world so he could best learn how to help. He came to believe that the lack of investment capital was one of the root causes of the poverty that plagued these people. In the villages, Yunus found poor folks who earned as little as two cents a day making bamboo stools, yet they paid exorbitant interest rates (as much as 10 percent a week) on the working capital they borrowed from moneylenders. Yunus was appalled. "I felt ashamed to be part of a society that could not make twenty-one dollars available to forty-two hardworking, skilled human beings so they could make a decent living," he said.

So he started lending tiny amounts of money—as little as ten dollars—to destitute people from his own pocket. They invested their money in building small businesses like poultry farming, rickshaw pulling, stool manufacturing, and other cottage industries. He created the Grameen Bank (Grameen means "village") to give the villagers something they could count on. Twenty years later, more than 2 million people—mostly women—have received loans from the Grameen Bank. On an average working day, Grameen disburses more than 60 million Bangladeshi taka, or roughly $1.5 million. The return on Yunus's first investment has been astounding. Ninety-nine percent have paid their loans back in full.

The bank's secret is to get poor people to help themselves while they help one another, in borrowing support groups. They meet in their groups every week to troubleshoot their challenges and celebrate their successes. Each borrower also has a real financial stake in all the others in the group; if anyone defaults on a loan, the other group members must repay it. With the help of the Grameen

Bank, millions of Bangledeshis are working their way out of poverty, building lives of promise for themselves and their families.

Yunus is spreading this simple story—and its success—to people around the world. In 1986, Governor Bill Clinton invited him to come to rural Arkansas to see if it was possible to start a similar program in the United States. At first, poor people couldn't believe that anyone would lend to them.

Yunus asked the welfare recipients and unemployed people he met in Arkansas to imagine what they would do with the money if a bank agreed to give them a loan. Almost everybody said that a bank would not give them money, so there was no point in talking about it. So he decided to take a more direct approach. "Look," he said, "I run a bank in Bangladesh that lends money to poor people. Governor Clinton asked me to bring my bank to your community. I am thinking of starting a bank right here. Now I am trying to find out if somebody is interested in borrowing money from me." He explained that they didn't need any collateral, or anything else usually required for bank loans. All they needed was a good idea.

One woman who had been listening very carefully answered, "I would like to borrow some money from your bank!" When Yunus asked her how much, she said $375. Yunus was surprised at the precise figure, so he asked her what she wanted to do with it. She said that she was a beautician and that her business was limited because she did not have all the right supplies. If she could get a box of supplies costing $375, she was sure she could pay him back with the extra income, and she did not want to take a penny more than what the box cost.

Another woman, unemployed since the textile factory she had worked at closed and moved to Taiwan, requested a few hundred dollars for a sewing machine. Another wanted six hundred dollars to buy a pushcart to sell hot tamales.

For years Yunus had been saying that his program would thrive anywhere poverty existed, but many experts had told him that America was different. "Poor Americans are lazy Americans," they told him. After his trip to Arkansas, Yunus knew these experts were wrong. Convinced that his program would work in

America, he charged a handful of mavericks working for nonprofit organizations with making it happen. Within months they established the Good Faith Fund in Pine Bluff, Arkansas. At about the same time, the Women's Self-Employment Project started making loans to women in the Englewood section of Chicago.

Since then, nearly forty American nonprofit organizations have started "peer lending" programs based on the model of the Grameen Bank. They serve African Americans and Mexicans in south central Los Angeles, Native Americans in South Dakota, poor whites in Arkansas, North Carolina, and New England, and refugees from Southeast Asia—a whole spectrum of disadvantaged people in the United States. Traditional bankers dismiss the idea that poor people can start businesses. They think a destitute village woman in Bangladesh or a welfare recipient in inner-city Chicago should settle for a job, while banks give loans to wealthy people and companies to create employment. The Grameen strategy turns this idea upside down. It gives the poor and jobless the opportunity to create their own jobs rather than waiting for someone else to give them jobs—and take them away.

When Muhammad Yunus started lending, two decades ago, he sought a fertile middle ground between rugged capitalism and ragged socialism, between lending to wealthy individuals and to mismanaged cooperatives. He found one, and today, in addition to Grameen's 2 million borrowers in Bangladesh, another 6 million poor people in fifty countries around the world—in the Philippines and South Africa and in cities such as Brooklyn and Paris—are part of a powerful group of peers who are changing the entire banking industry.

Grameen's goal for the year 2005 is to have 100 million of the world's poorest families join them—with access to credit and the opportunity to create their own livelihood. They hope it will be one of the greatest humanitarian campaigns in history.

> *Never doubt that a small group of thoughtful, committed citizens can change the world. Indeed, it's the only thing that ever has.*

> MARGARET MEAD

Help end poverty in the world, one woman at a time. Join the campaign to give 100,000 poor families access to microloans by 2005. To learn about the campaign and about how you can develop partnerships with the Grameen Bank, contact the **Grameen Foundation** at www.gfusa.org.

VI

THE HEALING POWER
OF DOING GOOD

Sometimes the impulse to help can heal our deepest wounds. Migdalia Ramos lost her husband, Harry, on September 11, when he helped an injured stranger on the eighty-seventh floor of 1 World Trade Center. Left with two small children, a half-built house, a six-figure mortgage, and a flood of bills, she was angry. She couldn't understand why her husband had put a stranger's welfare ahead of his own family. Three weeks later she found herself running into a smoke-filled stairway, intent on saving her mother's elderly neighbor from a fire. In that moment she understood why Harry had done what he did.

The stories in this chapter feature people who discover the healing power of helping others. A busy mother finds the time to hold babies at a hospital nursery and experiences the magical healing power of love. A cynical student fills the emotional and spiritual hollowness in his life by volunteering in a soup kitchen. Inner-city teenagers help others gain self-esteem, dignity, and personal mastery in their lives. Being part of something greater and more meaningful than themselves brings them the kind of happiness they've always wanted. It's a phenomenon too often overlooked by the prophets of "self-help."

Research shows that when we help others, we feel better; we are energized, both physically and mentally. People who habitually behave selflessly and give from their hearts usually have less pain, depression, and disease, and more energy to enjoy their lives. The "helper's high" is like the runner's high: By helping others, we can actually improve our body's immune system and our health. By helping others for as little as two hours a week, we get a rush of warmth, energy, euphoria, and longer-lasting feelings of self-worth, calm, and peace of mind. With the smile on a beneficiary's face, the joy in her eyes, or a simple thank-you in return, we realize what it is we really live for.

Sometimes we find it easiest to help strangers. We feel less burdened by expectations and freer to choose how we want to give. Yet, as a wise friend once told me, if we want to change the world, the best place to start is with our own families. Given the daily ups and downs of family life, they offer an ideal training ground for learning how to care for others. And those with "helper's burnout" may feel revitalized by getting to know their helpees better as human beings, thereby allowing the healing benefits of the relationship to flow both ways. True healing happens for the giver and the receiver when we slow down and come close enough to touch each other. In our fast-paced world, we are often too busy for each other, too busy to see what really matters, to find out what people really need. When we take time for one another, our families and our neighbors, we receive many blessings: loving relationships, happy children, healthy communities, and a safer world. Each one of us has special gifts we can give. What are yours?

A pessimist, they say, sees a glass of water as being half empty;

an optimist sees the same glass as half full.

But a giving person sees a glass of water

and starts looking for someone who might be thirsty.

"If you don't, who will?"

G. DONALD GALE

FROM A CYNIC TO A SERVER

Told by Andrew Carroll

Despite the benefit of a Quaker education and two extraordinarily generous and loving parents, at the age of eighteen Andy Carroll left home for college a rather cynical young man. He wasn't bitter or angry; he just believed that the world, especially as it appeared on the nightly news, was a brutal place, and that nothing would ever change.

Cynicism, as he saw it, was the easiest route to happiness. It seemed daring and adventurous, unrestrained by rules or responsibilities, and he found humor in its irreverence. Best of all, it demanded nothing of him. It didn't ask him to sign petitions, recycle old newspapers, or feed the homeless.

Andy didn't have the energy to get involved anyway. He was too busy having fun and living for the moment to commit himself to any cause, belief, or person. It was all very intoxicating. But his carefree lifestyle was not without its emotional hangovers. Underneath his cavalier confidence was a noxious suspicion that something enormously significant was missing in his life.

Then he came across a book that seemed to point right at him, at the guilt, restlessness, and emptiness he was used to swatting aside. Robert Bellah's *Habits of the Heart: Individualism and Commitment in American Life* almost miraculously changed the way he saw the world and his place in it.

This book, which explores the emotional and spiritual hollowness of selfish living, helped Andy own up to his desire to give back to others and believe in something greater than himself. After reading it, he began to look at people differently, seeing their positive qualities, not just their flaws and offenses. He also noticed how many people—those whom he had previously ignored—were working to improve their communities.

Urged by their example, he decided to give something a try.

He volunteered at a soup kitchen in the basement of a local church, where he learned quickly about real compassion and sacrifice up close, in action. The cooks, servers, and organizers who were his fellow volunteers went about their work quietly and dependably, without asking for recognition or appreciation. For the first time in his life, Andy felt he was part of something greater and more meaningful than his own cramped universe; his world, in turn, was un-cramping.

To his surprise, it wasn't difficult to find the energy to volunteer—in fact, volunteering gave him energy, reviving his optimism and invigorating his faith in humanity like spiritual oxygen. With a new, heartier sense of humor, he was especially delighted to find something potent enough in its goodness to excite hope in him. It was easy to have hope, however, when things were going well. He wondered whether he would be so optimistic during hard times.

He didn't wait long to be tested. One year, just a few days before Christmas, his home burned to the ground. He had never been a big fan of Christmas as a religious holiday. He liked getting gifts well enough, but the spirit of the season eluded him. In fact, he found it maddening, always the same songs over and over. If he'd ever known the magic of Christmas, he'd forgotten it.

After the devastating fire, he had more reason to hate it. Everything he'd owned was destroyed. Books, clothes, and CDs could be replaced, but letters he'd kept from friends and loved ones, a silver pocket watch from his grandfather, generations of photographs, and other precious things were gone forever.

But as Andy was mourning the loss of all his material possessions, he realized that something more important remained—his newfound idealism, which in turn enabled him to see other things that had survived the fire, too. Everyone, even his cat, Claude, had escaped unharmed.

Thanks to insurance, Andy and his family found a place to stay over the holidays and while their house was rebuilt. But, comfortable as they were, the fire made him think about people who didn't have a home to go to any time of the year. When he returned to school after the break, he kept volunteering at the soup kitchen, and he wanted to do more.

The following Christmas, remembering what it was like to lose everything, Andy decided to get presents for poor and homeless children. Thinking "the more the merrier," he decided to get others to do it, too. With the help of some friends and their school's volunteer program, using the national Toys for Tots progam as a model, they started the ABC Project, for "A Better Christmas." They put up flyers around campus and spread the word in classes, churches, everywhere they went. They persuaded the college newspaper to print a full-page ad asking for donations, and soon toys and books came pouring in from students and professors, fraternities and sororities, and people who lived in the neighborhood. Andy was overwhelmed by the community's generosity. He realized how much people wanted to give of themselves, when given the opportunity. He just had to ask.

For Andy, ABC was all about giving, and it wasn't too long before he realized that the more he gave, the more he received. The day before Andy left to go home for Christmas break—almost exactly one year since the fire—he received a handwritten note with no return address. A woman wrote, "Thank you ABC for the toys you gave my children. All we had was stolen last week. I had no toys to give them, but now I do. You don't know how much I appreciate it. Thank you so much, and have a Merry Christmas."

Quite simply, this was the best Christmas gift Andy had ever received.

Altruism is like a muscle. It must be used or it atrophies. Reach out and help the person nearest you. You'll feel the good feeling, the shock of recognition—and as you help, the helping will spread.

NORMAN COUSINS

Help promote literacy by supporting **The American Poetry & Literacy (APL) Project**'s distribution of free poetry books in public places like hospitals, schools, train stations, day-care centers, and jury waiting rooms. Write to P.O. Box 53445, Washington, DC 20009.

BABY MAGIC

Told by Allan Luks

Adapted from his book *The Healing Power of Doing Good,*
written with Peggy Payne

Twelve years ago, Lynn was suffering from chronic back pain. No matter
what she did, the pain just wouldn't go away. One day she found herself lying in
traction in a hospital bed, listening to her doctor recommend surgery. Lynn listened carefully and thought about her options. She'd heard about a program
where people learned how to cope with stress and control most back problems.
Lynn decided against the surgery, opting to join the program instead. She found
that the relaxation techniques did help ease the pain, but the periodic flare-ups
continued—until she began to help with the babies.

At first Lynn didn't think she would have the time. She lived a full and fast-
paced life. In addition to being a wife and mother of two teenagers, she carried
heavy professional responsibilities. As the director of a private preschool, she
worried about competing for students, pleasing worried parents, and placating
her school's supervisors. It seemed her schedule couldn't hold another thing, but
it did.

Now, once a week after work, Lynn takes a fifteen-minute walk to the Rusk
Institute of Rehabilitation Medicine in a nearby urban medical center. There
she puts on gloves and a bright yellow sterile gown, and for the next two hours
she holds, feeds, and diapers new babies who have no one else to care for them.
Most days, Lynn arrives to find ten babies in the room, four being fed and the
rest crying. They are so small that it sounds more like the mewing of kittens.
Some of the babies, abandoned by drug-addicted mothers, are shaking with with-
drawal symptoms. Many were born outside of a hospital, to mothers without

medical care. Here they sleep in metal cribs, each tagged with a sticker displaying a name and a few statistics.

Even with all of their problems, these babies are uncommonly beautiful. Their huge eyes and little bodies remind Lynn how precious and fragile life really is. She leans over a waist-high crib and picks up a baby. Today it is Madison, a tiny, dark-skinned, seven-day-old baby boy. He is awaiting the results of a drug test, then placement in a foster home. She can feel his tiny bones in her hands. *It's so scary to hold some of them,* Lynn thinks as she cradles him. As they rock back and forth, Madison latches onto a bottle with surprising vigor. When he is finished, she gently pats him to sleep and puts him to bed. Someone brings in a new baby, half an hour old, big, pink, and howling. This little linebacker looks so unusually healthy, he makes the others seem even smaller. Next to him, Sanchez, born with heart and liver problems, lies helpless in an incubator. At birth, Sanchez weighed a little over two pounds.

Leaning over to pick up another, Lynn makes no effort to protect her back. Dupree has curly black hair and features that look almost grown-up. He is two weeks old and trembling, sometimes faintly, sometimes in shudders that move through his whole body. "I'm sorry, I'm sorry," Lynn whispers as she holds his little body.

Lynn spends her entire two hours in the nursery, lifting and lowering babies, feeding and diapering. When she arrived, her back had been a little stiff, but the pain has vanished. As she gets her coat to leave the hospital, she notices her hands still smell of babies. "Baby magic," she says, taking a sniff. "Baby magic has changed my life."

A baby is God's opinion that the world should go on.

CARL SANDBURG

Discover the joy and experience the healing of holding babies. Call your local hospital volunteer program and ask how you can join their volunteer program, helping out in their nursery.

THE QUILT

There is a quilt on Cleve Jones's bed; he's had it all his life. In one corner, stitched in yellow thread on a blue background, you can find the words "Emma Rupert—age 78—1952." Emma was his great-grandmother, born in Bee Ridge, Indiana, in 1874. The quilt she sewed for him, her first great-grandchild, was a wonderful quilt for a little boy: a crazy quilt sewn from scraps of Grandpa's pajamas, with hundreds of brightly colored tigers, horses, dolphins, and dragons.

Cleve was thinking of this quilt the night of November 27, 1985, as he stood in the San Francisco Civic Center Plaza, in a sea of candles flickering in the chilly fog. Thousands of people marched that night, as they march every November 27, holding their candles as they proceed down Market Street in memory of City Supervisor Harvey Milk and Mayor George Moscone.

Harvey Milk was California's first openly gay elected official. He and Mayor Moscone were assassinated in their City Hall offices on November 27, 1978. As word of the murders spread throughout the city, first hundreds, then thousands, then tens of thousands of San Franciscans made their way to Castro Street to join the silent march to City Hall.

In November 1985, as they prepared for the annual tribute to Milk and Moscone, the *San Francisco Examiner* reported that one thousand San Franciscans had thus far died of AIDS. Cleve knew many of them. They were his friends, neighbors, and colleagues. They were dying too quickly, too painfully; and often, they died alone.

As he stood at the corner of Castro and Market Streets, he knew he was at the center of tragedy, a plague accompanied by a parallel epidemic of hatred, bigotry, and fear. It seemed to Cleve that he and his friends would all be dead long before the world awoke to the awful challenge of this disease. He wanted to give a voice to those who were silently disappearing.

As the marchers gathered with their candles for Harvey and George that evening, Cleve asked everyone to take a placard and write the name of someone they knew who had been killed by AIDS. They marched to City Hall and stood in silence there for several moments; then on to the Federal Building, where Cleve and some friends had earlier hidden extension ladders and rolls of tape. They placed the ladders against the gray stone walls of the Federal Building and climbed three stories up, taping the placards with the names of the dead to the walls.

When it was done, the walls were covered, and Cleve stepped back and looked at the patchwork of names spread over the building. *It looks like a quilt,* he thought. It reminded him of his great-grandmother—and of the gentle ladies who brought their quilts to Quaker meetings in Indiana to raise money for the poor. To Cleve it seemed the perfect symbol of traditional middle-class, middle-American family values. A potent symbol to match with this disease that was killing gay men, black children, hemophiliacs, and drug users. An antidote, if not to the virus, then perhaps to the hatred and fear poisoning the country.

A year later, Cleve created the first panel of the AIDS Memorial Quilt in memory of his best friend, Marvin Feldman, who died in October 1986. And on October 11, 1987, the Names Project AIDS Memorial Quilt was first unfolded, on the National Mall in Washington, D.C., displaying 1,920 names.

When Cleve returned to San Francisco, he found letters from all over the world—from anguished parents who had lost their children, from community leaders uncertain how to mobilize their communities against the epidemic, from gay men who had been abandoned by their families—imploring him to bring the Quilt to their hometowns.

So he and his friends bought a truck named Stella, loaded up the Quilt, and set out across this country and around the world, displaying the Quilt as the centerpiece of local educational and fund-raising campaigns. Out of their travels grew an extraordinary network of chapters and international affiliates, uniting diverse peoples from every nation in the global struggle against the HIV disease. While they had first thought of quilting as a particularly American folk art, they learned that similar traditions existed in many other cultures. Today the names of Cleve's gay friends from San Francisco are stitched in next to panels memorializing housewives from New Jersey, farmers from Uganda, shopkeepers from Thailand, street kids from Brazil—men, women, and children of all races, faiths, and nationalities.

In 1987 Cleve created The Names Project Foundation to preserve, care for, and use The AIDS Memorial Quilt and promote healing, heighten awareness, and inspire action in the struggle against HIV and AIDS.

Over the years, more than 7 million people have visited the Quilt in its thousands of displays worldwide. Wherever it goes, the Quilt sparks a dialogue between those who make the panels and those who view them. A gift from the hearts and hands of Americans has touched millions of people and moved them to act, caring for the sick, comforting the dying, building hospices, joining speakers' bureaus, writing checks, signing petitions, demonstrating, testifying, getting arrested, wearing red ribbons, sewing Quilt squares for their own loved ones, and raising their own candles against the darkness.

Nominated for the Nobel Peace Prize in 1989, the Quilt is the largest piece of community folk art in the world—and a living memorial to a generation lost to AIDS. It illustrates the enormity of the worldwide AIDS crisis by revealing the individual lives behind the statistics, giving us a powerful symbol and eliciting a compassionate response. In October 1999, the Quilt was displayed once again on the National Mall in Washington D.C.: It had grown to 49,000 panels, weighing fifty-four tons, covering more than thirty acres, the size of thirty-five football fields. Two thousand readers read out 86,000 names, a litany of the dead that took three entire days.

Recently in Edinburgh, Texas, a small town on the banks of the Rio Grande, Cleve witnessed a display of panels created for people from south Texas, joined by several panels sent from Mexico City. Thousands of families from both sides of the border moved silently through the fabric walkways of the Quilt: young parents with small children, gay and lesbian couples, grandparents, teenagers. A hot wind blew up dust from the desert, but no one complained; they were listening to the names. A woman approached Cleve with a bundle of fabric in her arms. "This is my son," she said, and handed him the cloth. "He's gone now, but he lives on—in my heart and in the Quilt."

The Names Project urges you to join the fight for a world without AIDS. For information on how to get involved with the AIDS Memorial Quilt, call 404-688-5500, or visit the Quilt Web site, www.aidsquilt.org.

CHANGING PEOPLE'S MINDS
Told by Susan Keese

Joseph Rogers could be mistaken for Santa Claus. This forty-five-year-old man, with his bushy white beard and robust manner, is often called "the Mother Teresa of the consumer movement" or "the Martin Luther King of mental health." But despite all that he's accomplished, Joe still struggles with his illness.

Joe remembers the day when he was diagnosed as a paranoid schizophrenic. "It was like a death sentence," he says. He was only nineteen when he was told he'd spend most of his life in a mental institution. "While most people my age were planning for their future, I was told, 'You might as well apply for social security.'" But Joe surprised almost everyone. Thirty years later he is a nationally recognized leader in a movement that's reforming the entire mental-health-care system. He confers with presidents, testifies before Congress, and consults with foreign governments. It's hard to believe that this man was once homeless, wandering the streets of New York City, fishing through Dumpsters looking for food.

Raised in a troubled household on the outskirts of Orlando, Florida, Joe left home at thirteen. As he drifted, he became increasingly disorganized, isolated, and depressed. Near suicide, he turned for help to an understanding youth worker, a call that probably saved his life.

During his twenties, Joe bounced around from one mental hospital to another and had many painful experiences in the system. Between hospitalizations, he struggled through beginning classes at a New Jersey community college. "I got lots of insights into my life from the courses I took in psychology," he says. But his recurring bouts of mental illness made it difficult for him to finish his degree.

One day a professor persuaded him to use his insider's knowledge of how the system works—and, too often, doesn't—to make it better. Joe decided to volunteer at a small community mental health center in New Jersey, which, since all the states were downsizing mental hospitals to cut costs, was struggling. "Suddenly this little center, designed for family counseling, was expected to take care of people with serious mental illness. Many had been institutionalized for a long time," Joe says. "Folks at the center weren't prepared for this new challenge. Something needed to be done, so I said, 'Let me work on this.'"

Joe remembered how he had felt when he first came out of the hospital. He spent time with the newcomers, sharing his story and listening to theirs. People found it comforting to talk with others who had "been there." It made them feel less alone, less afraid, better able to help themselves.

Joe turned these conversations into programs for people in halfway homes. He created a model and set up a number of self-help groups in which former patients supported one another in rebuilding their own lives. His reputation spread as he continued to develop new programs. Ironically, he had to hide his own background. "I had all this experience with inpatients and outpatients, but I couldn't tell anyone how I got it," he says.

He moved to Philadelphia, to accept a job with the Mental Health Association of Southeastern Pennsylvania (MHASP), where he created Project SHARE (Self Help and Advocacy Resource Exchange) to help people who had lived with mental illness in designing programs to meet their own needs. "Hearing the success stories of people whose problems are similar to your own gives a kind of hope you can't get from professionals," Joe maintains. He adds, "Many professionals don't really see these people as equals. They see them as children at best, or mentally retarded at worst. It's a threat to them to have former patients saying, 'This is what I want,' or 'This works best for me.'"

Through Project SHARE, more than five thousand mental health "consumers" have transformed themselves from helpless recipients into helpers and wage earners, become advocates for mental-health care as well as role models for others. Project SHARE has spawned hundreds of peer counseling/support groups and serves as an umbrella organization for twenty projects run by mental-health clients—such as housing programs, drop-in centers, job training, outreach, and advocacy. They've also created a national clearinghouse to help consumers around the country organize their own self-help and advocacy groups. "Many people come into our programs, literally homeless and hopeless," Joe says. "They start as volunteers, then become paid facilitators. They go to school, get new skills, and end up with a new lease on life." The basic principle is "Helping others is often the best therapy." It's the best economy, too. "It costs up to $1,500 a day to hospitalize someone. For what it once cost to warehouse five hundred people in the state hospital, we're now serving three thousand in a community setting."

"Joe Rogers is a visionary who saw the future and pushed for it to happen," says Ilene Shane, director of the Disabilities Law Project. "He's made Pennsylvania a model for consumer-run mental-health programs around the country and the world."

Joe still suffers from random hallucinations and sometimes hears voices that no one else hears. Every day he and millions of others must try to make it through life while they wait for a cure. But, thanks to Joe and Project SHARE, at least the wait is more hopeful, and life is certainly more meaningful. By helping one another, they are a shining example of what it means to be "our brother's keeper." And by educating others about the reality of mental illness, and advocating for change, they are building the road to a better future.

> *Whatever you can do or dream you can, begin it:*
> *Boldness has genius, power and magic in it.*
>
> GOETHE

Help yourself! If you have a mental illness, believe in your abilities: Organize a self-help/advocacy group for yourself and others who are working toward recovery. Call the **National Mental Health Consumers' Self-Help Clearinghouse** for information about organizing, getting funding, and more, 800-553-4539; or visit their Web site, www.mhselfhelp.org.

CARING FOR OUR FAMILIES

Caring for others has always been a tradition in the Carey family. We greeted new neighbors with a loaf of Grammie Carey's pecan rolls. New mothers would find my Aunt Betty's lasagna on their doorstep. Lonely friends were invited to share a Thanksgiving meal, and grieving families got sweet treats and warm hugs.

As children, we often begrudged the exporting of goodies from our kitchen, calculating that someone else's gain must be our loss. But whether we realized it sooner or later, we were learning one of life's most important lessons. Caring for others multiplies love, like the loaves and fishes.

For many years, our extended family came together for christenings, graduations, weddings, and funerals. Since the four Carey siblings had twenty-eight children, there were lots of special occasions to celebrate. We laughed and cried, ate and drank, sang and danced together. Together, pain was more bearable, joy more wonderful; those gatherings were like glue.

Like many families who grew up between the 1950s and the 1990s, we struggled to find ourselves. As each of us searched for his or her own uniqueness, our differences sometimes collided. Often, we'd end up confronting each other on the happiest occasions and parting with deep resentments. As the years went by, we lost track of what we had in common, forgot how much we needed each other, and somewhere along the way, our family's tradition of caring seemed to fade.

But, as a wise friend once told me, if we want to change the world, we can start with our families. They're the best place to start learning how to care for our communities. I wasn't sure how to begin with my own family, but I knew I had to try.

One day my mother, my Aunt Betty, and I confided in one another our concern, sadness, and sense of loss. Over the years we had had our share of heartaches. Loved ones, fathers and children, had been taken too soon, some before we got to say good-bye. We couldn't bear to lose anyone else, and we couldn't wait any longer for healing to happen on its own. We longed to put the family together again.

We decided it was time for a family reunion to revive the true Carey spirit. We sent a flyer inviting all twenty-eight cousins (and their thirty-five children) to a Fourth of July celebration at Aunt Betty and Uncle Connie's camp on Lake Champlain in Vermont. We were eager to see how our family would respond, and to our great delight, they came! From California, Florida, and all over New England, they came to see if the magic was still there. Some hadn't seen each other for years. Many had never met their cousins' new spouses or children. People who hadn't spoken in ages gave up their resentments and renewed old friendships. An annual tradition was born.

Pretty soon we outgrew the camp. Now, each year, we search for the perfect spot, somewhere in New England: a secluded campground with a big fireplace, picnic tables, and a swimming hole for the kids. There'll be no shopping for thirty miles, and no televisions or telephones. Instead, for a few days we chop wood, carry water, cook over fires, pitch tents, and sleep on the hard ground. Each family brings their favorite food, and vegetables from their garden. Out of a basket someone pulls a tablecloth, some candles, and good wine. *Voilà!* Stone Soup! Somehow nature demands that we all pitch in.

After dinner around the campfire, everyone listens as people tell stories from their childhood. When my Uncle Francis was a teenager in the 1930s, he worked with FDR's Civilian Conservation Corps to build these campgrounds. I, who grew up in the idealist sixties, exchange notes with Nancy, who came of age with sex, drugs, and rock and roll in the seventies. Ben, a teenager now, helps us prepare for the future. As we share our stories and responsibilities, we renew our common values and vow to raise our children with them.

We welcome new babies into the clan. In such close quarters, their early-morning whimpers trigger instincts in other mothers. One mother takes another's cranky child for a walk, or for a swim in the lake. Last year's toddlers are running with the "big kids" now. Two five-year-old cousins meet and become friends.

"Mom, that boy keeps following me," says Simon, a bit confused. His mother patiently explains, "That's your cousin, Taylor, and he wants to play with you." Once Simon understands he has a new playmate, they are inseparable. They explore the woods, play monster in the water, and bury themselves in the sand. They giggle and laugh, and tease and torment each other. Their contagious friendship causes aunts and uncles to smile, remembering the fun they had together with young cousins. Our family spirit is reconnected and rekindled. There are hugs—lots of them: We stock up for months.

When it's time to leave, everyone is too busy packing to notice that Simon and Taylor aren't around. Suddenly, Simon's watchful mom calls out the alarm. The entire family joins in a frantic search for the boys, until someone follows a trail of Hershey bar wrappers to the hiding place of two chocolate-covered smiling faces. The boys are surprised by all the fuss. They're just "packing up" the eight candy bars left over from last night's s'mores.

And then, it's time to say good-bye, but the boys don't want to go. As Taylor walks off and cries quietly to himself, Simon is puzzled once again. Not knowing what else to do, he sits beside his cousin and puts his tiny little arm around his shoulder. We never know what words, if any, transpired. He is just there with him, caring. After all, that's what cousins do.

How many years has it been since your extended family got together? Take the time to organize a family reunion, and try to make it a regular event. You'll be glad you did.

WISE BEYOND HIS YEARS

Told by Robert Wuthrow

Adapted from the Independent Sector Report, *What It Means to Volunteer; Lessons from America's Youth*

Dexter Wellman lives with his mother, father, and sister in the low-income area of a prosperous Midwestern city. Their home is a tiny, one-story clapboard house with walls so thin, the ice-cold winter air blows right through. Dexter sleeps in a small room with a mattress on the floor, a couple of posters on the wall, and some plastic milk crates stuffed with books. There is no other furniture. It isn't much to look at; but as Dexter points out, at least it's a home. That's a luxury this ninth-grader hasn't always had.

When Dexter was twelve, both his parents lost their jobs. After falling too far behind on rent and utilities, the Wellmans were forced out into the street. They stored what few belongings they had at his aunt's apartment and, with no other choice, declared themselves homeless. Fortunately, the African Methodist (AME) church to which they belonged ran a shelter for the homeless.

The facility provided refuge; but as Dexter quickly learned, it was no place for a child. Surrounded by so many unfortunate people who seemed to have lost their will to live, Dexter was terribly afraid. Not wanting to end up like them, he looked for a way to stay busy and keep his spirits up.

One day, while wandering around the church building, Dexter noticed some unused classrooms. Seeing the empty spaces, he thought of the many children in the shelter, most of whom couldn't read or write. He remembered playing "school" in the park near his old home. He'd always enjoyed helping other kids with their homework. Perhaps, Dexter thought, he could do it again.

When the woman who ran the shelter agreed to his plan to create a tutoring center, Dexter went to see his school principal. He got some workbooks that were going to be thrown away. Then he asked a community agency to bring over a few desks. Dexter was in business. Soon, every afternoon, evening, and all day Saturday, the kids would come, about twenty at a time. Dexter helped them with their homework, taught them to read, and had them practice in their workbooks.

He fondly remembers one of his first pupils. "When I first started living at the shelter, I met a four-year-old girl named Sarah. She was the youngest student I ever had. At first she couldn't read or write. But within three days she was reading easy books, like *Cat in the Hat* and *Green Eggs and Ham*." It felt really good, knowing that he had done something to help someone.

Her progress was remarkable, thanks, in part, to Dexter's creativity. "I taped myself reading a book. Then, she played the tape and read along with it." During the next nine months, while he lived at the shelter, he grew very close to the other children.

It was painful for Dexter when his pupils moved on, going from shelter to shelter. "Just when you'd get used to someone, they'd move out," Dexter says. Of little Sarah he recalls, "I was really upset when she and her mom left for another shelter. But I gave her the tape and the book and told her to keep on reading."

Although two years have passed since Dexter and his family moved out of the shelter, he still goes back every day to tutor his kids. When he's not with them, he can be found helping the children in his own neighborhood with their schoolwork. The plastic milk crates in his bedroom hold his lending library.

Now nineteen, Dexter is wise beyond his years. Of course, he has already experienced more as a child than most people would ever want to in a lifetime. When asked why he does volunteer work, he replies, "Like they always say, you do something for somebody else, you always get something back." Then he pauses, thinking this over. "People have always helped me," he adds. "So I thought that it was time to give something back."

It is not possible for civilization to flow backwards while there is still youth in the world.

HELEN KELLER

About one-third of all homeless kids can't attend school regularly. Let Dexter's actions inspire you to spend a few hours a week at a homeless shelter, helping kids keep up and receive the extra emotional support they need. For a referral, call your local homeless organizations or your county Homeless Coalition, or visit www.nationalhomeless.org.

LEARNING TO LOVE AGAIN

Told by Judith Thompson

For the first eight years of his life, Arn Chorn enjoyed the luxury of a peaceful childhood. Each night he would lie in his bamboo house in Cambodia's Battambong province and watch stars blaze in the warm and silent sky.

Then came his ninth birthday. He remembers the moment the Khmer Rouge first rode victoriously into town. At first the people welcomed them. But when they got a closer look, they noticed something hard and cold about the faces of these young warriors, as if their very souls had deserted them.

This fanatical Cambodian communist group sprang up in the countryside during the troubled years of the U.S. war with Vietnam. Boys hiding in the jungle with their brutal leader, Pol Pot, were schooled in layer upon layer of hate. Each learned to ignore the voice of his own conscience. The day the Khmer Rouge took over in Cambodia began one of the cruelest bloodbaths in history. Those who survived watched in horror as their beautiful homeland earned a new name, "the killing fields."

Little Arn Chorn was taken from his family, marched into the countryside, and forced into a child-labor camp. He describes the next four years as "a living hell." The Khmer Rouge began the systematic slaughter of millions of Cambodians. People were executed for wearing glasses, for having light skin, for being teachers or monks. People were executed for crying when a family member was killed, thrust into the front lines of combat. Forced to witness the murder of thousands of children, Arn says, "I had to kill my heart in order to survive."

In the chaos that followed the Vietnamese invasion of Cambodia in 1979, Arn was able to escape into the jungle, where he lived alone for many months. His only friends were the monkeys. Arn learned how to survive in the jungle by watching the monkeys, seeing what they ate and eating only what they did. In fact, he came to trust those monkeys more than he could human beings. The tenderness and unconditional love they showed him was the first he had experienced in years. Inside, a tiny part of him started to heal.

Perhaps someone was guiding this little one. One day Arn stumbled across the border into Thailand. He was close to starving to death when rescue workers discovered him and brought him to Sakeo, a large refugee camp. Arn could scarcely believe his fortune when he became the first Cambodian orphan permitted entry into the United States.

Arn arrived in America in October 1980 and thought it was truly amazing. To Arn, America had always seemed at least as far away as the stars. When I met Arn, shortly after his arrival, I was impressed by his willingness to share his story and his struggle to heal his past. For one so young, Arn had an extraordinary desire and ability to inspire others.

Over the years I had met many young people deeply wounded by violence. Arn was exceptionally eager to reach out to those who, like himself, had "endured the nightmare of human madness." Together we founded Children of War, to help children heal their lives and reclaim their futures, and began by working day and night with young people from Cambodian refugee communities.

In 1982, when he was just sixteen, Arn spoke before an enthralled audience of ten thousand people in New York's Cathedral of St. John the Divine. "It seems almost unbelievable that I could forgive and forget what happened to my people," he said. "Sharing with other young people who've endured similar horrors has helped me to feel again—their pain as well as my own." He concluded, "I'm alive after all these years, because I can love again." Those simple words carried more power than Arn could possibly have imagined. Before he knew it, he was sharing his story at the United Nations, before Congress, with people from across the United States.

For the next several years, Children of War provided the vision, training, and support for young people from Beirut, South Africa, and Guatemala, as well as from U.S. inner cities, to heal from their deep grief and rebuild their lives. In the process, they discovered what Arn calls the "common bonds of suffering" and the common dream of peace that unites them. Surprisingly, their own painful sharing gives way to a much deeper joy. They see themselves in each other's stories and dreams and realize that they are not alone.

Strengthened and empowered, these young people become Children of War leaders, like Arn, traveling across the United States, educating and motivating their peers.

That's how Arn met Jacob Smith, a boy from Bedford-Stuyvesant, one of Brooklyn's toughest neighborhoods. For several years Jacob had gone the way of guns, drugs, and violence and ended up in the juvenile-justice system. "When I met Arn and all the other Children of War, I began to dream again about my future," says Jacob. "When I was acting out, I didn't have time to dream. But when I met Arn and began thinking again, I just started to feel real good. Every time my good feeling increased, I realized the violent feelings decreased."

Now Arn and Jacob work as a team in inner-city high schools, helping victims of violence become visionaries. For his work with Children of War, Arn received the Reebok Human Rights Award and the opportunity to travel worldwide on behalf of children whose lives had been torn apart by violence.

In 1990, the Reebok Human Rights Award made it possible for Arn to return to the killing fields of Cambodia. "Sometimes I feel like I want to die," Arn said. "The weight of the past is so great. But then I tell myself that I can do something good to help other people, and that keeps me going." Today, fifty thousand young Cambodians make up Cambodian Volunteers for Community Development. Arn works at the Cambodian Mutual Assistance Association in Boston, helping Cambodian youth form partnerships with those back in Cambodia. "These people have all suffered so much. It will take a while for them to learn to trust and love again," he says. "The Khmer Rouge took that away from us. It will take time, but I am committed. We have to learn to love each other again. That's the only way."

May you live all the days of your life.

JONATHAN SWIFT

Learn more about Arn's work in the film *Strong in the Broken Places* or visit the Cambodian Mutual Assistance Association online at www.asianabc.com/users/cmaa/. If you want to help young people heal from violence in this country and around the world—and help them rebuild their lives and reclaim their futures— visit www.global youthconnect.org.

A HEALING MOMENT

Told by Brother David Stendl-Rast

New York City had never seen anything like it: close to a million people demonstrating against the insanity of nuclear arms. It was 1982. The Cold War was quietly raging.

The people marched from the United Nations headquarters to Central Park, taking half a day to walk those few miles slowly, deliberately, claiming the streets with their banners, charts, signs, and songs. Among them was a quiet band of Buddhist and Christian monks, including Brother David and his companion, the Vietnamese Zen monk Thich Nhat Hanh.*

---

*A leader in the nonviolent movement for peace in Vietnam, Thich Nhat Hanh believed that mindfulness, insight, and altruistic love should be the foundation for any political action. His vision was so powerful that after meeting him in 1966, Martin Luther King Jr. strengthened his commitment to nonviolence in the Civil Rights Movement, and, in solidarity with his new friend, King took the controversial step of supporting the anti–Vietnam War movement. King nominated Thich Nhat Hanh for the Nobel Peace Prize with characteristic eloquence: "His ideas for peace, if applied, would build a monument to ecumenism, to world brotherhood, to humanity."

They were enjoying the crowd: the colorful array of streamers and signs, masks and costumes, clowns surrounded by children, musicians and singers. There were Veterans of Foreign Wars, Grandmothers for Peace, parents wheeling babies, and dogs displaying peaceful slogans on their backs—a day of pure joy in solidarity. On the evening news, New York City's chief of police praised the demonstrators for cleaning up every scrap of trash along their route, right down to the gum wrappers.

Why not leave it at that? A group of students from Columbia University with whom Brother David set out the next morning had grappled all night with this question. They decided there are times when we can—and should—forget what divides us; but other times we must take an active stand for our beliefs. We must make a clean cut, when necessary, so healing can take place. In this spirit, that morning, Brother David and the students would obstruct access to the office of the French delegation to the UN, as other groups were doing the same at offices of the other countries that kept the arms race going. There was to be no violence, even if they were attacked.

As a symbol of their message, they brought bread to share, baskets of fresh, fragrant, home-baked bread. The banner above them read BREAD NOT BOMBS. They sang and prayed and broke the bread, offering it to people rushing by on their way to work. Occasionally someone stopped long enough to read their banner and eat some bread. Homeless people, drawn to the food and company, pulled up with their shopping carts full of belongings.

Soon a police squad moved in and surrounded the entrance to the building. The police asked the protestors to clear out. They stayed. "Do you want to get arrested?" an officer asked. "We want to stay here," a protestor answered, "even if that means getting arrested." The police lowered the visors on their helmets and grabbed their clubs. The protestors knelt down and refused to move.

It was a strange scene, those two lines of people confronting each other, face to face, less than two feet apart. In Brother David's mind, it became a figure in a dance, one position suspended in time. An hour went by, then another. They stood. They sang. They prayed the Lord's Prayer aloud, over and over: "Give us this day our daily bread, and forgive us . . . as we forgive." Another hour passed.

They came to know the buttons on the police uniforms in greater detail than they'd ever known the buttons on their own coats. They were close enough to hear one another's breathing, had it not been for the city noises. Behind the bars of the visor opposite him, Brother David looked into the eyes of a young man. In a different context, he might have called those eyes gentle. He imagined the man's mother proudly showing her neighbors a photo of her son in uniform. By now, he felt like a brother to him. He wondered if the feeling could be mutual.

He didn't understand why they hadn't been arrested and taken off in a paddy wagon hours ago. Why this deadlock? Later they learned that more arrests had been made that day than ever before in the history of New York City. Every police van, and even schoolbuses, had been pressed into service to cart off the demonstrators. Perhaps, when it was their turn, no vehicles were available to take them to jail.

Employees of the French offices came and went. Then one small, silver-haired gentleman in a gray three-piece suit and tie stopped. Looking down the gauntlet—a long row of helmets facing a long row of unprotected heads—Brother David could see the man's face, timid and anxious, exactly where the lines converged. Then something happened, as if a high voltage had built up between the two poles, and suddenly a spark jumped. The man's face lit up. He read the banner, BREAD NOT BOMBS, took off his hat, and—bravely, proudly—held out his hand. He took a piece of bread and put it in his mouth, solemnly almost, as if it were Holy Communion. And in a way, it was.

Shortly after that, the police took off their helmets, shook hands with the demonstrators, and let them go. One of the officers raised his hand in the victory sign. But what Brother David will never forget is the moment when that clerk's face lit up—the victory of his own private conviction—and his own healing.

Touching the present moment is the door to everything.

THICH NHAT HANH

Your gift to the hungry may be small. Find out how you can give it the greatest leverage by contacting **Bread for the World** at 800-82-BREAD, or by visiting their Web site, www.bread.org.

If you want to learn mindfulness with Thich Nhat Hanh by attending a retreat, or to receive a list of his books and tapes, contact the **Community of Mindful Living** at Parallax Press, P.O. Box 7355, Berkeley, CA 94707; or visit www. plumvillage.org.

MINNA MEANS LOVE

Kristin Pauly had never realized one of her most important dreams. She'd always wanted to be a mother. Every time she had a glimpse of motherhood, the door was shut. When she was twenty and pregnant, she had to place her son for adoption. It nearly broke her heart. Later, when she got married, she couldn't get pregnant.

After her childbearing years passed, Kristin hoped that somehow there would be other children in her life. Twenty-one years later she and her biological son, Philip, reconnected. Kristin was thrilled to meet her two beautiful grandchildren. Now, she was a happy grandmother.

At age fifty-one, Kristin was feeling settled, living a happy life. She had a job that she loved as an advocate for the Chesapeake Bay and lived in a beautiful spot. She'd had a life full of adventure and rising to challenges.

One Saturday in March, she went to a baby shower for her friends who had adopted a sweet baby girl. The parents of this child were extremely happy, and they spoke about how Kristin's reunion with her son had touched them, and how they would always be grateful to their daughter's birth parents for entrusting her to them. Kristin's heart was opened that day.

During the reception, chatting with another guest, Kristin asked the young woman if she had any children. "Well, yes, we have a six-month-old daughter," she said. "We just came back from China, where we adopted her." She went on to explain that with China's one-child policy, many little girls have been abandoned. The Chinese tradition of preferring male children is so strong that if a family can have only one child, they want a boy. If their first child is a girl, she may be abandoned so they can try again.

Kristin was stunned. It took her a while to comprehend fully what the woman was saying. Then she felt tears welling up inside, and the room felt like it was floating away. She sat down for a moment in the nearest chair to collect herself. In an instant, the door of motherhood that had been closed to her for so many years opened. With a rush, the thought came to her: *I could do that, too. I could go to China and bring back my daughter.*

Kristin amazed herself with the idea that she could be a mother at fifty-one, and that a little girl was waiting for her in China. But maybe she was too old, maybe they wouldn't let her adopt a child at her age. Still, she knew she was going to try, and joy filled her heart.

The next morning, Kristin called the woman from the party. "I don't know if this is even possible," she began. "Do you think I could adopt a little girl from China, too?" The woman said, "I think so. The Chinese have a different respect for age; their regulations specify that adoptive parents must be *over* a minimum age, and I don't think there is an upper age limit. I'll give you the name of the agency we used, and you can call them tomorrow."

Kristin started going through all the steps required for an international adoption—making lists, filling out forms, and waiting for documents to arrive from government agencies. The adoption process is not an easy one; it took nine months to complete the paperwork, to take the parenting classes, and to go through all the necessary steps. In August, Kristin received the long-awaited photograph of her little girl. Her name was Chang Chun Da, which means "spring arrives." It was hard to believe that a flesh-and-blood child would emerge from all of this paperwork, but there she was! On October 24, Kristin and her sister-in-law boarded a plane for the thirty-six-hour trip to China.

They landed in Beijing, and after a few days of sightseeing and acclimatization, on a Sunday, the ten other families who were adopting from her agency took a four-hour bus ride through the Chinese countryside to Changzhou. At 8:00 A.M. on Monday, they went to Changzhou Children's Welfare Institute, where they were escorted to a narrow room lined with banquettes and doilies. There were bowls of fruit piled on the tables, and many officials and nurses were present. There were speeches (and translators), and gifts were exchanged. After too much ceremony, the families were lined up in a certain order, and when everyone was in place, caretakers poured in with a beautifully choreographed parade of babies! A woman in a white coat handed Kristin a little baby girl dressed in a yellow knitted outfit. She couldn't quite hold her head up. But Kristin recognized her from her photo and knew this was her little girl. From the first moment, she was Minna—Kristin's great-grandmother's name, which means "love" (in Finnish).

The quiet room erupted in happy chaos as people who had wanted children for years actually held their hearts' desires. There were babies everywhere—some in yellow like Minna, some in blue—but they were all little girls. The new parents left with a bag of formula and bottles, and a list of the things the babies liked to eat.

Eventually, Kristin and Minna arrived back at the hotel—at last they were alone together. But Minna didn't seem to want to eat. Kristin was worried about her and had trouble falling asleep. Around four in the morning, she woke up and heard the baby stirring. Kristin leaned over, picked up little Minna, and put her on her chest. There they were, the two of them, in a dark hotel room in China. As Minna lay on her chest, Kristin felt Minna open her heart to her. In that intimate, dark space she said, "I'm here. I trust you." And Kristin answered,

"I'm here, too. It has taken a long time to get to you, but now I am here. And from now on, I will always be here for you." In that moment, Kristin and Minna became mother and daughter.

The next day they went back to the orphanage to take some pictures, and as they were leaving, one of the caretakers leaned over and said, "This baby loves to laugh!" Kristin was overjoyed, since of all the major characteristics that she hoped her daughter would have, this was most important to her. Just a few weeks later, during an episode of the TV program *World's Funniest Videos*, when Minna was only six months old, the two of them laughed together until tears ran down their cheeks.

Kristin has discovered that she's a very good mother. She kept waiting for the meltdown or the sense of inadequacy to come flooding in—but it didn't. She found her own reserves of calmness, patience, and wisdom. The shift from single life to being a family is momentous, but there's nonetheless an easy flow to their lives.

Minna is now six years old and comfortable being a Chinese American. Kristin and Minna keep in touch with the families who adopted that same day in Changzhou. With other families in their town who have adopted Chinese daughters, they've started a Chinese-language class and get together often. Kristin herself feels physically bound to China now and studies its history, cuisine, and traditions. It is especially painful for her to think about Minna's sisters who weren't in the favored orphanages that benefit from international adoptions. In both cities and rural areas, many of them don't get enough to eat and cannot go to school. Only 10 percent of the hundreds of thousands of little girls abandoned in China find homes.

As they build their lives together, Kristin and Minna will always be sensitive to women's rights, to their struggles for independence and self-esteem, and to the rights of all different kinds of families outside the young, racially homogenous, married heterosexual model. Over the years, China has changed its adoption policies, making it much more difficult for single parents to adopt. However, there are children in other countries in need of loving families. One day recently, a manila envelope arrived at Kristin's house—the forms to start the process of adopting a sister for Minna.

Kristin is committed to helping anyone—especially older or single people—go through the process of adoption. "Adoption is a wonderful way to create a family—at any age," says Kristin. Minna loves being a "little aunt" to her grown brother's children. And pretty soon she will have a new baby sister! "Every girl and every woman deserve an opportunity to love and be loved, and to have a chance in life," she says.

> *And as they held you close they whispered into your open, curving ear,*
> *"We're so glad you've come."*
>
> DEBRA FRASIER, *On the Day You Were Born*

Learn how you can adopt a Chinese girl and bring joy to both of you. Contact **Families with Children from China.** Call your local chapter, or visit www. fwcc.org. Contact Kristin Pauly via e-mail at kapauly@aol.com.

VII

DOING WELL
BY DOING GOOD

A

few years ago, Ted Turner stunned the world with his announcement that he was giving the United Nations a billion dollars over ten years. It all started with a lunch he had one day with Claude Rosenberg. The founder of a $26-billion investment company who had discovered the joy of giving back, Rosenberg had an idea: to get Bill Gates and others to agree to give away a billion dollars a year for three or four years. "They can easily afford to do that and set an example for others," he told Turner.

Until then, Bill Gates had lived by the old adage "Make your money while you are young and give it away when you are old." But when Ted Turner called and invited him to "join the club," he had a change of heart. Soon afterward, Gates created the largest foundation in the nation, with over $23.5 billion in assets. People around the world benefit from his generosity: millions of children in Africa immunized, thousands of schools equipped with technology, and researchers making breakthroughs in AIDS vaccine development.

People in the business world were also inspired by Howard Lutnick, Cantor Fitzgerald CEO, who promised to pay the salaries for all seven hundred of the firm's employees who lost their lives in the collapse of the World Trade Center. After the disaster on September 11, this hard-driving businessman softened. "My view of business is different," he said. "We've got to make our company take care of my seven hundred families."

Whether corporate humanitarians choose to do good because of "enlightened self-interest" or as smart business practice, many companies have discovered the power of being more socially responsible. Coca-Cola is leading a global coalition to address the AIDS crisis in Africa. Unilever bought environmental champion Ben & Jerry's and is learning about their tradition of doing well by doing good. More than three hundred large companies have pledged their support to the United Nations' Global Compact on human rights, labor standards, and environmental protection.

This chapter offers successful examples and a wealth of ideas for how to begin. Paul Newman started out by bottling and selling his favorite salad dressing and donating the proceeds to charity. This year Newman's Own celebrates its twentieth anniversary as a business that donates 100 percent of its profits to humanitarian and envionmental projects, totaling an amazing $125 million. Business heroes like Aaron Feuerstein, Judy Wicks, and Arnold Hiatt use their heads and hearts, their moral and economic resources, to improve their communities. Bank of America finds that building partnerships with community organizations to help first-time homeowners multiplies its investments and maximizes its effectiveness. Bonneville International offers listeners to their radio stations opportunities to give back to their communities.

Consumers are paying attention to the broader implications of their purchases. Studies show that, all things being equal, people prefer to spend their dollars with companies that are doing good in the world. Members of Business for Social Responsibility find that doing good helps them to do well—enhancing their public image, attracting better and more-motivated employees, lowering their risks, and boosting their stock prices. Companies conduct "social audits" to impress the public and monitor their own behavior. Even the Dow Jones Sustainability Index now tracks social and environmental as well as economic performance. Some companies realize that the highest good of doing business can ultimately be the good of all.

Companies are also doing well by giving their time as well as their money to do good. More than 50 percent of Fortune 500 companies have workplace volunteer programs. Even when times are tough—with an uncertain economy and layoffs—employees continue volunteering. Helping those less fortunate helps them put their own situations in perspective.

Home Depot finds that when employees volunteer in their communities, it builds a strong team spirit in the workplace. Multinational companies like EDS extend their tradition of being good neighbors as they expand their business abroad. This year, EDS celebrates its tenth anniversary of Global Volunteer Day. "One of my dreams for EDS goes way beyond financial success and service excellence," says its chairman, Dick Brown. "I want us to be the most admired company—to have a heart and soul and give back something to the communities we work in." A lifelong volunteer, he encourages all 130,000 employees to participate in EDS's Global Volunteer Day—living out the company's philosophy that healthy communities and healthy business go hand-in-hand.

Money is one of the most important tools we have to create positive change in the world. While we can't all be Ted Turner or Bill Gates, there are hundreds of ways each of us can invest our time and our money in our communities. We will make the world a better place when we revolutionize the way we think about gain and giving.

What if more businesspeople championed socially responsible business? What if investors insisted upon it? What if the best, the brightest, and the most powerful supported what is working for everyone in the world? Just imagine what the world would look like, what an inheritance for future generations!

There comes a time in each of our lives

when we must choose:

to continue on the path we're on,

or take a look at the world and ask ourselves:

What is most important in my life?

What kind of life do I really want to live?

What kind of world do I want for my children and my grandchildren?

Now is the time. And it's your turn to choose.

Don't wait. Dare to share.

Act with your pocketbook.

Write the check. Just do it!

STONE SOUP MAGIC
Told by A. E. Hotchner

Think of him as a master chef cooking up magic for the whole world. "I like to take what I've got and spread it around," Paul Newman says. He has the old-fashioned notion that a man whom the world did good by ought to do good by the world. So he does. He donates every penny of his after-tax profits from his company, Newman's Own, Inc., to good causes. Since 1982 his charitable contributions have totaled over $125 million.

"Newman's Own began as a lark, a joke more or less, and soon became a challenge," says the movie star. "I had no idea that my salad dressing would outgross my films. Today there's an entire generation that may know me more for my popcorn than for my movies," he adds with a grin.

"Newman's Own furnishes people with wholesome, all-natural foods that they enjoy," Newman explains. "The after-tax profits from the company are then given to organizations serving people who, because of poverty, sickness, old age, or illiteracy, desperately need assistance." Newman has funded programs for health, education, the homeless, the environment, the arts, and children. Thousands of organizations have received grants from the company, the majority of them smaller, obscure organizations that are often overlooked by mainstream donors. "What makes this business great is the mutually beneficial recycling from the haves to the have-nots," says Newman.

Among his favorite endeavors is the Newman's Own and Good Housekeeping Recipe Contest, in which winners receive ten thousand dollars to donate to their favorite charity. When a first-grade class at the Terra Linda School in Beaverton, Oregon, learned about the recipe contest, they decided to try their luck.

That week, during story time, their teacher, Mrs. Clement, read them the classic children's folktale "Stone Soup": *A hungry traveler feeds himself and a whole village, starting with just one magic stone and a pot of water. When each of the villagers gives a little, there is plenty for everyone.* Twenty-four six-year-olds listened carefully, sitting cross-legged on mats surrounding their teacher, studying with wide eyes the pictures she showed them. When she'd finished reading, they talked about the book. The children agreed that their favorite illustration was the very last one. Above "The End," an entire village feasted together upon this extraordinary soup.

Mrs. Clement had a great idea: What if the class entered their own recipe for Stone Soup in the contest? The kids were enthusiastic. Working together, they chalked a list on the blackboard of all your basic soup ingredients, except for two: a twenty-six-ounce jar of Newman's Own Sockarooni Sauce, and a stone. "It wouldn't be right without a stone from Oregon," said Jessica Stewart.

Stone Soup made them winners. "When Mrs. Clement told us we had won the contest," Jessica, now thirteen, remembers, "we screamed, shouted, and danced around the classroom."

The students knew exactly what they would do with their ten thousand dollars in prize money: They would give it back to their own school. They purchased books for the library, keyboards for the music department, and a weather station. They stamped every new item with the words "Newman's Own." Now, checking out a book or playing the keyboards reminds Terra Linda students of their legacy of innovation and generosity.

As for Jessica, her days of giving have just begun. "Winning ten thousand dollars as a kid made a big difference in how I feel about giving. It made me want to help others now and when I get older," she says. "Now that I'm in the fourth grade, I'm on the student council. Each year we give our time and energy to help others. We've collected money to buy school supplies for the flood victims in the Oregon flood. We've collected pop cans to raise money for Keiko the whale. We bring in Campbell's Soup labels to get balls for our playground."

"An important part of what we teach in the classroom is sharing, giving, and helping others," Mrs. Clement confirms. "The students also learn that to be successful in life, it's necessary to listen, work together, and solve problems." The Stone Soup story was a feast of food for thought, and the contest invited the children to make it real. "The books and keyboards will grow old and out of date, but the memory of what the students were able to do for their school will stay with them always," she says. "Paul Newman could have just made his own donation, and does, but by helping others to give, he gives so much more than just money. The greatest gift Paul Newman gave my students was a lesson in the value of giving. He planted the seeds for them to do great things in their lives."

MRS. CLEMENT'S FIRST-GRADERS' STONE SOUP RECIPE

1 magic stone
10 cups water
1 10½-oz. can broth
1 tsp. salt
1 tsp. pepper
2 lbs. stew meat
1 large onion, sliced
1 26-oz. jar Newman's Own Sockarooni Sauce
4 carrots, sliced
4 celery stalks
10 small new potatoes, cut in small chunks
1 12-oz. package Italian green beans
1 cup uncooked ABC pasta

Place stone in small amount of water (2 cups) with broth, salt, pepper, stew meat, and onion in an 8-quart soup pot. Simmer on low heat for approximately 2 hours. Add Newman's Own Sockarooni Sauce and vegetables. Continue to simmer for 20 minutes, until vegetables are tender. Add ABC pasta and cook for another

10–15 minutes until pasta is al dente. **Don't forget to remove stone before eating, or teeth may get hurt.** Serve with warm bread and butter. Serves one first-grade class of 24, or 8 adults.

Cook up a winner for your favorite charity. Enter your best recipe using a Newman's Own product in the **Newman's Own and Good Housekeeping Recipe Contest.** For more information, call 800-272-0257, or visit <u>newmansown.com</u>.

FROM STREET KIDS TO WALL STREET
Told by Matthew Malone

Show Steve Mariotti a young person bright enough to rob someone and get away with it, and he'll show you a potential business leader needing direction. Inside a rundown classroom on the uncertain streets of the Bedford-Stuyvesant section of Brooklyn is probably the last place most people would look for America's entrepreneurial future, but Steve is trying to change all that.

It was a dark night when he first saw the light. Jogging down a busy New York street, dodging the city's normal hustle and bustle, Steve was stopped abruptly by a gang of youths who wanted his money. They roughed him up and he handed over his wallet, and, though still somewhat dazed, as he watched them run away he was jarred by an improbable thought: What if the talents and energy these kids spent on illegal and destructive activities could be channeled productively?

A successful businessman himself, Steve recognized their creativity and drive, however misguided, as the same qualities needed in the business world. They were aggressive, focused—and they were working together to achieve a common goal. Unfortunately, tonight their goal was his wallet. But Steve had a hunch that with the proper training, these kids could reach higher. He decided to leave his successful import-export business behind and follow a dream.

Steve had always wanted to be a teacher. He taught one of his first classes at the Central Ward Boys & Girls Club in Newark, New Jersey, where one of his first students was fifteen-year-old Felix Rouse. Felix was instantly impressed by his teacher, a short white man carefully explaining such business concepts as supply and demand, buying wholesale, and profit. To this bunch of kids, the business world looked like another planet. As Steve talked, he laid the groundwork for his "mini-MBA," enticing the students with his enthusiastic delivery and promising ideas.

He taught them the basics of running a business. They opened checking accounts, designed business cards, and discussed the delicate art of customer relations. They visited Wall Street, met with wholesalers, and developed plans to start their own businesses.

Steve used somewhat unusual techniques to get his students to think beyond today to what they could become. One day when they came to class, he greeted them with a challenge: "If you want something badly enough, you'll reach high enough to get it!" They followed his gaze upward and saw a five-dollar bill dangling from the ceiling. As his classmates and teacher looked on, Felix made several unsuccessful attempts to grab the bill. He stopped for a moment to think, then he climbed up on a chair as his friends chanted, "Fe-lix, Fe-lix, Fe-lix!" He leaped through the air, snatched the money, and landed safely back on the classroom floor. Money in hand, Felix sashayed back to his chair, and Steve said again, smiling, "If you want something badly enough, you'll reach high enough to get it!"

A few months later, Felix reached for his dream, too. He and a friend had a passion for comic books, and they decided to open their own comic-book store. First they developed a detailed business plan, outlining their costs, prices, and strategy. Steve gave them one hundred dollars to open their own store. For two years they ran their business out of office space provided by the Boys & Girls Club. The boys did all the buying and selling, bookkeeping, and inventory.

"Though we didn't make a ton of money, I never had to borrow any," Felix says. "I learned very quickly to take care of myself and developed the skills to be successful."

In 1986, Steve created the NFTE (National Foundation for Teaching Entrepreneurship) to expand his successful program to reach other inner-city youth. NFTE now has 45,000 graduates, 400 active and 2,000 trained teachers, 14,000 sponsors, and 12,000 students each year in the United States as well as in India, Belgium, the United Kingdom, and Argentina, breaking through the dead ends of drugs, crime, and teenage pregnancy in vigorous pursuit of success in business. In partnerships with Goldman Sachs, Microsoft, and Koch Industries, as well as major universities—Harvard, Stanford, Yale, Columbia Teacher's College, and Babson College—NFTE is making inroads beyond Steve's wildest dreams.

While inner-city kids learn about business, hone their personal ambitions, and even begin to count their profits, the personal attention and respect they're getting from someone who really cares is invaluable. "Steve was always in the mix," Felix says. "He knew about my struggles and was always there to listen. He cares about all of us on a very personal level."

Like many other NFTE students, Felix has experienced some bumps along the road. During his senior year in high school, his father passed away. A year later his older brother was shot and confined to a wheelchair. But Felix stayed on course and followed his dream to college. In 1996 he graduated from the University of Pennsylvania with a degree in political science. He became the first NFTE student to be trained as an entrepreneurship teacher, teaching at the Boys & Girls Club where he first encountered Steve. He's working on his MBA at Cornell University.

The outlook for thousands of kids like Felix who find their way through the NFTE program is not "underprivileged." Their new knowledge, skills, experience, and hope skyrocket their chances of success. As one graduate put it, "My dream is not to die in poverty, but to have poverty die in me." Day by day, student by student, so it is and so it does.

A coach is someone who tells you what you don't want to hear, and has you see what you don't want to see, so you can be who you have always known you could be.

TOM LANDRY

Want to help a child learn how to start a small business, get NFTE's entrepreneurial curriculum into the hands of at-risk youth, or sponsor a teacher to be NFTE trained? Visit the NFTE Web site, www.nfte.com.

THE ROBIN HOOD OF WALL STREET
Told by Terry Mollner

All the world was built by dreamers—and Wayne Silby was a dreamer. Born and raised in a small Iowa town, he was nevertheless introduced to the world of high finance at the age of eight. When his father bought him twenty shares of stock, he carried the confirmation slip around with him—knowing it was "important." He treasured it more than his baseball cards. By the time Wayne was fourteen, he was picking his own stocks. By age thirty, he was the youngest CEO of a billion-dollar investment fund.

In the late 1970s, Wayne and his buddy John Guffey borrowed ten thousand dollars from Wayne's dad and created an all-government (and tax-exempt) money market fund. They rented a desk at a law office so they would have the prestigious address of 1700 Pennsylvania Avenue, Washington, D.C., and Wayne, who was a lawyer, did their legal work himself. They asked some respected finance people to be on their board and got the approval of the Securities and Exchange Commission. Friends and other supporters invested the necessary $100,000 start-up money to launch the First Government Securities

Fund. Because of the variable-rate government loans they found, within a couple of months it was the top performing fund of its kind in the country.

One day, Wayne came to Boston to meet with Terry Mollner and explore ideas he and his colleagues had been working on to stimulate socially responsible investing. They took a long walk in a park and talked about the state of affairs in the world and what they could do about it. They were thinking out loud about how nice it would be to have an investment fund that was "an expression of something from our generation—finance according to our values." Suddenly their feet stopped, and they turned and saw the future spark and crackle in each other's hopeful eyes.

They decided they would invest only in companies that had healthy relationships with their employees, the community, and the environment. They were earnest, doing what they thought was right—not expecting that it would grow to become a $2-billion fund, spawn a new industry, and attract millions of supporters. "That's what happens sometimes when you just do the right thing," Wayne would later say.

Less than a year later, when Wayne's company, now called The Calvert Group, had established its success, he called Terry and said, "Let's create a socially responsible mutual fund." Wayne invited Terry to be on its Board of Trustees, and they conceived the Calvert Family of Socially Responsible Investment Funds, what is now the largest and oldest family of such funds in the world, with over $2 billion under management.

When Wayne and John first presented the idea to their management team, it was rejected. They were told that their small company would be laughed out of the Wall Street community. "Well," Wayne said, "since John and I own the company, we will do it as a special project." To set it up, they spent hundreds of thousands of dollars—knowing there would be many years of losses before they reached the $30-million break-even point.

They started with a particularly bold decision: They would not invest in any company doing business in South Africa. Calvert was the first mutual fund to make such a commitment. For decades, apartheid had been South Africa's official policy of discrimination against black Africans. In 1982 there weren't very many people in the world bothering to take a stand against it. But within a few years, a huge movement of investors—city and state governments, universities, and other business and financial institutions—also came to refuse to invest in companies doing business in South Africa. And since Calvert was initially the only one they could invest in with a clear conscience, Calvert reached the $30-million target long before they thought it would. The impact this had on South Africa was historic. "The disinvestment movement in America was a significant factor in ending apartheid," says Nelson Mandela. "The Calvert Group deserves a great deal of credit," says the late Dr. Leon Sullivan, founder of the anti-apartheid movement's Sullivan divestiture principles. "They were the first to pressure companies—and to help us confront the government of South Africa."

Today, in the United States over $2 trillion is invested with a social con-science—one of the fastest-growing areas of investment. You can walk into any brokerage firm and ask for someone to help you set up a "socially screened port-folio." In 1975 you would have been sent to the offices of a local charity. The trend is also spreading rapidly to other countries around the world.

The Calvert Social Investment Fund had some unusual ground rules: Up to 10 percent of the funds' assets could be loaned directly to new, socially respon-sible businesses and organizations. Eventually, they wanted to bring together into one movement or industry the socially responsible investment community, which invested in stocks and bonds, and the community investment community, which invested in poor communities. They wanted to offer people the same financial return while being socially responsible and also to respond to investors who would accept a lower return on a very small portion of the fund so it could provide investment dollars to poor families to work their way out of poverty.

In 1988 Calvert began making loans with less than 1 percent of the assets in their socially responsible mutual funds at low (3 percent) interest rates to local community loan funds around the world. These funds would then re-loan the money to poor families in "micro-loans"—initially as small as twenty-five dollars—to help them start their own businesses. The program was so successful that they created an investment program within a foundation they established alongside The Calvert Group. This makes it possible for anyone in the world to invest in ending poverty. Thousands of people's lives have been transformed by these loans, like Joite, a woman Terry met in a Bangladesh village. "A few years ago my children and I were living under a tree by the road. We had nothing. Nothing," she said to him emphatically, then added, "With your help, I now have a house, chickens, goats, cows, a fish pond, banana trees, and a husband. My children go to school. We are happy—and alive."

While Robin Hood stole from the rich to give to the poor, Wayne and Terry and the people they have brought together invite the rich to join together in giving to the poor. And many have—beyond their most ambitious dreams.

These investors are creating a new, mutually respectful "hand-up rather than hand-out industry." A few years ago you couldn't find any legitimate socially responsible investment options on Wall Street; today you can choose among many. Follow your heart and fatten your wallet and know that your choices are changing the world. "People want to do the right thing," Wayne says. "If they are given a choice, many will choose to make money by helping the good guys. All we did was give them a choice."

The next time a great idea catches fire when your eyes meet another's, believe in it, and your ability—your responsibility—together to make it happen. Then do.

Invest your money with companies that have healthy relationships with the environment, their employees, and the community. Contact the **Calvert Family of Socially Responsible Mutual Funds** at 800-368-2750 or their Web site, www.calvert.com. If you want to invest to help people work their way out of poverty permanently, contact the **Calvert Foundation** at 800-248-0337, or visit www.calvertfoundation.org.

JIM'S BIG SECRET
Told by Sheila Richardson

Jim Guest was a great guy with a big secret. For fifteen years he'd worked hard to be a valued employee at Ames Rubber. His supervisors knew they could count on Jim to learn just about any job. They knew he would get it done—and in record time. What they didn't know was that Jim couldn't read. But he isn't alone. More than 40 million adults in our country live with this challenge every day.

Jim will be the first to admit that he was never very interested in school. He had other things to do. As a child, it was playing. Then, as a teenager, it was partying and hanging out. No one knew Jim couldn't read or write, and he tried to keep it that way. "When you don't know how to read, you find ways of getting around it," he explains. "People who can't read have a bag full of tricks to hide their handicap. To pull it off, you actually have to be pretty smart. Being illiterate is definitely not the same thing as being stupid."

Jim hid his secret well, until one day, when it came crashing in on him. He was chosen to participate in a special company project and was asked to take notes at a meeting. Jim was trapped, there was no way out. He decided to tell his boss, Bob Kenna, the truth—the three words he had been hiding his whole life: "I can't read." He didn't know what to expect. Would his boss understand? Would he trash years of hard work and loyalty?

To Jim's huge relief, his boss said, "Don't worry about it, we'll work something out," and a great weight was lifted from his shoulders. After hiding the truth for so long, Jim was finally free. A few months later, Bob asked Jim if he'd like to learn to read, explaining that several Ames employees were tutors trained by

Literacy Volunteers of America. He could work with one of them and learn to read on company time. Jim was overjoyed. "I jumped at the chance," he says.

Jim met with his tutor, Sandy Rocheleau, for an hour and a half every week to learn skills most people acquire in grade school. At first his progress was slow, but gradually he improved. For two years Jim was faithful to his weekly tutoring sessions, working toward a special goal that kept him going: to read to his new son, Kyle. Soon enough, he did.

"It's hard to express how I feel," Jim says. "Words like pride, accomplishment, self-respect, self-confidence, and security come to mind, but also hard work, drive, challenge, and commitment. It has not been easy, but it sure was worth it."

Several months passed, during which Jim and Sandy hadn't spoken. Then one day Sandy received a phone call from Jim, to say that he had just finished reading his first novel, *Robinson Crusoe*. "Thanks for making it possible," he said. Sandy remembers that as one of the golden moments of her life. "It just doesn't get any better than that," she says. "I'm so proud of him. And I've gotten as much out of it as he has."

Following Jim and Sandy's success, Ames extended this gift to others. Their tutors work with employees and local residents who want to learn to read and write. Jim has become their greatest cheerleader, encouraging everyone to learn to read. "There is no shame in not being able to read," Jim tells others. "The shame is in not taking advantage of an opportunity to learn.

"When you can't read, your whole life is a continuous balancing act, memorizing on the one hand, and hiding the handicap on the other. What's frightening is that I couldn't even read medicine-bottle labels for the correct dosage. Thanks to Sandy and Ames, I don't have to hide anymore.

"At bedtime, as I hold my son in my arms, a lot of things go through my head," he adds. "I have to change the oil in my car. What will I plant in the garden this year? I need new work boots. But all these thoughts fly out of my head when Kyle tosses *The Cat in the Hat* in my lap. A few short years ago, I couldn't read even the simplest story to him. It won't be long now before his mother finds us sitting at the kitchen table doing homework together. Tonight he said, 'Come on,

Daddy, let's read *Green Eggs and Ham* next.' You can't imagine how good it makes me feel to be able to do that for him."

The Boulder

All through my life, a boulder was in my way.
I tried to move it. It wouldn't budge.
I tried to pick it up, or break it.
I could only chip at it.
So, for most of my life, I managed to work around it.
Then one day, there was no way out.
I looked at it, and admitted it was a problem.
Help came.
Together we chipped away at the boulder.
Then, we pushed it, tugged at it.
We managed to move it, slowly at first.
It started to roll, then faster and faster.
It rolled off a cliff and broke in pieces.
Today I can read.
And though I still have some problems, there's help.
Thanks for the help.

JIM GUEST

Give someone the gift of reading; call **Literacy Volunteers of America, Inc.,** at 800-LVA-8812 for the LVA group nearest to you; or visit LVA at www.literacy volunteers.org. If someone you know could benefit from their free and confidential services, have them call us, too.

GIVING THEM A CHANCE

Told by Diane Valletta

Ladell Johnson was just another one of the unemployed in an inner-city Chicago neighborhood. A casualty of a factory shutdown, this earnest African-American woman faced a bleak and uncertain future. Quiet and timid, Ladell's potential was shrouded in a deep-seated lack of confidence, but the thought of going on welfare went against everything she believed in. All she wanted was a fair chance.

Thanks to Rachel Hubka, she got it. The owner of Rachel's Bus Company, Rachel has a knack for recognizing people's hidden talents. When she interviewed Ladell for a job, Ladell's life switched tracks. "Rachel stirred something inside me," Ladell says. "Her faith in my abilities woke me up to what life was all about. For the first time I felt I could really live, instead of just going through the motions."

For Rachel, interviewing an unemployed person with no related job experience was not unusual. After all, she chose to locate her company in North Lawndale, a Chicago neighborhood where unemployment is more or less stable at 60 percent. She recruits seemingly unemployable people and many welfare recipients to drive her schoolbuses.

Blessed with loving and supportive parents, Rachel grew up convinced that "I could do anything, as long as I had an opportunity." She now extends that same confidence and enthusiasm to her employees. "When I opened my business, I wanted to create opportunities for those the system had left behind. They needed work, and I needed employees. I knew that with the right training they could become valuable members of society."

Rachel believes in helping people help themselves. Her guiding principle is "Bloom where you are planted." With her training, inspiration, and encouragement, her employees reach for more responsibility and move up in the company. Rachel fosters an entrepreneurial spirit by offering commissions to drivers who bring in charter business. She helps men and women with marginal work histories and minimal skills grow into proud, productive, and committed employees.

Helping others work has worked for Rachel. Her seven-year-old company has expanded to a staff of more than 140, and a fleet of 125 buses. In 1995 she received the prestigious Business Enterprise Award, which honors business owners who build their success with their social conscience.

Rachel did more than just give Ladell a job. From the start, she encouraged Ladell to stretch herself. She gave her new opportunities and guided her along the way. Rachel asked Ladell to take her place at important meetings with school administrators, CEOs, and other business and community leaders.

Ladell had lived a life of solitude, rarely interacting with the community around her. So at first she went reluctantly, then with increasing self-assurance and enthusiasm. She developed a natural ease with others. From her first job as a personnel clerk, Ladell rose to become head of the human resources division. Now she looks for ways to contribute to the company, her co-workers, and the community.

In only a few years, Ladell has lowered employee turnover by carefully screening applicants and matching them with the right jobs. She helps get people registered to vote and urges other employees to take active roles in their community. On her own time, as a lay minister, she helps those who are ill, or just want someone to talk to.

Ladell, someone whom society might have written off, recently received the Sister Thea Bowman Humanitarian Award, given to people who do things for others "just because." She credits Rachel for the opportunity and inspiration to make her life a successful one. In a note of thanks she sent to Rachel straight from her heart, Ladell wrote, "I recently met two young women who reminded me of the old me, both in their early twenties, their lives in a downward spiral.

One, a mother of two, was in an abusive relationship; the other was struggling to find her way as an adult. I reached out to them. Now the three of us are finding our way by enriching the lives of others. And it all began with you."

Give **Welfare to Work** reform a chance, and make a positive impact on your community and the nation's economy. Help people off the welfare rolls and onto the tax rolls. Call the Welfare to Work Partnership at 202-955-3005, or visit www.welfaretowork.org.

A CULTURE OF GIVING
Told by Ann Bauer

For eight years, Esther Diaz rose early two days each week and dressed for her job at the Target store in Lavern, California. There she served customers from behind the counter on "Food Avenue," folded towels, hung clothes, marked prices, and always earned the highest marks from her superiors. Esther is a remarkable employee who just happens to have a mental disability and happens to have a job because of Target Stores' recruiting program, "I Can Do That."

It began in 1988 when Dwight Bonds, a high-school teacher, devised a plan to help Esther and three of her classmates who were developmentally disabled make the transition from graduation to the workforce.

"I called Target's regional office and explained what I was looking for," Bonds says. "My students need an opportunity and a little extra support transitioning into the workplace." He was pleased with Target's response. "They said, 'We'll make them a part of our family,'" he says. "They offered them regular jobs, with the same benefits and wages paid to other employees."

The store came through with frontline jobs as well as job coaches. Bonds drilled the students on skills they would need, such as money counting and alphabetic filing. At work, Esther Diaz's managers discovered she was dependable and attentive to every job she was assigned, including those in which other workers tended to lose interest. "You never see Esther just standing around," commented her supervisor, Hope Cantwell. "She's always working hard." Within five months the arrangement proved so successful, Target placed twenty-five more mentally challenged students in thirteen California locations.

Bonds calls it a win-win-win situation. Young people get jobs. Parents who feared their kids would be dependent for life see that they are able to work and be productive. And businesses find out that the disabled can make great employees.

The program grew by leaps and bounds, eventually benefiting more than 1,500 severely disabled workers in 736 Target stores nationwide. Customer response was fantastic. Letters poured into the national office complimenting the workers and praising the company for giving them a chance. The company incorporated the program into their everyday hiring process.

Minneapolis-based Target Corporation has been a national leader in charitable giving and social action for more than fifty years. George Draper Dayton began this culture of giving in 1909 by donating $500,000 from his department store to charity. "Success by contribution is open to everyone," wrote Dayton. "The thrills of relieving distress, of encouraging the young or ministering to the aged, of easing the footsteps of the weary—are these not rewards greater than the knowledge you have added thousands of dollars to your hoard?"

Fortunately, the heirs to Dayton's growing empire inherited their grandfather's generous spirit. In 1946 they created the "Five-Percent Rule," under which 5 percent of the corporation's pre-tax profits are set aside and reinvested in the community. In 1974, a particularly hard year for the retail industry, Dayton employees voted to keep the five-percent covenant even if their salaries had to be cut. Today this amounts to $1 million a week given back to the communities Target serves.

Thanks in part to Dayton's leadership, the Twin Cities ranks as one of the most giving corporate communities in the United States. The Greater Minneapolis Chamber of Commerce sponsors the 5% Club for over two hundred other members.

In 1996, Target Corporation celebrated its fiftieth anniversary of giving with the "50 Acts of Giving Day." Volunteers from more than one hundred Target stores across the country helped their communities by cleaning up parks, assisting the elderly, and removing debris from the Mississippi River Bank. "Employees rolled up their sleeves, donating time and energy," says Laysha Ward, director of the Target Foundation. "Our team member volunteers reflect the heart of this company and our commitment to our communities."

When a district team leader, Kim Dicicco, and her Southern California colleagues learned that the Special Olympics would be held on the same day as the 50 Acts of Giving Day, she rallied to take them on as a joint cause. Thanks to her recruiting efforts, more than four hundred Target employees from seventy stores volunteered for the weekend events. On opening night they formed a huge cheering section to welcome the athletes. For the next two days, during the competitions, they shouted encouragement from the sidelines and handed out medals. "We did a lot of screaming, yelling, and high-fiving," Kim remembers.

Ian Eaton, a young man hired through the "I Can Do That" program, ran with the Olympic torch in front of the store where he works as a cart attendant. The street was lined with people cheering him on.

"When Ian was coming down the street, we announced it over the loudspeaker in the store. Everyone just poured out the doors," recalls his supervisor, Karla Burgess. Even customers left their shopping carts and ran outside to cheer for Ian.

"That was fun!" Ian told his supervisor. "I saw you waving to me!"

The week after the race, Ian's supervisor had to slow him down a few times, because he was still running through the store. Karla smiles. "He just forgets he's not still on the track with all of us cheering him on."

Small kindnesses make a community whole and lift up all of its members.

ANN BAUER

Create a culture of giving. Strengthen your own community by becoming involved; meet your neighbors; volunteer for school functions and community events; or become a **Special Olympics** coach. Call 800-700-8585, or visit www. specialolympics.org.

WAKING UP TO COFFEE
Told by Co-op America

For ten years Paul Katzeff had worked as a social worker and community organizer with street gangs in East Harlem and New York's Lower East Side. He was tired and wanted to get back to the land. In 1969 he moved to Aspen, Colorado.

When he couldn't find a job as a social worker, Paul decided to open a coffee house, Greenwich Village style. He bought an old roaster in New York and learned how to roast his own beans.

This was long before the gourmet coffee boom, and Paul soon discovered he was too far ahead of his time. When the café failed, he migrated to Mendocino, California, where he met his wife, Joan. They set up the old roaster and peddled their "gourmet coffee" by the pound. From these humble beginnings was born Thanksgiving Coffee Company.

In those early days, Paul and Joan didn't realize the effect the American coffee industry was having on people in other parts of the world. Francisco Javier Saenz, a coffee farmer in Nicaragua, lived with the reality every day. As a founding member of the Specialty Coffee Association of America, Paul invited Francisco to speak to members about "Coffee, Human Rights, and the Third World Economy." Francisco then invited all 120 members to come visit his Nicaraguan coffee fields.

Paul accepted Francisco's invitation. When he arrived in Nicaragua, it didn't take him long to see through Francisco's eyes. As they left the airport, homeless street children in filthy, tattered clothing chased after his car, begging him to purchase cookies or drinks.

The next day, in the mountains, Francisco introduced him to coffee pickers who were even more destitute. Their huts had dirt floors and cardboard roofs. The only windows were holes pushed out of the walls. In the corner of one hut, an exhausted, barefoot woman was making tortillas. Francisco explained that the women didn't own shoes and often spent three hours a day pounding out tortillas for their families.

Paul took an honest look at the coffee industry. He was distraught to realize that his company, Thanksgiving Coffee, was selling a product that was actually harming rather than helping people. Nicaraguan coffee growers had no choice but to sell to a handful of giant coffee brokers, which resulted in coffee prices so low that it was hardly worth selling the beans. For every pound of gourmet coffee sold in the United States for six to ten dollars, the farmers received only thirty-five to fifty cents. A coffee picker's family might earn four hundred to six hundred dollars per year, barely enough to buy food and soap. It was especially disturbing because Paul had been raised and educated never to tolerate a situation like this one. As a social worker in New York, he had fought for tenants against unscrupulous landlords. His parents, hardworking Russian immigrants in New York City, had been deeply involved in labor union organizing, political activism, and war relief for Jews in the Soviet Union. "My family taught me that you can accomplish anything if you try," says Paul. Seeing the plight of the Nicaraguans, he realized that the coffee industry needed to do more than just sell great-tasting coffee—it needed a conscience. But what could he do?

Paul decided that he wanted to give something back to the coffee pickers.

After much soul-searching, he created the company's first "social justice" program, "Coffee for Peace." For every pound of coffee sold, he returned fifteen cents to the Nicaraguan coffee farmers' organization to buy trucks and build schools and health clinics. Coffee for Peace was an important first step in personalizing coffee, connecting buyers to a product—and eventually changing the entire coffee industry.

But paying the farmers a fair price for their coffee wasn't enough. Americans' growing appetite for coffee introduced a host of environmental problems. In the 1970s, biotechnologists introduced a new kind of high-yield coffee plant, which grew only in the hot sun. To keep up with first-world demand, farmers cut down their forests to make way for huge coffee plantations. Sadly, this forest was home to thousands of animals and birds including 150 species of songbirds per acre— the same delicate songbirds that migrate north to the United States and sing to us so sweetly every spring. Something had to be done before this lush tropical forest, with all its biodiversity, was completely destroyed.

So, Paul would offer Song Bird Coffee from plants that grew in the forest under large shade trees, his eco-friendly promise to the consumer (and to the songbirds). He invited the American Birding Association to join him. Thanksgiving Coffee developed a unique marketing strategy targeted to the 63 million birders in America who eagerly await the annual migration. They created a line of Songbird Coffees and invited bird lovers everywhere to buy it.

The Company now gives to the American Birding Association fifteen cents from every package of coffee sold, to help preserve migratory bird habitats. With forty thousand ABA members, this adds up fast. In 2000, the company donated $25,000 to the ABA, matched by the National Fish and Wildlife Foundation, to support education and conservation programs for neotropical birds.

By pioneering shade coffee, Paul sparked an entire industry to realize the link between coffee and the environment, between the farmer's quality of life and the quality of their product. Today most specialty coffees are shade-grown, and the open-sun-coffee trend has ended. Over time, many of Paul's "radical" ideas have become industry standards. Coffee companies are learning from and working with the farmers. Starbucks, Seattle's Best, and other industry leaders had to reassess their buying practices and now offer fair-trade and certified organic coffees. By 2000, the Specialty Coffee Association was the world's largest coffee trade association—with more than three thousand members. They created a "fair trade" certification system that guarantees coffee farmers a fair price for their harvest. As president, in 2001, Paul commissioned a Fair Trade Task Force that would unify trade and increase the demand for fair-trade coffee.

Wanting to level the playing field so that farmers could taste their coffee, determine its value, and improve its quality, he brought nine Nicaraguan farmers to visit U.S. professional coffee labs. "Once they had the vision," Paul says, "they were ready to take it back to Nicaragua." With a grant from the U.S. Agency for International Development, they built nine coffee-tasting "laboratories." Now, more than six thousand co-op members can taste, evaluate, and improve their coffee—and command a higher price. On October 24, 2001, the community celebrated with all-day fiestas: Thirty-two teens received their official co-op "cupping" certification.

Today, Thanksgiving Coffee is a $6-million-per-year business, with dedicated employees who share Paul and Joan's vision for social justice for all. Thanks to their hard work and determination, hundreds of thousands of farmers are now living better lives and protecting the Earth for generations to come.

A little awareness goes a long way. Next time you're drinking coffee, raise your cup to Francisco, to "not just a cup, but a just cup."

> *If you give a man a fish, it feeds him for a day;*
> *If you teach a man to fish, it will feed him for a lifetime.*

Buy fair-trade and certified organic, shade-grown coffee. Ask for it wherever you go. To learn where you can buy Thanksgiving Coffee, call 800-648-6491, or visit www.thanksgivingcoffee.com. Buying Songbird Coffee helps save trees for millions of birds that would otherwise have no place to live. To learn more, visit their Web site, www.songbirdcoffee.com.

THE POWER OF GIVING
Told by Gregory S. Gross

Seven-year-old Van Truong Le looked over the rail. His homeland, Vietnam, was quickly disappearing from view. He and his family had fled on a boat with a hundred others, running from war, seeking peace. When Van arrived in America, he felt as if he were in a movie. There were no bombs, there was no war—just lots of big cars.

Before the war, Van's father had been a successful businessman and landowner in Vietnam, but he had lost everything and had to start over in America, as a janitor. He moved his family around the country, searching for a new place to call home. At the time, Van couldn't even dream of the life that lay before him, or of Arnold Hiatt, the man who helped make it happen.

Hiatt has helped make things happen for lots of people. As president of the Stride Rite shoe company, he wanted to do more than just make a profit. He wanted to make a difference. By serving employees, stockholders, and the community as one, he built his business on a solid foundation of reciprocal values and principles. He firmly believes in "doing unto others as we would have them do to us"—and has discovered that it's given him a great business advantage.

Hiatt never went to business school or received an MBA; he studied history and literature instead. Later he learned about the world of business at an executive training program. But when he found little civility there, he decided to start his own company. His start-up children's footwear company prospered, despite his on-the-job training. When the Stride Rite Corporation wanted to acquire his company, and have him assume the presidency, he agreed—on his terms.

Under Hiatt's leadership, Stride Rite also set a precedent for how business could make a difference in the community. He persuaded his directors first to give 1 percent, and then 5 percent, of the company's pre-tax earnings to social initiatives in the community. By creating the nation's first on-site corporate day-care program, he helped Stride Rite workers and gave jobs to residents of down-trodden and crime-ridden Roxbury, Massachusetts. Stride Rite was also the first company to establish an intergenerational center—providing opportunities for seniors and children to be cared for together. A strong advocate for mentoring, he also encouraged Stride Rite employees to work with inner-city youth, at the company's expense, during work hours.

Stride Rite's sales increased dramatically, and for several years the company was in the ninety-ninth percentile of financial performance on the New York Stock Exchange. "People started to wonder if there was a correlation between treating people fairly and doing well," Hiatt remembers. Over the years he became one of the nation's champions for greater corporate social responsibility. He founded Business for Social Responsibility to help other companies become more responsive to their workers, their community, and the environment.

But Hiatt's favorite program, and the one that changed Van Truong's life, is the least well known. He was especially concerned that young people learn to be responsible citizens. And he believed that students would learn more about this by doing than by listening to someone in a classroom talk about ethics and personal responsibility. So he invited his alma mater, Harvard, to become a partner in providing scholarships so that low-income students could do public-service work in the inner city. The Stride Rite scholars now reach beyond classrooms and textbooks to face tough, real-life situations; instead of flipping burgers to support themselves through school, these future leaders volunteer in homeless centers, AIDS wards, juvenile-offender programs, and shelters for abused women and children.

Van Truong, whose hard work and tenacity earned him a place at Harvard, was one of the forty students who won a Stride Rite scholarship that year. When he realized that there were housing projects near Harvard, he used his scholarship funds so he could work at one of them, Jefferson Park. He wanted to put his experience to work helping other young people overcome obstacles.

So, every summer for four years, Van Truong lived with the youngsters—right in the housing project. He started by earning their trust. "These kids live in a tough inner-city environment," he says. "Because of my own childhood experiences, I could relate to them." As a living example of what they could become, Van gave hope to those who had none. He tutored them and took them on field trips, opening up views of different worlds. By teaching them to write their intimate feelings and personal observations in journals, he helped them find their "voices." Van was happy to see that "at nine or ten years old, these kids had great dreams for themselves and for their future."

During the course of his work in the projects, Van was amazed that Hiatt, the head of a multinational corporation, would take the time to meet with him, ask about his summer, and get to know him. Hiatt wanted to see for himself how these scholarship students were making a mark on their community. During one of his visits, Van told him about a serious problem that was undermining the program. Harvard had reduced financial aid for students receiving the Stride Rite scholarships, pulling out from under them the very ground they'd gained.

Hiatt was troubled by what he heard. He informed Harvard officials that Stride Rite funds would continue only if they were never used to displace other student aid. He challenged Harvard to match Stride Rite funds, generating additional funding for work-study grants. He also created a fellowship program for graduating students to continue their public-service work. With his strategic support, public service has become a multiplying force for change at Harvard and in the community, and the lives of many young people have improved.

Van Truong, for one, was profoundly influenced by his mentor, Hiatt, and his commitment to public service: "Arnold Hiatt showed us how to be public-spirited and not forget our community. Working closely with him strongly affected my beliefs, my values, and my career goals. He actually altered the course of my life. In the money-crazy 1980s, he was a visionary role model for us all."

Van has since decided to dedicate his life to public service. A recent law-school graduate, he is now a clerk for a Boston federal court judge. One of Van's former Jefferson Park students is aiming to go to college. Van is grateful for Hiatt's example of a life lived in pursuit of something more than material wealth. His aspirations are quieter, richer, for a life given to serving others. Van says, "Arnold Hiatt taught me the power of giving back, one person at a time."

Everyone can be great, because everyone can serve.

DR. MARTIN LUTHER KING JR.

Companies who want to launch or improve community-service initiatives should phone **Business for Social Responsibility (BSR)** at 415-537-0888 for information, tools, resources, and technical assistance, or visit their Web site, www. bsr.org.

REACHING FOR THE DREAM
Told by Jonathan Roseman

The final notes of the closing ceremonies hovered in the humid air over Centennial Olympic Stadium in Atlanta as Day 17 came to an end. The best athletes in the world—more than eleven thousand of them from 197 countries—were enjoying their final farewell party. At that moment there were no winners or losers, only champions who had reached for their Olympic dreams.

Down the road, in a three-bedroom home, another celebration kicked off. In the community known simply as Peoplestown, Wrandell Jackson had reached his own gold. For the first time in their lives, he and his family owned their own home.

Jackson had struggled to hold down two jobs to pay the rent and feed his five children. During the day he worked in a kitchen, then cleaned office buildings at night. The mortgage meant he could quit the night shift and be home for his family when they really needed him, and his new home came with a sense of belonging to a neighborhood where everyone was beginning all over again.

The wood-framed house at 899 Washington Street is a tiny piece of the extraordinary legacy that grew out of the 1996 Centennial Olympic Games. Over the preceding six years, local businesses transformed a blighted swath of downtown Atlanta into a twenty-four-acre urban park. The rights to televise the games helped fund construction of a state-of-the-art stadium. Meanwhile, Habitat for Humanity deployed an army of volunteers into impoverished inner-city neighborhoods to build one hundred homes for those who had none, an unparalleled undertaking that the worldwide nonprofit organization had given itself eighteen months to accomplish. As a partner, Home Depot constructed one of the original houses and also built the hundredth home, for thirty-four-year-old Wrandell Jackson and his family.

In less than twenty years, Home Depot has opened nearly five hundred do-it-yourself stores in the United States and Canada. Its volunteer force, made up of 100,000 associates, helps communities in any way needed. They partner with local nonprofit organizations, such as Habitat for Humanity and Christmas in April, to build and repair homes for low-income families, the elderly, and the disabled.

No one keeps track, but it seems as though everyone at Home Depot volunteers—sales associates, managers, and officers alike. When company president and co-founder Arthur Blank put out the call for volunteers to build the hundredth home in the company's hometown, forty-five officers from across North America and thirty-five of their spouses signed up to help. Together they worked side by side with Wrandell in the sweltering heat and "blitz built" his home in six days. Vice-President Suzanne Apple hammered nails, hung trusses, and installed windows.

"It was a phenomenal experience," says Suzanne. "We'd pick up our tools just after sunrise and finish around dinnertime. It seemed every day was hotter than the last. But as a team we kept on going, hammering, measuring, and making things fit." On Monday morning, 899 Washington Street was just a concrete foundation. By Saturday afternoon it was a home. When they handed Wrandell his keys, there wasn't a dry eye present. The paint was still fresh on the peach-colored house when Suzanne signed up to help build another Habitat home.

In Peoplestown, with the Olympic stadium in full view, the Jackson household realized their dream with a lot of reaching and a little help from their friends. As a family, now they're fixing screen doors and learning how to care for daisies and pansies.

"Before we moved in, we would drive by here all the time," says Wrandell. "The kids were always asking, 'When are we moving in, Daddy, when are we moving in?' And now we're here, living in our own home. It's a dream come true."

Help a low-income family realize their dream of building a home. Find your local **Habitat for Humanity** affiliate by calling 800-422-4828, or visit www. habitat.org. You can learn more about Home Depot's community initiatives at www.homedepot.com.

FOCUS: HOPE

Told by Jim Young

Maia Cherry, a twenty-five-year-old African-American student, is a ray of hope in Detroit. But when she first came into this world, there wasn't much hope there. Five years earlier, race riots had nearly torn the city apart.

Born to a single mom, Maia is the youngest of five children. She was a bright student, loved sports, and got good grades in school—most of the time. But when she didn't get the attention she needed from her busy mom, she had lots of problems. "I didn't have any motivation, so I wasn't consistent," she says. "I wasn't happy. Sometimes I was even suicidal." Fortunately, Maia found a way through the darkness. "I knew there had to be more to life," she says. "So I started reading the Bible, going to church, and letting God direct my steps." She's glad her steps led her to Focus: HOPE.

Focus: HOPE was born on the road from Selma to Montgomery, Alabama. In 1964, Father Bill Cunningham had traveled south from Detroit in response to Dr. Martin Luther King's call for help and joined him on that historic march. Three years later, in the summer of 1967, Father Cunningham saw his own hometown destroyed by race riots, and drawing on the hope instilled in him by Dr. King, he devoted himself to building racial harmony in Detroit.

One of his parishioners, Eleanor Josaitis, a housewife raising five children, was so moved by his passionate commitment to overcoming racism, poverty, and injustice that she uprooted herself from her comfortable life in the suburbs and planted her family back down in Detroit's volatile inner city. Father Cunningham quit his teaching job. They started simply, feeding people in a church basement. "We felt we had a moral responsibility to feed the children and the elderly," Father Cunningham said. People have to be properly nourished before they can be productive members of society. Since then they've been training underprivileged young people for good jobs.

Father Cunningham invites everyone he meets to join him in this work, and thousands have. One of them was Hulas King. He came for a visit and stayed for a year. The director of Industrial Partnership programs for EDS Unigraphics Division, Hulas was a "loaned executive" to Focus: HOPE. The loaned-executive program is just one of the ways that EDS helps communities. "One of my dreams for EDS goes way beyond financial success and service excellence," says chairman Dick Brown. "I want us to be the most-admired company—to have a heart and soul and give back something to the communities we work in." A lifelong volunteer, he encourages all 130,000 employees to participate in EDS's Global Volunteer Day—living out the company's philosophy that healthy communities and healthy business go hand-in-hand.

"EDS is known as a systems integrator. We're helping to integrate urban minority youth into mainstream society through technical training," says Hulas. "Our corporate partnership with Focus: HOPE helps us achieve this goal." At Focus: HOPE, students use the most advanced equipment, get real work experience, and learn from the best teachers. Retired engineers from Detroit supervise them, helping them to become well-rounded manufacturing engineers and the best machinists in the world. "Since the technology center's founding in 1981, more than five thousand young people have completed their programs, moving out of poverty and forward in their lives. For kids once on welfare and walking the streets, that's an incredible future," says Hulas.

During Hulas's year at Focus: HOPE, he spent lots of time with the students. When Maia first saw him, she was surprised. "We deal with thousands of important people at Focus: HOPE, even presidents of companies. But they are usually white. Hulas is one of the top people—and he's black. I was impressed!" she says.

Early on, Hulas reached out to Maia, and they developed a special mentor relationship. "He would ask me how was I doing, how my grades were, and give me some advice. He told me, 'Stay focused and do your job, be on time and be responsible. Be a 110 percent kind of person,'" she says. "He told me that as a young black woman, I might face racism and sexism, but I should hold my head high and never lower my standards." Hulas also helped Maia gain a realistic perspective about life. "Don't look for somebody to shake your hand after you do something," he'd say. "Your rewards will come. Just do your best, keep on moving—and enjoy your life." What Maia appreciated most was knowing Hulas was there for her. "If you need anything, anything at all, let me know," he told her.

Hulas certainly knows the importance of helping the next guy—or gal. "I grew up in East St. Louis, one of the most deprived cities in America. We all shared the same poverty, so we stuck together. When a kid got out of line, the whole community stepped in to discipline him," Hulas says. "To be able to help students and then have the pleasure of watching them assume positions of responsibility is really wonderful," he adds. "When you nurture them to be on their own, they can then reach back and help someone else." This continuity is part of what makes the mentoring such rewarding work.

Maia has big plans for how she wants to give back to other young people in Detroit. Having finished her undergraduate studies, she is working on her doctorate. After that, she plans to build her own business and work in the corporate world for a while. Eventually she plans to teach what she calls "The Three A's"—Academics, Attendance, and Attitude. "I want high-school students to learn that engineering isn't as hard as people make it seem," she says.

"There are so many smart young people—and they don't even know their potential. A lot of kids stop themselves by thinking, 'I can't do it.' I want them to know they don't have to be the cream of the crop to learn it." Maia readily admits that she isn't a math whiz. It just takes practice, she says. "If you have the desire, you can do it!"

Carrying on Father Cunningham's tradition, Maia invites others to come to Focus: HOPE. "If we all give back, we can make Detroit really great," she says. From Dr. King to Father Cunningham, from Hulas to Maia: a chain of people strong enough to make their hopes come true.

In thirty years, Focus: HOPE has grown into a charitable empire including a state-of-the-art technology center with an engineering-degree program and a manufacturing company, as well as a food-distribution center and a Montessori-based day-care facility.

Over the years, Father Cunningham and Eleanor Josaitis faced many challenges at Focus: HOPE. When things were difficult, they shared a ritual that gave them the courage to carry on. Quietly, without anyone noticing, they would pass a penny between them. The simple inscription on the penny—"In God We Trust"—and the exchange with each other helped them remember that they were never alone. Continuing her leadership at Focus: HOPE, Eleanor told a special story at Father Cunningham's funeral. She asked the gathered mourners to think of him when they saw a penny—so his spirit would live on forever. The next week, the U.S. Army, a long-time supporter of Focus: HOPE, delivered more than a million pennies to Focus: HOPE, donated by army families, for the millions of lives Father Cunningham had helped.

Make a career of humanity . . . and you will make
a finer world to live in.

DR. MARTIN LUTHER KING JR.

Reach out and help someone get on the road to success. Companies that want to give young people the gift of technology and bring hope to their communities can call **Focus: HOPE** at 313-494-5500, or visit www.focushope.edu.

WE CAN DO IT
Told by Anne Colby and William Damon
Adapted from their book *Some Do Care*

What makes Cabell Brand different from the average ambitious business-man who builds a small family company into a multimillion-dollar corporation? The best answer can be found in a tour of Roanoke Valley in Virginia. But just in case you're not planning a visit soon, here is the next best explanation.

Like most businessmen, Cabell believes in the American system of entrepre-neurship. While most of his colleagues are interested in how well the system works for them, however, Cabell wants to make it work for others. While running his shoe business, he gave over 25 percent of his time to community activities. Since he sold it in 1986, he's spent nearly all his time helping others—some say as a kind of "community entrepreneur."

It all started for Cabell in 1965. "I'll never forget watching a *Today Show* interview with Sargent Shriver, who had just been appointed director of the War on Poverty. 'What the hell is this—this War on Poverty?' I thought. I'd seen poor people in slums but had never really thought of it as a serious problem. When I read about President Johnson's Economic Opportunity Act, I thought, 'I didn't realize all this was going on.'" Cabell learned that "the federal government was going to make money available, but that local people had to get organized to benefit. If you didn't get organized, the money went somewhere else." He began to think about the poor people he'd seen in the poverty-stricken Roanoke Valley.

Cabell was scheduled to make a major presentation to Roanoke Valley's prestigious Torch Club. He dropped the topic he had planned and talked instead about the new poverty program. To apply for the federal funds, he took three months off from his business, anticipating that the program would bring desperately needed resources to Roanoke Valley. His time paid off: The funds were granted and put to good use. The community revived.

But Cabell didn't stop there; he's been gathering similar resources ever since. For the last thirty years he's been the volunteer president and chairman of the board of a local group called Total Action Against Poverty (TAP). They are as committed to building a profitable community as any corporate board is committed to profits. For Cabell, TAP, and the people of Roanoke Valley, that means starting from the ground up, with early-childhood education, high literacy, low unemployment, and accessible health care. It requires programs that offer new beginnings for ex-convicts, drug users, and dropouts, as well as home weatherization and food banks for the tough times, and community centers for the good times. It's ultimately about preparing for the future—dealing with people's real problems, not just the symptoms of poverty.

Cabell likes to take full advantage of promising opportunities. Concerned about the well-being of a depressed, low-income neighborhood in Northwest Roanoke, he led a community movement to open up a supermarket. He got the head of a major supermarket chain to donate the facilities. Under Cabell's leadership, TAP enticed others to bring in economic-development projects. By

matching local funds with federal funds, their success has expanded local business activity and multiplied their federal financial aid.

Perhaps TAP's greatest endeavor was bringing running water to the tens of
thousands of valley homes that had none. As Cabell describes the situation, getting water to the rural areas was the beginning of the magic. "Once there was
water in the area, all kinds of good things began to happen. Roads were built,
developers came in, and there were new job opportunities. When people went
to work, their families were no longer isolated, and they kept their kids in
school." When Charles Kuralt showcased them on CBS *Sunday Morning*, viewers saw a thriving community.

The battle is far from over. "Can you believe it?" Cabell asks. "We've still got
over 79,000 families with no water, no wells, nothing!" If anyone can find a solution, though, he's the one. "He's a walking brainstorm," says TAP executive director Ted Edlich. "He never stops thinking; he never stops generating ideas. He's
got more energy than any human being I know." According to Cleo Sims,
Roanoke Valley's Head Start director, "He works very quietly, behind the scenes.
But he's a giant in the community. He paves the way for us, making the contacts,
reaching out to leaders in the community, saying, 'Come, let's work together.' He
lives by the motto, We can do it." That's saying quite a lot, when you consider
that Cabell is nearly seventy-five years old. From time to time he does get a little
tired and discouraged. Then he leans on his wife, Shirley. "She has always been
there for me. She challenges me to keep going and sustains me in the difficult
times."

"Now that the government wants us to get our communities to help people,"
Cleo explains, "we need more businesspeople like Cabell—people who ask us,
'What can I do?' and 'What needs to be done?'" She adds, "We also need advocates, to speak up for the children—in the boardroom or on the golf course—to
reach out and see what our communities can do collectively to make things
better for everyone."

Cabell likes to quote the popular slogan "Think globally, act locally" to
describe his approach of applying local solutions to social problems. "I have

always been conscious of what I'm going to leave as a legacy," he says. "It's the everyday lessons, the building blocks of progress and the community process." From his perspective, "The bigger the problem is, the bigger the challenge is, and the more important it is to get started." If you could see the changes put in motion by this one man's efforts, you'd understand where his optimism comes from.

> *This country will not be a good place for any of us to live in unless we make it a good place for all of us to live in.*

> THEODORE ROOSEVELT

There are one thousand **Community Action Agencies.** Work with the one nearest you to build partnerships that last. Call the National Association of Community Action Agencies at 202-265-7546. To reach the **Roanoke Valley Community Action Agency,** phone Cleo Sims or Ted Edlich at 540-345-6781.

SERVE FIRST

Told by Larry C. Spears

Many years ago there lived a gentle man named Leo. He was an unassuming man who joined a group of spiritual travelers as their servant. He fixed the meals, carried the heaviest of their belongings, and did many other chores for the group. Leo was also a musician, keeping the travelers' spirits high with his joyful songs. All went well with the journey, until one day Leo disappeared.

At first, the group of travelers thought they could continue on their way without him. However, they soon discovered the good spirit they shared had disappeared overnight. People who had been the best of friends began to argue over little things. Before they knew it, no one could agree on much of anything. The group fell apart and abandoned their journey.

Many years later, one of the travelers happened across Leo and was overjoyed to see him. Leo took the seeker to the headquarters of the spiritual organization which had originally sponsored the journey. Once inside, the seeker was surprised to discover that Leo, whom he had known as his servant, was in fact the head of this organization, its guiding light. Leo was a great and noble leader.

Hermann Hesse, *Journey to the East*

Some years after this story was written, an American Quaker businessman named Robert Greenleaf read it. Greenleaf, a former AT&T executive, had been on a similar journey, searching for a new kind of leader. He found him in Hesse's story.

Greenleaf tried to imagine a world where the people we value most highly are those who best serve others: the teacher who inspires a student, the nurse who cares for a patient, the boss who takes a few minutes to ask about an employee's sick child. Greenleaf's quest sparked the simple yet profound idea of "servant-leadership," and he strove to follow its path.

He created a series of questions to guide his life decisions as a servant-leader. Do those I serve grow as people? Do they become healthier, wiser, more autonomous, and more likely to become servants themselves? And how am I benefiting the least privileged in the group? Then he wrote a small book, *The Servant as Leader*, introducing the concept. Over the years, it became popular at business schools, and the humble questions it contained worked their way into the minds of the greatest corporate leaders.

Over the past few decades, servant-leadership has influenced hundreds of thousands of people and has revolutionized companies and organizations around the globe. TDIndustries, a construction and service company in Dallas, Texas, is just one. Their CEO, Jack Lowe Jr., enthusiastically shares his stories of enlightened corporate management.

"My dad, Jack Senior, was a servant-leader before it was even called that. He was a bighearted man who gave much to his employees and his community. In 1946 he built this company to be owned by its employees. He thought that was only fair.

"In the 1970s he stumbled across Bob Greenleaf's book on servant-leadership and felt a special kinship with its author. Dad started giving away copies of the book, hundreds of them, to employees in discussion groups, and to leaders at community meetings." One day Bob called him, Lowe recalls with a laugh. "He was wondering why a construction company was his biggest customer." "What are you doing down there in Dallas?" he wanted to know.

"For the past twenty-five years we've been using Greenleaf's work as the foundation for our training programs. Before then, many of our supervisors were struggling as leaders. They were highly skilled in their trades, but unprepared as managers or foremen. The construction business is tough, and so are the men who work in it. Some of the guys thought being a supervisor entitled you to be a bully, or that getting promoted went hand-in-hand with getting respect. They didn't understand that you've got to earn respect."

By learning to serve first, TDPartners, as TDI employees are called, have done just that. The result: Everyone wins. The partners feel valued, they support their supervisors, and together, they build a stronger team and a healthy company.

Lowe offers a case in point. "Twenty years ago, Tom Creed, a burly construction superintendent, had participated in many of our training programs centered around servant-leadership. He recently told me, 'I came here as a cop, but I see myself now as a coach and a cheerleader.' Today 93 percent of our partners say their supervisor is fair in dealing with them, compared to only 60 percent nationally.

"Servant-leadership has helped us build a great company," Jack explains. "If you're going to succeed in today's business world, you've got to have a lot of trust, between employers, employees, suppliers, and customers. Servant-leadership has helped us build a trusting culture and has allowed us to create change, embrace diversity, enhance quality, and integrate technology. It's also gotten us through some horrible situations."

In the late 1980s the construction market collapsed and every major bank in Texas failed, including TDIndustries'. "When our bank went under, we owed the Feds $16 million. We didn't have it," Jack remembers. "We did everything we could to stay afloat. We even asked our partners to consider investing their own retirement funds back into the company. It was a lot to ask, since they would be risking everything to help us try to turn the company around. We were amazed, and deeply moved, when nearly every associate said yes. Our partners took over $1,250,000 out of their retirements and invested it back into the company. In less than a year, with everyone's help, we made it," says Lowe.

The TDPartners were not just making a financial investment. They were making a statement. TDI's service supervisor, Jerry Lynn, says, "What surprised me was how much people gave back to the company. The seeds for their generosity were planted by a company that built trust with its people."

And the human benefits are as powerful as the financial ones. A few years later, Sylvia Stephens, a credit manager and second-generation partner, suffered a heart attack. "When I came by the office during my recuperation, I left feeling renewed," she remembers. "My healing process accelerated because I had been around people who really loved me."

"Today, business is fabulous!" exclaims Jack. "TDIndustries celebrated its fiftieth anniversary, and *Fortune* magazine honored us as one of the top five best companies to work for in America." A high level of trust, built on servant-leadership, has supported them through both the good and the bad times. But Lowe isn't resting on his laurels. He's always looking for ways to make his employees happier and his business better. "Our best years are yet to come," he promises, "and it's going to really be fun."

To learn more about servant-leadership programs and publications, contact **The Greenleaf Center for Servant Leadership** at 317-259-1241, or visit its Web site, www.greenleaf.org.

THE TURNING POINT

"Don't wait for a crisis to happen to change your life," Claire Nuer said to a group of business leaders. They'd come to learn how to build better companies. What could personal crises and changes have to do with that?

The mother of two children, wife of a successful businessman, Claire ran an optical shop in Paris. In May 1982, she got a life-threatening wake-up call. "I think you need to change my glasses," she told her doctor. "I have a black area in my vision." Her exam revealed cancer, an ocular melanoma. She was given only a few months to live.

In French, *claire* means "clear." And the cancer was in her eye. Interesting coincidence. So began her fascinating journey, on which she learned to make meaning out of life's bad breaks, and help others to find meaning in their own lives.

In those days the prognosis was indeed terrible. Claire wanted desperately to live, so her two children would have a mother. As a hidden child during the Holocaust, she'd lost her own father. Some days her fears would just about paralyze her. "I'm not a very brave patient," she would say. "I'm going to die in twenty minutes—this time it's for sure." Her husband, Sam, would remind her, "It's been three years since you're going to die in twenty minutes, so come on." Claire could be adamant in her despair: "Precisely, it's been three years, so this time it's going to happen!"

Then, one day, Claire had an epiphany: "Okay, I'm going to die in twenty minutes. So what?" she asked herself. "What do I want to do with the next twenty minutes of my life?" Without hesitating, she replied, "To hug my children." From then on, when she felt this fear taking over, she would pull herself out of bed and go to her sleeping children's room. Often she didn't think she'd make it, but little by little the breath of life came back into her lungs. The fear would subside—and her passion for her life grew more vigorous than ever. From this simple exercise, Claire learned how her fear of dying could disconnect her from what was most important. She also received a great gift: the present moment.

As Claire came to see that she could learn from her cancer, she became less preoccupied with it as a death sentence and more interested in seeing where her curiousity and revelation would take her. She discovered what unconscious obstacle was in the way of her happiness. She started sharing her experiences with others, urging people to live fully in the moment. Over time, Claire pieced together a methodology that became the foundation for her educational seminars. She taught people to look beyond symptoms and appearances for the fundamental issues and solutions, challenging and then changing their thinking and communication habits. She encouraged them to take each opportunity to improve the quality of their relationships, and to transform their lives, their families, their organizations.

As Claire's seminars became richer, their impact greater, the opportunities multiplied. She facilitated intercultural dialogues, led business seminars, and spoke at such prestigious venues as the Commonwealth Club and the State of the World Forum.

Claire vividly remembers V-E Day, the end of World War II. Everyone in Paris was celebrating at the Arc de Triomphe. Planes flew overhead in a V-for-victory formation. While Claire was grateful for her freedom, she was devastated since her beloved father had died at Auschwitz-Birkenau. That day, this twelve-year-old decided never to let such a thing happen again. On her healing journey, she anchored her life with a goal: "to co-create a healthy context for humanity."

At a gathering convened by MIT visionary Peter Senge in honor of the fiftieth anniversary of the 1944 Bretton Woods Conference, Claire asked an audience of three hundred business leaders, "Fifty years from today, looking back, what decisions would we each have been proud to make to create the future we all want?"

Whatever the business leaders went on to do, this question led Claire to the most important work of her life, the Turning Point Project. In August 1995, fifty years after the liberation of Auschwitz, Claire brought together 367 people from thirty-three different countries near the site of the concentration camp in Poland. "Our 'never, never again' can be a starting point," she told them, "to start learning, to start doing whatever is necessary—in each moment of our lives—so this never happens again. We can be a strong anchor for humanity."

In 1996, Claire developed a mass in her liver. Undaunted by her physical pain, she brought the lessons learned from the Turning Point to help companies align their goals, implement their missions, and develop healthier work environments. They learned about "ecosystem" leadership rather than "egosystem" leadership. "We don't see the cost of the actions from our ego—the pain we cause ourselves and others—or we would do something about it," she would tell participants in her seminars. "In an ecosystem, we operate beyond competition, beyond being 'stars.' We are each a link in the chain, adding to each other's strengths.

"This work on our ego takes a lifetime," Claire told them. "But the shift, the decision, requires just one second and can happen at each moment, which can be a turning point in our lives, in our families, in our companies, and in the world."

Rick Fox is one leader who turned at such a point. When he met Claire in 1997, he was struggling. An asset leader on Ursa, Shell's largest deep-water project in the Gulf of Mexico, Rick and his team had faced a series of setbacks. A drilling problem had delayed operations for six months and cost him 250 million dollars, putting pressure on Rick and his team to achieve what they thought were impossible objectives. He knew it would take something extraordinary for his team to overcome these challenges. When he traveled to San Francisco for his first Learning as Leadership training with Claire, he was looking for a way to prepare his team and deepen their commitment.

Rick realized in the first workshop (a self-discovery process through guided journaling, experimental exercises, and sharing with other participants) how he was limited by his fears and how his reactions to those fears provoked fears in others. He was shocked to see how he was creating exactly the opposite of what he intended.

When Claire explained that "one person can be the rock that changes the course of a river," and that "it starts with me," Rick suddenly realized that *he* was the one who needed to be more committed. "I had lots of tricks to preserve my image as a visionary leader instead of a work-through-the-details leader," he admits today. Claire's commitment to Rick and his team was a guiding light. "If I want to be trusted, I need to trust," Rick realized. "If I want commitment, I need to commit. If I want love, I need to create it."

With newfound courage, Rick invited eleven members of his team, including his boss, to take Claire's next seminar. He also decided to do something about his other big problem, his seventeen-year-old son, Roger. A high-school senior, Roger had taken up training for the "Ultimate Fighting Championship," and Rick worried about his son's "ultimate" safety.

Rick asked Roger to join him and his team at the seminars. "Instead of trying to force or convince Roger," Rick says, "I asked him in a way that was clear and respectful. I told him how much he meant to me and how I wanted this opportunity for our relationship." Roger listened carefully to his father and said, "Okay, I'll go. You can make the reservations." When Rick admitted shyly, "I already did," they both laughed.

Rick knew he was taking a big risk. He knew he'd have to be honest with his team, including his boss—and all in front of his son. But he was determined to be in the "learning process" since this was too important for him. "What would I lose by taking risks, being vulnerable with people close to me?" Rick asked himself. "And how much could I gain by improving those relationships?"

When, during the seminar, Rick shared his struggles at work, and admitted his own shortcomings, his son was touched by his honesty. "Dad, you say what you need to say and do what you need to do," he said, putting his arm around his father. "If we end up in the ditch, I'll be there with you." The other parents in the room longed to get as close to their children.

After that seminar, things started to change. Today, Roger is a peaceful guy. His friends come to him for honesty and support, instead of for protection. He's on his way to medical school. "He's a great role model for his brother, Rabun," says Rick proudly, "and for me, too!"

Rick's team has also made remarkable progress: They've set new goals, one of which is to cultivate their "ecosystem." What may sound like soft ideals directed them to solid results. They completed the Ursa project four months ahead of schedule and $40 million under budget. Their operating performance is "Best in Class," and their uptime performance of 99 percent leads the industry. Their safety record is outstanding, and they pride themselves on achieving aggressive environmental goals. "This tiny woman, who spoke only French, was one of the most courageous people I've ever met," Rick says. "She inspired me by always aiming for what she wanted to create and saying 'so what' to her fears."

Claire kept working to the end. She died in 1999, but her spirit lives in those who carry on her work. The Learning as Leadership team continues to offer seminars so that more people can thrive together in a global ecosystem. "Claire was not religious, but she was one of the most deeply spiritual people I've ever met," said her close friend George McCown, a founding partner of McCown De Leeuw & Co., at her funeral. "She taught what all the great prophets taught: the power of love and connection."

To learn more about **Learning as Leadership** training programs, phone 415-453-5050, or visit www.learnaslead.com. **The Nuer Foundation**'s mission is to empower people, projects, and communities to make a difference for the future of humanity. Visit their Web site, www.nuerfoundation.org.

A MENSCH

Told by Jeanne Wallace

The telephone had been ringing for hours in mill owner Aaron Feuerstein's kitchen when he and his wife, Louise, opened their front door and Feuerstein answered the phone. He had been quietly celebrating his seventieth birthday at a small surprise party thrown by his family. During the celebration, one of his top managers had gotten word of a fire at the mill. He told a few others, but nobody told Feuerstein. They didn't want to ruin his party. "The mill's burning, Aaron. The whole mill's on fire," said the voice on the phone. Feuerstein hung up, pale and shaking.

News of the fire raced through the mill workforce the next morning, December 12, 1995, as fast as the flames had destroyed the mill the night before. Many stood outside in the bitter cold, drawn to the devastation as though the mill were a dying member of their family.

Joseph Melo, a thirty-three-year-old machine operator, had worked in the mill since high school. His father, Manuel, had spent his life in the mill, and his stepfather, sister, and cousin had also worked there. As he stood outside that morning, looking at the damage, Joseph wanted to believe the mill would be saved and everyone would come back to work.

Meanwhile, Feuerstein calculated more than three thousand people without work in the city of Lawrence, and he shuddered at the specter of a ghost town. He vowed to rebuild the plant in the city—the twenty-sixth-poorest in the nation. In the days and months ahead, this third-generation mill owner, driven by pride, religious conviction, and a sense of family, did something nobody in modern times had attempted: rebuild a giant textile plant in an old New England mill city. Feuerstein and his mill became a national media event as people warmed to the story of a devout Jew whose heroic generosity at Christmastime distinguished him dramatically in an era of corporate greed and downsizing. But behind the sentimental headlines, the battle for the body and soul of a new Malden Mills was a tough fight with wide-ranging implications for workers and American industry.

In the 1950s, Feuerstein stayed put while nearly every other textile mill in New England shut down or moved away. He survived recession and a bankruptcy in the early eighties. Founded in 1906 by Feuerstein's grandfather, Henry, Malden Mills had nearly gone out of business than one of its mainstay products, fake fur, went out of fashion, forcing the business into bankruptcy protection. Feuerstein battled back, restructuring the mill around two revolutionary new products, Polartec and Polarfleece. These uniquely light and warm wool-like synthetics, developed by his workers out of recycled plastic, were a hit. It was Polartec that put Malden Mills in the forefront of textile technology, generating $200 million in sales in 1995, about half the company's total.

Rebuilding the mill when he could have settled for the insurance money was certainly a noble thing to do. But what brought Feuerstein to national acclaim was his commitment to his employees while the mill was being rebuilt. Three days after the fire, in a local high-school gym, he announced that he would pay all 3,200 employees for thirty days—at a cost of $15 million, with health benefits extending two months beyond that.

To rebuild fast, Feuerstein insisted, "We need to keep our people together." Malden Mills' "people" reflect the city of Lawrence. Rich in textile and labor-union history, Lawrence had become a city of vacant mill buildings and poor workers with too few jobs and too little hope. The exception was Feuerstein's mill. It made dreams as well as cloth—providing a way for countless blue-collar workers to become part of America's middle class. Many had limited English language skills or trade skills outside textile-making. More than 25 percent of the workers were minorities—black, Hispanic, Asian, and Native American. Many were first-generation immigrants, from twenty-one different countries. Like Joe

Melo, white and unskilled, they found in Malden Mills and its average $12.50-an-hour pay (the highest in the industry)—plus overtime and benefits—a way to earn a good living and raise a family. Nobody could afford not to go back. They needed something to go back to.

"It's the right thing to do." That was how Feuerstein reassured his managers. "There is a need to know that corporate America could be interested in the welfare of the worker as well as the shareholder," he said. "I consider our workers an asset, not an expense. If you close a factory because you can get work done for two dollars an hour elsewhere, you break the American Dream. It would have been unconscionable to put three thousand people on the streets and deliver a death blow to the cities of Lawrence and Methuen."

Feuerstein's employees repaid his loyalty with their own. "If he had the guts to rebuild," said one, "we decided we would do whatever we could." By the end of February the entire mill complex—the scene of utter destruction just two months earlier—had come alive with its mission. And people across the country rallied to help. State, federal, and local licenses and zoning parted like the Red Sea.

In order to keep the business open, employees had to meet production demands with only a fraction of the pre-fire staff and equipment. "Our people became very creative," said Feuerstein. Incredibly, they began running Polartec off the first fire-damaged machine just three days after the fire. It was only a test, but it had symbolic importance. "We're back in business," a manager said. Before the fire, one plant had produced 130,000 yards of the fabric a week. A few weeks after the fire, it was up to 230,000 yards in a temporary facility. And the people were committed. "They were willing to work twenty-five hours a day," said Feuerstein. He sees this as "a direct result of the goodwill and determination of our people to show their gratitude to Malden Mills."

Nearly five months after the fire, Feuerstein had to convince the furniture retailers in South Carolina—who accounted for 50 percent of the mill's business—that he could deliver. He traveled there, knowing that his promise to his 3,200 workers in three states to rebuild his mill and bring everyone back to work hung in the balance.

In High Point and elsewhere in North Carolina, Feuerstein was already famous for his generosity. His picture adorned the front of many showrooms in the furniture-crazy town. He had a big reputation and a lot of friends here. He needed both when he met with his customers and asked them to stick with him now. "Absolutely," said one company president, greeting Feuerstein like an honored relative. "Anything we need to do to make it work, we'll do." Another had heard all about it and was impressed. "Anything we can do to be part of it, we will." One company used the now-famous Malden Mills name in its marketing. "They are like 'Made in America' tags. People feel good about it, because of Aaron."

In a just world, such fame and good feeling would be enough to keep Malden Mills profitable. In a perfect world, the laws of business karma would ensure the company's growth and flourishing. As it happened, after years of rebuilding and rehiring, honors and innovation, since the fire, Aaron and his mill filed Chapter 11 in November, 2001. This is not the end of the story.

Not only does Aaron carry no regrets for the decisions he's made so far, he affirms that Malden Mills' market position is nonetheless "enviable" and sees this period of reorganization as a chance to write a "new chapter" of its life, to refocus and strengthen its brand. As a former employee points out, "They've been through bankruptcy before, in the early '80s, which is how Polartec was born." Like President Clinton before them in his 1996 State of the Union Address, government officials continue to publicly praise Aaron's example. Consumers aren't sitting around waiting for the mill to rise again, either. Since November, they've received thousands of letters, checks, and other expressions of solidarity—one professional car-racing team offered free title sponsorship. Such strong, all-weather friendships are enviable indeed.

In Yiddish there is a word for a decent human being: *mensch*. But Aaron downplays his own role in his company's recovery. It is the workers, he says, who are responsible for that. "They wanted a miracle to happen, and it did. That's all I can tell you—it did."

To learn how Malden Mills is strengthening social services in its community, contact **ALMA** (Action for Lawrence, Methuen, Arlington), c/o Malden Mills, 46 Stafford Street, Lawrence, MA 01841. (*Alma* means "soul" in Spanish.) To communicate your support of everything Aaron Feuerstein and Malden Mills stand for, visit www.polartec.com and make the "Polartec Promise" to look for Polartec labels when you buy clothes.

A LITTLE COMPANY MAKES A BIG DIFFERENCE

Told by Kevin Berger

Laura Scher could barely contain her excitement. The thirty-seven-year-old chief executive officer of Working Assets had a $50,000 check to present to Planned Parenthood's president, Pamela Maraldo, at their headquarters in New York, and she was standing next to women's rights leader Gloria Steinem, one of her heroes.

The check was one of thirty-six donations totaling $1 million made by the company to nonprofit organizations in 1993, but to Scher it represented much more. Eight years earlier, as the one and only employee of Working Assets, Laura had dreamed of the day when her "little company" could make a big contribution to a cause she "believed in with her heart and soul." As Laura handed over the check, her nervous excitement gave way to a beaming smile. Her dream had come true.

"I was so proud when we gave $55,000 to Planned Parenthood, especially since AT&T had abruptly stopped contributing to them," says Laura today. "Our donation has helped Planned Parenthood keep up its great work for women's health and freedom. We also showed the world that you really can create a successful business *and* be committed to social change."

Laura has turned Working Assets from an idealistic vision into a $140-million company. Founded in 1985, the long-distance, wireless, and credit-card company was designed to give customers the opportunity to contribute to social change. Today Working Assets donates ten cents of every credit-card purchase and 1 percent of all long-distance bills and wireless charges to nonprofit groups.

Remembering the excitement of its inception, Laura says, "It's such a perfect product: Just by people talking on the phone or buying a book, we can build a community of kindred spirits with enormous impact."

Over time, Working Assets has built such a community. Since 1985, it has raised $30 million for nonprofit groups. In 2001 alone it generated over $5 million. Practicing what Laura calls "democracy in action," their customers nominate the organizations they want to receive the donations, and then vote on how much money each one receives.

"Working Assets has created a wonderful vehicle for supporting social change," remarks Pamela Maraldo. "Their contribution helped us increase access to reproductive health care for women, troubled teens, the sexually abused, and the underserved. We were particularly grateful to be the highest vote-getter on a long list of very effective and worthwhile grantees. To us, it's a vote of confidence from the American people."

Working Assets customers can also increase support to nonprofit groups by "rounding up" their monthly phone bills to the highest dollar. In this way, in 1999 they sent extra money—more than sixty thousand dollars—to the humanitarian group Kosovo Women's Fund, which aids women and their families in Kosovo and neighboring countries. Laura says she was impressed that "a simple message on a bill like 'Round up your check' can change the lives of people who live half a world away."

Working Assets also helps its customers stay informed. Each month's phone bill contains copy highlighting two crucial issues, explaining what's at stake and whom to contact to make a difference. If you have something to say, all you have to do is pick up the phone and speak your mind, and Working Assets will pick up the tab. Or for a small fee, the company will send a "Citizen Letter" on your behalf. By flooding Congress and corporate boardrooms with their calls and letters, customers have brought attention to sweatshop conditions, wasteful government spending, and America's vanishing wilderness.

Laura always wanted to "work for a company that treated its employees well and was conscientious about the environment and developing countries." But her ambitions cast her as a lone wolf among her classmates at Harvard Business School. After all, Laura had graduated in the top 5 percent of her MBA class at the height of the greedy eighties. Even before she graduated, she was wined and dined by recruiters from Fortune 100 corporations, who promised her salaries of over $100,000 a year, right out of school.

"But I didn't want to sell laundry detergent," she says. "And I didn't want to work on Wall Street. I wanted something valuable to come out of my work. We don't need one more company to figure out how to invent one more breakfast cereal. We need to figure out how to solve some of the world's problems."

So, instead of "sitting in an office on Wall Street with a view of the Hudson River," Laura and her husband furnished a dusty one-room office with an old desk and a filing cabinet. "We didn't have enough money to pay the landlord to renovate the space," she says, "so we had to live with orange shag carpet and bright orange bookcases. But I did talk them into at least cleaning the curtains."

As its chief executive officer, Laura's challenge has been to demonstrate to vendors that Working Assets is legitimate. The banks that issue its credit cards and the major phone companies that lease its fiberoptic cables are tough business folks. "People in the business world have a hard time believing that consumers will make buying decisions based on their social convictions," she says.

"But time after time we've convinced them that people will use a credit card and choose a phone company based on their beliefs." Indeed, Working Assets' annual revenues recently topped $140 million. As Laura guides the company forward, she wants the company to reach an annual donation budget of $10 million.

Laura is proud of the success she has achieved on a "road less traveled" and credits her parents with teaching her that "responsibility means taking your social values into the workplace." Her father, who ran a water-based chemical company, and her mother, an economics professor, taught her to have "concern for others and the world around us, instead of being self-absorbed," she says.

Laura wants to pass on to her children the same values she learned from her parents. "I want them to know that they can do anything they want with their lives," she says. "And I want them to understand that not everyone has the basic comforts of life. So it's up to the rest of us to create a more just and equitable world."

It is by spending oneself that one becomes rich.

SARAH BERNHARDT

To join Working Assets, call 800-788-8588, or visit their Web site, www.working assets.com.

TABLE FOR SIX BILLION, PLEASE
Told by Susan Dundon

One sunny spring morning in 1957, a ten-year-old girl with a feisty spirit and a passion for softball was just itching to play on the first day of the season.

"Class," her gym teacher announced, "it looks like a great day out there. Time to play ball!" The girl excitedly jumped from her seat.

"Guys down to the field," said the coach. "Girls go over there and practice cheerleading." The girl was dumbfounded. She stood dejectedly behind the backstop watching the boys play. She didn't know enough to be angry.

For Judy Wicks, now the owner of the White Dog Café in Philadelphia, her first experience with discrimination was a definitive moment. As soon as she found her voice again, she was outraged by the notion that anyone should be excluded. And for the ensuing forty years, she's been bringing people together, making sure that everyone gets to play the game.

Judy loves to tell another story, about something that happened when she was five years old. She ran a string of extension cords down the driveway and hooked up her record player. Then she turned it up to full volume, sat in a little chair, and waited to see who might come along. That was the opening of her first "restaurant." She will never forget the excitement she felt when her first customer, Johnny Baker, a boy her age with big feet and big ears, walked shyly up the driveway.

Running a restaurant may seem like a perverse enterprise for a woman who once refused to cook, who leaped out the classroom window to avoid having to take home economics. But then, Judy doesn't run "just a restaurant." For her, food is the magic that brings people together.

The White Dog Café started simply, as a take-out muffin shop. One morning, when Judy leaned out her apartment window above her shop, she noticed there was a line of people waiting to be served. She brought a table and some chairs from her apartment and invited everyone to take a seat. It was an impulse that came naturally.

The muffin shop grew: Judy now has two hundred chairs in her restaurant, situated in three attractive town houses on a lovely, tree-lined street. The music that brought Johnny Baker up the driveway is always part of the festival atmosphere at the White Dog, whether it's Noche Latina (Latin Night), or tunes for other multicultural, intergenerational events there. But, the real heart of the White Dog Café, where people gather for fun and lively conversation, lies as much outside of its walls as within. Judy throws back her head and laughs when she says that she uses good food "to lure innocent people into social activism."

Judy had always wanted to create "one big, city-wide community." She thought that by getting people to sit down to a good dinner together and talk, they could begin to understand and appreciate their similarities, rather than fear their differences. When she asked around, community leaders suggested that she talk to Daphne Brown, the owner of Daffodil's Home Cooking, another café in North Philadelphia. Daffodil's is sandwiched between a sad-looking Shiloh Apostolic Temple and a garage whose door is badly in need of repair. Outside, a broken milk carton serves as a basketball hoop. Nearby, vacant lots are strewn with broken bottles. A telephone pole on the corner bears a sign: DRUG FREE SCHOOL ZONE. The local media has dubbed it "the Badlands."

Daphne remembers Judy walking in the door one day, introducing herself, and sharing her idea about bridging cultural and ethnic groups by bringing people together to join in a meal. To start, they arranged an evening of entertainment at the Freedom Theater, one of the oldest African-American theaters in the country, followed by dinner at Daffodil's. Several dozen mostly white and affluent White Dog customers came and had a lot of fun. As the first participants in the White Dog Sisters Restaurants Program, they still come, from time to time, and they've brought Daphne new catering jobs. With the addition of more "sister restaurants" in Philadelphia, a Latino restaurant in the barrio, and a Korean-American restaurant in Olney, Judy sees her community dream growing.

But Judy's dream isn't confined to Philadelphia. She is adding more chairs for her extended "community" around the world. Her invited guests include people from Nicaragua, Lithuania, Vietnam, Cuba, Thailand, and Mexico. Her tongue-in-cheek name for her international "sister restaurants" program is "Eating with the Enemy." Most come from nations that have policy misunderstandings and disputes with the U.S. government. Judy wants to know why.

To find out, she takes an educational scouting mission to "enemy" territory each year, under the auspices of a nonprofit organization such as Global Exchange. The following year, she and some of her White Dog customers return. During their two-week visit, they look for a suitable "sister restaurant," where they get to know ordinary people. Through their explorations, they learn how U.S. policy affects people in that country. They come to appreciate the country's hardships and learn firsthand about the misunderstandings that exist between cultures and nations.

Harriet Behringer is a White Dog customer who has accompanied Judy on trips to Vietnam, Cuba, and Mexico. "These experiences have increased my understanding and knowledge of my world," she says. "I've laughed and learned and cried. Above all, I've discovered that we are not eating with the enemy, but with friends."

It isn't certain yet what new friends will join Judy's community, or what countries they live in. Bosnia, perhaps, or Palestine, China, Iran, Iraq, North Korea, or Indonesia. Wherever Judy goes, extension cords will connect; music will play. There will always be room for another chair at the table, a place for everybody in the world.

This is Judy's vision: "Table for six billion, please!"

> *Most politicians will not stick their necks out unless they sense grass-roots support . . . neither you nor I should expect someone else to take our responsibility.*
>
> KATHARINE HEPBURN

Learn how to mix social activism with sound business practices and good food. Call 215-386-9224 and ask to receive the **White Dog Café**'s quarterly newsletter, *Tales from the White Dog Café*, or visit their Web site at www.whitedog.com.

IF YOU DON'T, WHO WILL?

Told by G. Donald Gale

An elderly couple came through the door at Broadcast House in Salt Lake City, holding hands. The man carried a small coin purse. They opened the purse and together emptied a few coins into a slotted wooden box labeled "KSL Quarters for Christmas." Their smiles were warm, satisfied, happy.

"We don't have much," the man explained. "And we never had children of our own. We save coins to help buy shoes for youngsters who need them. It makes Christmas more meaningful for us."

For thirty years, KSL Radio has conducted the Quarters for Christmas campaign to raise money for shoes for needy children. Every cent collected goes to buy shoes, and each year thousands of listeners contribute.

In New York City, hundreds of children and their parents gather in a Salvation Army auditorium. It's the week after Thanksgiving. At the front of the auditorium are piled thousands of children's coats—some new, some used and freshly dry-cleaned. People from social-service agencies distribute the coats to needy youngsters, while at the back of the room stands Mark Bench, manager of radio station WDBZ, beaming. "Look at those youngsters smile. For some, this is the first warm coat they've ever had. What a joy to be the voice for 'Coats for Kids.' Our entire radio family feels lucky."

In New York as in Salt Lake City, the Bonneville station gives voice to the needs of less fortunate children and offers a way for listeners who want to help. On-air announcements urge listeners to deposit new or used coats in bins set up in area shopping malls. In fact, every one of Bonneville International Corporation's nineteen radio and television stations can tell a similar story. Every year Bonneville publishes a "Values Report" that chronicles the community-service activities of company stations in eight cities, from New York to Los Angeles.

"We don't have the resources to respond to every request for help, but we can reach out to bring together the people who do, and who want to help those who need it. So often, people want to help but don't know how to go about it," says BIC president and CEO Bruce Reese. "They need only a little encouragement and assistance to complete the circle. We think of ourselves as facilitators. Our broadcast stations give us a voice in the community, and we use it to say, 'Sure you can help, and here's how.' It works every time."

Like most people, Bonneville employees care about their communities, and just a little nudge moves their caring to action. The company's mission is to "Make a Difference" in communities where it operates. Employees know that when they volunteer in their communities, the company will back them with time and resources. Bonneville believes it takes both individual involvement and corporate commitment: People must want to serve, and the corporate culture must give service high priority.

Bonneville's public-service campaign, "If You Don't, Who Will?" which it runs on all its broadcast outlets, talks about simple solutions—slowing down in school zones, voting, reading to children, discarding fast-food wrappings in waste containers instead of on the sidewalks. It speaks to everyone, at every level—whether it's shoes for disadvantaged children or millions of dollars for sick children's care.

The elderly couple with their purse full of coins know they cannot afford to buy even one pair of shoes for a needy child, but by pooling their quarters with the quarters of many others, KSL multiplies their gift.

The benefits go beyond simple problem-solving to the personal rewards of serving. A pessimist, they say, sees a half-empty glass, which to an optimist appears half full, but a giving person who sees water in a glass starts looking for someone who might be thirsty.

"If you don't, who will?"

Channel your goodness by tuning in to one of the **Bonneville** stations in New York, Washington, Chicago, Dallas, Houston, Salt Lake City, Los Angeles, or San Francisco. To learn about their community-service projects, phone 801-575-5690, or visit their Web site, www.bonnint.com.

FOOTPRINTS IN THE SANDS OF TIME
Told by Jan Boylston

Driving by the four hundred boarded-up apartments of Dallas's Wynnewood Gardens, it was easy to see why neighbors wanted it torn down. The former public housing complex was an eyesore and a security threat to surrounding homes. But Duane McClurg, president of Dallas City Homes, saw something different. "I could imagine children playing and hearing the neighbors chatting," he said. He saw the need for affordable housing, but he knew that turning his vision into reality wasn't going to be easy. First, Duane had to convince neighbors that a mixed-income apartment community would enhance the area. Second, renovations would take a huge investment. Duane turned to a bank with a wealth of experience in community development: Bank of America.

Almost twenty years earlier and nearly one thousand miles away in North Carolina, Hugh McColl, Bank of America chairman and CEO, had similar visions. When he considered the Fourth Ward, an area of deteriorating Victorian homes and increasing rates of crime in Charlotte, McColl decided to try to reverse the neighborhood's deep downward spiral.

The bank formed a Community Development Corporation, the first of its kind. In partnership with city government, citizens, and preservationists, the CDC led the way for a transformation. They restored shabby and haunted-looking flophouses to their original decorative grandeur. Like a spring garden, new life blossomed in fresh paint in pinks, blues, and yellows. Snow-white accents on the gingerbread lattice said WELCOME HOME.

The changes intrigued Dr. Mildred Baxter Davis, who'd lived in the nearby Third Ward for more than twenty years. Her neighborhood also was declining from various social and economic pressures. Prostitutes walked the border streets. A thirteen-acre working scrapyard ground away inhospitably. Fed up, Dr. Davis organized a small group of concerned residents and asked for McColl's help.

McColl seized the opportunity. The CDC constructed new town homes and converted an abandoned foundry into offices, galleries, and pubs. The well-manicured practice fields of the Carolina Panthers and the stadium just beyond replaced the scrapyard, smoothing over that blight.

"We wanted a community for all people—a place for anyone and everyone—black, white, young, and old," Dr. Davis says. "What we've achieved is really wonderful. People here care about their homes and their neighbors. This is what a neighborhood should be."

When Charlotte's assistant city manager, Del Borgsdorf, compares the before and after, he says, "Both of these neighborhoods were places no one wanted to walk through, let alone live in. Now they're vibrant places—real neighborhoods where people really *want* to live."

As Bank of America grew, it carried its vision to other floundering communities, like the Parklands in Washington, D.C., Atlanta's Summerhill neighborhood, Baltimore's Lexington Terrace, and Nubia Square in Houston. Now, migrant-worker families in Immokalee, Florida; low-income families in East Point, Georgia; and senior citizens at Villa de San Alfonso in San Antonio have decent, affordable rental housing as a result of the CDC's loans and investments: more than $90 billion and nearly 100,000 affordable homes and apartments over the past decade. "Businesspeople generally don't leave many footprints in the sands of time," McColl says. "Projects like these are real footprints."

A wise businessman, McColl points out that "profits give us the resources to get things done—like investing in the lives of our neighbors. By strengthening our neighborhoods, we strengthen our communities. And that's good for business."

But the real success is measured in people's lives. Thousands of first-time home buyers or low-income renters now enjoy clean, safe, affordable homes. "What's heartwarming," McColl says, "is that we always find residents who still have hope of improving their neighborhoods. They just need help."

For many years, Rodney and Colette Brown lived in Richmond, Virginia— never thinking it would ever be possible to own their own home. Then one day they attended a course sponsored by the bank and the NAACP for first-time home buyers. They learned how to straighten out their credit and save for a down payment so they could buy a house and put down roots in their community. "God used Bank of America and the NAACP to plant seeds in our lives," says Colette. "We learned how to make our dream come true. Our whole family now has a sense of pride and belonging. We call our home our 'lighthouse'—it draws us together as a family and with our neighbors."

McColl says, "Rebuilding our most troubled neighborhoods is essential for the health of our cities and our country. No one company, nonprofit group, or government agency can do it alone. Each has an important role to play; each has certain resources and expertise to bring to the table." Challenging other corporate leaders, McColl says, "More players need to get off the sidelines and join in. At the end of our careers, the real test will be 'Did we matter?' I think everyone wants to be able to answer 'Yes!' "

When Duane McClurg celebrated the reopening of The Parks at Wynnewood in Dallas, he could see what mattered. Oak trees shade the trimmed lawns where children's laughter fills the air. Neighbors meet regularly at the community center. Residents exchange greetings as they go to and from the laundry rooms. A neighborhood has been reborn.

Bankers can make a big difference in their communities by collaborating with their local or state Community Development Department to provide mortgages to low-income people—so they can become first-time homeowners and long-term contributing citizens. Call the **National Congress for Community Economic Development** at 202-282-9020, or visit their Web site, www.ncced.org.

THE HUNDREDTH MONKEY

This is a popular tale by the Japanese storyteller Yukio Funai. It has taken on a life of its own in the decades since its original telling based on the scientific research that inspired it. Ken Keyes Jr. adapted it as a slogan for the nuclear-freeze movement. Combined with the Stone Soup folktale, it reminds us of the power we have to change the world, one person—or monkey—at a time.

As the story goes, a group of curious scientists were observing the eating habits of the Japanese monkey, *Macaca fuscata*, on the island of Koshima. They fed the monkeys by flying over the island and dropping sweet potatoes in the sand. While the monkeys liked the taste of the potatoes, they didn't care for the sand.

Imo, an eighteen-month-old female monkey, figured out that she could wash the potatoes in a nearby stream. She taught this to her mother and to her playmates, who taught their mothers. After a few years, all the young monkeys on the island had learned to wash off the sandy sweet potatoes so they would taste better. But only the adults who imitated the children learned this trick. The other adults kept eating their potatoes with sand.

After a while, more and more monkeys were washing their sweet potatoes—nobody knows for sure how many. For the sake of the story, let's suppose that when the sun rose one morning there were ninety-nine monkeys who had taken to washing their sweet potatoes. Let's further suppose that later that morning, a hundredth monkey learned to wash his potatoes.

Then something remarkable happened. It seems that the additional energy of this hundredth monkey created a spark—an ideological breakthrough—that advanced the entire species. By that evening, nearly all the monkeys in the tribe washed their sweet potatoes before they ate them.

The scientists soon observed that the new habit of washing sweet potatoes had somehow jumped overseas. Colonies of monkeys on nearby islands, and even the mainland troop of monkeys at Takasakiyama, were all washing their sweet potatoes!

The "hundredth monkey" phenomenon shows what can happen when someone has a good idea. First, a few others recognize its value and put it into practice. One by one, others join in, too, until, at a certain point of "critical mass," everybody gets it, and the entire species can advance thanks to the ones who dared to do things in a new and better way.

Just think what this can mean for humankind. Each one of us who changes our ways, adopts a more generous habit or a sustainable way of doing things, increases our collective wisdom and benefits the entire planet.

Who knows? The hundredth one, the one who tips the scale, could be you!

STONE SOUP RESOURCES
The Stone Soup Leadership Institute

The Stone Soup Leadership Institute is the learning-in-action arm of the Stone Soup Foundation, a 501(c)3 international, nonprofit education organization founded in 1997. Proceeds from this book help support Institute projects such as the development of the *Stone Soup for the World* educational curriculum. The Institute provides technical assistance and training to organizations to prepare future and emerging leaders to use our educational curriculum to develop public/private partnerships that build healthier communities and a healthier world.

The Institute is an America's Promise Partner whose supporters include the Annie E. Casey Foundation, Bank of America, City Lights Inc., EDS, Fairchild Semiconductor, General Motors Foundation, Learning as Leadership, Shinnyo-En Foundation, Smith Family Foundation, Sun Microsystems, Unagraphics Solutions, and the United Way of Central Maryland.

Contact the **Stone Soup Leadership Institute,** P.O. Box 3694, Half Moon Bay, CA 94019; or visit our Web site, www.soup4world.com.

Educational Curriculum

An exciting multicultural program featuring people from all cultures and twenty-nine countries, for introducing positive role models to youth. Curriculum includes the book, Leader's Guide, videotape with Walter Cronkite, audiotapes, and Web site.

The *Stone Soup for the World* educational curriculum is a toolbox and an action resource, inspiring young people to catch the "Stone Soup spirit" and get involved in helping their communities.

Stone Soup for the World Web site

www.soup4world.com

An interactive global education resource, featuring a monthly Call to Action and Hero of the Month; with information about volunteer opportunities, cross-cultural exchanges, and educational programs in conflict resolution, peace and social justice, environmental and ecotourism, as well as community and economic development.

Proceeds from *Stone Soup for the World*

Proceeds from *Stone Soup for the World* help support the Stone Soup Leadership Institute, our educational curriculum and Web site. We also dedicate 10 percent of the book's proceeds to make *Stone Soup for the World* available to others in schools, libraries, prisons, and churches. We invite you to join with us in this goal.

PUT SOMETHING IN THE POT

We would love to hear from you about how the stories in this book have touched you. We're collecting new stories for future editions of *Stone Soup for the World*. E-mail your story to the Stone Soup Leadership Institute, info@soup4world.com; or send by regular mail to P.O. Box 3694, Half Moon Bay, CA 94019.

OTHER RESOURCES
National Days of Service

Pick a day to join millions of Americans and experience the joy of volunteering.

The Big Help Campaign   212-258-7080
The Big Help is **Nickelodeon**'s year-round campaign to get kids involved in their communities through volunteering. Each year, Nickelodeon airs The Big Help-a-Thon, a live, televised extravaganza in which kids call 800 numbers to pledge their help. Nickelodeon also provides teachers with the Big Help Classroom Kit, and local community leaders with educational materials and information about local volunteer activities through a traveling Helpmobile. They partner with twenty-three national organizations dedicated to helping kids serve. The Big Help Week is the third week of April. Visit www. NICK.com.

Rebuilding Together   800-4-REHAB9
Deliver a dream to an elderly neighbor who needs you—grab a hammer or a paintbrush to restore joy and hope in homes across the country. Rebuilding Together preserves neighborhoods, reduces institutionalizations, and builds stronger communities in partnership with community groups, business, labor, and everyday Americans. Lend a hand and make a difference. "We're love in action." Phone, or visit online at www.rebuilding together.com.

The United Way's Day of Caring   703-836-7100
The **United Way** conducts one or more Days of Caring in over 400 communities each year, typically in the fall, in which individuals and groups volunteer to work in daylong projects at local agencies—delivering meals to the elderly, reading to children, repairing and painting houses—even rebuilding a baseball field. The day combines the camaraderie of side-by-side work with co-workers, friends, and new acquaintances with exposure to the good work of agencies in your community. Visit www.unitedway.org.

Make a Difference Day   800-VOLUNTEER
An annual day of doing good in which more than a million Americans volunteer and organize service activities in their communities. The event, created in 1992 by *USA Weekend* magazine in partnership with **The Points of Light Foundation,** rallies corporations, government leaders, charitable organizations, and everyday Americans. Volunteer efforts that capture the spirit of the day receive charitable awards from a pool funded by *USA Weekend* magazine and Newman's Own products. The day takes place the fourth Saturday of each October. Visit www.usaweekend.com and click on "Make a Difference Day info."

Martin Luther King Jr. Day   202-606-5000
In the spirit of Dr. King's commitment to service, the King Holiday in January is a national day of service. This day, sponsored by the Corporation for National and Community Service, is an opportunity to raise awareness about human rights, interracial cooperation, and youth antiviolence initiatives. Visit www.cns.gov/index.html.

National Youth Service Day   202-296-2992
Celebrate the power of young people. National Youth Service Day is the largest service event in America, engaging 2 million young volunteers in more than 9 million hours of community service. An annual public education campaign sponsored by **Youth Service America** in collaboration with thirty-four national youth organizations, it promotes the involvement of youth in their communities. Visit www.SERVEnet.org.

Stand for Children Day   800-663-4032
Stand for Children is a national network of grassroots children's activists who are building a strong movement called Leave No Child Behind. Each year they plan local activities all across the country on June 1. To learn how you can help the children in your community, visit www.stand.org.

Take Our Daughters to Work Day   800-676-7780
On the fourth Thursday of April, parents and other adults across the country take their daughters or other young girls to work for the day. Sponsored by the **Ms. Foundation for Women,** this day lets girls see firsthand what the workday looks like and promotes girls' work by educating them about their wide range of life options. Call Gail Maynor, or visit online at www.ms.foundation.org.

Trick or Treat for UNICEF   800-252-KIDS
For over fifty years, children across America have celebrated Halloween by collecting coins to help provide medication, vaccines, clean water and sanitation, nutritious food, and basic education to millions of children in more than 106 countries. During October, the **U.S. Committee for UNICEF** provides educators and families with myriad opportunities to teach children about global issues and celebrate cultural diversity. To order the free trademark orange "Trick or Treat for UNICEF" cartons or educational materials, visit www.unicef.org.

Organizations

Alliance for National Renewal   800-223-6004
The Alliance is a unique coalition of 194 community-building organizations, institutions, communities, and people from the public, private, and nonprofit sectors who are re-engaging citizens in community life and working together toward a shared vision of improving communities. ANR is a program of the National Civic League. Call 800-223-6004, or visit www.ncl.org/anr.

America's Promise: The Alliance for Youth   800-365-0153
Launched at the Presidents' Summit in April 1997, America's Promise: The Alliance for Youth mobilizes communities, organizations, businesses, and volunteers across the country to help provide young people with fundamental resources of caring adults, safe places to live, a healthy start, marketable skills, and opportunities to serve. Call 888-55-YOUTH, or visit www.americaspromise.org.

Connect America   800-VOLUNTEER
Connect America is a collaborative effort that brings together the energies and resources of nonprofit organizations, businesses, and community volunteers to help build the connections that are critical to solving many of society's problems. To learn about volunteer opportunities in your community, call 800-59-LIGHT, or visit www.pointsoflight.org.

Corporation for National and Community Service   800-942-2677
A public-private partnership that collaborates with local and national nonprofit organizations to sponsor service projects that respond to the needs of the communities they serve. They oversee three national initiatives: **AmeriCorps,** a year of community service for seventeen- to-twenty-three-year-olds; **Learn & Serve,** educational resources and models

for kindergarten through college; and the **National Senior Corps** for people fifty years and older. Call 800-424-8867, or visit www.cns.gov.

The Giraffe Project   360-221-7989

The Giraffe Project is a national nonprofit organization that finds, honors, and publicizes people who "stick their necks out" for the common good. The **K-12 Giraffe Heroes Program** provides educational materials to students in all fifty states and American schools abroad. E-mail office@giraffe.org, or visit www.giraffe.org.

The Independent Sector   202-223-8100

Comprising eight hundred nationally oriented foundations, nonprofits, charities, and philanthropies, the Independent Sector researches and reports on trends in giving and volunteering; labors to safeguard advocacy rights for nonprofits; educates the public on the integral role of nonprofits in society; and provides a forum for interaction and collaboration among the nonprofit, business, and government sectors. Visit www.indepsec.org.

One to One: The National Mentoring Partnership   202-338-3844

One to One serves as a resource for mentoring initiatives nationwide and advocates the benefits of expanding mentoring programs. To start or expand a mentoring program, visit www.mentoring.org.

The Points of Light Foundation Volunteer Centers   800-VOLUNTEER

The Points of Light Foundation is a nonpartisan, nonprofit organization dedicated to engaging more people more effectively in volunteer service to help solve social problems. The Volunteer Centers connect more than 1 million people each year to volunteer opportunities. To learn about volunteer opportunities in your community, call your local Volunteer Center, or visit www.pointsoflight.org.

American Association of Retired Persons   202-434-3219

AARP has a national Volunteer Talent Bank that matches people ages fifty and older with volunteer opportunities based on their interests, skills, and geographical location. Their database matches volunteers with service opportunities in literacy, sciences, legislative and legal assistance, health, housing, arts, and cultural, intergenerational, and environmental activities. To become a volunteer, call for a registration packet, or visit www.aarp.org.

Big Brothers Big Sisters of America   215-567-7000
Big Brothers Big Sisters of America's five hundred agencies nationwide provide more than 100,000 children from single-parent homes with positive adult role models. Become a caring friend to a child in your community so he or she can succeed in the world. To join BBBSA's One-to-One mentoring program or the School-Based Mentoring Program, visit www.bbbsa.org.

Boys & Girls Clubs of America   800-854-CLUB
Boys & Girls Clubs of America is a nationwide affiliation of organizations working to help youth of all backgrounds, especially those in disadvantaged circumstances, to develop the qualities needed to become responsible citizens and leaders. Visit www.bgca.org.

Catholic Charities USA   703-549-1390
Catholic Charities USA is a national nonprofit network of 1,400 local, independent agencies that provides social services to more than 12 million people in need—regardless of religious, ethnic, or social background. As the largest private social-services network, they provide housing, refugee and immigration assistance, employment programs, pregnancy and adoption services, counseling, and food. Visit www.catholiccharitiesusa.org.

Alliance for Children and Families   414-359-1040
Alliance for Children and Families strengthens family life through local agencies throughout the United States and Canada. Volunteers mentor young people to reduce teenage pregnancy and drug/alcohol abuse, serve as counselors for marriage and parent-child relationships, and help with foster care, adoption, and crisis hotlines for family pressures related to aging, child abuse, and family violence. Visit www.alliance1.org.

Jewish Community Centers Association of North America   212-532-4949
The Association offers a wide range of services and resources to enable its 275 affiliates— Jewish Community Centers, YMHAs and YWHAs, and summer camps across the United States and Canada—to provide educational, cultural, and recreational programs to enhance the lives of Jewish people. E-mail info@jcca.org, or visit www.jcca.org.

The Association of Jewish Family and Children's Agencies   800-634-7346
The Asssociation of Jewish Family and Children's Agencies provide family services to people in need, regardless of their faith. Volunteers help feed the hungry, visit hospital

patients, serve as companions to the elderly, and work with disadvantaged children, at-risk youth, and people with disabilities. They also help resettle Jewish families from other countries and work at improving intercultural relations. Visit www.ajfca.org.

The United Black Fund   800-323-7677

There are thirty-nine United Black Funds around the country that work with nonprofit organizations to meet unmet needs in communities such as child care, literacy, crime prevention, drug and alcohol programs, mentoring programs for youth, and support programs for the elderly people and those with disabilities. Visit www.unitedblackfund.org.

American Red Cross

The American Red Cross is a volunteer emergency services organization with more than 2,600 chapters throughout the United States and its territories. Volunteers help in blood centers and food banks, in providing transportation for people with disabilities and translation for new immigrants, and in caring for the elderly and children of working parents, as well as in repairing homes after fire, floods, and tornadoes. Visit www.redcross.org.

Girls Inc.

Girls Inc., a national youth advocacy organization, helps girls become "strong, smart, and bold" in an equitable society. Professionally trained staff members provide educational programs, such as developing leadership skills and encouraging science, math, and technology studies, to 350,000 young people at one thousand sites, especially in high-risk, underserved areas. Visit www.girlsinc.org.

Girl Scouts of the U.S.A.   212-852-5000

The Girl Scouts are committed to helping all girls from every background develop the confidence, determination, and skills needed to thrive in today's world. Visit www.girlscouts.org.

National 4-H Council   301-961-2800

In 4-H, teamwork and leadership skills are developed through hands-on learning projects in the environment, gardening, nutrition, and raising animals, as well as in public speaking and citizenship. More than 5.6 million youth, ages five to nineteen, participate in 4-H's coeducational programs every year. Visit www.fourHcouncil.edu.

Ronald McDonald House Charities

By supporting Ronald McDonald Houses in communities around the world, and by making grants to other nonprofit children's programs, this organization lifts disadvantaged children to a better tomorrow. Visit www.rmhc.com.

The Salvation Army   703-684-5500

The Salvation Army is a national nonprofit organization motivated by a love of God and a concern for people in need, regardless of color, creed, gender, or age. Volunteers in ten thousand centers help with crisis hotlines, emergency disaster services, day-care centers, summer camps, and youth programs for low-income children, as well as food banks and shelters for the homeless. During the Christmas season they distribute food to the homeless, along with toys and clothing to disadvantaged children. Visit www.salvationarmy usa.org.

Volunteer Centers of America   800-899-0089

Volunteers of America serves over one million people each year through our community-based affiliates, which offer a variety of programs including day-care centers for abused and neglected children, emergency shelters for the homeless, and "meals on wheels" for the frail elderly. They are also the nation's largest nonprofit affordable-housing provider for low-income families, the elderly, and persons with disabilities. Visit www.voa.org.

YMCA (Young Men's Christian Association)   312-977-0031

The YMCA helps men and women of all ages, incomes, abilities, backgrounds, and religions grow in body, mind, and spirit. The 2,400 YMCAs nationwide provide tutors and mentors and offer alcohol and drug prevention programs, health and recreation programs, day camps and child care, food banks and job training. Visit www.ymca. net.

YWCA of the U.S.A. (Young Women's Christian Association)   212-614-2700

The YWCA is dedicated to the empowerment of women and girls. With 363 member associations in thousands of sites in all fifty states, the YWCA helps more than a million women, girls, and their families nationwide with parent and peer counseling, child and health care, teen pregnancy prevention, domestic abuse issues, and career counseling. Visit www.ywca.org.

United Neighborhood Centers of America, Inc.   216-391-3028

United Neighborhood Centers of America serves 153 neighborhood centers by cultivating leadership and accrediting quality day-care, youth, family, and elderly programs, as well as providing other services improving conditions for all neighborhood residents. Visit www.unca.org.

Co-op America   800-58-GREEN

Co-op America is a national, nonprofit membership organization that links socially responsible businesses and consumers in a national alternative marketplace. Through its *National Green Pages, Co-op America Quarterly,* and *Financial Planning Handbook,* it educates people on how to vote with their dollars and use their purchasing and investing power to create a just and sustainable society and provides information and services to help people make spending and investing decisions that are in harmony with their politics and values. The *National Green Pages* features 2,500 socially and environmentally responsible companies and organizations. Visit www.coopamerica.org.

The World Business Academy   415-227-0106

WBA urges members to avoid or solve our most pressing problems, including sustainability. An international membership organization, it is open to anyone committed to maximizing our human potential and implementing the new paradigms. Visit www.worldbusiness.org.

Social Venture Network   415-561-6502

SVN is a part of an international organization of business and social entrepreneurs dedicated to promoting progressive solutions to social problems and changing the way the world does business. SVN members strive to be effective businesspeople and catalysts for social change by integrating the values of a just and sustainable society into their day-to-day business practices, and by using their enterprises to create new ventures to improve the world. Visit www.svn.org.

Institute for Food and Development Policy: Food First   510-654-4400

Food First empowers citizens to address the root causes of hunger, poverty, and environmental decline. Their research and educational materials teach people how to change antidemocratic institutions and belief systems that promote hunger and environmental deterioration. E-mail foodfirst@foodfirst.org, or visit www.foodfirst.org.

Grassroots Leadership   704-332-3090
Be passionate for justice. Learn the skills of community empowerment. To receive books, tapes, and CDs from Grassroots Leadership, write to P.O. Box 36006, Charlotte, NC 28236, or visit www.grass-roots.org.

National Civic League   800-223-6004
Help your community prepare for the future through a citizens' visioning and strategic planning process. Call the National Civic League and ask for their catalogue of books, conferences, and tools, including 98 *Things You Can Do for Your Community*.

National Coalition for the Homeless   202-775-1322
NCH is a national advocacy network committed to meeting the urgent needs of those who are (or are at risk of becoming) homeless, as well as creating systemic and attitudinal changes to prevent and end homelessness. The network includes homeless persons, activists, and service and housing providers. E-mail nch@ari.net, or visit www.national homeless.org.

Robert Wood Johnson Community Health Leadership Program   617-426-9772
Each year the Community Health Leadership Program honors ten outstanding heroes of community health care. Call to nominate an outstanding health leader, or visit www.communityhealthleaders.org.

Teaching Tolerance
This project of the Southern Poverty Law Center helps teachers promote interracial and intercultural understanding. Half a million educators receive its free magazine, and more than fifty thousand schools have used its free multimedia kits. For more information, write to 400 Washington Ave., Montgomery, AL 36104, or visit www.splcenter.org/teaching tolerance/tt=index.html.

Conflict Resolution Center International, Inc.   412-687-6210
CRCI is a worldwide network of cutting-edge mediators, teachers, arbitrators, and dispute-resolution specialists bridging conflict and peace on every continent. They draw on a large body of accumulated wisdom and experience so that wherever you are, whatever your problem, the solution may be available to you. For information, visit www.conflictres.org.

Educators for Social Responsibility   617-492-1764
ESR is nationally recognized for promoting children's ethical and social development to

shape a safe, sustainable, and just world—through conflict resolution, violence prevention, intergroup relations, and character education. A leading voice for teaching social responsibility as a core practice in the schooling and upbringing of children, they offer professional development, networks, and instructional materials to educators and parents. Visit www.esrnational.org.

Quaker Information Center   215-241-7024
The Center provides a list of volunteer/service opportunities, internships, work camps, and life-changing experiences with a wide variety of Quaker and non-Quaker organizations such as the American Friends Service Committee and others around the world. Visit www.quakerinfo.org.

Heifer International   800-422-0474
Heifer International helps more than 4 million struggling families worldwide to become self-reliant by giving the gift of livestock and training in its care. Heifer joins with people of all faiths to work for the dignity and well-being of all people. Visit www.heifer.org.

Mennonite Central Committee   717-859-1151
MCC connects people around the world who suffer from poverty, conflict, oppression, and natural disaster with volunteers in North American churches. The Committee strives for peace, justice, and dignity for all people by sharing our experiences, resources, and faith. Visit www.mcc.org.

Save the Children   202-221-4079
Save the Children Federation empowers 2 million disadvantaged children and their families in thirty-nine countries and fifteen U.S. states to take control of their lives. Their two thousand professionals provide education, health, economic opportunities, humanitarian response, and community self-help assistance. Visit www.savethechildren.org.

Trickle Up Program   212-362-7958
We give the poorest of the poor the opportunity to start their own businesses. In the past twenty years, more than 250,000 people in 112 countries have lifted themselves out of poverty by starting over 47,000 businesses. Visit www.trickleup.org.

U.S. Fund for UNICEF   800-FOR-KIDS

UNICEF works for the survival, protection, and development of the world's children through fund-raising, education, and advocacy. In more than 160 countries and territories, the organization provides lifesaving medicine, better nutrition, clean water and sanitation, education, and emergency relief. Visit www.unicefusa.org.

Peace Pals Program/World Peace Prayer Society   212-755-4755

Unite with people all over the world through the universal prayer "May peace prevail on Earth." To bring the Peace Pole Project to your community, or to learn about the Peace Pals program for children, contact Deirdre Fisher, Director, 26 Benton Road, Wassaic, NY 12592, or visit www.worldpeace.org.

Web site addresses and other contact information were current at the time of publication but may have changed since. The author and publisher would greatly appreciate being notified of any such changes.

RECOMMENDED READING
Books

Ackerman, Peter, and Jack DuVall. *A Force More Powerful: A Century of Nonviolent Conflict*. New York: St. Martin's Press, 2000.

Bellah, Robert, et al. *Habits of the Heart: Individualism and Commitment in American Life*. New York: Harper & Row, 1985.

Chappell, Tom. *The Soul of a Business*. New York: Bantam Books, 1993.

Church, Dawson, and Alan Sherr, eds. *The Heart of the Healer*. New York: Aslan Publishing, 1977.

Clinton, Hillary Rodham. *It Takes a Village*. New York: Simon & Schuster, 1996.

Coles, Robert. *The Call of Service*. Boston: Houghton Mifflin Company, 1993.

De Tocqueville, Alexis. *Democracy in America*. New York: Vintage Books, 1945 (1834).

Dolphin, Laurie. *Neve Shalom/Wahat al-Salam: Oasis of Peace*. New York: Scholastic Books, 1993.

Earth Works Group. *50 Simple Things You Can Do to Save the Earth*. Berkeley: Earth Works Press, 1989.

Edelman, Marian Wright. *The Measure of Our Success*. New York: HarperPerennial, 1992.

Gardner, John W. *On Leadership*. New York: Free Press, 1990.

———. *Self-Renewal: The Individual and the Innovative Society*. New York: Harper & Row, 1965.

Goleman, Daniel. *Emotional Intelligence*. New York: Bantam Books, 1995.

Jackson, Jesse. *Straight from the Heart.* Philadelphia: Fortress Press, 1987.

Kanter, Rosabeth Moss. *World Class: Thriving Locally in the Global Economy.* New York: Simon & Schuster, 1995.

King, Mary. *Mahatma Gandhi and Martin Luther King Jr.: The Power of Nonviolent Action.* Paris: UNESCO Publishing, 1999.

Kretzmann, John, and John McKnight. *Building Communities from the Inside Out.* Chicago: ACTA Publications, 1993.

Lappé, Frances Moore, and Paul Martin Du Bois. *The Quickening of America.* San Francisco: Jossey-Bass Publishers, 1995.

Lewis, Barbara. *The Kid's Guide to Social Action.* Minneapolis: Free Spirit Publishing, Inc., 1998.

Lipkis, Andy and Katie. *The Simple Act of Planting a Tree.* Los Angeles: Jeremy P. Tarcher, Inc., 1990.

Mariotti, Steve. *The Young Entrepreneur's Guide.* New York: Times Books, 2000.

Newman, Nell, and Ursula Hotchner. *Newman's Own Cookbook.* Chicago: Contemporary Books, Inc., 1985.

Peck, Scott M., M.D. *The Different Drum.* New York: Touchstone, 1987.

Shore, Bill. *Revolution of the Heart.* New York: Riverhead Books, 1995.

Sklar, Holly, and Peter Medoff. *Streets of Hope.* Boston: South End Press, 1994.

Young, Andrew. *A Way Out of No Way.* Nashville: Thomas Nelson Publishers, 1994.

Magazines and Other Publications

Hope Magazine
A bimonthly magazine about humanity making a difference; phone 207-359-4651, or visit www.hopemag.com.

Fellowship of Reconciliation Publications
Phone 845-358-4601, or visit www.forusa.org or www.nonviolence.org.

The Utne Reader
Phone 800-736-UTNE, or visit www.utne.com.

Yes! A Journal of Positive Futures
Subscribe to *Yes!* magazine and connect with thousands of others in the United States and around the world who are turning hope into action for a sustainable, just, and compassionate future; phone 800-937-4451, or visit yesmagazine.org.

ABOUT MARIANNE LARNED

Marianne Larned is a dynamic speaker who inspires people to help make the world a better place. She has served great leaders and worked with people from all walks of life, many of whom are featured in this book. After overcoming a life-threatening illness, she realized that if we can each heal ourselves, together we have the power to heal our planet.

As founding Director of the Stone Soup Leadership Institute, Ms. Larned collaborates in developing public-private partnerships to build healthier communities. She's assisted corporate, government, civic, and community leaders including Fortune 500 companies, health-care systems, chambers of commerce, and the Foundation for Education & Economic Development in the Philippines. As the guest columnist for "The Business of Education," a year-long monthly column for the *San Francisco Business Times,* she helped create an educated constituency of companies prepared to be active participants in education-reform initiatives.

For her pioneering and humanitarian work, Ms. Larned has received numerous awards including Outstanding Young Woman of America and World Intellectual, 2000 Notable American Women, and the World's Who's Who of Women. Her undergraduate studies at the University of Massachusetts, Amherst, and the Rudolph Steiner Center in Aberdeen, Scotland, prepared her to become a teacher. Her graduate work at Boston University and California State University gave her the tools to advise leaders of corporate America in practicing socially and environmentally responsible business.

To schedule Ms. Larned or another speaker from the *Stone Soup for the World* Speakers Bureau, please call 415-646-0416, or e-mail speaker@soup4world.com.

THE AUTHOR'S JOURNEY

For many years, I've been a Stone Soup traveler, living and working in communities across the country and around the world.

In 1990, I met Claire Nuer, a Holocaust and cancer survivor, who became my mentor. She would ask people in her leadership trainings a provocative question: "What changes could you make in your life today to create a more humane world fifty years from now?" It was a powerful wake-up call for me.

To ponder this question, I took some time off from my fast-paced life and returned to my New England roots. Walking the beaches of Martha's Vineyard, Massachusetts, I asked myself what I could do.

One day I found a "magic" stone on Lucy Vincent Beach. Its fossilized imprint looked like the tree of life. It fit perfectly in the palm of my hand. Each day I would hold it, remembering Claire's words: "One rock can change the course of the river."

When my mother reminded me of the Stone Soup folktale, she inspired this book. My dream is for each of us to discover our own magic stone and find a way to give our gifts to the world.

For curious, first-time travelers, I hope this book gives you new ideas, inspiration, and direction. For fellow seasoned travelers, I hope these stories nourish your soul and give you strength to carry on. For all of us, may these stories rekindle the joy of giving and the power of working together to build a better world. May our children be inspired to join us.

STORYTELLERS

Jonathan Alter is a senior editor and columnist at *Newsweek* and often writes about community service. This is the first time he's written about his mother, Joanne Alter.

Karen Anderson is the director of Public Liaison for the U.S. Agency for International Development. She has developed its Lessons Without Borders program so that U.S. communities can benefit from lessons they have learned from developing countries.

Sarah Bachman is a freelance writer whose work has appeared in magazines and newspapers in the United States and abroad. She has reported on women, development, and child labor in Bangladesh and other countries. She dedicates her story to all those she met while volunteering in Bangladesh.

Masankho Banda, co-vice-president of Pathways to Peace, is a graduate student in theology at Berkeley. Through dance and theater, he helps children work for peace and justice in the U.S. and Europe.

Rosalind E. Barnes, a vice-president and marketing manager at Wachovia, serves as president of the INROADS/Atlanta Alumni Association. Since her experience interning with INROADS, she mentors and encourages young adults to pursue a lifetime of excellence.

Ann M. Bauer is a Minneapolis-based writer and communications consultant to the Dayton Hudson Corporation. She is actively involved in making public schools inclusive for all children.

Melba Pattillo Beals is a communications consultant in San Francisco, former NBC reporter, and author of *Warriors Don't Cry*, her memoir about the struggle to integrate Central High School in Little Rock, Arkansas. A mother of a grown daughter, she has recently adopted four-year-old twins.

John Bell is a founding staff member and Director of Training for YouthBuild USA, the proud husband and work partner of Dorothy Stoneman.

Nancy Berg is an award-winning writer and poet living in Woodland Hills, California, who teaches at the University of Phoenix and with California Poets in the Schools. She was an editor of *Stone Soup for the World*, *Chicken Soup for the Woman's Soul*, and other books.

Kevin Berger is executive editor of *San Francisco* magazine. He says he found the subject of his story, Laura Scher, a business leader concerned with social and environmental issues as much as with the bottom line, "a breath of fresh air."

Jan Boylston is Senior Vice-President for Public Policy at NationsBank. She consistently volunteers with numerous community and civic programs in Charlotte, North Carolina.

Patricia Broughton was a freelance writer and photographer before joining Bethel New Life as its Director of Resource Development. She has learned the power of transforming silence into language and action.

Laura Brown is a freelance writer living in Washington, D.C. She urges you to join her in buying from businesses that do well by doing good.

Sharon Burde is director of LINCS, Lasting Interfaith Network Connections, a conflict-resolution training program for urban clergy at Baruch College of the City University of New York.

Jeb Bush is the governor of the State of Florida, and **Brian Yablonski** is deputy chief of staff to the governor.

Andrew Carroll is the executive director of the American Poetry and Literacy Project, based in Washington, D.C., and is the author of *Letters of a Nation*.

Jimmy Carter, former president of the United States, is the founder of the Carter Center. He dedicates his time to Habitat for Humanity and other nonprofit organizations.

Anne Colby is co-director of the Preparation for the Professions Program and the Project on Higher Education and the Development of Moral and Civic Responsibility at the Carnegie Foundation for the Advancement of Teaching. She has co-authored *Some Do Care: Contemporary Lives of Moral Commitment* with William Damon.

Alex Counts is the executive director of the Washington, D.C.–based Grameen Foundation. He remains in close contact with the men, women, and children in Bangladesh who befriended and inspired him when he lived there for more than five years.

Leslie Crutchfield is editor of *Who Cares* magazine, the toolkit for social change, the nation's leading magazine for community leaders who want to make a difference.

Ram Dass is founder of the Seva Foundation and the Hanuman Foundation. He is co-author of *How Can I Help?* with Paul Gorman and dedicates his time in service to others.

Richard Deats is an author, lecturer, workshop facilitator, and editor of *Fellowship,* and coordinator of communications for the U.S. Fellowship of Reconciliation. He has worked all over the world for nonviolent social change and reconciliation.

Tom Dellner is a freelance writer and the West Coast editor of *Links* magazine. He dedicates this story to his mother, Jeanne, who taught him the value and rewards of community service.

Susan Dundon is the author of a novel, *To My Ex-Husband,* and an essayist whose work appears in numerous magazines and newspapers. Her face, however, frequently appears at the White Dog Café.

Jonah Edelman is the co-founder and executive director of Stand For Children. He helped organize Stand For Children Day and developed the concept of Stand For Children's local chapter organizing approach, then moved to Oregon to field-test it. Stand For Children has 1,400 members, four active chapters, and four more chapters-in-formation. It has helped increase access to dental and mental-health care and after-school programs and has pushed for increased compensation of qualified early childhood educators at the local and state levels.

Gil Friend is president and CEO of Natural Logic, Inc., a strategy, design, and software firm helping companies and communities prosper by putting the laws of nature at the heart of enterprise.

Donald G. Gale, Ph.D., was vice-president of Bonneville International Corporation and a former university professor. He serves on the boards of a dozen community service organizations that emphasize education and young people.

Arun Gandhi is the grandson of Mahatma Gandhi. Founder/director of the M. K. Gandhi Institute for Nonviolence, he is an author and lecturer on the philosophy of nonviolence.

Rick Glassberg and Susan Spence, longtime summer visitors to Martha's Vineyard, became year-rounders in 1993. They were "Barn Busters" for the new Agricultural Hall and recently authored *Magic Time,* a family guide to the best of Martha's Vineyard.

Gregory S. Gross, Ed.D., Foundation consultant, was the founding president of the Jacksonville Jaguars Foundation and co-founder of the Sports Philanthropy Project. He dedicates this story to Arnold Hiatt and others who have taught him by example.

Marc Grossman, a storyteller for *By Giving Our Lives,* and a media consultant in Sacramento, California, was Cesar Chavez's longtime personal aide and spokesman. He supervises press relations for the United Farm Workers.

Jane Harvey is a freelance writer and the editor of *Volunteer Leadership* magazine, published by the Points of Light Foundation. She teaches Sunday school and volunteers at a food pantry.

Jo Clare Hartsig is a United Church of Christ minister living in Minneapolis/St. Paul. She is a regular columnist for *Fellowship* magazine.

A. E. Hotchner is a longtime friend and cooking conspirator of Paul Newman. They founded Newman's Own, Inc., and the Hole in the Wall Gang Camp for seriously ill children. "Hotch" has authored screenplays and books such as the best-seller *Papa Hemingway.*

Janet Hulstrand, an editor and writer, lives in Washington, D.C. She has worked on books written by Caroline Kennedy, Paul Robeson Jr., and Andrew Young. She likes to read the Stone Soup folktale and other stories from this book to her two children and their friends.

Dawn M. Hutchison is the co-founder of KaBOOM! She is passionate about building healthy and vibrant communities. Her role model is seven-year-old Ashley, who used her faith and vision to lead when others doubted. Dawn is currently a consultant and writer in Madison, Wisconsin.

Rosabeth Moss Kanter, a professor at the Harvard Business School and author of several prize-winning books, is a proud member of City Year's National Board of Trustees and loves to participate in their annual Serve-a-Thons.

Leslie Kean is a journalist and coauthor of *Burma's Revolution of the Spirit: The Struggle for Democratic Freedom and Dignity.* For two months in 1996, she attended Aung San Suu Kyi's weekend speeches. She has reported on Burma for the *Boston Globe, The Nation,* and a host of other media around the world.

Susan Keese is a freelance writer and columnist who has written for numerous newspapers and magazines. She was inspired by Joseph Rogers while working as a reporter for the American News Service.

Ken Keyes Jr. is a successful author whose books have sold over a million copies. They include *The Handbook to Higher Consciousness* and *The Hundredth Monkey.*

Nina Mermey Klippel has written for *House & Garden, House Beautiful,* and other magazines, as well as for newspapers throughout the United States. She learned about Neve Shalom/Wahat al-Salam at a benefit hosted by Richard Gere and loves to share her excitement about the Oasis of Peace.

Frances Moore Lappé's efforts to understand the roots of needless suffering led her to co-found two national organizations, Food First: The Institute for Food and Development Policy and The Center for Living Democracy. With her daughter Anna, she wrote *Hope's Edge: The Next Diet for a Small Planet,* the thirtieth-anniversary sequel to her 1971 bestseller, *Diet for a Small Planet.*

Trude Lash was Eleanor Roosevelt's friend and co-worker for over forty years. She is co-chairman with Arthur Schlesinger Jr. of the Franklin and Eleanor Roosevelt Institute and former director of the Eleanor Roosevelt Institute. Her late husband, Joseph Lash, wrote many books about the Roosevelts and received the Pulitzer Prize for *Eleanor and Franklin.* Mrs. Lash recently received the first Eleanor Roosevelt Medal.

Allan Luks is executive director of Big Brothers Big Sisters of New York City, the author of four books on social and health issues, and a lawyer who has initiated laws that have become national models. He also volunteers regularly.

John McKnight directs the Asset Based Community Development Institute at Northwestern University. He is committed to discovering the gifts, capacities, and resources in local neighborhoods.

Jeffrey Madison is a Harvard-educated writer who volunteers at Food from the 'Hood, where he discovered that he is the sum of everyone around him and they are the sum of him. He's now turning that into action.

Matthew Malone graduated from Connecticut College with an economics degree and is pursuing a writing career in Colorado. As he developed business stories for *Stone Soup*, he discovered that when "capitalism is coupled with compassion, it's a marriage with an exciting future."

Nelson Mandela, author of *A Long Road to Freedom*, is an international hero whose lifelong dedication to the fight against racial oppression in South Africa won him the Nobel Peace Prize and the presidency of his country.

Peter Mann is international coordinator for World Hunger Year. He works with hunger activists around the world and is a proud member of a community-supported farm in New York.

Robert Marra is coordinating an immigrant health and access coalition at Health Care for All, the nationally recognized health-advocacy organization. He came to Boston as a medical student and then worked with Judith Kurland, Boston's Commissioner of Health and Hospitals.

Jenny Midtgaard is the former "Lifestyles" editor for the Gavilan Newspapers and has been a Garlic Festival volunteer for the past thirteen years.

Terry Mollner, a pioneer of socially responsible investing and community development for over twenty-five years, is the president of the Trusteeship Institute, a founding board member of the Calvert Social Investment Fund, and co-chair of the Calvert Foundation.

Dennis Morgigno, as a broadcast journalist and station manager of Channel 4 San Diego, reported on Father Joe Carroll's attempts to reinvent homeless shelters and became a believer in Father Joe's crusade and a supporter of his cause.

Robert Muller, chancellor of the University of Peace in Costa Rica, former assistant secretary general to three secretaries-general of the United Nations and the author of several books, is a great humanitarian and prophet of hope for the twenty-first century.

Suki Munsell, Ph.D., is an inspired colleague of Anna Halprin for twenty-three years. She brings transformational healing into her fitness programs at the Dynamic Health and Fitness Institute in Corte Madera, California.

David Murcott is a former vice-president of the Journey Foundation, a nonprofit resource group helping college students prepare for the road ahead. He is currently a partner in a professional development company in San Diego.

Carrie Caton Pillsbury, formerly with MEDISEND, is now a project manager on EDS Community Affairs team helping nonprofit organizations and the communities they serve. She and her husband volunteer at her local church, mentoring college students.

Jennifer Pooley is an editor at HarperCollins Publishers. A 1997 graduate of Colgate University, she lives in New York City.

Kimberly Ridley is the senior editor of *HOPE*, a magazine about humanity making a difference, based in Brooklin, Maine. She writes about people in communities working together to solve local problems.

Sheila Richardson is an editor, book reviewer, freelance copywriter, and children's story writer who believes that books are windows to the world. Sheila is a trained tutor for Literacy Volunteers of America.

Joseph L. Rodriguez is Vice-President of Human Resources for the Home Depot Northwest Division and lives in Seattle with his family. He wishes to thank his family and God for his success.

Jonathan Roseman, Director of Community Affairs at Home Depot, is active in the Atlanta community, serving on the board of the Fernbank Museum of Natural History, Trees Atlanta, the Study Hall, and the Atlanta Foundation Center.

Richard Russell is a Boston-based author and an award-winning environmental activist. His latest book is *The Eye of the Whale*. A personal friend of Alejandro Obando, his story is dedicated to the children he met on a memorable visit to Nicaragua.

Diane Saunders is vice-president of the Nellie Mae Foundation for Education. After six years volunteering in Botswana, she wrote short stories for two anthologies, *Eyes on Africa* and *Patterns of Africa.*

Bill Shore is the founder and executive director of Share Our Strength. In his book *Revolution of the Heart*, he describes his personal transition from traditional politics to innovative community service and his prescription for community change.

Marion Silverbear, a development consultant, artist, and poet, wishes to thank Ada Deer and everyone else who helped with her story, and the Encampment for Citizenship community for contributing all of their unique flavors to the soup.

Holly Sklar, a widely published Boston-based writer, is the author of *Street of Hope: The Fall and Rise of an Urban Neighborhood*, the story of the inspiring Dudley Street Neighborhood Initiative. Her latest book is *Raise the Floor: Wages and Policies That Work for All of Us.*

Larry C. Spears is executive director of the Greenleaf Center for Servant Leadership and editor of four books on servant-leadership. He also serves on the board of *Friends Journal*, a Quaker magazine.

Steven Spielberg, a principal founder of DreamWorks SKG, produced, executive produced, or directed eight of the top twenty highest-grossing films of all time. He touched millions of people's hearts with *E.T. The Extra-Terrestrial* and dedicated his Academy Award–winning *Schindler's List* to the memory of the Holocaust so that it would never be forgotten or happen again.

Brother David Steindl-Rast, a Benedictine monk, author, and lecturer, is a charter member of Bread for the World. His books include *Gratefulness: The Heart of Prayer, A Listening Heart,* and, with his Buddhist counterpart, Robert Aitken Roshi, *The Ground We Share.*

Judith Thompson, co-founder of Children of War and Global Youth Connect, has been a leader in human rights, peace education, and leadership training for over twenty years in Israel/Palestine, Cambodia, and the Americas. She is co-producing a film, *From Victims to Visionaries,* about social healing work being led by survivors of political violence.

Robert Thurman is professor of Buddhist Studies at Columbia University, a friend of the Dalai Lama for thirty-five years, the father of five children, and author of many books. As a co-founder of Tibet House in New York, he works for the freedom of Tibet and the future of life on earth.

Peggy Townsend is a features writer for the *Santa Cruz County Sentinel,* where she focuses on children's issues, especially in neighborhoods where Nane Alejandrez began his work.

Skye Trimble is a writer and associate producer working in the documentary film industry in Washington, D.C. She was inspired by Frances Vaughn and Christmas in April.

Diane Valletta, owner of a Chicago-based communications firm and member of the National Association of Women Business Owners board of directors, often writes about the contributions of women-owned businesses in service to the community.

Elaina Verveer, publications assistant at the Corporation for National Service, is pursuing graduate studies in English. In the spirit of the Foster Grandparent Program, Elaina currently tutors children at a local elementary school.

Jeanne Wallace spearheaded public relations, community affairs, and employee outreach for Malden Mills, working side by side with Aaron Feuerstein. Today she is the president of Jeanne Wallace Marketing and Public Relations in Newburyport, Massachusetts.

Reverend Cecil Williams is Minister of Liberation of Glide Memorial United Methodist Church in San Francisco. He has been in the forefront of change for more than thirty-four years as a minister, community leader, activist, advocate, author, lecturer, and television personality.

Harris Wofford, president of America's Promise and former president of the Corporation for National Service, has dedicated his life to making citizen service a common expectation and experience for all Americans. He served as a U.S. senator from Pennsylvania and assisted President Kennedy in creating the Peace Corps.

Robert Wuthnow is a Gerhard R. Andlinger professor of sociology at Princeton University and director of the university's Center for the Study of American Religion. He is the author of a number of books, including *Acts of Compassion* (1991) and *Learning to Care* (1995).

Andrew Young was a close friend of Dr. Martin Luther King Jr. An ordained minister of the United Church of Christ, he was the executive director of the Southern Christian Leadership Conference. He has served as a congressman and as mayor of Atlanta, Georgia, as well as U.S. ambassador to the United Nations and as co-chair of the Atlanta Committee for the Centennial Olympic Games.

CREDITS

Grateful acknowledgment is made to the following for permission to reprint previously published material:

Alfred A. Knopf: Excerpt from *How Can I Help?* By Ram Dass and Paul Gorman. Copyright © 1985 by Ram Dass and Paul Gorman. Reprinted by permission of Alfred A. Knopf, a division of Random House, Inc.

Alfred A. Knopf and Alexander Counts: Excerpt from *Give Us Credit* by Alexander Counts. Copyright © 1996 by Alexander M. Counts. Reprinted by permission of Alfred A. Knopf, a division of Random House, Inc., and the author.

Leslie R. Crutchfield: "Teaching Jazz, Creating Community," is adapted from "Democracy=Participation With Style" from *Who Cares Magazine* (Fall 1995). Reprinted by permission of the author.

Dutton Children's Books: Excerpt from *Talking Peace: A Vision for the Next Generation* by Jimmy Carter. Copyright © 1993 by Jimmy Carter. All rights reserved. Reprinted by permission of Dutton Children's Books, an imprint of Penguin Putnam books for Young Readers, a division of Penguin Putnam Inc.

Fellowship of Reconciliation: Excerpt from "The Forgiveness Party" by Jo Clare Hartsig, from *Fellowship* (July/August 1995). Excerpt from "Shine On Montana" by Jo Clare Hartsig, from *Fellowship* (January/February 1995). "A Miracle in Montgomery," is adapted from "God Makes the Crooked Places Straight" by Joseph Lowery, from *Fellowship* (July/August 1995). Excerpt from "Adagio in Sarajevo" by Richard Deats, from *Fellowship* (March 1993). Reprinted by permission of the Fellowship of Reconciliation, www.forusa.org.